WOOLLY WISDOM

How to Tie and Fish Woolly Worms,
Woolly Buggers, and Their Fish-catching Kin.
Tying Recipes for 400 Patterns!

BY GARY SOUCIE

Foreword by
Lefty Kreh

Fly photographs by
Jim Schollmeyer

Additional photographs by
Peter Frailey

WOOLLY WISDOM

How to Tie and Fish Woolly Worms,
Woolly Buggers, and Their Fish-catching Kin.
Tying Recipes for 400 Patterns!

by Gary Soucie

Foreword by
Lefty Kreh

Fly photographs by
Jim Schollmeyer

Additional photographs by
Peter Frailey

Frank Amato
PORTLAND

This book is respectfully and thankfully dedicated to all the fly-fishing men and women around the world who keep coming up with new fly patterns to fish and new ways to tie old favorite patterns. Their creative genius keeps hope flickering in our hearts and smiles curling on our lips.

Published in 2006 by
Frank Amato Publications, Inc.
PO Box 82112
Portland, Oregon 97282
(503) 653-8108
www.amatobooks.com

Softbound ISBN: 1-57188-351-7 • Softbound UPC: 0-81127-00185-9
Hardbound ISBN: 1-57188-352-5 • Hardbound UPC: 0-81127-00186-6
Limited Hardbound ISBN: 1-57188-355-X • Limited Hardbound UPC: 0-81127-00189-7

All fly-pattern photographs taken by Jim Schollmeyer unless otherwise noted.
Frontispiece Photo: Mark R. Tompkins
Book Design: Tony Amato

Printed in Hong Kong

1 2 3 4 5 6 7 8 9 10

TABLE OF CONTENTS

Acknowledgments

Many people helped during the research and writing of this book by giving me patterns, flies, fishing information, advice, and moral support. In the last category, moral support, two stand out: my wife, Marina Brodskaya, and my publisher, Frank Amato. Without their infinite patience, this book never would have been written.

Fortunately for you, dear reader, I had plenty of help tying the flies for this book. A cursory glance inside will reveal that the flies tied by yours truly are the worst-looking specimens herein. I tie flies for fishing, not for show-and-tell. Now and then, even fish don't think much of my tying. Many tiers furnished camera-ready samples of their Woolly creations; their contributions are noted within. A few pitched in more heavily. In addition to their own Woolly wonders, Peter Frailey, Alberto Jimeno, and especially Bob Balogh volunteered to help out by tying quite a few other flies. Peter Frailey also made the tying-steps and tying-tips photo sequences for both Woolly wonders. Martin Jørgensen, Jens Larsen, and Paul Milstam graciously agreed to tie several Scandinavian and other patterns not of their own creation, in addition to their own patterns. And Mike Connor was kind enough to tie a few Woollies that are popular on the German side of the Baltic. Although they have no original patterns in the book, Wayne Mones and Ian Ricketson also helped lighten the burden by tying a few patterns.

Russell Blessing of Harrisburg, Pennsylvania, who tied the first Woolly Bugger, graciously tied a Bugger for this book. He also let me pester him with questions about his development of the pattern and the evolution of his tying and fishing those first Woolly Buggers.

You might think that companies in the business of selling flies would be loathe to part with recipes for their patterns. But that was generally not the case. The following were particularly helpful, not only in furnishing pattern recipes and sample flies, but also in answering all sorts of questions about how their proprietary patterns are tied and fished: Randall Kaufmann of Kaufmann's Streamborn, John Bailey of Dan Bailey's Fly Shop, Kevin Sloan and Tom Rosenbauer of Orvis, Mike Mercer and Mike Michalak of The Fly Shop, Mike Hogue of Badger Creek Fly Tying, Monte Malzahn of Cabela's, Jim Lake of Round Rocks Fly Fishing, Adam Trina of Montana Fly Company, and Rick Pope of Temple Fork Outfitters, as well as such independent commercial tiers as Tony Spezio, Steve Schweitzer, Jay "Fishy" Fullum, Jack Gartside, Philip Rowley, and others.

A great many tiers furnished patterns and recipes, as did the webmasters of quite a few fly-fishing and -tying sites on the Internet, and I thank them all. Thanks, too, to Sean Sonderman, curator of the American Museum of Fly Fishing, who helped me find things in the museum's library and collections. Ernest Schwiebert, a veritable encyclopedia of fly-fishing and -tying history and lore, always seems ready to answer my questions and steer me in the right directions.

Jim Krul, formerly of English Angling Trappings in Fairfield, Connecticut, and Dick Talleur, tier, teacher, author, raconteur, and friend, helped out with a variety of materials when time, patience, and money were running short.

For several years now, I have refused to carry a camera when fishing, but Mark R. Tompkins, and Erling Olsen were kind enough to send me a few of their photographs of Woolly Worms and Buggers at work.

Jim Schollmeyer's considerable artistry and skill with a camera not only lent this book utility and grace it otherwise would have lacked, he also spared your having to endure the rotten fruits of my photographic labors.

And a very special thanks to Lefty Kreh, who somehow managed to find time in his whirlwind schedule to read the manuscript and write the Foreword. (Lefty, I don't know how you keep it up when all the rest of us are slowing down. Maybe that bald pate of yours really *is* a solar collector panel!)

Nor should I forget Thomas Barker, Charles Cotton, Walter Bales, Don Martinez, Ray Bergman, Charles Brooks, Dan Bailey, Barry Beck, and all the others whose pioneering, proselytizing, and popularizing put Woolly Worms and Woolly Buggers on our fly-fishing map.

Thanks and tight lines to them all!

—*Gary Soucie*
Williamstown, Massachusetts

FOREWORD

I've been asked to write many Forewords to fly-fishing books. So when Gary Soucie e-mailed me to write one for his new book on Woolly Worms and Woolly Buggers, I agreed. I expected a small book. Instead, what arrived was a two-inch-thick manuscript. I wondered, "How could anyone write more than 400 pages on two somewhat similar flies?" Gary did and I am grateful he did.

I started fly fishing in 1947. The first few fish I caught were smallmouths on a popping bug. Joe Brooks, my mentor, said, "You should try fishing under water," and handed me some Woolly Worms. They resembled caterpillars and had a buggy appearance. Arriving at Big Hunting Creek, near Thurmont, Maryland, I crawled to a deep pool and, while lying on my stomach, noticed two nice brook trout holding at the tail of the pool. I carefully cast the Woolly Worm upstream and let it drift down toward the trout. The Woolly Worm, hackles undulating, approached the brookies and one of the trout rose, sucking it in. It was at that moment I became hooked on Woolly Worms.

Later, I found out about Woolly Buggers, and these two flies have allowed me to catch fish all over the world, both in fresh and salt water. From tiny brook trout to giant tarpon, these two fly patterns have helped fly-rodders everywhere to put a bend in their rods.

I can recall many times when the Woolly Worm or Woolly Bugger saved the day. The Montana outdoor writer Charley Brooks and I were fishing the Bow River in Alberta, Canada, many years ago. We were doing okay, but not getting the big trout. Our guide tied onto our tippets heavily weighted purple Woolly Buggers dressed on 4XL, size-2 hooks and the big trout came to dine. Once, while fishing in the Bahamas, the bonefish were being finicky. I tied on a sand-colored Woolly Bugger dressed on a 2XL, size-4 hook. I cast it out and allowed it to fall to the bottom. The bonefish approached. I barely twitched the fly and the finicky bones no longer hesitated. If I am having trouble coaxing my favorite freshwater fish—smallmouth bass—to bite, switching to a black or chartreuse Woolly Bugger will usually turn the trick.

No one has given a good explanation of what the Woolly Worm and Woolly Bugger are meant to imitate. Certainly, either can imitate a leech, hellgrammite, stonefly, caterpillar, grub or worm, nymph, or baitfish, or just act as an attractor pattern. Even the Griffith's Gnat is a miniature Woolly Worm.

So, how could Gary Soucie write an entire book about these two flies? You really have to read it to understand that he has done a magnificent job. After a brief history of the flies, Gary explains what materials are used in these patterns—and there are many. There is a superb treatment of the various hooks used in building these woollies and how and why you tie them differently for a variety of species—and fishing conditions.

There are detailed instructions on how to fish the Woolly Worms and Woolly Buggers—for different species and fishing conditions. A comprehensive index allows you to locate almost anything quickly.

Jim Schollmeyer is a complete master at photographing the flies so you can see the vast range of fish attraction in the huge number of patterns that Gary has written about. And Peter Frailey has done an excellent job of photographing the tying steps necessary to build good, sturdy Woolly Worms and Woolly Buggers.

All fly fishermen should read this book (for even a novice can tie most Woolly Buggers and Woolly Worms). Fly fishermen everywhere owe a debt of gratitude to Gary Soucie for writing this most useful book.

—Lefty Kreh

INTRODUCTION

A couple confessions are in order.

First, I'm not a good tier. I tend to put too much material on a fly. When wrapping or dubbing the body, I often crowd the front of the shank, leaving precious little room for collars, wings, and heads. I'm lazy and impatient at the vise. I simply can't get the hang of certain techniques. I never was a very good tier, and now osteoarthritis and other ailments of aging have left my fingers even less nimble than they used to be. Nor is my eyesight as sharp as it once was. All of this may be painfully obvious in the photos of the flies I tied in the pages that follow, for which I apologize. (But look at the bright side: Try one of those patterns and, your first time out of the gate, you'll tie a nicer-looking fly!)

I didn't even start tying until rather late in the game. Prior to a six-week trip to Arctic Russia for Atlantic salmon in 1994, I figured I'd better learn, because salmon flies for one-week trips usually cost me upwards of a couple hundred bucks. So, I asked my friend Wayne Mones (one of the best tiers I know) to show me the ropes. He even gave me my first vise, a Griffin, and later the one I now almost always use, a Regal rotary. After a couple hours of Wayne's tutelage, I figured I was ready. So, doubtless with fingers crossed behind his back and a lump in his throat, Wayne sent me off into the brave new world with aforesaid Griffin vise and two hen necks.

Second, for the first few years of my fly fishing, I hardly ever fished Woolly Worms and Woolly Buggers. Because of all the glowing accounts in books and articles, I *carried* both patterns, but they just didn't seem to work for me. (The same was true of the Muddler Minnow, but that's a whole other story. Perhaps even a whole other book.) Then I stumbled upon the Miller Woolly Worm (page **32**), which actually caught fish and which my friend Chuck Tryon was willing to tie for me. A bit later, I discovered the fish-attracting qualities of the Brown Bivisible (page **92**) and the Lectric Blue Leech (page **134**), both of which I could readily find in fly shops. I realized the problem had been with *me*, not the patterns. (As my grandson might say: *Du-u-u-h-h-h-h-h!*)

Anyway, once I finally started tying (and got past all those hairwing salmon flies, some of which even worked), I recognized that Woolly Worms and Buggers are among the easiest of all flies to tie. And among the most forgiving of faulty skills. No wings to set *just so*. No fussy microfibbet tails. No expensive, exotic materials. No spinning and packing of deer hair. And not so tiny they hide behind my fumbling fingertips. For me, almost perfect patterns.

Gradually, I went from Woolly skeptic to Woolly missionary. I certainly don't fish Woolly Worms and Buggers exclusively, or even a majority of the time. I take too much pleasure in experimentation for that. But my exper-

imental tendencies have led me to discover—either by accident or happenstance, and more lately by dint of research—just how many ways you can tie and fish these Woolly wonders. And that discovery has led directly to my writing this book.

When I announced my intention to write a book on Woolly Worms and Buggers, most of my fly-fishing and fly-tying friends politely (or not so politely) raised their eyebrows. The first book publisher I mentioned it to said it sounded more like a magazine article than a book. (Both reactions filled me with a sense of *déjà vu*, as I had received similar reactions when I announced plans for my first book, on terminal tackle—first published in 1982 and still in print, if somewhat out of date, as of this writing.) But when I contacted Frank Amato, he immediately saw the possibilities. He even told me that when he caught his first wild British Columbia steelhead—lo, these many years ago—he found, after finally wrestling it to submission, someone else's red-tailed black Woolly Worm hanging from the fish's jaw.

I know or at least *know of* fly-fishers who spend most of their time fishing with Woolly Buggers. Hardly what I would call adventurous souls. Look in their streamer boxes and you will see row after row of black, olive, and black-and-olive Buggers, maybe even a few purple or white or white-and-grizzly Buggers. Even if they are devotees of catch and release, they remind me of meat fishermen for whom the catching is more important than the fishing. These are not the kind of people with whom I particularly like to fish. When I lived in suburban Maryland, just outside the District of Columbia, I got so sick of reading *The Washington Post* fishing columnist's accounts of catching fish on Woolly Buggers I stopped reading his column altogether. What's to learn from a guy like that?

On the other hand, I delight in reading of this fly fisher's innovative adaptation of the basic Woolly Bugger pattern or that one's experimentation with different ways of tying and fishing the venerable Woolly Worm. Even British fly fishers, so often mired in tradition, have found a myriad ways to tie their beloved palmer flies.

My point? Woolly Worms and Buggers may not be for those who want to show off their meticulous small-motor skills at the vise, but they are perfect patterns for people who like to experiment, to pioneer, to try new things. And they are perfect patterns for people who like to actually *catch* fish while they are having fun pushing the envelope.

If fly fishing and fly tying were simply about catching fish, we could end this book right here with these two generic patterns, noting that, in either case, colors (or even materials) may be varied to suit the angler or the angling and that either a bead or cone head may be slipped onto the hook before tying on, or that beadchain or dumbbell eyes may be lashed to the shank:

	WOOLLY WORM		WOOLLY BUGGER
1X-long wet-fly, sizes 8–16		**Hook**	4X-long streamer, sizes 2–12
Black 6/0		**Thread**	Black 6/0
Optionally, lead wire on shank		**Underbody**	*Optionally, lead wire on shank*
Hackle fibers, hackle points, or yarn, a gap-width long		**Tail**	Marabou, shank length
Optionally, tinsel (or wire)		**Rib**	*Optionally, tinsel (or wire)*
Chenille		**Body**	Chenille
Hen hackle, glossy side to rear, palmered over the body in 4 to 7 turns, barbs angled forward		**Palmer hackle**	Saddle hackle, palmered fairly closely over the body
Tying thread		**Head**	Tying thread

It would be tough to fault either of those two patterns, without modification or adornment, for fish-catching efficacy. However, half the fun of fly fishing and fly tying lies in their almost endless variety of opportunity for exploration and self-expression. Hence, all the pages and patterns that follow.

Although I have tried to be as logically orderly as possible in assigning patterns to chapters, a certain amount of coin-tossing and second-guessing was involved. If a pattern has a medium-length marabou tail (somewhere between gap-width and shank-length), is it a Woolly Worm or Bugger? I did not try to define and apply hard-and-fast rules. Sometimes I put them in the first part of the book and sometimes, the second. For a perfect example, look at the Soft-Hackle Woolly Worm (page 37) and Tom's Best Bet (page 177), a Great Lakes steelhead pattern. Each could have, just as logically, been placed in the other half of the book. While the classic Woolly patterns are easy to separate, the myriad modifications and mutations are not always easy to pigeonhole. As with the rest of life, there are more grays than blacks and whites.

Similarly, I could not be consistent in assigning patterns to chapters and sections within chapters. For example, several steelhead Woolies use bodies of long-fibered tinsel chenille and omit the palmer hackle altogether. Some of them were used to illustrate steelhead patterns and others to illustrate the tying of hackle-free Woolies. The same thing goes for flies with eyes and heads.

As you study the pictures and patterns in the pages that follow, you will notice a smattering of awfully similar, even virtually identical patterns, separated only by color, size, the addition of some flash material. I intentionally included a few, but by no means all, of these close relatives, to illustrate three things: (1) how tiny details can make the difference between an effective and a so-so pattern; (2) how those same details can separate a panfish pattern from a steelhead fly; (3) how tiers separated by hundreds of miles or tens of years could come up with similar solutions to similar or dissimilar fly-fishing problems. In the last chapter of the book I have included three ostrich-and-marabou patterns that *look* a lot alike but that were, as far as I know, developed independently of one another: the Itty Bitty Bugger, Bluegill Bugger, and Mini Leech (pages 199–200). Whether they fish alike, I don't know because I've never tried using all of them in identical situations.

Chances are, each would work but that each would work better when fished to its own design strength.

Pattern books such as this one somewhat resemble cookbooks. We even use the word "recipe" for the listing of ingredients in a pattern. You *can* cook a meal or tie a fly by slavishly following a recipe. But good cooks, like good tiers and fly fishers, are creative, tweaking and adjusting according to experience, intuition, and just plain hunch. Don't think you can't tie a pattern because it calls for burgundy and all you have is maroon.

Purists who might consign you to some fly-fishing purgatory of people they won't talk to if you put a hot-orange body or potato-chip-bag wings on a Hendrickson won't much mind what you do to these palmered patterns. Purists are largely disdainful about such patterns anyway. If it doesn't match a hatch, they don't want to know about it.

You might live a thousand miles away from the nearest steelhead or Pacific salmon stream, but if you get an itch to combine fluorescent chartreuse, deep cerise, and metallic black, go ahead and whip up your own Woolly Worm or Bugger. Odds are pretty good that it will catch fish, particularly if you are willing to settle for sunnies, say, or needlefish. But, who knows? You might have created the next world-beater fly for brown trout or bonefish. You just never know until you try it.

One last note: Even though both patterns are fundamentally easy to tie, I strongly suggest that you read, re-read, and thoroughly digest Chapters 1, "Tying Woolly Worms," and 8, "Tying Woolly Buggers," before you pore over the patterns and recipes. Sprinkled therein are tying tips from a variety of experts—tips that can help you at the vise and on the water. To save space, I have not gone into great detail in each pattern, as to how the materials are tied in and wrapped and finished off. That sort of detail is covered in the tying chapters just mentioned. To save time, I didn't always follow those sages's good advice in tying the flies illustrated herein. So, don't try to figure out why I didn't mention a tail-supporting loop or hair platform every time I described or tied a Woolly Bugger with an extra-long tail. Once you've discovered what a good idea it is, you'll automatically add it to recipes that need it.

On your marks. Get set. Go!

WOOLLY WORMS

Apparently thinking that Woolly Worms look like Woolly Buggers without the lively marabou tails, many fly fishers surmise that Woolly Worms must therefore be less effective and don't even carry them. Such Izaaks-come-lately don't know what they are missing.

In *The Trout and the Stream* (1974), the late Charles S. Brooks wrote:

"There are fishermen around here, darn good fishermen, who say that if you can't catch fish on the Woolly Worm, you might as well give up. One fellow I used to know, now deceased, used nothing but this fly, in 3 sizes and 4 colors. He caught as many trout as any of us, and as many big ones. George used brown, olive green, black, and orange Woolly Worms, in sizes 4, 6, and 8, all 4X long, all weighted. He said he never felt a need for anything else. He called dry flies 'feather dusters.' Spend more of your time fishing the water, he would say, and less sorting through your fly box and you'll be a lot better fisherman."

I don't think anyone actually knows who tied the first Woolly Worm, but Ernest Schwiebert recalls a 1950ish *Saturday Evening Post* article in which a young woman from Denver claimed to have originated it. "Her company was called Sure-Strike Flies, as I recall," he says. Although some trace the Woolly Worm's origin back to Izaak Walton's day and beyond, the eminent British fly-fishing authority Charles Jardine says the Woolly Worm is a North American pattern, not merely another English Palmer Fly. Another English authority, Taff Price, says, "The Woolly Worms differ from other palmered flies in that the hackle slopes towards the eye, not towards the tail." But nobody ever seems to attribute the innovation of forward-sloping palmer hackle to anyone in particular. Palmered wet flies have been around a long, long time under other names. In his 1932 book *Just Fishing*, Ray Bergman mentioned "the old-time Pool Hackle which I have fished wet for a good many years." He didn't say whether its soft, oversize palmer hackle sloped one way or the other.

A. J. McClane, in *The Practical Fly Fisherman* (1953, revised 1975), said the Woolly Worm "made its reputation as an Ozark bass fly back in the 1920's. Actually, this pattern was first described by Izaak Walton back in 1653 *[Actually, it wasn't, as we shall see later.—GS]* and has three centuries of recommendation to its credit." McClane also wrote, "When it was first introduced in the Ozark rivers, the Woolly Worm had a yellow body. The dressing changed to black after the pattern went west.... I'm not sure how the Woolly Worm became known as a Western trout pattern. A fellow by the name of Walter Bales from Kansas City, Missouri, snaffled a prize-winning rainbow on it back in 1935 and passed the pattern on to Don Martinez in West Yellowstone, Montana. At any rate, Don nursed it along, and the Worm became synonymous with Western trouting."

As Martinez told Ray Bergman (quoted in the 1978 third edition of *Trout*), "This is probably the most popular number that was ever commercialized. They were not original with me … but were derived from a very old Missouri bass fly of somewhat similar design. I was merely the first to make them commercially available as a trout fly, or to be more accurate, trout lure. Black is perhaps the best number."

Just what is a Woolly Worm, anyway? Is it a wet fly, a nymph, or a terrestrial? Is it an attractor or an imitator, an impressionistic or a suggestive pattern?

It is all of the above, and then some. As Bergman wrote in *Trout*, "It isn't a true wet fly, a nymph, or a dry fly. … It has proved to be a great fish-catcher."

Although most classify the Woolly Worm as a wet fly, it can be and often is fished as a nymph. Charlie Brooks included a lot about the Woolly Worm in his *Nymph Fishing for Larger Trout* (1976), and Gary Borger devoted the last chapter of his first book, *Nymphing: A Basic Book* (1979), to the "Secret of the Wooly Worm."[1]

In his masterful *Aquatic Entomology* (1981), the entomologist W. Patrick McCafferty says Woolly Worms are "likely to be accepted as stoneflies by trout," and he certainly didn't mean adult stones. Three Woolly Worm patterns made it into Eric Leiser's and Bob Boyle's *Stoneflies for the Angler* (1982). On the other hand, in a 1940 letter to Preston Jennings, Don Martinez wrote that he thought the pulsating palmer hackle of this "horrible looking grub … a made over bass and croppie [*sic*] fly" simulated the breathing action of the gills on mayfly nymphs "and others." Charlie Brooks once discovered that trout found a size 4, olive-green Woolly Worm a perfectly acceptable imitation of riffle-beetle larvae.

Fishing Woolly Worms one day on the Yellowstone, Brooks wrote in *The Trout and the Stream* (1974), he, his wife, sister, and brother-in-law caught and released "about 150 trout, running from twelve to seventeen inches. Most people nearby caught nothing or small fish. I believe it was because they were not using the right fly." Prior to that experience with the Woolly Worm, he'd "always thought of it as nonimitative."

Ernest Schwiebert agrees with Brooks. When I asked the author of *Matching the Hatch* (1955) if he ever fishes so humble a pattern, Ernie laughed and said, "Yes, but slightly modified. You know I'm into imitating things rather than 'covey-shooting.'" Ernie said he ties Woollies with short-barbed palmer hackle—"no longer than the hook gap, or shorter." Tied that way, Ernie says, Woolly Worms look a lot like the larvae of riffle beetles and certain other aquatic beetles, which dwell in lakes and ponds as well as in streams.

Brooks (surely the Woolly Worm's Boswell) wrote in *Nymph Fishing for Larger Trout* that the pattern is "suggestive of many kinds of underwater creatures—stoneflies, dragonflies, riffle beetle larvae, hellgrammites, damselflies, and who knows what."

---

[1] Unfortunately, Borger could not resist trying to improve on the pattern. His misspelled Hair Leg Wooly Worm is one fine, buggy-looking, fish-catching nymph, but it's a Woolly Worm in name only. Not only does it lack the requisite palmer hackle, it is utterly bereft of feathered parts. Constructed completely of hair, yarn, thread, and wire, it looks less like a Woolly Worm than like Polly Rosborough's Casual Dress or Randall Kaufmann's Hare's Ear. So we don't really know whether Borger's praise of the Woolly Worm extends to the fly we're concerned with here.

At first glance, the Woolly Worm looks very much like any of several fuzzy terrestrial caterpillars, especially if the hackle is densely palmered by wrapping it too closely. As McClane wrote, "The Woolly Worm is said to imitate a caterpillar, commonly called 'woolly worm' or 'woolly bear' in our central and northern bass states." Brooks, who favored a sparsely palmered fly—five rather than the standard seven wraps of hackle—wrote, "Doubt if it is ever taken as a caterpillar." At the risk of being damned to fly-fishing's nether world for the sin of presumption, I think Brooks may have been mistaken on this last point, and for a couple reasons.

Aquatic-moth larvae of the family Pyralidae are usually called aquatic caterpillars. Fairly widespread across the continent, pyralid larvae dwell on algae-covered rocks in streams with moderate to strong currents, or in still and calm waters around fish-producing vegetation: water lilies, pondweed, eel grass, duckweed, water-milfoil, sedges. Most are poor swimmers, but a few of them swim reasonably well at or just below the surface. Judging by one of the color plates of a pyralid larva in *Aquatic Entomology*, I think a chartreuse or lime-green Woolly Worm tied with brown thread and sparsely palmered with a white or cream hackle would probably pass muster with a hungry fish. (See my Pyralid Woolly Worm on page 39.)

But Brooks probably meant he didn't think trout ever took Woolly Worms for fuzzy *terrestrial* caterpillars. I'm afraid he might have been wrong there, too, because even terrestrial caterpillars have their piscatorial advocates. Izaak Walton advocated the use of caterpillar-imitating flies in *The Compleat Angler*'s "Fourth Day." After having named nine flies worth knowing and imitating, and suggesting there were far too many others to list all the possibilities, Walton's Piscator told Venator:

> And, yet, I will exercise your promised patience by saying a little of the caterpillar, or the palmer-fly or worm....
>
> ...this is called a pilgrim, or palmer-worm, for his very wandering life[2] and various food: not contenting himself, as others do, with any one certain place for his abode, nor any certain kind of herb or flower for his feeding, but will boldly and disorderly wander up and down, and not endure to be kept to a diet, or fixed to a particular place.
>
> ... Mr. Barker commends several sorts of the palmer-flies, not only those ribbed with silver and gold, but others that have their bodies all made of black, or some with red, and a red hackle....

"Mr. Barker" was Thomas Barker, an angling cook whose *Barker's Delight, or, The Art of Angling* (1651) beat Walton into print by more than two years. Until his later partnership with Charles Cotton, Walton cited Barker as his fount of fly-fishing knowledge, as we have just seen in his mention of the good cook's advocacy of the caterpillar. But let's go right to the horse's mouth, to see what Thomas Barker wrote. The following comes from the discussion of trout fishing with the fly in *The Art of Fishing*'s second ("much enlarged") edition of 1657. (I don't have a facsimile of the first edition.)

> Let us begin to angle in March with the flye. If the weather prove windy or cloudy, there are severall kinds of Palmers that are good for that time.
>
> First, a black Palmer, ribbed with silver. Secondly, a black Palmer ribbed with an orenge-tawny body. Thirdly, a black Palmer made all of black. Fourthly, a red Palmer ribbed with gold. Fifthly, a red Palmer mixed with an orenge-tawny body of cruell. All of these flies must be made with hackles, and they will serve all the year long morning and evening, windy or cloudy. Without these flyes you cannot make a dayes angling good.

That sounds like a ringing endorsement of the caterpillar as trout "bait," as well as a pretty good description of some ancestral Woolly Worms.[3]

In Part II of *The Compleat Angler*, fifth edition (1676), Charles Cotton gave us several more palmer-hackled patterns:

> "... a plain hackle, or palmer-fly, made with a rough black body, either of black spaniel's fur, or the whirl of an ostrich feather, and the red hackle of a capon all over ...."
>
> "... a lesser hackle, with a black body, also silver twist over that, and a red feather over all ...."
>
> "...a great hackle, the body black, and wrapped with a red feather of a capon untrimmed; that is, the whole length of the hackle staring out ...."
>
> "...another great hackle, the body black and ribbed over with gold twist, and a red feather over all ...."
>
> "... a hackle with a purple body, whipt about with a red capon's feather."
>
> "... a gold-twist hackle with a purple body, whipt about with a red capon's feather."
>
> "... a green grasshopper; the dubbing of green and yellow wool mixed, ribbed over with green silk, and a red capon's feather over all."
>
> "... a black hackle; the body made of the whirl of a peacock's feather, and a black hackle-feather on the top."

If you want to tie Cotton's forerunners of the Woolly Worm, know that his "red" hackle is not a red-dyed feather, but what British tiers call natural red and we call fiery brown.

---

2 This meaning for the word "palmer" dates back to the Holy Crusades. Returning crusaders often brought back with them the fronds of the palm trees they had so admired, so came to be called "palmers." The word later was applied to religious pilgrims generally, and finally to wanderers of a more worldly sort. Even in Slovenian, the word *romar* means both "pilgrim" and "palmer fly" or "palmer hackle."

3 Oddly enough, Dame Juliana (or whoever it was really wrote *The Treatyse of Fysshynge with an Angle*, first published in 1496) didn't suggest a single palmer fly. All 12 of her recommended monthly patterns are winged flies.

By 1892, when Mary Orvis Marbury's *Favorite Flies and Their Histories* appeared, palmer flies had apparently fallen out of favor, because she lists just two of them, the Soldier Palmer (page 102) and the Ashy (page 26). Thankfully, all that began changing within the next 50 years.

Modern Woolly Worms usually sport chenille bodies of various colors and red tails of yarn, hackle fibers, hackle points, or quill slips. Don Martinez, as responsible as anyone for the Woolly Worm pattern we know today, didn't tail them that way. Ernie Schwiebert told me he thought he remembered grizzly-hackle tails on the first Woolly Worms he saw in West Yellowstone in the 1950s. That sent me scurrying up to the American Museum of Fly Fishing in Manchester, Vermont. With the help of curator Sean Sonderman, I managed to find four Martinez-tied Woolly Worms in the museum's Preston Jennings Collection. Ernie had remembered well. All four had long tails: two of grizzly-hackle fibers, one of grizzly-hackle points, and one of golden-pheasant tippets. Not a red tail in the lot. Three were tied on 3X- or 4X-long streamer hooks in sizes 4 or 6, the fourth on a size 4, 6X-long streamer hook. All

had hackles that were considerably longer than the hook gaps. None was ribbed.

The Martinez color combinations included: grizzly palmered over green and grizzly palmered over brown, both with hackle-fiber tails and black heads; grizzly palmered over yellow, with a hackle-point tail and a red head; and black palmered over bright red, with tippets for the tail and a black head.

While the paternity of the modern Woolly Worm remains unknown, surely Don Martinez deserves full credit as its godfather.

Although I urge experimentation and creativity throughout the book, you can't put wings on your Woolly Worms. If you do, you will have to call them something else: Beaverkill, Brook Fin, Lady Merton, Neverwas, Queen of Waters, Rich Widow, Wickham's Fancy, whatever. Maybe even, Elk Hair Caddis. Of course you *can* wing a palmered fly and fish it quite successfully, but then it's no longer a Woolly Worm. We have to draw the line *somewhere*.

By almost universally accepted definition, the prototypical Woolly Worm has a cylindrical body of chenille (wool yarn, if we go back a few centuries) over the length of which is palmered a forward-slanting hackle (usually grizzly, but even some sticklers will allow badger or furnace), all of it usually tied on a long, or at least longish, hook. (Shank length, lack of body taper, and barb angle are the major distinctions between the Woolly Worm and the otherwise very-much-look-alike Palmer Flies.) Most of us classify the Woolly Worm as a wet fly; others think it's more nymph, and some few iconoclasts call it a streamer. It can be fished all three ways, and there are dry- and waking-fly versions as well. Some say the original Woolly Worm had a tail; others, that it didn't. Each camp can claim a complement of heavyweight adherents. Ditto for ribs. McClane claimed the tinsel or wire rib is an important element; Brooks said the rib was a later development or innovation.

Without further ado or argument, let's take a look at tying the Woolly Worm.

Black Woolly Worm

Like the basic black dress, the Black Woolly Worm is at home almost anywhere and is rarely a bad choice. (Just as chic women accessorize their basic "little black dresses" with colorful scarves, fancy belts, single-rope pearl necklaces, or gem-studded pins, so do fashion-conscious fly tiers dress up their basic Black Woolly Worms with red tails, silver ribs, shiny bead heads, or other fish-attracting fillips.)

Black Woolly Worm[1]

Hook: 2X- or 3X-long, standard to 2X-heavy wet-fly, sizes 2 to 16, say (6 to 12 being the sizes most often cited)

Thread: Black, in a size appropriate to the hook: 8/0 for sizes smaller than 16, say, 3/0 for a size 4 or larger, 6/0 for most sizes

Tail: Red or grizzly hackle fibers or point(s), a quill slip, or a short tuft of red yarn; *some tiers consider the tail optional in a standard Woolly Worm*[2]

Body: Black chenille—fine, medium, or large, to suit the hook

Hackle: Long grizzly hen hackle—neck or saddle, your choice—palmered the length of the body, with the dull underside of the feather facing forward and the barbs angled forward

Head: Tying thread, tied fairly large; *cement, varnish, lacquer, fingernail polish, or other protective coating is optional*[2]

Tying Steps (Tied and photographed by Peter Frailey)

In the photo sequence that follows, the body color has been changed to make the tying steps more easily visible.

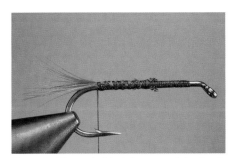  

Step 1: Tie on behind the eye of the hook and lay the tail material—if used—along the top of the shank and wrap the thread down to the bend, binding the tail material to the shank to form a smooth underbody.

Step 2: Strip one end of the chenille by pinching and pulling the fuzzy stuff away with the nails of your thumb and forefinger, exposing about 1/4 inch of the string core.

Step 3: Tie in the stripped end of the chenille at the bend, with the rest of the chenille hanging back behind the rear of the hook.

[1] In this recipe, and throughout the book, I have listed the materials in the order in which they are tied in (added to the hook), not the order in which they are wrapped. The order is important if you want neat, durable flies. Tie in the materials at the wrong stage, and your flies may be lumpy in appearance and prone to come apart in use. (Note that in the case of dubbed bodies, the listed order cannot be precise because the tying thread has already been tied on and the fur or other dubbing is added just prior to wrapping.)

[2] Here and elsewhere throughout the book, I have listed *optional ingredients in italics*. If you decide to coat a thread head, you may use head cement, clear or colored fingernail polish (the cheaper, the better, because it will dry harder and shinier), lacquer, varnish, or whatever else pleases you. In the recipes that follow, I list whatever my source listed, or the traditional "lacquer" or "varnish" to cover all bases. Use whatever you have or suits you best.

Step 4: Prepare the hackle feather by stroking most of the barbs perpendicular to the hackle's center stem, then trim the feather square at its tip, leaving a small triangle.

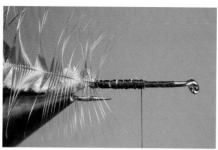

Step 5: Trap the aft-facing hackle feather (its dull, concave side facing up) by its triangular tip to the top of the hook at the rear of the shank, just ahead of the tied-in body material. Wrap the thread back up the shank in neat, close spirals, forming a thread base that will keep materials from slipping around on the slippery steel shank.

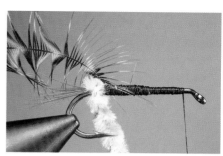

Step 6: Holding the hackle up and out of the way, take one wrap of chenille *behind* the hackle.

Step 7: Wrap the chenille forward in close spirals, each abutting the preceding wrap without overlapping it. Just behind the eye, tie off the chenille and clip the excess. Be sure to leave enough room between the chenille and the hook eye to tie off the hackle and build a head in step 8.

Step 8: Wind the hackle forward in evenly spaced, close, open spirals. Wrap with the shiny, convex side of the feather toward the rear, if you want most of the hackle barbs to angle forward. (Seven turns are traditional, but Charlie Brooks liked to use just five turns for a sparser look. When in doubt, opt for the fewer number of turns.) When you reach the front of the body, secure the hackle with three or four tight wraps, and clip the excess

feather. It's a good idea to anchor the hackle with a half hitch or two before clipping the excess. Build a neat, smooth, rather large head (larger than for most trout flies) with the tying thread. Whip-finish or use three half hitches. Clip the excess thread and—if you wish, it's not altogether necessary—apply a drop of head cement ("lacquer") to the thread. Once the head cement has dried, go out and catch a fish!

Charles Cotton's Great Hackle

A blast from the past, this is the black palmer fly listed by Charles Cotton in the 1676 fifth edition of Izaak Walton's *The Compleat Angler.* It clearly is the ancestor of the Woolly Worm pattern just listed.

Charles Cotton's Great Hackle

Hook: Long-shank wet-fly, size to suit your quarry or your local caterpillar fauna
Thread: Black
Body: Black wool, dubbing, or ostrich herl
Palmer hackle: Natural red (fiery brown) or brown hen hackle, clipped or unclipped, to suit

TIPS FOR TYING BETTER WOOLLY WORMS (Photos by Peter Frailey)

Even in so straightforward a tie as the Woolly Worm, a few tying "tricks" separate the good tiers from the rest of us.

Wrapping over the tail material

If you are using fairly bulky material for the tail—yarn, marabou, or the like—tying it in at the rear of the shank will produce a lumpy fly. To avoid this, lay the tailing material atop the whole length of the shank and overwrap it with thread all the way down the shank. This will produce a smooth, even, reasonably thin base for the body.

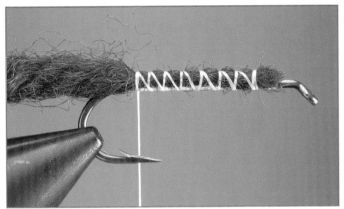

When using bulky tail materials, lash them atop the shank to keep the body neat and free of lumps.

Tying in the body material

If you want a slender fly body, strip the fluff from the end of the chenille (as described in Step 2 on page 13) and tie in the stripped core of string at the rear of the shank. If you want a fatter body, lay the chenille along the top of the shank, lash it to the shank with tying thread, and wrap the body forward over the chenille-and-thread base.

For neat, smooth, *thick* bodies, lash the body material atop the tail material the length of the shank.

Wrapping the body

As described in the Black Woolly Worm's tying steps 3, 5, and 6 (pages 13-14), you should usually tie in the body material before the hackle, and make the first wrap of the body *behind* the tied-in hackle. This way, the hackle doesn't have to climb up onto the

body from the shank at the rear. The same thing goes for ribs: They are usually best tied in *after* the body material (unless the rib is used to catch and tie down a reverse-palmered hackle). Palmer hackles and ribs that have to climb up the body's butt end often come loose. Do this on all your ribbed or palmered flies, not just chenille-bodied Woolly Worms and Buggers.

Peter Frailey adds three more reasons for tying in the body material first: It gives the hackle a little protection from fish teeth, making the fly a bit more durable. It also keeps the hackle from having to climb over the first wrap of chenille and compressing it, thus giving the fly a tapered butt—not necessarily bad, but a departure from Woolly Worm tradition. Finally, a hackle wrap behind a chenille or other bulky body tends to splay the hackle barbs, giving the hackle an unruly look and almost guaranteeing you won't be able to angle the barbs forward as the palmer the hackle forward. Good points, all.

To make your Woolly Worms neater and more durable, tie in hackle *after* the body material.

Palmering the hackle

In keeping with Woolly Worm tradition, I have usually specified that the hackles be palmered so the barbs angle forward. This is one of those easier-said-than-done or do-as-I-say, not-as-I-do things. Look at the flies I tied in the first half of this book and you will see that I seldom succeeded in getting the barbs to angle forward. Nor am I alone in this predicament. Tiers far more competent than I—Peter Frailey, for one—freely admit defeat when it comes to consistently angling Woolly Worm barbs forward. On the other hand, Orvis's Tom Rosenbauer says he doesn't have any trouble with the technique. Different strokes, I guess. Many tiers tell me they don't bother with such old-fashioned tradition, their rationale being that it seems to make no difference on the water; I suspect the real reason is frustration at the vise.

If you want *all* your barbs to angle forward (or at least in the same direction), you will have to (a) strip the barbs from the side of the feather than will be wrapped against the body

To ensure that your hackles all lean one way, you must fold the feather or, much easier, strip the barbs from one side of the stem.

Palmering the hackle shiny-side-down and burying the stem between the body wraps will help keep your hackle upright.

(which takes a little time) or (b) fold the feather in half lengthwise along the midrib, or quill, as you go (which takes considerably more time, dexterity, and practice).

If your hackle feathers are too anemic to give you a nice-looking, forward-leaning palmer hackle when you strip the barbs from one side of the quill, here are two things that those of us who are fumble-fingered often do: (1) Tie in the hackle feather *by the butt behind the eye*, tie in the body material up front, take the thread to the rear (or dub the body to the rear), wrap the body to the rear and tie it off (unnecessary in the case of a dubbed body), *reverse-palmer the hackle* to the bend, and rib the hackle with the tying thread. (2) Before tying in the hackle by its tip at the bend, strip several barbs from the side of the center quill that will make contact with the body (or shank); this will keep you from getting off to a bad start. However, neither method can guarantee success in angling those barbs forward (as you can see).

If you are content with having the barbs stand more or less erect, with merely *half* of them angled slightly forward, here's a neat trick I picked up from reading Dave Whitlock, John Merwin, and Eric Leiser: When you palmer the hackle, turn the

Stripping a few barbs from the body side of the hackle can help you get your palmer hackle started neatly.

hackle sideways so the shiny, top side of the feather is making contact with the body and the dull, underside of the feather is facing you (the barbs will now face directly backwards and forwards along the shank before they are wrapped). Try to bury the quill stem *between the turns of chenille* as you wind the hackle. In *The Book of Fly Patterns* (1987), Leiser clarifies that you should force the *shiny side of the feather down* into the chenille to make the barbs stand more upright. (In both cases, I have added italics for emphasis.)

Ribbing the fly

Some of the patterns described later use a rib of wire or tinsel; often, it is listed *in italics as an optional ingredient*. Whether the pattern calls for one or not, you may decide you want a rib, either to protect the palmer hackle from fish teeth or to give the fly an extra bit of attractive flash.[3] If the rib is there just for looks, you can rib the body before or after the hackle is palmered.

But if you want to reinforce the fly to make it more durable, you must cross-rib the fly—that is, wind the hackle in one direction and the rib in the other. If you palmer the hackle forward, then try to counter-wrap the rib over the palmer by spiral-winding in the opposite direction (counterclockwise, as viewed from the front end of the hook, rather than clockwise), you will discover how difficult it is to tie down the rib tightly and neatly at the front of the fly. The clockwise wraps of the thread tend to loosen the counterclockwise-wrapped rib. The key here is to reverse-palmer the fly by hackling backward and ribbing forward.

To reverse-palmer a fly, first tie in the hackle at the front of the shank, then take the thread to the rear, and tie in the body and ribbing materials.[4] Take the thread back to the front, wrap the body forward, tie it down, and clip the excess chenille or other material. Reverse-palmer the hackle to the rear. When you come to the rear of the body, use a couple or three tight wraps of the ribbing material to tie

---

[3] Paul Milstam, the professional tier from Malmö, Sweden, says he always ribs his flies, whether the pattern calls for it or not. "I add some rib to get an effect of curiosity on the fish. And it works very well."

[4] If you find the hackle feather gets in the way, tie in the body and ribbing materials first, wrap the body about three-fourths of the way forward, trap it with a couple of wraps, then tie in the hackle feather. Continue wrapping the body, tie it down, clip the excess, reverse-palmer the hackle, and continue and described above.

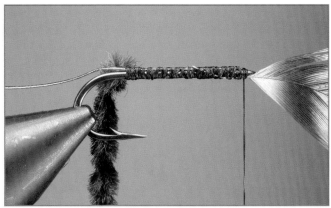

When ribbing a palmered fly, it's a good idea to tie the hackle in up front and the body and rib at the rear.

After wrapping the body material forward, and tying it off, you are ready to reverse-palmer the hackle.

Wriggle the rib as you wind it forward through the reverse-palmered hackle and you won't have as many trapped barbs to pick out.

down the hackle. Rib the fly forward in open spiral turns in the usual clockwise wrapping technique. Wriggle the rib back and forth as you go, to keep to a minimum the number of hackle barbs you trap. Tie down the rib and clip or break off the excess. Form a head and whip-finish. Carefully clip the excess hackle at the rear.

Make no mistake about it: You will trap barbs as you cross-rib the hackle. You can try picking them out later, using a bodkin or a needle, but it won't be easy—especially not with a wide or thick rib, such as was used in the photos for illustrative purposes. The more care you take while winding the rib,

the fewer hackles you will trap and the less frustration you will have to endure later. Many good tiers will not cross-rib their palmer-hackled flies because they'd rather tie a larger number of flies (to replace the ones damaged by toothy fish) than spend time wriggling ribs through hackles and picking out barbs. It's your decision which course to follow.

Tying off materials

Whenever you can, it's a good idea to tie off materials on the underside of the shank. It matters not to the fish, but your flies will look better—and you will feel better, more confident about them—if any lumpiness caused by the tying off and trimming is less visible under the shank.

Here's a great tip from Peter Frailey that will make your Woolly Worms (and Buggers, as well as other wet flies, streamers, and hackled nymphs) look ever so much neater: "For wet flies I almost always use a piece of drinking straw to aid in tying off with a whip-finish tool. It eliminates barb entrapment. I collect plastic straws in a variety of diameters and cut them in short lengths. I then slit the pieces along one side. The slit allows me to slip the straw-piece over the hanging thread, up and over the eye, and finally over the body, pushing the barbs toward the rear and out of the way. When I am done whip-finishing, I pull the straw-piece off by slipping a bodkin needle or tweezers under the straw on the opposite side of the slit and lifting."

If you have succeeded in getting your barbs angled forward, you might want to use the slit straw to push the hackle out of the way while building the head, even before the whip-finisher comes into play. This is such a good idea, I am still slapping myself on the side of the head for not having thought of it myself! I sure wish I'd learned it at the beginning rather than the end of the tying for this book. *Darn!*

Tying it altogether

Some of the best, most detailed instructions I know of for tying the Woolly Worm can be found on Kidfish, a web site subtitled "All About Lakes—and Fly Fishing Too! A Web-based tool for teaching Grade 5 to 7 students about our environment, fish, insects, and stewardship." Yes, I'm steering you to an educational site for kids. But what a site it is! Would that all tying books and sites intended for adults could be this cogent, thorough, and intelligent.

Go to the Basic Skills page in their Basic Fly Tying section (www.kidfish.bc.ca/tying/basic_skills.htm), and go through steps 6 through 8: *Wrapping materials and tying off, Controlling the materials when finishing the fly*, and *Finishing the fly*. You'll be glad you did, and be a better tier for it.

Woolly Worm Hooks

Tiers use a variety of hooks for tying Woolly Worms. Most use long-shank hooks, mostly 1X- and 2X-long, but some patterns go up to 6X-long. Standard, heavy-wire, and light-wire hooks may be used according to the depth at which you wish to fish your Woollies. If you are going to weight the fly for subsurface fishing, the hook's wire gauge doesn't much matter, except for strength.

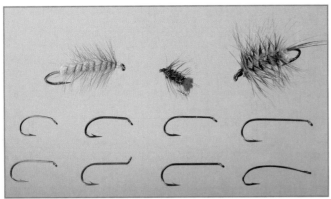

Woolly Worms can be tied on a variety of hook styles, lengths, and weights. Use your imagination and your fishing savvy.

If you are interested in experimenting with Woolly Worms in salt water better use stainless-steel or other corrosion-resistant hooks. I sometimes tie **Miller Woolly Worms** (page 32) on such hooks, because I find that snappers and other saltwater fish take them as well as they take similarly hued shrimp patterns of similar size. Saltwater tiers should have little trouble figuring out how to add Woolly Worms to their quivers.

When the recipe I found specified a particular hook, I listed it. But don't waste your tying and fishing time, running all over the county trying to find something like, say, a Kamasan 170. Use a close equivalent. You can find equivalents for most of the specified hooks in the Appendix beginning on page 223. And quite a few hook-equivalent charts are posted on tiers' web sites; find them by doing a Google (www.google.com) search. What they lack in comprehensiveness they make up for in being free. But if you tie a lot of flies, you should invest in a copy of Bill Schmidt's excellent *Hooks for the Fly: A Tier's Reference Guide* (Stackpole Books, 2000). In a pinch, use your imagination. I've tied Woolly Worms on some pretty bizarre hooks, and only a few of them turned out to be duds on the water.

Tying Variations

Naturally, you can tie the Woolly Worm in a wide variety of colors. In his authoritative but modestly named *Flies* (first published in 1950, and not-so-succinctly subtitled *Their Origin, Natural History, Tying, Hooks, Patterns, and Selections of Dry and Wet Flies, Nymphs, Streamers, Salmon Flies for Fresh and Salt Water in North America and the British Isles Including a Dictionary of 2,200 Patterns*), J. Edson Leonard listed the pattern's ingredients as badger, furnace, or grizzly hackle palmered over a black, yellow, or brown chenille body, with a red tail. But you can use any colors you like; the fly-tying police won't come after you. The palmer hackle can match, complement, or contrast with the body. For the tail, many tiers of Woolly Worms omit it or use colors other than red and such materials as hackle fibers and points, yarn, floss, short tufts of marabou, hackle fluff, stubs of peacock herl, peacock sword, short strands of Krystal Flash or Flashabou—separately or in combination. Tie Woolly Worms light or dark, bright or dull, drab or glitzy—whatever you think the fish might like. I haven't yet found a Woolly Worm color or color combination that didn't, sooner or later, catch some kind of fish, somewhere. And usually sooner than later.

If you want a fly that lands with a *plop!* and that fishes deep, weight it. Western anglers often tie their Woollies that way for their brawling mountain streams and fast-flowing big rivers. You can wrap some heavy wire (lead or, preferably, a nontoxic lead substitute) on the hook shank as an underbody before wrapping the chenille, or slip a glass or metal bead or a cone head on the hook before tying on the thread.

As you add or substitute materials, the old Woolly Worm may merit a new name.

Use a short-barbed (or clipped), aft-angled brown hackle over an olive-chenille body and you will have tied Charlie Brooks's **Riffle Devil** (page 50). Use the same brown hackle (tied or clipped to taper) over a dubbed or peacock-herl body, add a forked, goose-biot tail (or, lately, a short tuft of marabou), and thank Randall Kaufmann for his **Simulator** (page 52).

Use red wool for the tail and black floss rather than chenille for the body, palmer a black hackle so it leans toward the rear, add a fine oval silver tinsel rib, tie it all on a standard-length wet-fly hook, and you will wind up with a **Zulu** (page 102), one of the most widely used British wet flies. Had you used burnt-orange floss for the body, and a ginger hackle, you'd have tied an **Orange Asher** (page 71)

Make splayed tails with two gray goose biots, wrap the shank in dark-brown chenille (slightly thicker in the thorax), palmer black, grizzly, or furnace hackle through the thorax area only, clip the hackle on the top, and you have Ted Trueblood's **Stonefly Nymph**, which isn't a true Woolly Worm because it's only semi-palmered.

Substitute peacock herl for the body in a red-hackled, fiber-tailed, grizzly-hackled Woolly Worm, and such fly-tying gurus as Eric Leiser insist it becomes the **Gray Hackle (Peacock)** wet fly instead. Most of us would just call it a **Peacock Woolly Worm** (see page 105 for a Norman Irvine pattern from Scotland that bears the PWW moniker).

Omit the tail, wrap a peacock-herl body on a tiny dry-fly hook, palmer a stiff grizzly rooster hackle through the body—*et voilà!*: **Griffith's Gnat** (page 79), arguably the most popular and effective adult- or cluster-midge imitation. The same pattern is known throughout the U.K. and much of Europe as the **Peacock Palmer**, in German-speaking countries as the **Stubenfliege** ("house fly"), and in Slovenia as the **Grey Palmer**. Add a few strands of Krystal Flash for a tail, and instead of George Griffith's Gnat you have Charles Jardine's **Sparkle Gnat**. Down on New Mexico's San Juan tailwater, they tie huge (sizes 6 and 8) Griffith's Gnats and call them **Dead Chickens**. Palmer a blue-dun hen hackle over a diminutive peacock body and you have a Welsh pattern called the **Blue Bomber.**

As we shall soon see, the Woolly possibilities are almost without end.

Whether classified as a nymph, a wet fly, or something else, the Woolly Worm suggests a great many aquatic creatures, from many kinds of larvae crawling on the bottom to caterpillars struggling nearer the surface. Whether it actually imitates any of them is not very important. Whatever else a fish may see in the Woolly Worm, it often sees a lively bugginess that fairly shouts, "*Food!*" Its vague suggestiveness makes the Woolly Worm more versatile than most truly imitative patterns.

Charles Brooks wrote, "Not all wet flies are as consistently successful as the Woolly Worm. I have never failed to take at least one fish with this pattern in any waters where I have fished it." I wish I could say the same, but I have been skunked while Woolly Worming. The longer I fish, the more convinced I become that skunk-proof patterns don't exist.

But I have caught a lot of fish on Woolly Worms, and caught them every which way—even by accident. Woolly Worms have attracted savage strikes when I was just letting them dangle downstream while trying to decide what to do next. Once, in the middle of a fishless day on the Esopus Creek in the Catskills, I let a Miller Woolly Worm trail behind me in the water as I trudged back up through a long riffle I had just fished to no effect. *Wham!*—brown trout. The only fish of the day, as it turned out. On the Sava-Bohinjka, high in the Julian Alps of Slovenia, while walking down through some ankle-deep water on the way to deeper, more promising-looking water, I cast a Woolly Worm ahead of me just to keep it from fouling. In about a hundred meters of walking, I caught six or seven small trout, both browns and rainbows. Can I credit the pattern? Perhaps not, because I have had similar results on other flies, including Wulffs, Muddlers, ants, and other patterns, wet and dry. But perhaps more often on Woolly Worms, especially if we consider the Bivisible a variation on the Woolly Worm. I'm not sure, because I don't have the patience or self-discipline to keep fishing logs. I know I should, but I don't.

Usually considered a trout fly, the Woolly Worm also sees a lot of duty for sea trout (sea-run browns), steelhead, Pacific and even Atlantic salmon, large- and smallmouth bass, panfish, carp, and—tied on stainless-steel or other corrosion-resistant hooks—a variety of smaller saltwater species. If it swims, you can probably catch it on a properly presented Woolly Worm of appropriate size and color. In *Flyfishing Around the World*, Tony Pawson refers to an article in which a fly fisher mentions having "watched a local catch [a sea trout] of 19 pounds on a fuzzy Woolly Worm" in Argentina's justly famed Rìo Grande.

There are almost as many ways to fish a Woolly Worm as to tie it. You can fish it on floating, sinking-tip, or sinking lines; as a point or dropper fly in a tandem or multifly rig. Fish it in or just below the surface film, on the bottom, or anywhere in between. Fish it weighted or unweighted. The weight may be added at the vise—in the form of a wrapped-wire underbody, dumbbell or bead-chain eyes, or a bead or cone head—or you can add it later, by pinching shot on the leader, sliding a bead on the tippet before tying on the fly, or using a weighted leader or sinking leader section. Dry Woolly Worms also can be tied on light-wire hooks, using dense, stiff rooster hackles and a thinner, lighter, more water-resistant body.

You can dead-drift a Woolly Worm, like a nymph, or swing it across the current, like a wet fly. At the end of the swing or drift, a twitch or two often entices strikes. Twitched or not, you can lift the fly out of the water into a back cast at the end of a swing or drift, or you can strip-retrieve it in long, strips or in short, stop-and-go strips.

However and wherever you like to fish, you can fish a Woolly Worm. Don't worry about breaking the rules. There aren't any.

Dead-drift fishing

Because of its "active" palmer hackle and its suggestive resemblance to any number of aquatic creatures, a Woolly Worm can tempt curious or hungry fish even when it isn't doing much more than drifting along in the current, anywhere in the water column from bottom to top.

Dead-drift nymphing

Dead-drifting Woolly Worms as if they were nymphs works well. And it's easier than dead-drifting more imitative nymphs. For one thing, the drift need not be truly dead. An imitative nymph pattern that is being fished too fast or too slow, in relation to the current, may raise doubts in a fish's pea-size brain. But its palmer hackle gives the Woolly Worm some built-in "action," so an extra bit of motion in the water seems to attract rather than to alarm. For another, fish that are locked onto nymphs may be so bottom-oriented that an artificial drifting just a few inches above the bottom goes ignored, both by the nymph-feeding zombies as well as by other fish that, for some reason or other, have decided they'll pass on the nymphs for now. Dead-drifted Woolly Worms seem to appeal to opportunistic feeders as well as to nymph-feeding fish.

When dead-drifting in slow to moderate currents that lack turbulence, I will nearly always give a few twitches or tugs on the line, a single long strip, or a long, slow lifting of the rod before launching the fly into a back cast. It's when I seem to get most of my strikes when dead-drift fishing. A merely curious fish that was content to watch the strange thing drifting along in the current can suddenly turn into an active predator if the unidentified object of its idle curiosity suddenly moves as if to escape.

When the water is fast, I usually choose to drift Woolly Worms that are weighted (or I more often use high-density leaders and short tippets). On floating lines and mono leader, the unweighted ones fish awfully close to the surface, where I often find that winged wet flies, drowned dries, and other patterns work better for me.

In pocket water and other turbulent flows, try casting a Woolly Worm upstream and let it tumble downstream toward you; as it nears you, lift your rod tip high and then lower it again as the fly continues tumbling downstream. (Brits sometimes call this technique "long-tumble nymphing." In America, it's more often called "high-stick nymphing" or just "high-sticking.") When fishing this way, I like to use one of Airflo's thin, fast-sinking Light Leaders with a very short tippet—never more than 2 feet long, and sometimes as short as a foot.

Dead-sinking

In lakes and ponds, in large eddies, and even in deep pools with hardly any current, I like to fish unweighted Woolly Worms on weighted leaders, usually a slow sinker. You don't get much drift this way, but there's something about a slowly sinking Woolly Worm that really turns fish on. After I have let the fly sink all the way to the bottom, or as deep as it will sink or I want it to sink, I usually give the fly a few short twitches or a long, slow pull before lifting it into the back cast. Again, this tends to make a passively attentive fish decide to grab the strange thing before it can get away. And, who knows, something else may also be at work in those fishy little brains.

Most who have considered the matter agree that properly tied Woolly Worms look a lot like aquatic beetle larvae. With about three dozen genera and more than 400 species widely distributed across the continent, the predaceous diving beetles of the family Dytiscidae are far and away the beetle larvae most likely to be encountered by trout and other predators. They occupy almost every type of habitat, including brackish water. A few species inhabit swift-running water, but most prefer quieter waters. And here's the piscatorial pay-off: Most species are air-breathers, which means they must periodically swim to the surface to breathe. Fish that have been feeding on dytiscid larvae are used to seeing them travel both directions between substrate and surface.

If you want to more closely imitate the larvae of predaceous diving beetles, use a 2X- to 4X-long streamer hook and tie in a tail of hackle fibers or a sparse tuft of yarn because most species have two long, "hairy" tails. The palmer hackle strongly suggests their six long, prominent legs up front and the filaments short in some species, long in others on their rear body segments. Some of them are pretty big—to 48 mm, nearly 2 inches.

Active-retrieve fishing

When fished actively, the Woolly Worm must be considered a general attractor. It matters little to the fish. Movement through the water, especially stop-and-go movement, really gets those palmer-hackle barbs pulsating. What, if anything, it might suggest to fish, I don't know. But it certainly seems to suggest food.

If you have a tendency to over-hackle your flies, using hackle feathers with barbs that are too long or wrapping too many turns as you palmer the body—and who among us hasn't at some time or another been guilty of either or both?—you may find that your Woolly Worms work better when actively fished.

Wet-fly swinging

Like other wet flies, Woolly Worms fish well on the swing. Depending on the speed of the current, the weight of the fly, and where I think the fish are feeding, I may cast the fly up and across, directly across, or slightly down and across the current.

In *Nymphing*, Gary Borger said the "slow draw" technique described by Charlie Fox for fishing wet ant patterns in slow water works as well with Woolly Worms: Cast down and across the current to a sighted fish or likely holding lie, and let the current slowly draw the fly away. In riffles and runs, Borger suggested using the same technique, jiggling the rod tip as the fly swings across the current.

Steelhead fishers, particularly Great Lakes steelheaders, have adopted Woolly Worms. So have some Pacific salmon fishers, although they show a heavy preference for Woolly Buggers—especially in Alaska. Most Atlantic salmon fly fishers still haven't attained Woolly wisdom, but they ought to. Those noblest salmonids will jump all over big, fat Woolly Worms fished on the swing or waked in the surface film.

Twitch-retrieving

In *Superior Flies* (1989), Leonard M. Wright, Jr., concludes his chapter on wet flies with a paragraph that begins, "Woolly Worms and girdle bugs—flies with lively, built-in action—are excellent when retrieved with slow twitches." Amen. Fast twitches work well, too, and so do mixed-speed twitch retrieves. The hackle on a properly tied Woolly Worm responds immediately to a twitched line, often turning a curious fish into a taking fish.

Strip-retrieving

Because of the palmer hackle's action, an actively retrieved Woolly Worm can work when all else fails. But I wouldn't go to the well too often with this method. It's never the first technique I use when fishing Woolly Worms in water with any current at all. It's something I try when things get slow and I get impatient.

And speaking of "slow," that's the top speed you should use with a Woolly Worm in still water. Of this pattern (which he ties in sizes 2 to 16, "from a monster to a mere morsel"), John Merwin has written, in *Stillwater Trout* (1980), "The fly has accounted for untold numbers of trout over 10 pounds from lakes when fished with a sinking line and a slow, stripping retrieve."

A few patterns fish well fast, and I have tried to note that in the pattern discussions.

Hand-twist retrieving

The great English fly fisher Charles Jardine, in his *Classic Guide to Fly-Fishing for Trout* (1991), says the Woolly Worm "is imitative of dobson, fish, and alder flies and is ideal for early-season bottom-searching tactics with a floating line, long leader, and ultra-slow retrieves." If you can't get the hang of hand-twist retrieving, just use short, slow, steady strips by using the fingers of your line hand to pull the line along, without moving the hand itself very much. It isn't as pretty as the hand twist, but it's almost as effective. Just be sure you don't completely lose control of the line when you drop it. I usually catch the dropped line between the little finger (pinky) and the butt of my palm as I rotate the wrist forward to catch the line with my thumb and forefinger. (Whether this is actually any less tricky than a proper hand-twist retrieve, seems to depend on the individual's particular dexterity or deficiency thereof.)

"Dapping"

Heavily palmered dapping flies have always held great sway among British and Irish dappers. True dapping requires a long rod (10 to 12 feet, anyway), and a 6- to 15-foot "blow line" or "floss" (a long piece, knotted every 12 to 18 inches, of the same poly yarn used to make spinner wings) between backing and leader. By raising and lowering his rod, the dapping fly fisher controls the way his fly dances and skitters along the surface as the wind moves the floss. (For an excellent discussion of dapping, see Charles Jardine's "Dapping: British Angling Eccentricity at its Finest" in the May/June 1998 issue of *American Angler*. I am proud to have commissioned that article.)

Both dry and regular Woolly Worms also work well for *American*-style dapping: presenting the fly without a cast, by swinging or lowering it onto the water from the rod tip. The keys to this technique are (1) keeping only as much leader (and line, if necessary) out of the tip guide as it takes to reach the water, (2) keeping the reel drag set very light, (3) waving the rod about over the trout's lie as little as possible, and (4) a quiet, stealthy approach. If you aren't wearing out your waders at the knees, you're doing it all wrong. Crawl behind bushes, reeds, trees, and boulders. Move slowly and quietly; fish can feel vibrations better than they can hear sounds from above the surface. Poke the rod tip out into place no sooner than you must, and as slowly as you can. You probably won't be able to see the fly as it lands on the water, but don't worry: the fish will.

Any Woolly Worm, Bivisible, or Palmer Fly will work as a dapping fly, but if you want to dap on the surface, choose one of the dry patterns in Chapter 6 and palmer it heavy with an extra-large, stiff rooster hackle.

3. A WORLD OF WOOLLY WORMS

Being so basic a tie, the Woolly Worm naturally lends itself to whim, fancy, and experimentation. So, indulge yourself. Just don't count on achieving fly-tying immortality. No matter what changes you make, chances are better than good somebody has already "invented" the same fly.

No one knows for certain what the original Woolly Worm looked like, so no one is in a position to call a foul on you for choosing the wrong colors, materials, or methods.

COLOR VARIATIONS

Colors can run the gamut, from gloomy to gaudy. Even the hook; you don't have to stick to bronzed hooks. If you tie Woolly Worms for salt or brackish waters, corrosion prevention will force you to go to stainless steel, tinned, cadmium-plated, or other such hooks. Try black-lacquered salmon hooks, gold- or nickel-plated or blued bait hooks, and those red, blue, green, and other brightly colored hooks just beginning to invade fly tying.

Thread color

Most tiers use black thread, but you may want to use another color for your weighted flies: red or brown, say. Or you may want to use a colored thread so you wind up with a head that better imitates a particular aquatic creature, that better complements the rest of the pattern, or that you think might be more attractive.

Tail color

Red is the color of first choice among tiers who tail their Woolly Worms with other than grizzly hackle, but I wouldn't hesitate to use other colors: orange, yellow, green, chartreuse, black, gray, whatever.

Body color

Black, brown, olive, yellow, orange, red, and green bodies inhabit a lot of fly boxes, but I've also seen Woolly Worms with white, pink, chartreuse, maroon, and purple bodies; with two- and three-color bodies; with mottled bodies caused by using variegated chenille or speckling the chenille with a permanent marker prior to palmering the fly.

Steelheaders like to use fluorescent chenille, sometimes in two colors, fore and aft.

Rib color

Those who rib their Woolly Worms often choose silver, but don't hesitate to use gold or copper tinsel or wire if those colors better suit your plans and purposes. And don't forget to try thread, tinsel, or floss in other colors. Or even stripped hackle quills or hairs from a moose mane. Here, too, the sky's the limit.

Hackle color

When it comes to hackling the Woolly Worm, grizzly wins hands down. The grizzly can be pale or dark, natural or dyed. The barring seems to many anglers to be part of the Woolly Worm's seductively suggestive, now-you-see-it, now-you-don't appeal. Sort of a subtler variation on the chiaroscuro theme so well played by the red-and-white Daredevle spoon. However, some tiers prefer to use other two-tone feathers: furnace, cree, badger, barred ginger. And some patterns may actually look and fish better with a ginger, dun, cream, brown, black, or other single-shade hackle feather.

MATERIAL CONSIDERATIONS

Material choices for the Woolly Worm tend to show more uniformity and conformity than color choices.

Hook

Your hook will doubtless be made of steel—carbon or stainless—both otherwise you have a lot of latitude. You will need to select its size, shape, weight, and strength for the job at hand, not to please some arbiter of pattern. Although 1X- and 2X-long hooks are traditional, don't be afraid to go longer or shorter, or to use a curved-shank hook. Unless you are tying for a juried exhibition or a competition, where conformity counts, let your fish sense be your guide in choosing the right hook style or size.

Tailing material

Most tiers use either hackle fibers or yarn, but hackle points, quill slips, herl stubs or points, biots, frayed floss, hair or fur, pinches of marabou, Craft Fur, and any number of other materials can be used, or are called for in some of the varia-

tions. Some tiers and patterns omit the tail altogether. Tail composition and length matter in dry Woollies, but for wet flies, the tail's main purpose is to help imitate or suggest the natural or to attract a fish's attention or curiosity. Brightly colored tails also help to direct strikes at the business end of the fly (what Don Gapen called a "striking point").

Body material

Chenille is far and away the favored choice (and fittingly so, as *chenille* is French for "caterpillar"), but many other materials may be used. Wool and synthetic yarns, tinsel and tinsel-blend chenille, fur and dubbing or dubbing brushes, floss, flat or oval tinsel, peacock herl, braids, and all the usual fly-body materials make their appearances in flies that still bear the Woolly Worm name.

Ribbing material

If you asked Woolly Worm traditionalists for a show of hands on this one, it would be a horse race between "none" and "silver oval tinsel." But if armoring the fly is the reason for ribbing, fine wire—or even tying or rod-wrapping thread or clear monofilament—may well be a better choice. Those who rib Woolly Worms for the sizzle rather than the strengthening often use flat or embossed tinsel, floss, Flashabou or Krystal Flash, colored or fluorescent monofilament, or other eye-catching materials.

Hackle material

To me, saddle hackles make the most sense, because of the relative length of the Woolly Worm's body. Others like to use long neck hackles. Some tiers prefer to use stiff rooster hackle, others like soft hen hackle. I use both, depending on my mood or my plan. On large Woolly Worms used for bass, pike, steelhead, salmon, or saltwater game fish, schlappen feathers often are used. Game-bird feathers also see duty in Woolly Worms of appropriate size—albeit more often as face hackles or collars than as palmer hackles.

When tiers use tinsel chenille, mohair yarn, shaggy dubbing, or certain other high-bulk body materials, some forego the palmer hackle. I doubt whether such flies should properly be called Woolly Worms. Gary Borger's Hair Leg Woolly Worm is a good case in point: great fly, but it really should bear another name. But we'll compromise and admit a few of the hackle-free patterns that particularly intrigue us.

Head material

Tying thread, coated or uncoated, is the material most often used. But proportionately larger-than-normal heads are standard on Woolly Worms, so you will see other materials used: peacock or ostrich herl, yarn or dubbing, and metal, glass, or plastic beads. Bass and saltwater fly fishers often add painted, stick-on, bead-chain, dumbbell, Optic, or doll's eyes.

Beads, bead-chain eyes, and dumbbell eyes make it easy to weight a Woolly Worm; dumbbell eyes provide the most weight. You may also pinch a split shot to the front of the shank. Because of the toxicity of the lead to birds and other creatures, and the tendency of pinched shot to come loose during casting, you might want to use tin-alloy shot, which isn't as heavy. Always use epoxy cement or superglue to secure lead shot to the shank, which ought to have a thread base to hold the cement.

Wire-weighted underbodies

Some tiers who like weighted Woolly Worms prefer to use lead, or nontoxic, lead-substitute, wire on the hook shank. In increasing order of weight, the wire-weighting methods include lashing a single length of wire atop or beneath the shank with tying thread; lashing a length of wire on either side of the shank; wrapping an underbody of wire around the shank; and lashing a length of wire along the shank and then wrapping an underbody of wire.

The heavy wire, however attached, can run the length of the shank, or just a portion, depending on the sink rate sought.

SOME WINNING WOOLLY WORM PATTERNS

Over the years I have come across a lot of Woolly Worms, and most of those that I fished, worked. And why not? They shared some winning characteristics, namely a mobile, buggy-looking palmer hackle and a generally larval look in size and shape.

I suppose this might be called a Tan Woolly Worm elsewhere in the country, but in Maryland it is always the Patuxent Special, and hardly any fly fisher in the Free State would think of venturing forth without this fly.

Despite its name, the pattern's birthplace was elsewhere in the state. Jay Sheppard described its origin in a sheet that is (or at least was, when I was a member) distributed to and treasured by every new member of the Potomac–Patuxent Chapter of Trout Unlimited: "The Patuxent Special was discovered in a desperate attempt to catch some trout on the Savage River in western Maryland in April 1979. After several hours with only one strike on a dozen different patterns, I tied on a #8 Michigan Wriggler and was immediately rewarded with two strikes on the first swing of the fly!" As the day wore on, Sheppard took more than a dozen trout on this fly and had three strikes on a single swing.

By 1981, after a lot of trial-and-error experimentation on the Patuxent River, his home water, Sheppard had arrived at his killer combo of colors and materials. Among the early field testers: Bernard (as in Lefty) Kreh and then-Congressman Berkley (as in the tackle company) Bedell.

Sheppard insists he didn't really invent this version of the Woolly Worm. "I have modified the Wriggler [a Hexagenia nymph imitation from Michigan—GS] by just eliminating the shellback." Refreshingly modest, perhaps, but Jay has put a lot of thought and fishing time into this pattern so that it catches fish and holds up well. "It is not unusual to catch 40 trout or smallmouth in a few hours on just one fly," he says.

Jay has tried a lot of color combinations, but none beats the one presented below. The best color for the chenille is a golden ginger. And the tips of the fox squirrel tail fibers should closely match the chenille; tails from adult animals work better than those from immature squirrels. Don't try to substitute red squirrel or red fox for that fox-squirrel tail—neither will work nearly as well.

This is one pattern in which the weight is not optional; it simply doesn't fish as well without plenty of weight. You've got to get this pattern *down!* Sometimes, Sheppard says, he uses cone heads on size 8s. When fishing deep or fast water, he also clips a large split shot about 12 to 15 inches above the fly.

Besides trout and smallmouth bass wherever they fish, a lot of P-P Chapter members also swear by this fly for steelheading in New York State's Salmon River. (In fact, when I contacted Jay about tying a fly for the book, he and Charlie Gelso were about to head north on their annual steelhead trip to Pulaski, New York, "with a bucket load of Patuxent Specials.") Sheppard says the pattern has taken several species of trout and salmon all over the U.S., including Alaska. (I can add to the list at least one

lenok, *Brachymystax lenok,* a char-like salmonid, in Siberia.) Besides bass, non-salmonid species that have fallen to the Patuxent Special include perch, crappies, and other panfish; bonefish and redfish (red drum) in salt water. In other words, and most emphatically, the Patuxent Special isn't "just" a Tan Woolly Worm.

Patuxent Special

Hook: Mustad 9672, a 3X-long nymph and streamer, sizes 8 to 12—10 being Sheppard's first choice

Thread: Black 6/0, tied on at the rear of the shank

Tail: Fox-squirrel tail, very bulky and as long as the body or shank, about 1/8-inch of the black band showing at the rear of the body; the butts should not extend beyond the nethermost wrap of weighting wire.

Underbody: .030- or .035-in lead or nontoxic wire wrapped from the butts of the tail hair to just behind the eye; "ramped down" in front of the lead with tying thread, which then wraps down and back over the wire before being taken back to the rear; coat the thread-covered wire and the wrapped butts of the tail and hackle with head cement or Hard As Nails or similar cheap clear nail polish

Body: Golden-ginger medium chenille

Palmer hackle: Golden-ginger, ginger, or very light-brown (to match the color of the body and tail), stiff, very-large neck hackle (barbs 2 to 3 gap-widths long or longer), tied in by the butt and palmered in 4 to 6 even turns with the dull side facing forward, the quill worked down between the turns of chenille; *after securing the palmer hackle with 2 tight wraps of thread, some tiers who use saddle hackles twist the feather so the shiny side faces forward and wrap a 3- or 4-turn wet-fly collar at the front*

Head: Tying thread—small, and cemented

Tying Tips

Try to find a golden-ginger chenille; it's worth the effort. "The original chenille was the old Orvis tan color, which was a golden ginger," Sheppard says. "Orvis changed that shade a few years back to a real tan, which does not work as well."

To properly clip the fox squirrel, pull the hairs at right angles to the tail bone and cut across the black band. Keep those tied-down butts short; don't wrap the weighting wire over them. After tying in the tail, take the thread to the front.

Once the weighting wire has been wrapped, wrap a slope of tying thread at the front, then take the thread to the rear by wrapping over the wire.

After tying in the chenille and hackle, wrap the thread forward again. Apply head cement or clear fingernail polish over the thread-wrapped wire and material butts and wrap the chenille forward while the stuff is still tacky.

As for selecting a hackle, "I like the large hackles toward the middle rear of a good neck," Sheppard says. He ties off with "a double-lock of the hackle tip: three to four thread wraps with the hackle forward, then three to four more wraps with the hackle pulled back."

Fishing Tips

As good as this pattern is, presentation is key to the Patuxent Special's success. *Don't* fish it dead-drift—except for salmon, steelhead, and carp if you put the fly "right down on the bottom in front of them." For trout and smallies, retrieve it rapidly, in fast, short strips, with the rod tip held close to the water. Sheppard says the pause between strips should be no longer than the time it takes to reach up and grab another 10 to 20 inches of line. Pause longer than a second, he says, and you can pretty much forget about catching fish.

Cast upstream or directly across the current. Let the fly sink or begin stripping as soon as it lands. "Rapidly jigging it directly in front of a log jam or pile of roots while standing upstream works well, too."

Strikes are often savage, so use a 4X tippet, no lighter. And check the tippet for abrasion or chafing after every fish or missed strike.

Because of the way the fly is tied and weighted, the Patuxent Special is easy to free up when you inadvertently cast it into a tree. "A gentle tug usually flips the fly back off the twig," Sheppard notes.

If you can't catch fish with a Patuxent Special, Sheppard says, either you aren't fishing over any fish or you aren't moving the fly briskly enough.

SPENCER Tied by R. G. Balogh

In *Trout* (3rd edition, 1978), Ray Bergman listed a **Gray Hackle** (body of peacock herl or yellow floss with grizzly palmer hackle) as one of his "essential wet flies." But he also wrote that the Spencer was one of three patterns that could take its place and, "in fact, are frequently more effective."

Spencer

Hook:	1X- or 2X-long wet-fly, "any size according to needs"
Thread:	Unspecified; *black 6/0 will suffice*
Tag:	Gold tinsel at bend, below tail
Tail:	Yellow wool tag
Body:	Gray fur, dubbed
Rib:	Gold tinsel
Palmer hackle:	Gray badger hen

PEACOCK WOOLLY WORM

I found this pattern of the late John Beams on the web site (www.flyshop.co.za) of The Flyshop, a South African company based in both Johannesburg and Praetoria. Gerhard Laubscher, one of The Flyshop's proprietors, says, "It is an extremely successful stillwater trout fly, especially if dressed very sparsely."

Peacock Woolly Worm

Hook:	Mustad 9671, a 2X-long nymph, sizes 8 to 18
Thread:	Black 6/0
Tail:	Black hackle tips, topped by a small, shorter clump of red wool or marabou
Underbody:	Lead wire
Palmer hackle:	Sparse, fine, extra-long-barbed black hen, tied in at the front and reverse-palmered to the bend in no more than 4 turns
Rib:	Copper wire, used to secure the palmered hackle before being spiraled forward
Body:	5 to 8 peacock herls, spun around the tying thread to form a "chenille rope"

Tying Tip

If your hackles are too well-barbed for this sparsely hackled pattern, pull all the barbs off one side of the hackle feather before tying it in.

It's worth repeating this advice from The Flyshop's web site: "Keep the hackle wraps down to no more than four; this will create a more lifelike effect, resulting in more fish."

ASHY

This palmer fly was listed by Mary Orvis Marbury in her 1892 *Favorite Flies and Their Histories* (1892). For the palmer hackle she specified "a dun or ash-colored hackle feather," then went on to note, "These feathers are worth more than their weight in gold...." Happily, dun hackle is no longer so difficult to come by, but they are still valuable assets in the fly tier's kit.

Ashy

Hook:	Unspecified; *use a 1X- or 2X-long wet-fly, size to suit*
Thread:	Unspecified; black 6/0 will do
Body:	Red or orange—*what, she doesn't say, but we can use floss, yarn, dubbing, Mylar tinsel, or whatever else falls to hand*
Palmer hackle:	Dun rooster saddle

ARROWHEAD Tied by R. G. Balogh

The creation of Earl Grunnett, of Duluth, Minnesota, the Arrowhead can be tied wet or dry. I'm listing the wet fly as described by Keith Perrault in *Perrault's Standard Dictionary of Fishing Flies* (1984), a valuable archive of fly recipes.

Arrowhead

Hook:	Standard or 1X-long wet-fly, sizes 12 and 14
Thread:	Black or brown
Tail:	2 hen hackles, grizzly and brown, tied in at the bend so their tips extend half a shank-length or more to the rear; do not clip!
Body:	Peacock herl
Palmer hackle:	The hackles from the tail, palmered together to the eye

Tying Tip

To tie the Arrowhead as a dry fly, start with 2 rooster hackles and substitute thread for the herl in the body.

ORANGE FLAME Tied by Peter Frailey

Peter Frailey calls his creation "a Woolly Worm with an attitude." He fishes this fly as both nymph and streamer when big orange dragonflies buzz over his favorite bass pond and "the big bass come to it like cowboys to a chuckwagon (okay, that is a bit exaggerated)."

Orange Flame

Hook:	2X-long nymph or streamer, size 8, "the only size I've ever tied it on"
Thread:	Yellow Danville 3/0, "to contrast against the orange collar"
Underbody:	8 to 10 wraps of .020-inch lead wire
Tail:	Orange neck hackle fibers, half again as long as the hook gap
Palmer hackle:	Furnace brown rooster saddle
Body:	5 peacock herls twisted together as a chenille rope—*optionally, with 2 strands of Krystal Flash*—and counter-wrapped forward after coating the top of the hook shank and lead wraps with head cement or thick nail polish
Collar:	Orange neck hackle, 3 to 5 turns

Tying Tips

By counter-wrapping the body and then palmering the hackle normally, the hackle effectively serves as a rib reinforcing the relatively fragile peacock body. Recently, Peter sent me this e-mail: "Tested the Orange Flame against sunfish on Sunday. I tied the O.F. with the 5 herls twisted together with 2 strands of Krystal Flash, then counter-wrapped forward over a shank that was first lightly coated with Sally Hanson nail polish. I think it passed the durability test. It remained perfect until fish number 20, when one herl broke loose. Also the herl had lost

a lot of its bushiness by then, but no amount of reinforcement can prevent that. After number 24, four herls were broken but the fly looked basically the same in the water. That sounds durable enough for me. No need for a wire rib, I conclude."

From a separate message: "My guess is that this might also be a killer pattern as a **Red Flame** or **Yellow Flame**, as red and yellow are well-known attractor colors. Besides orange-colored dragonflies, we also have a huge hatch of blue-colored damselflies. Some day I will try a **Blue Flame**."

.56%ER

Pronounce it "Point Fifty-Six-Per-Center." This fly is the creation of the late Tom Nixon, the warmwater fly-fishing legend from Lake Charles, Louisiana, but this pattern dates back to when he lived in Missouri, where he also fished for trout. The .56%er was featured in Nixon's landmark book *Fly Tying and Fly Fishing for Bass and Panfish* (1990). His son, Tom, Jr., explains that the name came from Ivory Soap's claim of being 99.44% pure: "There was a bunch of dry-fly purists on the White River in Arkansas who decided, when trout wouldn't rise to a dry fly, that maybe they were only as pure as Ivory Soap. When nobody was looking, they would tie on a wet fly to catch fish. And the fly they used became known as the .56%er." I certainly wouldn't hesitate to use this on bass or trout—or, tied on appropriate hooks, with perhaps something a bit more durable for the tail, on steelhead, salmon, or saltwater species.

.56%er

Hook:	4X-long bronzed or gold-plated, Aberdeen streamer with a turned-down eye, sizes 8 to 16
Thread:	Unspecified, but black 6/0 would suffice
Underbody:	Lead wire, wrapped on the shank; 10 turns of .025-in for a size 10 hook, and adjusted accordingly for larger or smaller hooks
Tail:	Lemon wood-duck flank fibers, fairly thick and nearly as long as the shank
Belly:	Yellow single-ply yarn, tied in at the bend on the underside of the shank and pulled forward under the body before palmering the hackle
Body:	Oxford gray yarn, wrapped "long and lean"
Palmer hackle:	Grizzly saddle, the barbs about a gap-width long and stripped from one side of the quill; palmered forward in about 5 or 6 open spirals for a sparse look

DUCK LAKE WOOLLY WORM

George F. Grant, in *Montana Trout Flies* (1972), wrote of this tail-less, olive-and-grizzly fly that "its size and general coloration strongly suggests that it was created to simulate the nymph of the Dragon Fly that is often so prevalent in shallow, weedy lakes." That, or damsel-fly nymphs. When I fished Duck Lake (which is on the Blackfeet Indian Reservation a few miles east of Glacier National Park in northwestern Montana), the well-fed rainbow trout there showed an exceptionally strong preference for olive damsel-fly nymphs.

Duck Lake Woolly Worm

Hook:	Mustad 79580, or similar 4X-long streamer, sizes 2 to 8
Thread:	Olive or black
Body:	Dark-olive chenille—*wrapped fat to imitate dragonflies, slender for damsels*
Palmer hackle:	Grizzly hen

YAKIMA WHITEFISH FLY

With a name like this I don't know whether this is supposed to imitate whitefish fry or be used to catch whitefish.

Yakima Whitefish Fly

Hook:	1X-long wet-fly, sizes 10 and 12
Thread:	Black or brown
Body:	Yellow floss
Palmer hackle:	Brown hen

VOSS BARK NYMPH Tied by Wayne Mones

The English fly fisher Conrad Voss Bark has had several careers: as parliamentary correspondent for the BBC, as the first "news reader" (that's English for "anchor man") on British television, as the fishing correspondent for *The Times of London*, as top-drawer fly angler in English competitions, and as the author of numerous articles as well as the book *A Fly on the Water* (1986). Charles Jardine calls this fly "a wonderful all-rounder suggesting damsels, shrimps, and olive nymphs. Fish it on a floating line and long leader, either blind or to observed fish."

Voss Bark Nymph

Hook:	Standard nymph, sizes 10 and 12
Thread:	Brown
Underbody:	Lead wire
Tail:	Cream rooster-hackle fibers
Abdomen:	Olive seal fur or substitute, dubbed
Thorax:	Brown or claret seal fur or substitute, dubbed
Palmer hackle:	Fiery-brown rooster

Tying Note

Perrault listed a **Palmer Nymph** attributed to Voss Bark that differs in most respects: sizes 8 to 12, either 3 peacock-sword or gray-hackle fibers for the tail, a tapered body of yellow floss, a green or clipped brown palmer hackle, a yellow thread head, and *an optional antenna of dark-gray hackle fibers forming a V over the eye.*

HAIG-BROWN CATERPILLAR Tied by Ian Ricketson

Roderick Haig-Brown tied his Caterpillars—tailless Woolly Worms, really—in at least four colors (black, brown, fiery brown, and orange) which he fished for rainbow and cutthroat trout and summer steelhead. I am listing the **Black Caterpillar** (which he called "an A-1 ant imitation"), but you can tie the others simply by substituting the appropriate colors.

Haig-Brown Caterpillar

Hook:	2X-long nymph or wet-fly, sizes 10 to 2/0, mostly 4 to 8
Thread:	Black 6/0
Rib:	Fine, oval gold tinsel
Palmer hackle:	Black hen, long and soft ("ragged black or metallic green" Haig-Brown wrote in a margin note, according to the British Columbia fly-fishing historian Arthur James Lindgren)
Body:	Black seal's fur, dubbed

COSMIC WOOLLY WORM Tied by George Vosmik

George Vosmik (rhymes with "cosmic"), of Rocky River, Ohio, just calls this a Woolly Worm, but I think it's sufficiently different to deserve a distinct name. Anyway, some of his colleagues call him Cosmic Vosmik, not only because of the rhyme, but in part because of his "artful deceivers."

Fishing a placid little meadow stream in Maine one day, George and some buddies found that brook trout and chain pickerel would "decimate" these flies on alternate casts. Since then, he has discovered that his Cosmic Worms will catch almost everything that swims, from bluegill to big bass.

Cosmic Woolly Worm

Hook:	Mustad 9671 or 9672, or equivalent 2X- or 3X-long nymph or streamer, sizes 10 to 14
Thread:	Black 6/0
Tail:	Fluorescent-red y vertical loop and
Underbody:	6 wraps of lead
Body:	Chenille, in thirds always black, the fluorescent-green,
Rib:	Optionally, silver
Palmer hackle:	Soft, webby grizzl

Tying Tips

Vosmik says he palmers his Wooll both ways, although he more ofte the rear. "I know the old tying b should be tied with the dull side of but I never could figure out the log

"Don't be afraid to change fron hackle," George says. "You may find that tan or orange or white or black feathers palmered over the body will be effective as well." Just make sure the hackle is nice and soft, so it will move with the water or when you strip-retrieve the fly.

Fishing Tips
"Woolly Worms have been a mainstay for many years with me," George Vosmik writes. "Trout, bluegills, bass, and almost everything else eat them readily. Whether fished dead-drift like a nymph or stripped vigorously like a streamer, there are times when the Woolly Worm has no equal."

When he plans to strip the fly in imitation of a baitfish, Vosmik says the ribbed versions work best—especially the version with chartreuse amidships. However, he warns, "You may find that on certain days silver or gold ribbing is just what the fish want. On other days, the ribbing seems to scare anything in sight. Perhaps you need to carry a supply of ribbed and plain flies in the sizes and colors that work for you. I do."

GREEN GRUB Tied by Alberto Jimeno

This is the first fly that Alberto Jimeno, of Nashua, New Hampshire, learned to tie—from a beginner's tying kit he bought on eBay just a few years back. Since then, Alberto has quickly become an excellent tier; you will find several of his ties in this book. His first fly-caught fish, a 7-inch sunfish, was also caught on the first of these flies (originally, chenille-headed) that came out of his vise. Ever since, the Green Grub has been one of Alberto's go-to panfish patterns. Later, he added the bead head, so he wouldn't have to use split shot to get the fly down where the fish are.

Green Grub

Hook:	Mustad 9672, a 3X-long streamer, sizes 10 and 12
Head:	Black bead
Thread:	Black 6/0
Tail:	Brown or dun hackle fibers
Body:	Olive chenille
Rib:	Fine gold wire
Palmer hackle:	Brown or dun hen neck, tied in behind the bead and reverse-palmered over the body to the bend

Fishing Tip
"I fish this fly as a nymph," Alberto wrote on Peter Frailey's fine Fishing With Flies web site (www.fishingwithflies.com), "letting it sink to the bottom and then slowly stripping it back to me. … This fly has caught sunfish, crappie, largemouth bass, and even a few catfish. I'm not sure what nymph this fly imitates, but like the original Woolly Worm the Green Grub catches a lot of fish."

SHAGGY TAIL

I have literally translated *Korosep*, what this pattern is called in Slovenia, whence it comes. The difference between it and the better-known **Zulu** (page 102) from the U.K. is indeed slim. The Shaggy Tail is just one of several simple, yet effective palmer flies widely used in Slovenia. Others include the **Romar** (Palmer, or Pilgrim, see page 78), a brown- or ginger-hackled dry, and the **Carnik** (Witch, or Sorcerer), a peacock-bodied, ginger-palmered, gold-ribbed fly with either a red hackle-fiber tail or a gold tip.

Shaggy Tail

Hook:	Standard or long-shank wet-fly, sizes 12 and 14
Thread:	Black 6/0
Tail:	Short tuft of red wool
Rib:	Flat silver tinsel
Palmer hackle:	Black hen saddle
Body:	Black wool yarn

BOSTWICK Tied by Alberto Jimeno

This venerable wet fly was listed by Ray Bergman in *Trout*.

Bostwick

Hook:	Unspecified; use your favorite Woolly Worm hook
Thread:	Unspecified; black 6/0 will do
Tail:	Barred mandarin-duck fibers; *alternatively, in case you don't have or can't find mandarin duck, try using barred wood duck—according to Eric Leiser, they're virtually identical*
Body:	Flat silver tinsel
Palmer hackle:	Brown and grizzly hen hackles, mixed (palmered one through the other)

TWISTED WOOLLY

Besides palmering one hackle through another, as in the pattern preceding, you will find other twin-hackled recipes that call for palmering the hackles together, with or without folding them one inside the other. During the course of researching patterns for this book, I discovered yet another method of palmering two feathers, for which I shall be forever indebted to George Bodmer and Terry Hellekson (see the **Cased Caddis** on page 54 in the next chapter). Here's my generic-pattern approach to this wonderful technique:

Twisted Woolly

Hook:	1X- to 3X-long nymph or wet-fly, sizes 8 to 14
Head:	*Optionally, bead or cone head to suit*
Thread:	Black, brown, or other suitable 6/0
Rib:	Fine wire—gold, silver, or copper, to suit the rest of the pattern
Body:	Yarn, dubbing, chenille, peacock herl—something to cushion the twisted hackle
Palmer hackle:	2 saddle hackles, tied in by their butts at the front, twisted together, and reverse-palmered in close turns to the bend; *optionally, one or both tips left unclipped as tail*—use contrasting hackles: black and white, grizzly and blue dun, fiery brown and cream, furnace and ginger, black and olive, blue dun and purple-dyed grizzly, etc.

Tying Tips

Select saddle hackles with reasonably flexible stems. Even so, always counter-rib the palmered hackles with wire, because the torsion on the twisted stems may make them somewhat more likely to break under the stress and strain of a struggling fish.

If you don't use a bead or cone head, coat your thread head with head cement or clear nail polish to reinforce it. If you decide to use beadchain or dumbbell eyes, start the palmer hackle behind the eyes and use yarn, chenille, dubbing, or herl to build a head around and over the eyes.

Call me conservative, but I think a tinsel chenille body detracts from the effect of the twisted palmer hackle.

Don't forget to try twisted dual hackles on Woolly Buggers as well.

YELLOW WOOLLY WORM

Other, similar patterns bear the same name. This one, listed by Perrault, offers a few touches of its own.

Yellow Woolly Worm

Hook:	1X-long wet-fly, sizes 10 and 12
Thread:	Black
Tail:	Peacock sword, with red floss on top
Body:	Yellow chenille
Palmer hackle:	Furnace hen

FURNACE WORM

With colors as hot as a glowing furnace and palmered with furnace hackle, what else could I call it?

Furnace Worm

Hook:	Standard to 2X-long wet-fly or nymph, sizes 6 to 14
Thread:	Fluorescent-orange 6/0
Tail:	Hot red-orange egg yarn tuft, a gap-width long
Body:	Fluorescent red-orange chenille
Palmer hackle:	Furnace hen—neck or saddle to suit
Head:	Tying thread, large

COCK-A-TOUCHE Tied by Wayne Mones

Despite the French name, this Woolly Worm pattern hails from Japan.

Cock-a-Touche

Hook: 2X-long wet-fly, sizes 8 to 14
Thread: Red
Palmer hackle: Badger or light-furnace rooster saddle, tied in at the front and reverse-palmered to the bend
Tail: Red hackle fibers, topped by the tips of the peacock herl used to make the body
Rib: Silver wire or flat tinsel
Body: 2 to 4 strands of peacock herl

CRAPPIE WORM

Fish this one in still water with a stop-and-go, rising-and-falling action. If the very idea doesn't gag you, try jigging it under a floating strike indicator—the way bobber fishers tempt crappies.

Crappie Worm

Hook: 1X- or 2X-long wet-fly, sizes 8 to 12
Thread: Red
Tail: Bright-red yarn, frayed floss, hackle point, or hackle fibers
Body: Yellow chenille
Palmer hackle: White, closely palmered

RAUPE Tied by R. G. Balogh

The name is German for "Caterpillar." Other colors may be used to match the caterpillar "hatch" in your area.

Raupe

Hook: 3X- or 4X-long streamer, sizes 8 to 12
Thread: Olive
Tail: Red hackle fibers, yarn, or frayed floss, full and slightly more than a gap-width long
Body: Olive or green wool yarn, the surplus left untrimmed until the end (see Head)
Palmer hackle: Brown, badger, or furnace saddle, palmered forward in 4 or 5 turns with the barbs angled forward
Head: The butt end of the body yarn, trimmed flush over the eye, the way the wing butts are trimmed on Al Troth's Elk Hair Caddis; before finishing, take a couple of thread wraps around the shank under the yarn, then whip-finish

GRIZZLY BEAR

Unlike most of the fuzzy patterns designed to imitate the woolly-bear caterpillar, this panfish pattern from the Missourian Denis Hancock (whosoever modestly "makes no claim of originality or uniqueness") is a slow sinker rather than a dry fly. Because of the heavily palmered hackle, it will float for a while—long enough to attract strikes. If a bluegill doesn't take it within half a minute, he says, give it a twitch. If that doesn't work, start stripping it in, slowly at first but speeding up as you go.

Grizzly Bear

Hook: 2X- to 3X-long streamer, sizes 8 to 14
Thread: Black 8/0 or 6/0
Tail: Red floss, tied in doubled then trimmed flat to about 1/4 inch
Rib: *Optionally, fine gold wire*
Body: Peacock herl, tied fairly full
Palmer hackle: Brown saddle palmered very closely over the rear 2/3 to 3/4 of the body, grizzly saddle the rest of the way forward—*both tied in earlier and reverse-palmered from front to rear, if you rib the fly*

This shellbacked variation has been my favorite Woolly Worm for several years now. I don't recall where I got my first one, which I just carried around unused for a long time. But once I started fishing it, the fly seldom let me down. It didn't seem to make much difference how I fished it; I've caught fish on it, fishing every way imaginable—even by accident (but of course, who hasn't, and on many a pattern?). I'd show my wonderful mystery bug to people and ask if they knew what it was called: "Well, it's *some* sort of Woolly Worm, but—."

Finally, I showed it to Chuck Tryon, Rolla, Missouri's fly-fishing and -tying guru. "*Waalll*," he said in that bass-baritone drawl of his, "where did you ever get a Miller Woolly Worm?" He told me it was an Ozark pattern—designed specifically for fishing Arkansas's White River, he thought. Even with a proper name, I couldn't find the fly in any catalogs or books.

Many writers attribute this pattern to Dave Whitlock, listing it as Dave's Woolly Worm or the Whitlock Woolly Worm. I believe they are wrong (see Tying Tips below); more likely, says Chuck Tryon, the pattern was originated by a Missouri fly

fisher named Charlie Miller, an itinerant, part-time preacher about whom little is known.

Until I started tying my own flies, Chuck kept me supplied with Miller Woollies, both weighted and unweighted. For old-times' sake, I asked Chuck to tie one for the book. I sometimes make adjustments to the pattern; they are listed in italics.

Miller Woolly Worm

Hook: Standard to 2X-long wet-fly, usually 1X-heavy; sizes 6 to 12

Head: *Optionally, when you want to weight the fly, but don't want to use a lead-wire underbody, a silver or brass bead*

Thread: Black 6/0, for unweighted flies; red or brown, for flies with a weighted underbody

Underbody: *Optionally, lead wire*

Tail: Grizzly hackle fibers; *alternatively, I sometimes use red hackle or yarn, the stubs of the herl back, a short bunch of pearl Krystal Flash, or nothing*

Shellback: Peacock herl, tied in at the bend and pulled over the top

Body: Yellow *(alternatively, cream)* chenille

Rib: Silver oval tinsel *(alternatively, fine silver wire)*

Palmer hackle: Grizzly saddle hackle, tied in at the front and reverse-palmered to the bend

Tying Tips

If I want a weighted fly, I sometimes slip a shiny glass or metal bead onto the shank rather than wrapping a lead underbody. Sometimes, I tie them as beadheads. More often than not, I tie them unweighted; to get them down, I use a weighted leader, a glass or metal bead slipped onto the tippet, or a shot pinched onto the leader.

To fish the Miller in salt water (where it is great for small snappers and other saltwater panfish), I naturally use a stainless-steel, tinned, or plated hook. In salt water, I've had greater success with the cream-bodied version, but your experience might prove otherwise.

In his *Guide to Aquatic Trout Foods* (1982), Whitlock did list three herl-backed Woolly Worms. We can probably call them **Whitlock Woolly Worms**, even though he uncharacteristically didn't stick Dave's, Whit's, or Whitlock in front of any

of them. Here are all five of the Woolly Worm patterns he listed, for all of which he specified "weighted, chenille or fur bodies on 3XL [3X-long] hooks with saddle hackle wrapped sparsely."

No. 1: Red wool tail; black body; soft furnace palmer hackle; peacock-herl back; sizes 4 and 8

No. 2: Grizzly hackle-point tail; peacock-herl body; gold oval-tinsel rib; grizzly palmer hackle; no back; size 10

No. 3: Short, red marabou tail; golden-yellow body; grizzly palmer hackle; peacock-herl back; size 10

No. 4: Grizzly hackle-point tail; peacock-herl body; darkest furnace palmer hackle, no back; size 4

No. 5: Fluorescent-red yarn tail; bright insect-green body; silver tinsel rib; grizzly palmer hackle; peacock-herl back; size 8

I found this souped-up hybridization of the **Miller Woolly Worm** (page 32) and the **Crackleback** (page 85), by Bill Hale of St. Louis, Missouri, on the Ozark Fly Fishers' web site (www.ozarkflyfishers.org). In Missouri and Arkansas, apparently everyone carries some variety of peacock-backed Woolly Worm. I think fly fishers in every state should take heed. Like Hale, I also like to tie with Purr-fect Punch yarn. But pay close attention to his tips on securing it. The yarn stretches a bit when wet, thus becoming loose, so the fly has to be tied tightly and carefully. Incidentally, this fly is named for the Busch Wildlife Conservation Area.

Buschback

Hook: 1X-long dry-fly, size 12

Thread: Fluorescent-orange or -red 8/0 UNI *(I had to use 6/0—GS)*

Underbody: 12 wraps of .020-in lead wire, overwrapped with thread

Tail: Fibers from lemon wood duck flank feathers, half the shank length, surrounding a few strands of pearl Krystal Flash, slightly shorter

Shellback: 3 to 5 strands of peacock herl, pulled over the body before palmering the hackle

Body: Lemonade (no. 62031) Purr-fect Punch yarn, a light-yellow, 2-strand acrylic punch-embroidery yarn; *alternatively, pale-yellow dubbing*

Palmer hackle: Furnace saddle, the barbs half again as long as the hook gap *("twice the gap to fish lily pads")*, tied in by the butt at the bend with the dull underside of the feather facing you and palmered forward in 4 to 6 open turns

Head: Tying thread, small and tapered, then cemented

Tying Tips

Hale explains his justification for using a dry-fly hook for a lead-weighted fly: "The light wire is much easier to pull out of logs, lily pads, fish, and human skin. The Dai-Riki 300 will also bend a little if it's really stuck. I can usually retrieve my fly, even with 6X fluorocarbon tippet. I *love* fluorocarbon!"

To form the tail, tie in 5 or 6 wood duck fibers, then 4 slightly shorter strands of Krystal Flash, and cover with 6 more wood duck fibers. Cement the tie-in wraps.

Hale lays the peacock herl along the entire top of the shank, securing it by wrapping the thread back from the eye to the bend, then forward again to the eye. He uses the same procedure for tying in the body yarn.

When thread-wrapping the herl and yarn, be sure you cover them completely. When the yarn or dubbing body is wet, the thread will show through, making the sides and belly appear pink. "I also like to try different thread colors," Hale says, "olive, black, and so on. Each gives the fly a different look and fish-appeal."

After tying in the materials for the tail, shellback, body, and hackle, Hale adds a drop of cement on the tie-in wraps at the bend, "which seems to help keep the herl and hackle from coming apart." He does the same thing on the tie-off wraps up front, before building the head: "If the fly is going to come apart—after catching many fish—this is where it would likely happen."

Pull the peacock herl tightly across the body before tying it off up front. "Fish have abrasive mouths, patches, or just plain teeth," Hale explains. "This gives them less to tear up when pulled tight." (Hale admits that he sometimes omits the peacock herl, just to save a step, but he likes the Buschback better with the herl.)

Fishing Tips

"Fishing techniques vary from person to person," Hale admits, "and the same goes for fish. A strip–pause variance usually works, with the strike coming on the fall. It seems that as summer grows longer, faster stripping works well, with the fish cruising right under the surface.

"In open water, bass and bluegill usually 'submarine' behind the fly before the take. When fished over lily pads, the fly drops butt-first. The larger-size hackle toward the rear acts as a weed guard and the Buschback will actually skitter across the pad, if fished slowly."

On most half-backed flies, the shellback is pulled over the thorax, to imitate the wing case. This one has the shellback pulled over the abdomen. I doubt the fish give much of a hoot. Adam Trina, president of the Montana Fly Company, says, "This is one of the best general imitations for a stonefly nymph."

Halfback Stone

Hook:	MFC 7002 Stimulator, slightly curved-shank n̶
Thread:	Dark-brown 6/0 UNI
Underbody:	Lead wire wrapped on
Tail:	4 to 6 ring-necked phe width long
Shellback:	Several long fibers from pheasant tail, pulled over palmer-hackling the abdomen
Palmer hackle:	Brown saddle, tied in by the tip at the bend and palmered in two stages: abdomen, then thorax; *alternatively, use 2 separate hackle feathers*
Rib:	Copper wire, over the shellback and through the rear palmer hackle
Abdomen:	Peacock herl, wrapped over the rear two-thirds of the shank
Thorax:	Peacock herl, wrapped thickly over the front third of the shank
Head:	Tying thread, coated with head cement or similar

Tying Steps

After wrapping and securing the lead-wire underbody, tie in the tail, then the shellback fibers (tied in by their tips, the butts facing rearward over the bend), the wire rib, and the herls for the abdomen.

Wrap the abdomen over the rear two-thirds of the shank, palmer the hackle through the abdomen, and leave the rest of the feather hanging.

Pull the shellback over the abdomen, tie down the forward ends of the pheasant fibers, then rib the abdomen, trying not to trap the palmer hackle.

Tie in the herls for the thorax, wrap the thorax, and palmer the rest of the saddle feather through the thorax. Tie down the hackle, clip the excess feather, form a head, and whip-finish. Coat the head with cement, lacquer, or clear nail polish.

Several British nymphs bear this name, but this one, by Bob Carnill, comes closest to Woolly Wormness. I found it in Taff Price's *Tying and Fishing the Nymph* (1995). It imitates the larva of a *Sialis* alder fly, at least 6 of which species are of angling significance in the U.S.

Alder Larva

Hook:	Mustad 79580, a 4X-long streamer, size 10
Thread:	Brown 6/0
Rib:	Copper wire or a long tag end of tying thread, spiraled over the abdomen and thorax, after the hackles have been palmered
Tail:	Brown goose biot (just one)
Shellback:	Brown or mottled-brown quill section or hackle fibers, pulled over the top after the hackle has been palmered
Palmer hackle 1:	Pale ginger hen saddle, palmered over the abdomen, as gills
Abdomen:	Brown and chestnut mole (*or, let's face it, a substitute*), mixed and dubbed over the rear 2/3 of the shank
Palmer hackle 2:	Brown partridge, palmered over the thorax, as legs
Thorax:	The body dubbing, only thicker
Head:	The thorax dubbing, without palmer hackle or shellback

The last shellbacked pattern in this chapter, I found it on Don's Flytying (http://mypage.direct.ca/d/dhaaheim/). It is Don Haaheim's variation on Chuck Moore's older **Horsehair**, a favorite pattern on British Columbia's Sheridan Lake, well known for its large rainbow trout. Haaheim says, "The main difference from Chuck's fly is that the Bear features a single strand of green Krystal Flash wound through the body and of course is tied with black bear hair rather than horsehair. I also add a few turns of lead near the hook eye to ensure that the fly will easily reach the depths where the big rainbows are often found."

Sheridan Bear

Hook:	Mustad 9672, a 3X-long streamer, sizes 2 to 8
Thread:	Invisible mending thread, a clear monofilament not unlike 1-lb-test spinning line or 7X tippet
Weight:	2 or 3 wraps of lead wire behind the eye
Tail:	2 barbs from a black goose quill
Shellback:	Black bear hair, tied in by the butts behind the eye, and secured to the top of the shank by winding the tying thread to the bend and back; it will be pulled over the body after the hackle has been palmered
Rib:	A single strand of green Krystal Flash, ribbed through the hackle
Body:	Black Phentex or similar yarn
Palmer hackle:	Black or dark-green saddle, tied in at the bend by the tip
Head:	The bear hair, extended above the hook eye, and clipped

Tying Tips

After wrapping the body and palmering the hackle, rib the fly with the Krystal Flash, taking care not to trap the hackle fibers. Then pull the bear hair forward and rib it with the tying thread. "It is a bit tricky to get the bear hair tight enough," Haaheim admits, "but you can do it by carefully winding your invisible thread back to the hook bend and forward to the hook eye, all the while keeping forward pressure on the bear hair and at the same time trying not to distort the hackle too much as you wind back and forth through it! Trim the bear hair ahead of the hook eye to form the antennae, cement, tie off, and you have finished the Sheridan Bear."

WOOLLY BEE

I picked up this Ernie Harrison pattern from Usenet's ROFFT news group (news.rec.outdoor.fishing.fly.tying). Don't add weight to this one, because bees don't sink like rocks when they fall on water.

Woolly Bee

Hook:	Standard wet-fly or nymph, size to match the bees, wasps, hornets, and yellow jackets where you fish
Thread:	Black or brown
Body:	Chenille, alternating bands of black (or brown) and yellow
Palmer hackle:	Brown

This pattern comes from Steve Meyers, a guide on the mountain streams of southwestern Colorado as well as on the San Juan River, and one heck of a writer. (His *Lime Creek Odyssey* is one of my all-time literary fishing-themed favorites—right up there with Norman Maclean's *A River Runs Through It*, William Humphrey's *The Spawning Run*, Sydney Lea's *A Place in Mind*, Thomas McGuane's *Ninety-Two in the Shade*, John Gierach's *Sex, Death, and Fly-Fishing*, and Harry Middleton's *On the Spine of Time*.) "The hackle, tied in by its tip at the bend, shows a gradually swelling 'body' as the palmer hackle's dark center widens toward the head of the fly," Steve says. "It's quick, simple, and effective."

Steve's Stonefly

Hook:	TMC 200R, a 3X-long, slightly curved-shank streamer, sizes 12 and 14
Thread:	Black
Tail:	Furnace or badger fibers, to match the palmer hackle
Body:	A single strand of wool or Antron yarn—in whatever color best resembles your local plecopterids
Palmer hackle:	Furnace or badger saddle, tied in by its tip, and palmered with the dull, concave side facing forward

Tying Tip

"I don't weight this fly when I tie the body thin," Steve reports. "If the natural is really chunky, I sometimes use chenille, and wrap it over a fuse-wire underbody."

JYSK CHILLIMPS Tied by Martin Jørgensen

This fly also is known in alternate spelling as Jydsk Chillimps—in either spelling, meaning a "chillimps" from Jutland. (See also **Orange Chillimps** on page 72 and the superficially similar **Red-Tag Palmer** on page 108.) As for "chillimps," no flyfishing Dane, Swede, or Norwegian I've asked has known what the word means. Although some claim the Chillimps originated in Sweden or Norway, most of them say the patterns hails from Hans Christian Andersen country; the Danish newsman Mogens Espersen has written that the Jysk Chillimps is "as Danish as bacon, salted butter, and minority governments." Espersen fishes the fly downstream to make best use of the pulsating hackles. Leaded, the Chillimps can be fished deep as a nymph.

This pattern is half a century old—invented by a Danish fly fisher named Valdemar P. Haugaard, according to Espersen, who submitted the pattern for inclusion in *The World's Best Trout Flies*. Espersen says that Haugaard invented the fly to match what he found in trout stomachs—using "materials at hand: a greenish-blue pile from [his] overcoat, medium brown cock hackles and whisks from a lady's hat."

Jysk Chillimps

Hook: 3X-long streamer, sizes 10 to 14
Thread: Black
Underbody: Optionally, for nymphing, a few turns of lead wire around the front of the shank
Tail: Scarlet soft-hackle fibers, almost as long as the shank
Body: Greenish-blue darning wool, tapering slightly toward the rear
Palmer hackle: Medium fiery-brown (natural red)
Hackle collar: Medium fiery-brown, a size larger; *alternatively, select a steeply tapered hackle feather and use it to palmer the body and to wrap several turns of the longer-barbed butt section to form the hackle collar)*

RAGGLE BOMB

I don't know who originated this pattern, but it's a broad-spectrum nymph that looks like a lot of buggy fish foods.

Raggle Bomb

Hook: 2X-long, standard, or heavy-wire streamer, sizes 8 to 14
Thread: Black 6/0
Underbody: Optionally, lead wire wrapped around the shank
Underbody: Dark-olive wool, tapered slightly
Body: Peacock herl
Rib: Optionally, fine gold wire
Palmer hackle: Ginger or brown, palmered sparsely (about 5 turns) through the body, with 2 extra turns at the front of the body; *tied in at the front and reverse-palmered from eye to bend, if you use a rib*

SOFT-HACKLE WOOLLY WORM Tied by Rich Osthoff

The Wisconsin writer and tier Rich Osthoff does a lot of fishing in the spring creeks of the Badger State's Driftless Area. There, outsize brown trout gorge on the crayfish, leeches, sculpins, chubs, and minnows that abound in the coulees (as spring creeks often are called in the Badger State). His Soft-Hackle Woolly Worm and essentially similar **Bi-Bugger** (see page 139) are designed to cover all these bases. As for colors and color combinations, let fishing experience or flights of fancy be your guide. It's best to color-match the yarn underbody to the dubbed body. Here's his Basic Black-and-Grizzly Soft-Hackle Woolly Worm:

Soft-Hackle Woolly Worm

Hook: TMC 5263, Dai-Riki 1702XL, or similar long-shank nymph or streamer, sizes 12 to 16
Thread: Black
Underbody 1: 8 to 10 wraps of lead wire
Tail: Short tuft of black-dyed rabbit fur (slightly more than a gap-width long)
Underbody 2: Black Purr-fect Punch craft yarn, to form a tapered foundation over the lead
Body: Black dubbing blend—2 parts rabbit to 1 part Antron or smilar synthetic—dubbed in 2 stages, the rear 1/3 first, and the front 2/3 after the first hackle has been palmered and the second hackle has been tied in by its tip
Palmer hackle: 2 webby grizzly hen hackles: barbs on the rear hackle a gap-width long; and 1-1/2 times the gap width on the front hackle which should be finished as a soft-hackle collar in front of the body
Head: Tying thread, lacquered

Tying Tips

"To achieve the buggiest effect possible," Osthoff says, "comb the finished fly with a stiff, nylon-bristle brush, stroking from head to tail and raking the fly from all sides." You can clip the nylon bristles short on a stiff tooth brush, or glue the hooked side of a Velcro strip to a Popsicle stick.

WOBBLING WOOLLY WORM

I don't recall where I first picked up the idea of using a sequin to give built-in action to a fly, but it might well have been from Roman Moser, whose Quiver Nymph is the best-known sequin-activated pattern. I have specified no colors, so suit yourself.

Wobbling Woolly Worm

Hook: 1X- to 3X-long wet-fly, preferably straight-eyed (I used an Orvis barbless beadhead nymph with a slightly curved shank), sizes 8 to 12
Head: The tiniest glass bead that can be slipped onto the barbless or debarbed hook (I used a root-beer–color glass seed bead), to keep the sequin from wobbling on the shank; *alternatively, a small lump of tying thread, right at the eye*
Collar: Sequin, the color of your choice (I used orange), slipped all the way up the shank, concave side facing forward against the bead
Thread: 6/0 or 8/0 (I used dark-brown [Camel] 6/0 UNI)
Tail: *Optionally, none, yarn, hackle barbs, hackle point, golden- or silver-pheasant tippet, peacock-herl stubs, frayed floss, pheasant-tail fibers, whatever (I used 2 long strands of root beer Krystal Flash)*
Body: Chenille or yarn, in a color you think will work (I used peach Petite Estaz)
Rib: *Optionally, fine wire, oval tinsel, floss, or thread (I used none)*
Palmer hackle: Grizzly (or other) saddle hackle (I used dark barred dun); tied in at the front and *reverse-palmered to the bend from front to rear, if ribbed*

Fishing Tip

For best effect, use a stop-and-go retrieve (alternating short twitches with longer strips) in pools and still or calm waters, or cast the fly down and across the current, and let the moving water pull the fly across the current on a tight line. If the current is too fast or turbulent, you may experience tippet or leader twisting, so check your monofilament after every few casts.

Strung-Bead Woolly Worm

Although I haven't listed a specific bead-bodied Woolly Worm, it shouldn't require a PhD in astrophysics to figure out a pattern: slip a bunch of beads onto the hook shank, tie on a short tail and a hackle feather, palmer the hackle over and between the beads, wrap a thread head, and whip-finish.

Beaded-body palmer flies have their piscatorial pluses, but they have their shortcomings, too. Stringing the beads separately, rather than on the hook shank, gives you several distinct advantages. First, you aren't limited to using relatively fine-wire hooks and large-diameter beads; if you are so inspired, you could use tiny seed beads with a 4X-heavy hook. Second, you can use bugle beads, oval beads, or other long shapes than can't be pushed around the bend of a hook. Third, you can combine the come-hither glitz of a beaded body with the shagginess of a soft body as well as the overall bugginess of a palmer hackle.

As with the **Bead-Chain Bugger** (page 148), I got the idea from Ted Leeson's and Jim Schollmeyer's *Fly Tier's Benchside Reference to Techniques and Dressing Styles* (1998). And you can tie this one as a Bugger, too; just tie in a shank-length marabou tail.

Depending on the relative size of the beads you are using, the toothiness of the fish you expect to encounter, and the violence of the battles you hope to fight, you can string the beads on heavy thread (I'd use Kevlar), monofilament, or soft wire (not fine dry-fly ribbing wire). I have not specified colors or other details in the listing, so choose the colors and materials that will suit your purposes.

Strung-Bead Woolly Worm

Hook: 1X- to 3X-long nymph, wet-fly, or streamer, sizes 6 to 12
Thread: Tier's choice
Tail: *Optionally, none or whatever suits your piscatorial fancy*
Body: Chenille, tinsel chenille, yarn, dubbing, dubbing brush, peacock herl, or other reasonably "buggy" body material, tied in at the bend and wrapped forward between the beads
Palmer hackle: Hen or rooster hackle palmered over the body, between the beads
Stringer: Kevlar thread, monofilament, or soft wire, lashed to the shank immediately ahead of the hackle tie-in point, facing to the rear—pulled over the body when the beads are strung and tied off behind the eye
Beads: Glass, plastic, or small metal beads threaded onto the stringer one by one as the body is wrapped *(see Tying Tips)*

Tying Tips

The method of stringing the beads depends on which body material you use. If you choose chenille or yarn or some other "free-standing" material (one in which the tying thread is not incorporated), the tying thread should be advanced along the shank just ahead of the body wraps, securing each bead with a thread wrap or two. But if the body material incorporates the tying thread (dubbing, dubbing loop, peacock "chenille rope," etc.) or a reasonable facsimile thereof (a dubbing brush or Softdub, say), you can take the thread all the way to the eye before stringing the beads; the strong core of the body material will be sufficient to securely bind the beads in place.

New Mexico Woolly Worm

J. Edson Leonard listed a lot of palmer flies and Bivisibles in his *Flies* (1950), but just four Woolly Worms: Black, Brown, Yellow (all of them red-tailed and grizzly-, badger-, or furnace-hackled), and this cheerfully monochromatic one.

New Mexico Woolly Worm

Hook: Long-shank wet-fly of appropriate size
Thread: Yellow 6/0
Tail: Yellow hackle fibers
Body: Yellow floss
Palmer hackle: Yellow
Head: Yellow ostrich herl

Tying Tip

For another geographic variation, try the **New Zealand Woolly Worm** listed by Keith Perrault in his *Standard Dictionary of Fishing Flies* (1984): grizzly hackle-point tail, chenille body in the color of your choice, and grizzly palmer hackle.

PYRALID WOOLLY WORM

This homely pattern is designed to suggest the larvae of certain aquatic moths in the widespread genus *Paragyractis*, the body color and palmer hackle varied to match the local species.

Pyralid Woolly Worm

Hook: 2X- to 3X-long wet-fly, sizes 12 to 16
Thread: Dark-brown 6/0
Body: Chartreuse or light lime-green chenille *(I used a green variegated chenille)*
Palmer hackle: White, cree, or pale grizzly
Head: Tying thread, wrapped larger than on other wet-fly patterns

Fishing Tips

Whenever you have reason to believe that aquatic-moth caterpillars of this color pattern are about, try slow-twitching this pattern just under the surface around emergent or nearly emergent aquatic vegetation, or drifting it among the large, algae-covered rocks in fast-running water.

Unless the current is awfully swift, I wouldn't weight this pattern. To keep it from planing to the surface, I use a fast-sinking leader (Airflo's braided leaders or Poly-Leaders) and a very short tippet.

WET SPIDER G. D. Tied by R. G. Balogh

This pattern was listed by Perrault. The "G. D." stands for "green drake," although when I get frustrated at the vise I confess I sometimes think of something else. The late Jimmy Darren listed a similar pattern in the *Noll Guide to Trout Flies and How to Tie Them* (1965). Darren's pattern used wood duck rather than mallard for the tail and face collar.

Wet Spider G. D.

Hook: Standard or 1X-long wet-fly, sizes 12 and 14
Thread: *Not listed by Perrault, but black or brown 6/0 would do*
Tail: Fibers from the side feathers of a "brown Nashua mallard"
Body: Flat gold tinsel
Palmer hackle: Yellow hen
Face hackle: 2 or 3 turns of brown mallard

TEX'S FAVORITE NYMPH

Keith Perrault said he wasn't able to identify "Tex," but he listed several "Tex's Favorite" patterns. This is the only wingless, palmered one of Tex's patterns in the book.

Tex's Favorite Nymph

Hook: Standard or 1X-long nymph, sizes 10 and 12
Thread: Brown or black
Tail: Brown hackle fibers
Body: Dark-olive chenille
Palmer hackle: Brown hen, sparse

Edgar Allen Poe fans may be disappointed by the absence of raven feathers in the pattern. But have you ever tried to find a raven skin or neck? Heck, crow is hard enough to come by—and, since the invasion of the West Nile virus, potentially downright dangerous, to boot. But it's worth looking for, because corvid feathers have a unique sheen and texture.

Nevermore

Hook: Your favorite nymph, size to suit
Thread: Black
Tail: Crow hackle fibers—*I like to use stiff fibers from tail or flight feathers*
Body: Black Vernille or thin strip of Ultra Suede
Palmer hackle: Large crow body feathers—*alternatively, the large, soft "hackles" from the forward part of the wings*

Tying Tip

The tip on using the wing feathers comes from the Norwegian tier Kenneth Ramstad. You're looking at proof. It began by my posting a question about a safe source of crow feathers on ROFFT, the rec.outdoors.fishing.fly.tying Internet discussion group. I have since purchased a nice, affordable—even with air shipping—pair of wings from Lathkill Fly Tying Materials & Rod Building Supplies in West Yorkshire, England: sales@lathkill.com. Thanks to such discussion groups (if you can stand the mostly off-topic ranting and raving your questions are almost certain to set off), you can find people like Kenneth Ramstad, or Tommy Olinsson of Denmark, who generously posted a few body feathers from his own supply of crow hackle. (Incidentally, if you are beginning to notice an emerging pattern of helpful cooperation from Scandinavia, it is no coincidence. Almost invariably, when I am in a fly-tying jam, help seems to come out of "nowhere"—by way of Norway, Denmark, or Sweden.) Other, nonfishing, discussion groups or Google searches might help you locate people who keep pet crows, who might be willing to put a few shed feathers in an envelope and post them to you.

Before wildlife conservation entered the law books and the public consciousness, this Southern from Appalachia trout and panfish classic was tied with the split wing feathers of the eastern color morph of the northern flicker, a woodpecker known to taxonomic splitters as the yellow-shafted flicker and to Dixieland traditionalists as the yellowhammer—"yallerhammer" in Southern *lingua franca*. (Less often, good-old-boy tiers used the flight feathers of golden plovers.) Nowadays, law-abiding, conservation-minded tiers use the primary flight feathers of bobwhite, grouse, and other game birds, often died yellow, splitting the quill down the center with a razor blade or X-acto knife. I've chosen a pattern from the late L. J. DeCuir's *Southeastern Flies* (Menasha Ridge Press, 1999) that uses yellow-died grizzly hackle.

The Yallerhammer was and is sometimes tied with a hackle collar rather than a palmered hackle, both wet and dry.

Yallerhammer

Hook: Mustad 9761, TMC 5262, or similar 2X-long nymph or wet-fly, sizes 4 to 14
Thread: Black
Underbody: 6 to 10 wraps of lead wire, centered on the shank over a thread base and ramped fore and aft with tying thread to make a cigar-shaped base
Body: Peacock herl—2 to 5 strands, depending upon hook size
Palmer hackle: Yellow-dyed grizzly hackle, tied in by the tip

Tying Tip

The modern version of the Yallerhammer dry fly is similar (without the lead, of course), tied on a Mustad 94840 or similar dry-fly hook in sizes 12 to 18. Just add a long dry-fly tail of mixed black and yellow *rooster* hackle fibers and be sure to use a yellow-dyed grizzly *dry-fly* saddle.

Fishing Tips

You can dead-drift the weighted Yallerhammer as a nymph, but DeCuir said movement makes the fly more effective. Fish it on the swing in a good current, he said; in still or slow waters, use a slow retrieve.

"It is a very good fly for getting down into deep holes where the big ones are hiding out," DeCuir added.

SMALBLAAR NYMPH

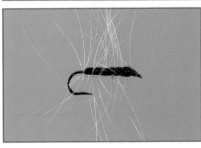

The South African fly fisher and tier Tony Biggs developed this unusual pattern for fishing easily spooked trout in clear streams. I found it in Taff Price's *Tying and Fishing the Nymph*. I don't know how durable this fly would be (especially with the golden pheasant crest palmered over floss), but it sure is interesting and buggy looking, in a daddy longlegs sort of way.

Smalblaar Nymph

- **Hook:** 2X- to 3X-long streamer, sizes 12 to 16
- **Thread:** Red
- **Body:** Tying thread or red floss
- **Palmer hackle:** Golden-pheasant crest, in 5 open spirals

Tying Note

In the same book, Price lists another South African pattern, the **Golden Heron Nymph**, that is essentially similar to the preceding fly. (Despite its name, the fly includes no heron hackle. Whether it originally did so, I don't know.) It uses the same hook and palmer hackle as the Smalblaar, but adds a tail of blue-dun hackle fibers, permits the use of either black or red thread, and substitutes peacock herl (wound thin) for the body.

BURLAP WORM

This pattern is as homely as the immediately preceding patterns are exotic. It's a fish-catcher, though.

Burlap Worm

- **Hook:** Standard to 3X-long wet-fly, nymph, or streamer, sized as appropriate
- **Thread:** Black or brown
- **Tail:** 2 or 3 splayed moose, deer, or elk hairs
- **Body:** Burlap strand, wrapped
- **Palmer hackle:** Furnace, grizzly, cree, or speckled ginger, to suit

WOODY WORM NYMPH Tied by Peter Frailey

I had originally used the name Woody Worm for a balsa-bod-
... Worm,
... on the
... few
..., but
... stan-
...es.)
... Bay
...od-
...his
other groundh... ...n-
flies.com), has ...s
this "combines ...
Worm and the ...

Woody Worm Nymph

- **Hook:** 2X-long nymph or wet-fly, sizes 8 to 12
- **Thread:** Color to suit, 3/0 for size 8, 6/0 for size 12, either for size 10
- **Underbody:** 10 to 12 wraps of lead wire on the shank ahead of the hook point
- **Tail:** Woodchuck guard hairs *(alternatively, underfur, if you prefer)*, plus or minus a gap-width long
- **Palmer hackle:** Brown rooster saddle or hen neck, palmered over the abdomen
- **Abdomen:** Woodchuck underfur, cut to 1/4 inch and mixed in a Mini-Chop or similar appliance, and dubbed over 2/3 of the shank; *alternatively, use a commercial hare's ear or rabbit dubbing*
- **Thorax:** Woodchuck underfur, full-length, dubbed in a dubbing loop, forming a thorax that is more like a furry "hackle" collar
- **Head:** Tying thread, varnished

Tying Tips

To make the collar-like thorax, place the underfur crosswise in the dubbing loop (perpendicular to the thread). Close the loop and position the underfur evenly within the loop. Spin and twist the loop to make a dubbing rope. After each wrap, stroke the fur back toward the hook bend to avoid trapping the fibers under the next wrap. Continue wrapping and stroking to cover the front third of the shank.

If you like beadhead patterns, slip a metal bead onto the hook before tying on, and eliminate the lead-wire underbody. "If you use shank-length woodchuck underfur for the tail," says Frailey, "you will have created a **Woody Bugger**."

In the Kaufmann's catalog, it says, "If we told you [about] some of the fishing we have had with these lately, it would border on fantasy. Excellent in alpine lakes." It is very similar to the **Red-Butt Woolly** of the Ontario tier Jay Passmore (page 69). Besides the black pattern listed, Kaufmann's also offers the pattern in white.

Hot-Butt Woolly Worm

Hook:	1X- to 3X-long wet-fly or nymph, size 8
Thread:	Fluorescent red
Palmer hackle:	Black saddle, tied in at the front and palmered to the bend
Underbody:	Lead wire
Tail:	Salmon-pink poly yarn, spun and less than a gap-width long, covered by longer strands of pearl Krystal Flash
Body:	Black chenille
Rib:	Fine copper wire
Head:	Tying thread, lacquered

SPITFIRE

Call this one an over-dressed Woolly Worm—overdressed in the sense of being less than faithful to the basic pattern. I include it for two reasons: first, to suggest ways you can take your Woolly Worms in various directions; second, so you will know that the late Don Gapen originated more fly patterns than the Muddler Minnow, for which he is deservedly best known.

Gapen designed and tied the Spitfire at streamside to solve the problem of short-striking fish. He named it for the English fighter plane that was so successful against the Luftwaffe during the Battle of Britain. Gapen used red and yellow tails as "striking points" to direct strikes at the hook point. This 1940 pattern was for a time second in popularity only to the Muddler in Ontario's Nipigon watershed. The writer David Lucca rediscovered the Spitfire and other forgotten Don Gapen patterns by interviewing Dan Gapen, Sr., Don's son.

Spitfire

Hook:	Standard or long-shank wet-fly, sizes 8 to 16
Thread:	Black
Tail:	Slip of red-dyed duck quill, tied in so it curves upward
Body:	Black chenille
Palmer hackle:	2 brown saddles tied in by their tips at the bend and palmered closely over the body
Collar:	Guinea hen, wrapped as a wet-fly collar
Cheeks:	*Optionally, a jungle-cock nail on either side, angled slightly above level*
Head:	Tying thread, *lacquered or cemented to help secure those expensive jungle-cock cheeks*

Fishing Tip

According to Dan Gapen, his dad's Spitfire is both a wet fly and a streamer. Fish it on the swing or retrieve it actively.

RUMMEL'S WOOLLY WORM

I wish I could tell you who "Rummel" is or was, but I found his or her pattern in Matt Supinski's *Steelhead Dreams* (2001). Tied on a normal-weight hook (as I did on the fly here), it ought to work as well on trout as on their bigger, brawnier steelheaded cousins.

Rummel's Woolly Worm

Hook:	Daiichi 1530, a 1X-short, 2X-heavy wet-fly— *alternatively, a standard wet-fly*, sizes 10 to 14
Thread:	Black 6/0
Tail:	Red yarn tag
Body:	Orange-and-black variegated chenille, medium
Palmer hackle:	Grizzly microbarb rooster saddle

RED SETTER WOOLLY

The Red Setter, a New Zealand standby, isn't usually tied as a palmer fly. Instead, the body sports two hackle collars—one amidships, as a body joint, and the other up front in the normal arrangement. But I saw a palmered version on an anonymous New Zealander's web site (the same tier who gave us the **Terrestrial** on page 91 and the **Black Moth** on page 83), and that's what I am presenting here. On that web page, the Red Setter is described as a "bully imitation that fishes well in freestone streams and lakes. Also an excellent fly to use on dark, moonless nights, fished slowly along the bottom on a sinking line."

Red Setter Woolly

- **Hook:** 3X- or 4X-long streamer, sizes 2 to 8
- **Thread:** Black 6/0
- **Palmer hackle:** Black—*traditionally, ginger*—hen saddle, tied in by the butt behind the eye and reverse-palmered to the bend
- **Tail:** Black squirrel—*traditionally, "brown or ginger" (but gray or fox squirrel will do)*—hook-length and medium sparse
- **Body:** Red—*traditionally, orange*—chenille
- **Rib:** Silver medium wire or oval tinsel
- **Head:** Tying thread, varnished

ZUG DUB WOOLLY WORM Tied by Peter Frailey

Even though Peter Frailey admits that he often ties his Zug Dub without a palmer hackle, here's a nice Woolly version.

Zug Dub Woolly Worm

- **Hook:** 2X-long nymph or streamer, sizes 12 to 16
- **Thread:** Black 6/0 or 8/0
- **Underbody:** 8 to 10 wraps of lead wire on the shank
- **Tail:** Several peacock sword herls, the tips extending about a gap-width past the bend, the butts lashed to the rear 2/3 of the shank, but left untrimmed
- **Palmer hackle:** Brown hen neck or soft rooster saddle, the barbs stripped from one side and tied in by the tip at the bend, to be palmered forward after abdomen, thorax, and wing case have been completed
- **Abdomen:** Hare's ear dubbing over the rear two-thirds of the shank
- **Thorax:** Hare's ear—*a shade darker or lighter than the abdomen, if you wish*—dubbed over the front third of the shank after the peacock sword butts have been pulled back (over the top of the abdomen) out of the way
- **Wing case:** The peacock sword butts from the tail, pulled over the top of the thorax, tied down behind the eye, and the excess clipped
- **Head:** Tying thread

PANCORA Tied by Umpqua Feather Merchants for Kaufmann's Streamborn

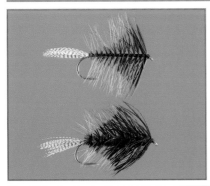

This pattern, which comes in both wet (bottom) and dry (top) manifestations, imitates a crablike Patgonian crustacean called the pancora.

Pancora

- **Hook:** 3X-long streamer or nymph, size 6
- **Thread:** Black or olive
- **Underbody:** Lead wire
- **Tail:** Teal flank feather, rolled, about half again as long as the gap width
- **Body:** Very dark olive wool, dubbing, or fine chenille; *alternatively, peacock herl*
- **Palmer hackle:** Dark furnace (a steeply tapered hen or soft rooster feather with lots of black), palmered closely (at least 9 or 10 turns)

Tying Tip

To tie a dry Pancora, use a fine-wire terrestrial hook, eliminate the lead wire and the chenille (or other body material), and palmer a tapered furnace dry-fly hackle in touching turns over the bare shank or a thread base, so the black part of the feather forms a "body." Tail is the same.

PANCORA WOOLLY WORM

On his web site (Killroy's Fly Tying and Fishing, www.killroys.com), the late Harley Bowler listed his pancora imitation this way. (FYI, the Killroy's site continues under the administration of Steve Scott, at the urging of Bowler's widow.) In his *Standard Dictionary of Fishing Flies* (1984), Keith Perrault lists a similar, Argentine **Pancora** pattern that uses a bunch of hot-orange hackle fuzz for the tail, black chenille for the body, and yellow-dyed grizzly for the palmer hackle. The lacquered black head also sports a yellow spot of paint on top.

Pancora Woolly Worm

Hook:	Orvis 1511, or similar 6X-long streamer, sizes 2 to 6
Thread:	Black 6/0
Tail:	Orange marabou tuft, about a gap-width long
Body:	Olive chenille
Palmer hackle:	Grizzly saddle

KILL DEVIL WOOLLY WORM

These cool colors often appeal to salmonids. And to other fish as well.

Kill Devil Woolly Worm

Hook:	Standard to 2X-long wet-fly or nymph, sizes 6 to 12
Thread:	Black
Tag:	Flat silver tinsel
Body:	Peacock herl, green
Palmer hackle:	Bright medium-blue hen, oversize
Head:	High-gloss finish over the tying thread

Tying Tip

The **Little Chappie** is a similar, but "warmer," pattern: Just substitute a gold tag and use bronze peacock herl for the body and a less-bright blue dun palmer hackle of normal size.

MAX VON DEM BORNE Tied by R. G. Balogh

But for the lack of a wing, this old-fashioned "fancy lake fly" listed by Keith Perrault almost resembles an Atlantic salmon pattern. The fly is named for the German author of the seminal books *Illustrirtes Handbuch der Angelfischerei* (*Illustrated Handbook of Angling*, 1875) and *Teichwirtschaft* (*Pondkeeping*, 1894), who was instrumental in introducing rainbow trout and both large- and smallmouth bass to Germany and other parts of Europe. The contemporary popularity of bass fishing on both continents has its roots in the pioneering work of Von dem Borne and the American James A. Henshall.

Max von dem Borne

Hook:	Streamer or salmon/steelhead, sizes 4 to 12
Tag 1:	Scarlet floss, tied in at the bend, extending toward the eye
Tag 2:	Flat gold tinsel, tied in at the bend, atop the floss tie-in, extending rearward and wrapped first, over both tags's tie-in wraps
Tail:	Golden pheasant crest, tied so that it curves upward, as in Atlantic salmon flies
Butt:	Peacock herl
Body:	In two sections: rear 2/3, yellow wool or dubbing; front 1/3, pink fur, dubbed and picked out
Rib:	Gold tinsel
Palmer hackle:	Yellow-dyed saddle

GENE GANTT MEMORIAL FLY

This pattern, found in Perrault's book, is by the late Tom Nixon, who was best known as a warmwater fly fisher in Louisiana. I think this dates back to his trout-fishing days in Arkansas and Missouri. Perrault called it a lake fly. I don't know who Gene Gantt was.

Gene Gantt Memorial Fly

Hook:	4X-long streamer, size 8
Thread:	Black
Tag:	Embossed gold tinsel
Tail:	Hackle fibers from a wood-duck flank feather
Underbody:	Lead wire wrapped on the shank
Body:	Lettuce-green wool yarn, wrapped over the lead underbody
Belly:	Lemon-yellow wool yarn, pulled over the body on the underside of the shank
Palmer hackle:	Ginger hen, sparse

YUK BUG Tied by Alberto Jimeno

Part Girdle Bug, part Woolly Worm, this squirrel-tailed, rubber-legged pattern comes from the master tier and fly designer Al Troth.

Yuk Bug

Hook:	Mustad 79580, TMC 300, or similar 4X- to 6X-long streamer, sizes 2 to 8
Thread:	Black 6/0, or 3/0 Monocord
Underbody:	Lead wire wrapped on the shank
Legs:	3 strands of white "rubber hackle" tied around the shank or lashed with figure-8 wraps of thread to the top of the shank, spaced at even intervals to produce 6 half-inch-plus legs that slant toward the rear
Tail:	Gray-squirrel tail hair, full and a gap-width past the bend
Body:	Black chenille
Rib:	Black thread or fine gold wire, in which case the hackle should be tied in up front and palmered to the rear; *some tiers consider the rib optional*
Palmer hackle:	Light-badger saddle, long and fairly soft

Tying Note

Several catalogs also list Brown and Olive Yuk Bugs, which are pretty easy to figure out. Also quite popular out West is the **Pepperoni Yuk Bug**: black chenille abdomen and orange chenille thorax (in a 50:50 or 65:35 ratio), and brown palmer hackle; some palmer the Pepperoni's whole body, but most palmer just the thorax.

BUBFLY Tied by Chuck Tryon

When Chuck Tryon was first trying to teach his late wife, Sharon, how to fly fish, he wanted to be sure she caught fish. He wanted something "real buggy-looking," with "a million moving parts." The result of his brainstorming was this big, ugly, black fly—the BUBfly. Since then, Chuck has come up with a myriad of other colors and color combinations, the first being the yellow **Banana BUBfly**, which I can personally attest Missouri smallmouths love, having been present for one of its first field tests. Chuck says a smallmouth-fishing buddy of his has lately been having great success on stream smallies with a bright-chartreuse **Brilliant Bosky BUBfly**. I came up with the **Brindle BUBfly**: variegated chenille body, speckled tails and antennae, grizzly hackle. *Please—Hold the applause.* Let your imagination run wild. Chuck simply insists that you give your creation a name beginning with the letter B: Brown, Bloody, Bilious, Beery, Bodacious, Bungled, Bearded, Buddy's—you get the idea.

BUBfly

Hook:	Mustad 9674, a 4X-long streamer, sizes 6 to 10
Thread:	Black 6/0
Tail:	2 long, black rubber legs, as long as the fly, in a V
Antennae:	2 black rubber legs, a little shorter than the tail, in a V over the eye
Underbody:	Lead wire
Body:	Black chenille
Palmer hackle:	Black saddle
Head:	Tying thread, coated with head cement

FORK-TAIL WOOLLY Tied by Jim Hester

I found this panfish pattern on the Chesapeake Fly & Bait Company's web site (www.chesapeakefly.com). The Fork-Tail Woolly somewhat resembles Chuck Tryon's BUBfly, but with a tinsel-chenille body and no antennae. In addition to the listed **Black-and-Chartreuse** (which may be tied with the body and hackle colors reversed), the Fork-Tail Woolly also comes in solid colors (chartreuse, black, brown, white, and olive), but you can safely use your imagination and experience.

"The Fork-Tail Woolly is simply a Woolly Worm with a two-strand, round rubber tail instead of the standard hackle fiber or yarn tail," Chesapeake's "Big Jim" Hester says. "The rubber really

vibrates when retrieved, and makes an already productive pattern a little better, at least most of the time. I only intended to use it as a panfish fly, but have also caught trout and bass."

Fork-Tail Woolly

Hook:	1X-long wet-fly or nymph, sizes 6 to 10
Thread:	Black or chartreuse 6/0
Tail:	Chartreuse rubber legs, tied in at the bend in a wide, shank-length Vee
Body:	Chartreuse Estaz or other tinsel chenille
Palmer hackle:	Black neck or saddle

Tying Tip

Use closed-cell foam for the body—either a ready-made cylinder or wrapping a thin strip—and you can make a slightly less glitzy **Floating Fork-Tail Woolly.** If you insist on the glitz, carefully apply a very thin layer of craft cement to the foam body and sprinkle with tiny flakes of craft glitter before palmering the hackle.

CAPE COD WOOLLY WORM

Eric Leiser listed this pattern in *The Book of Fly Patterns* (1987), and said he was introduced to this "ugly, yet tantalizing little morsel" by John Harder, while fishing Rhode Island's very trouty Wood River with the United Fly Tyers. Leiser observed that the fly is tied in a variety of sizes on a variety of hook styles, but always in black. He also said, "It is claimed that the less expertly tied this pattern is, the more fish it will take."

Definitely *my* kind of fly! I've often observed that shagginess often counts more than neatness in a fish's eye—a lame,

but convenient, excuse for my poor tying technique.

Cape Cod Woolly Worm

Hook:	Whatever wet-fly, nymph, or streamer pattern strikes your fancy, sizes 8 to 14 (larger for bass or saltwater species)
Thread:	Black
Tail:	Black hen hackle fibers or marabou, a gap-width long
Body:	Black wool, fur, or chenille
Palmer hackle:	Soft black hen hackle
Collar:	Black hen, oversize, wrapped as a wet-fly collar (use a separate feather or the longer fibers near the butt of a tapered saddle hackle used to palmer over the body)

WET MOUSE Tied by Jack Gartside

This odd, palmer-bodied pattern comes from the fertile mind and nimble fingers of the Bostonian iconoclast Jack Gartside. The palmered material is not chicken hackle but pheasant aftershaft feathers. "I had been working with pheasant for years," he writes on his web site (www.jackgartside.com), "and had handled thousands of aftershaft feathers before I ever gave a thought to putting these feathers to work."

Gartside says he invented the pattern almost by accident, having tired of the repetitious and time-consuming tying of Pheasant Hoppers for Bud Lilly's Fly Shop one summer. Nor would he probably have fished it, he says, except that a friend interrupted his tying to remind him they'd agreed to go fishing that evening. So, he hastily whip-finished the fuzzy-looking thing in his vise and stuck it onto his fly patch. He tied it on to

his tippet just to see what it would look like in the water. He was amazed. "It seemed that a heart was beating beneath those feathers; every fiber simply trembled with movement and life." On the third twitch of the first cast, his as-yet-unnamed fly took a big cutthroat. During a caddis hatch that evening, the Wet Mouse took a dozen or so fish. "Since that first day on Slough Creek, I've fished this simple fly ... with consistent success in many different types of water throughout the world." Gartside thinks the Wet Mouse probably looks like a dragonfly nymph or even a snail to a fish.

Wet Mouse

Hook:	Mustad 9671 or equivalent 2X-long nymph, sizes 4 to 12
Thread:	Gray or tan Danville 6/0
Body:	Pheasant aftershaft feathers, natural or dyed, palmered one after another on the shank
Collar:	Pheasant back feather, partridge, grouse, or long speckled-hen hackle wet-fly collar
Head:	Tying thread, neat

Tying Tip

Of using aftershaft feathers in this manner, Gartside writes, "It's important to tie this feather in at the butt, not at the tip (which is very fragile). In fact, after tying in the feather at the butt, it's wise to break off the tip before applying your hackle pliers." Gartside prefers to use E-Z Minihooks, those little electronic wiring tools that are, he observes, "a lot cheaper at places like Radio Shack than at fly shops."

SMART'S YELLOWTAIL

I found this "fancy" South African pattern in Taff Price's *Fly Patterns: An International Guide.* It's a bear to tie. In some listings, the order of the face hackles is reversed.

Smart's Yellowtail

Hook:	1X- or 2X-long wet- or dry-fly, sizes 8 to 14
Thread:	Black or yellow
Tail:	Golden pheasant crest, about as long as the shank
Rib:	Fine gold wire, spiraled through the palmer hackle
Body:	Yellow seal fur or substitute, dubbed
Palmer hackle:	Honey dun rooster, tied in about a quarter of the way back from the hook eye, leaving room for the three face hackles, then reverse-palmered to the bend
Face hackles:	From the palmer hackle forward, 2 to 3 turns of each: apple-green rooster, gray partridge, and white hen or rooster, each the same size or a bit longer than the palmer hackle

HEATHER MOTH Tied by Wayne Mones

Peter Deane's pattern can also be tied dry, substituting a fine-wire hook and blue dun or grizzly rooster hackle, and adding a long, dry-fly tail of brown mallard hackle fibers.

Heather Moth

Hook:	Standard or 1X-short wet-fly, sizes 6 and 8 (12 to 20 for grayling)
Thread:	Gray or black (8/0 for grayling)
Palmer hackle:	Grizzly hen, tied in at the front and reverse-palmered to the bend
Tag/Rib:	Silver wire or fine oval tinsel
Body:	Gray squirrel underfur, dubbed and picked out

Tying Tip

Brits also tie wet Heather Moths with tails, using barred teal fibers (and, sometimes, mallard flank or mandarin duck fibers). They also sometimes substitute olive or dark-gray wool yarn for the body, and blue dun ("light gray") for the palmer hackle.

ARMY WORM

Of the several patterns bearing this name, this one is the closest to a Woolly Worm in execution.

Army Worm

Hook:	2X-long nymph or wet-fly, sizes 6 to 10
Palmer hackle:	Grizzly or gray-dun hen saddle, tied in at the eye and reverse-palmered to the bend
Rib:	Insect-green floss
Body:	Yellow floss

BLOODY MARY

No relation to the Atlantic salmon fly of the same name, this trout-targeted Bloody Mary hails from Australia. According to Alan Shepherd, it was created in 1956 by his fellow Tasman, Max Christensen.

Bloody Mary

Hook:	Dry-fly, preferably round bend, sizes 6 to 10
Thread:	Black
Tail:	Tomato-red silk or nylon, frayed, as a tuft less than a gap-width long
Rib:	Fine gold wire
Body:	Orange-red Lurex, a flat Mylar tinsel (unable to find orange-red, I used red)
Palmer hackle:	Soft black, preferably game cock

Fishing Tips

Alan sent a passage from a 1971 book by Rodger Hungerford, *Guide to Trout Angling*, in which the author sings the praises of the Bloody Mary as a special kind of dapping fly "[w]hen the wind is so strong and gusty that all thoughts of a dry fly proper vanish from your mind, when all you can think of is bashing out a wet or retiring with hurt feelings to the pub...." Hungerford counsels greasing everything, including the 6-pound-test tippet and fly, and making short casts to drop the fly lightly near "a steepish bank with plenty of depth near the edge and the wind either blowing parallel to it or, better still, slightly off shore," where "the surface will be well ruffled, but not broken by active wavelets." Holding the rod high will let the wind belly the line, and a few twitches of the rod tip will let the fly dance and leap about on the rippled surface. After retrieving a yard or two of slack line, cast again and be prepared for a strike that is said to be always swift and savage.

Another good place to fish the Bloody Mary, according to Hungerford, is "where a good stiff breeze is blowing directly off a sloping lake shore." You want to work the area where the rippled water separates the calm water near shore and the rougher water under the winds offshore. Cast into the ripples and work the fly in toward the calm water.

GRADUATED WOOLLY WORM

This fly is based on the Idaho Nymph, which lacks the palmer hackle and uses the ostrich palmer rib only over the abdomen. I have tied an all-black version, but use the color or colors you think will work in your waters. Add a marabou tail, and you will tie a **Graduated Woolly Bugger**.

Graduated Woolly Worm

Hook:	3X- or 4X-long streamer, sizes 8 to 14
Thread:	To suit
Tail:	None; *alternatively, hackle points or fibers, a tuft of yarn tuft or frayed floss, hackle fluff, peacock herl stubs, flash material—whatever— about a gap width long*
Underbody:	*Optionally, lead wire on the shank—or use a bead head to weight the fly*
Palmer rib:	*Ostrich herl, tied in at the bend and palmered over the whole body in open spirals*
Palmer hackle:	Neck or saddle hackle, the barbs a gap-width long or clipped to length, tied in at mid shank and palmered over the front half of the body
Body:	Chenille, yarn, dubbing, peacock herl, floss, tinsel
Rib:	*Optionally, fine wire or tinsel, tied in at the bend and spiraled through the ostrich herl, before the hackle is palmered—in which case, tie in the ostrich herl at the front and reverse-palmer it to the bend*
Hackle collar:	Oversize hen neck, wrapped in 2 or 3 turns between the body and the hook eye as a wet-fly collar or soft hackle

GREEN CATERPILLAR Tied by Wayne Mones

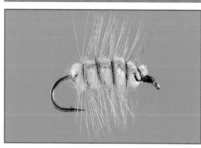

Keith Perrault lists two patterns by this name. One is simply green hackle palmered over a green chenille body on a size 10 or 12 streamer or wet-fly hook. He lists that one as an English pattern, but attributes it to Leonard West, who he later identifies as an "amateur tier of U.S. but better known as a fly pattern historian and writer." Be that as it may, it looks like a good pattern. This is the other pattern he lists.

Green Caterpillar

Hook:	Standard streamer or 2X- to 4X-long nymph, sizes 11 (English, indeed!) to 18
Thread:	Black
Body:	Mohair—green on top, yellow on bottom
Palmer hackle:	Short-barbed blue dun hen saddle

Tying Note

Perrault doesn't say how the two colors of mohair are applied, so you can experiment. I wrapped the yellow and pulled the green over the top, but you might want to try the reverse: wrapping the green and pulling the yellow under the belly. If you have more digital dexterity and better small-motor skills than *moi*, you could even try crocheting or braiding the mohair body.

Simpler than most western caterpillar patterns, this one you could probably fish in forested streams as a cricket. It's from Perrault, who listed it as a wet fly. (See also his clipped-hackle **Black Caterpillar** on page 55 as well as Haig-Brown's **Caterpillar** on page 28.)

Black Caterpillar

Hook: 2X-long wet-fly, sizes 6 and 8 (but you might go down to 10 for a cricket)
Thread: Black
Palmer hackle: Black hen saddle
Rib: Gold tinsel or wire, spiraled forward over the herl body, before the hackle is palmered
Body: Black ostrich herl, tied in at front and reverse-palmered to the bend, *and back, if you wish*

PISTOL PETE Courtesy of Yager's Flies; tied by Hi-Country Flies

Of the several unrelated patterns bearing this name, this is the one that most think of. Fly-fishing purists who look down their noses at the homely Woolly Worm will likely go ballistic over this variation. The spinner and the palmer hackle define this pattern. Everything else is your choice, including the social responsibility for tying and fishing it.

The Hi-Country Flies catalog shows 40 different Pistol Petes, including 6 salmon/steelhead, 6 saltwater, 12 Bugger-types (including an egg-sucking version), as well as 16 Woolly Worm-types. Several of the Petes are based on other patterns, among them the Babine, Seaducer, Clouser Deep Minnow, Lefty's Deceiver, Renegade, Bendback, Cactus Shrimp, Wiggle Tail, and Coho. So, after slipping that propeller onto the hook, let your imagination run wild!

Pistol Pete

Hook: 2X- to 4X-long nymph or streamer, preferably barbless or debarbed, sizes 6 to 10 for trout and panfish, 2 for salmon and steelhead, or 1/0 stainless for salt water
Head: A tiny glass or plastic bead, in the smallest size that will slip around the bend
Collar: Propeller-type spinner blade, sized to match the fly
Bearing: A glass or plastic bead (identical to the head bead); *alternatively, to fish deep, a larger bead or conehead*
Thread: Tier's choice
Tail: Whatever you like—hackle fibers, hackle points, yarn tuft, short or Bugger-length marabou, golden pheasant tippet or crest, a soft-plastic sickle tail—or nothing
Palmer hackle: Hen or rooster in the color of choice, tied in at the bend and palmered over the body; just don't crowd that bearing bead too tightly when you tie off, or the propeller won't spin
Body: Chenille, tinsel chenille, yarn, peacock or ostrich herl, floss, tying thread, monofilament, Larva Lace, dubbing—whatever

Tying Tip
Somewhere, I have seen a different version of the Pistol Pete with a Woolly Bugger's hook-length marabou tail augmented by even longer strips of Flashabou and a cone head between the propeller blade and the body.

Fishing Tips
Fish the Pistol Pete the way you would a wet fly, a streamer, or—perish the thought—a spinner: cast across or down and across the current and let the fly swing. At the end of the swing, twitch it back toward you before picking up for the back cast. Strikes can come at any time. If you are into trolling with a fly rod, Pistol Pete is your pattern.

To get the fly down deep, add weight in the tying or pinch a split shot about 6 inches up the leader. (Or use the conehead version described above.) If the propeller isn't giving you the right buzz, use your fingers to change the pitch of the blades.

This Len Holt pattern is a staple of the tailwater fishery on the San Juan River in New Mexico.

Dead Scud

Hook: Mustad 3906, a standard wet-fly, sizes 8 to 14
Thread: Orange 6/0 or 8/0
Tail: Fine tips of light deer or elk hair, about half a gap-width long, the butts used as a shellback
Shellback: The butts of the tail hairs, pulled over the body before the hackle is palmered
Body: Orange (alternatively, yellow) chenille
Palmer hackle: Grizzly rooster, the barbs not quite a gap-width long
Head: The butt ends of the deer or elk hair, clipped straight across, above the hook eye, after the tying thread has been whip-finished under the head

Tying Note

There are dozens, perhaps even hundreds, of shellbacked Woolly Wormish patterns out there, usually named Scud, Shrimp, Sow Bug, Cress Bug, or the like. While the details, and uses, of each pattern may differ, the principles are the same: A few hackle fibers, herl tips or stubs, strands of Krystal Flash, or something similar are tied in as a tail, often angling downward; in some cases (depending upon the critter being imitated), the tail may be omitted. Some sort of material is tied in early and pulled over the top later to suggest a carapace or shellback (the tail material, Flashabou, Krystal Flash, Swiss straw, clear or colored plastic, even a strip of sandwich bag). If the crustacean model is heavily segmented, a rib (wire, thread, monofilament) may be spiraled over the almost-finished fly. The scud may or may not be palmer-hackled, and the palmer may or may not be clipped. If a palmer hackle is used, almost anything can be used for the body (peacock herl, yarn, dubbing, beads, and so forth). If the fly is not palmer-hackled, the fluffy or bristly body may be made of ostrich herl, shaggy dubbing, hackle fluff, marabou blood feather, emu, or anything that will functionally substitute for a palmer hackle.

In the early 1970s, Charles Brooks had decided that the olive Woolly Worm was a perfectly adequate, if merely suggestive, imitation of the riffle worm, the large larva of the *Dytiscus* riffle beetle. A decade later, he was fishing a more imitative pattern, his Riffle Devil. This is his coy reference to imitating the *Dytiscus* larva in *Fishing Yellowstone Waters* (1984): "…either my Riffle Devil pattern, if you can find it, or a ginger-hackle, olive-bodied Woolly Worm in size 4, 4XL. Believe me, there will be times when one or the other is all that the fish will take."

Riffle Devil

Hook: 3X- to 4X-long streamer, sizes 4 to 8
Thread: Black or olive 6/0
Underbody: *Taff Price and Keith Perrault are silent on the subject, and Randall Stetzer merely specifies that the hook is weighted. If you like weighted flies, wrap a dozen or more turns of wire around the shank*
Body: Olive chenille, large
Palmer hackle: Ginger and brown saddles, palmered together (alternatively, a dark-ginger saddle), the barbs a gap-width long or slightly shorter, tied in by the tip and palmered more closely than in the sparsely hackled standard Woolly Worm; *some say the barbs should be angled toward the rear rather than the front, but suit yourself*

Tying Tip

If all your saddle hackles have long barbs, you can clip the hackle to length after you've finished.

And that brings us to our next general subject, clipped- and reduced-hackle versions of the Woolly Worm.

4. HACKLE-CHALLENGED WOOLLY WORMS

For uncertain reasons, clipping or otherwise reducing the palmer hackle to next-to-nothing sometimes increases the effectiveness of the basic Woolly Worm. You can always make this alteration on the water, but various tiers have devised patterns for severely clipped-hackle Woolly Worms. You can also palmer the fly with a variety of other materials, resulting in what I have lumped together as reduced-hackle Woolly Worms. Now, sticklers and purists will insist that a clipped- or reduced-hackle fly ought to be called something other than a Woolly Worm. They have a good point. But a few such clipped- or reduced-hackle flies are *called* Woolly Worms by their originators and by the people who tie and fish them, and a few otherwise-named patterns are so close to Woolly Worms in concept and construction, I have decided to include a bunch of the best ones.

CLIPPED-HACKLE WOOLLY WORMS

YELLOW GRUB

I found this Texas wet fly on Tony and Dottie Neal's Fly-fishing123.com web site, which was not operating last time I looked.

Yellow Grub

Hook:	Mustad 3906 or 3906B, sizes 8 to 12
Thread:	Black or red 6/0
Tail:	Red-dyed hackle fibers
Body:	Yellow medium chenille
Palmer hackle:	Gray saddle, clipped fairly short all around

ROCKWORM

This all-hackle pattern was listed by Keith Perrault in his 1984 *Perrault's Standard Dictionary of Fishing Flies*. I have changed the palmering technique to suit my style.

Rockworm

Hook:	Curved-shank nymph, sizes 8 to 14
Thread:	Black
Palmer hackle:	Black and white hackle feathers, tied in up front and reverse-palmered to the bend (either together, or one through the other), after the thread has been taken to the bend, then trimmed short, forming a fuzzy, bristly body
Rib:	Tying thread, taken forward through the palmer hackle
Hackle:	Badger soft-hackle collar

WATER CRICKET

Listed by Bergman in *Trout*, this is an early example of a shaped-hackle palmer fly. It is attributed elsewhere to one A. Ronalds.

Water Cricket

Hook:	Unspecified, but it looks like a 3X- or 4X-long streamer in the picture, sizes 14 to 16
Thread:	Black 6/0
Tail:	Black hackle fibers, a gap-width long
Body:	Pink or orange floss
Palmer hackle:	Black hen saddle, clipped to shape: sloping from a gap-width long in front to half a gap-width at the bend

SIMULATOR *Tied by Umpqua Feather Merchants for Kaufmann's Streamborn (left) and by Wayne Mones (right)*

Of late, the Kaufmann's Streamborn catalog shows Randall Kaufmann's Simulator with a marabou tail rather than the traditional pair of biots. I'm listing the bushy-tailed version (and showing it on the left, above), because that's the one Randall chose to be represented here. (If you want to tie it the original way—as Wayne Mones did on the right, above—just substitute a pair of dark-brown turkey biots for the tail and perhaps even clip the hackle a bit more aggressively.) Although the Simulator can be tied in a variety of body colors, the Peacock Simulator now dominates the scene.

Simulator

Hook:	TMC 5263BL, a 3X-long, 2X-heavy, barbless nymph, sizes 4 to 12
Thread:	Maroon
Underbody:	Lead wire
Tail:	Olive-brown marabou, thick and a bit longer than a gap-width; *alternatively, and traditionally, 2 dark-brown turkey biots, splayed*
Palmer hackle:	Furnace saddle, reverse-palmered, and more or less clipped at an angle
Body:	Peacock herl, fairly thick and tapered
Rib:	Copper wire, fine on the smaller sizes and medium on the larger

Tying Note

Tie the marabou tail longer than you need, and pinch it down to length. Besides marabou, try using blood feathers or hackle fluff (the "junk" that usually gets discarded from the butt end of the hackle quill).

The Simulator used to sport a rather severely clipped hackle, from more than a gap-width long at the front to about half a gap-width long at the rear. Nowadays, as you can see in the sample Kaufmann's sent me, it hardly gets clipped at all.

RED-ASSED RIES BUG *Tied by Dennis E. Smith*

I received this clipped-hackle pattern from Dennis E. Smith, a Colorado fly fisher and writer of skill and wit. He got it from "a cranky old guy who stays in a dilapidated pickup camper on Delaney Buttes Lake, and who ties these things to sell to any rookies silly enough to pay him $1.50 each for them."

"We called the old man Delaney Buttes Bob," Dennis writes, "but we named his fly after Pat Ries, a buddy who fell for the scam and bought a half-dozen of them, then proceeded to catch one fish after another on the stupid-looking thing while the rest of us went damn-near fishless. He really cleaned our clocks with the thing."

"If you ask me," Dennis says, "it's just a conventional Woolly Worm, clipped down to nothing, but the old man swears that his particular adaptation (mutilation) is what makes it a killer. I have no idea what it's supposed to represent, or what makes it so effective, but that day, on that lake, it was *the* fly."

Oh, yes: Despite having taken considerable verbal abuse from his buddies about buying the fly, Pat Ries did share his stash with his companions that day—demanding $2.75 a pop and an honest answer to his question, "*Now* who's ass is red?"

Red-Assed Ries Bug

Hook:	Mustad 9671 or similar 2X-long streamer, size 10 or 12
Thread:	Black
Tail:	Red yarn, tag-style, snipped short (about half a gap-width long)
Body:	Brown chenille: "Gotta be medium, goddamn it," according to the originator
Palmer hackle:	Grizzly, clipped to a stubble, and none too neatly at that

Tying Tips

When he ties them for himself, Dennis Smith modifies the pattern, using a larger and longer salmon/steelhead hook, trimming the tail a wee bit longer (maybe 3/4 a gap-width), and clipping the hackle at an angle (from nearly nothing at the rear to about tail-length at the front), even leaving a few of the barbs on the underside of the hook untrimmed up front. "I tie it solely to accommodate my taste for flies that *look* as though they might catch fish—as opposed to those that actually do but are so hideous I can't bring myself to knot one to my leader," Dennis explains. "I guess I'd rather fish all day with a 'good-looking' fly and catch nothing than bang hell out of them on a pattern that holds about the same cosmetic appeal for me as a chunk of stink bait. What can I say? I'm a fly fisherman, and we tend to be a bit eccentric—if not downright goofy at times."

For the dry-fly version, use a 3X-long, fine-wire terrestrial hook, omit the underbody and body, and palmer a stiff, steeply tapered rooster furnace hackle in touching turns.

I know this has to be a pattern *for* whitefish, which do not produce nymphs. Perrault lists three different patterns with this name.

Whitefish Nymph

Hook: Standard or 1X-long nymph, sizes 10 to 14
Thread: Unspecified
Body: Pale-yellow floss
Palmer hackle: Brown hen, clipped short

Tying Tips

Alternatively, use yellow, white, light-blue, or tan wool for the body.

If you prefer an unclipped palmer hackle, use brown floss for the body, according to Perrault.

REDHEAD

This damselfly nymph imitation was brought to the angling world's attention by Gary L. Fenwick, a freelance writer from American Falls, Idaho, who described his fishing buddy's pattern in the May/June 1997 issue of *American Angler*. Fenwick notes that "the fly has proved successful everywhere damselfly nymphs are numerous," in waters as varied as spring creeks and deep reservoirs such as Henrys Lake. The body color varies with the color of the damsel nymphs present.

Redhead

Hook: 2X- or 3X-long streamer, size 10
Thread: Red
Tail: Brown hackle fibers
Tag: Tying thread, from the base of the tail to opposite the hook point, head-cemented—*not* flexible cement, as it will dull the color
Body: Olive, brown, or variegated chenille or yarn
Palmer hackle: Brown rooster hackle, clipped flat on top and bottom, the sides clipped in a wedge, widening toward the front
Head: Tying thread, cemented

Fishing Tip

The Redhead should be fished on a sinking or sinking-tip line, depending on the water's depth. Cast it out, count it down to the fishing depth, and wiggle the rod tip from side to side as you strip-retrieve the fly.

HENRYS LAKE SPECIAL

Although he doesn't attribute the pattern to anyone in particular, Eric Leiser says in *The Book of Fly Patterns* (1987) that this fly "is a favorite on Henry's [sic] Lake and Yellowstone Lake."

(See also Ruel Stayner's **Henrys Lake Leech** on page 200.)

Henrys Lake Special

Hook: Mustad 9671, a 2X-long streamer, sizes 6 to 10
Thread: Olive
Tail: 2 brown-dyed goose biots, splayed out in a V, a gap-width long
Palmer hackle: Brown saddle, clipped to 1/8-inch in length
Body: Peacock herl
Palmer hackle: Brown saddle, clipped to 1/8-inch

Tying Note

I vaguely recall seeing a pattern of the same name that listed a short ginger hackle (barbs about a gap-width long) sparsely palmered over a wool body that was lettuce-green on top and yellow on the bottom (wrap the yellow and pull the green over). (See the **Gene Gantt Memorial Fly** on page 45, which is probably that same pattern, but with a clipped or reduced palmer hackle.)

Jim "Red" Chase of Toppenish, Washington, created this one. Polly Rosborough often tied the Nondescript, but he used a short tuft of dark-brown marabou for the tail.

Brown Nondescript

Hook: 3X-long streamer, sizes 8 to 12
Thread: Brown
Tail: Brown-dyed, barred mallard fibers *(dark-brown marabou, for the Rosborough version)*, slightly longer than a gap-width
Body: Dark-brown synthetic yarn
Rib: Heavy yellow thread, wrapped *between* the turns of saddle hackle
Palmer hackle: Dark furnace saddle, tied in at the bend by its tip; before tying it in, use scissors to taper it on each side of the midrib, from nothing at the tip to 1/2 inch at its widest

Tying Tip

After preparing the saddle hackle, tie it in by the tip, take one turn of yarn behind the hackle and rib, then closely wrap the body forward. After palmering the hackle, rib the fly by wrapping the yellow thread between the turns of palmered hackle.

I don't know whose pattern this is, but the name (riffle beetle larvae often are called fish flies) suggests it should be fished in riffles.

Fish Fly Larva

Hook: Standard or 1X-long nymph, sizes 4 to 8
Thread: Black
Body: Black dubbing, mixed seal (or substitute) and rabbit
Palmer hackle: Soft black hen, heavy in front, and clipped to a taper

Similar patterns of the same name abound, but this one—which Terry Hellekson wrote was "sent to me by George Bodmer of Colorado Springs, Colorado"—has an interesting twist (no pun intended). This twisted-hackle technique so excited me, I started tying a bunch of palmered flies that way (see my **Twisted Woolly** on page 30; see also the twisted-hackle technique there, and on page 123). I am listing it "as is," but I would reverse-palmer the hackles, because of the wire rib. I've also seen this pattern listed as **Cased Caddis Hazel**.

Cased Caddis

Hook: Mustad 9671, a 2X-long streamer, sizes 10 to 16
Thread: Black
Body: Dark-brown floss or yarn, tapered
Rib: Copper wire
Palmer hackle: Brown and black saddle feathers, twisted together and wrapped forward—*alternatively, tied in up front, twisted, and reverse-palmered to the bend*—clipped even with the ostrich herl
Head: Black ostrich herl

Tying Note

In British Columbia, they tie a fly of the same name, but use red thread, add a fairly thick tail of brown hackle fibers, wrap olive (or other hatch-matching color) chenille for the body, palmer a furnace hackle, and wrap a thread head. To rib or not to rib is apparently tier's choice in Pacific Canada.

HELLGRAMMITE

Many patterns by this name exist. This is the one listed by Terry Hellekson in *Popular Fly Patterns* (1977).

Hellgrammite

Hook: Mustad 79580 or similar 4X-long streamer, sizes 4 to 8
Thread: Black
Palmer hackle: Brown and black saddles, palmered one after the other over a thread base, then clipped flush top and bottom and angled at the sides from about 3/4-inch at front to just stubble at the rear

GUNNY SACK

Hellekson also listed this slightly more "elaborate" trout and summer-steelhead pattern.

Gunny Sack

Hook: Mustad 9671 or similar 2X-long streamer, sizes 8 to 14
Thread: Brown
Tail: Grizzly hackle fibers, at least a gap-width long
Body: Burlap fibers, tapered
Palmer hackle: Grizzly, clipped to a taper: about 1/4-inch long at front to a mere stubble at rear

BLACK CATERPILLAR (2)

According to Keith Perrault, this is an English pattern that is fished wet. It apparently represents the larval form of the tortoise-shell butterfly. See Perrault's other, unclipped **Black Caterpillar** on page 49 as well as Haig-Brown's **Caterpillar** on page 28.)

Black Caterpillar

Hook: 2X- to 4X-long streamer, sizes 12 to 18
Thread: Black
Body: Black wool
Palmer hackle: Black hen, clipped short

HUSMASK *Tied by Paul Milstam*

Husmask is Swedish for **Cased Caddis**. Relative to other insect patterns, caddis flies are much more important in Sweden than in North America—as both dry flies and nymphs. The Baltic countries—Sweden, Denmark, Finland, Germany—have some really dynamite caddis patterns.

"The important thing about the Husmask," writes Paul Milstam, "is to tie it in the right color to match the bottom. If the bottom is dark brown, make the Husmask dark brown. If the bottom is light, make the Husmask light. It's also very important to fish this fly on the bottom, so that it rolls over the bottom in the current. Therefore, it's normal to give it some extra weight—either lead or copper wire."

Husmask

Hook: Standard or long-shank streamer, sizes 10 and 12
Thread: 6/0, to suit the color of the hackle or head
Underbody: Lead or copper wire; *optionally, omit the wire underbody*
Body: Tying thread over the weighting wire
Palmer hackle: Rooster hackle "in the right color," palmered very closely and clipped to about 2 mm (1/8 inch)
Head: Partridge SLF dubbing in a color that's slightly lighter or darker than the rest of the fly

HACKLE NYMPH *Tied by R. G. Balogh*

Ingo Karwath presented this simple nymph clipped-hackle (in German *gestutzte Hechelnymphe*) in the magazine *Fliegen-Fischen*. I can't read German, but with the aid of a dictionary and some German-speaking, but non-fishing, friends, I was able to struggle through Karwath's fly recipes, if not the article accompanying them. Judging by the hook size, I figure this is a midge nymph. (I had it tied it larger for photographic purposes.) Hackle color should match the midge fauna in your local waters, anything from bright red to dark olive.

Hackle Nymph

Hook:	Standard, heavy-wire, or 1X- to 2X-long nymph, sizes 20 to 28
Thread:	Black
Palmer hackle:	Hen or rooster hackle, closely palmered over a thread base and clipped to half a gap-width or shorter

ANYTIME, ANYWHERE

Garry Merriman of The Fish Hawk in Atlanta, Georgia, submitted this pattern to Eric Leiser for inclusion in *The Book of Fly Patterns*. Merriman fishes it as a nymph for trout, steelhead, salmon, bonefish, panfish, and bass—hence, its name. Perhaps it's a variation on the **C. K. Nymph** pattern described three patterns below.

Anytime, Anywhere

Hook:	Mustad 9672, a 3X-long streamer, sizes 10 to 16
Thread:	Black 6/0, or 3/0 Monocord
Tail:	Wood-duck flank fibers, a heavy bunch as long as the shank
Body:	Black chenille
Palmer hackle:	Grizzly saddle, trimmed to a bushy stubble

LEHIGH UGLY *Tied by Mary S. Kuss*

Mary S. Kuss, a fly-fishing and -tying instructor at The Sporting Gentleman in Media, Pennsylvania, developed this easy and effective pattern from an older fly called the Ridley Ugly. (Historical note: Flies named "Ugly" should have clipped hackles.) She prefers to fish it as a bottom-bouncing nymph, but her friend Jay Everly, "a consummate streamer man, also found it very effective fished downstream with a fast, twitching, hand-twist retrieve."

Because Kuss refined the tying technique to maximize the tying speed and the fly's durability, I have decided to present her tying steps. You won't need photos to follow them. When I asked how the tail fibers stay in position and whether it might be easier to tie in a tail separately, she replied, "Believe it or not, the tail fibers stay in position once you start winding the hackle. Try it and you'll see. In fact, sometimes you get more rear-facing fibers than you want and have to trim some out! You certainly *could* tie in a hackle-fiber tail as a first step, but I find it quicker and easier to skip that and form the tail as indicated. Also, the final effect is somewhat different than you get by tying in a tail clump, and I like it better on this fly. Frankly, I don't think the fish would care one whit either way, but I tie to please myself as much as to please the fish. And they and I seem to be in reasonable agreement most of the time."

Lehigh Ugly

Hook:	2X-long nymph or wet-fly, size 10
Thread:	Black 3/0 Monocord
Tail:	Fibers from the palmer hackle (see Tying Steps), about as long as the fly
Palmer hackle:	Natural black rooster saddle or large neck hackle, clipped short (see Tying Steps)
Body:	Natural black wool yarn, wrapped
Underbody:	Hackle stem and body yarn, lashed to the shank
Head:	Tying thread, lacquered

Tying Steps

Tie on at the eye and take the thread back to the bend in open spiral wraps. Tie in the hackle by the butt, then take the thread to the front (leaving room behind the eye for the head, and binding the stripped hackle stem to the hook shank as you go).

With the thread at the "shoulder," tie in the yarn by its tip and bind it to the shank by wrapping the thread back to the bend and then forward once more to the shoulder.

Apply head cement or lacquer to the shank, thoroughly soaking the bound materials of the underbody, then wrap the yarn forward in even, touching (but not overlapping) turns, tie it off, and clip the excess.

Pull the hackle feather straight up with your right hand. Use your left hand to stroke several fibers rearward to form the tail. Palmer the hackle forward, so the stem gets pulled down between the wraps of yarn. Tie off the hackle, trim the excess, form a head, and whip-finish.

"You *could* just trim all the hackle to stubble length, but I like to do it as follows: With the fly still in the vise, use the thumb and forefinger of your right hand to stroke the bottom hackle fibers up on both sides of the shank. Grasp all the upswept hackle fibers between your left thumb and forefinger and hold them straight up. With one snip of your scissors, shear the hackle fibers to stubble length. Once the hackle stubs are groomed, you will have a fly with a hackle that graduates from very short on top to less than a gap-width long below. I think it looks kind of neat this way."

RIDLEY UGLY *Tied by R. G. Balogh*

This acknowledged ancestor of the Lehigh Ugly uses brighter colors. It can be tied the conventional way, or using Mary Kuss's technique described for the Lehigh Ugly.

Ridley Ugly

Hook: 2X-long nymph or wet-fly, sizes 8 to 12
Thread: Black or dark-brown 6/0 or 3/0
Tail: Brown hackle fibers
Body: Bright-yellow wool yarn, wrapped
Palmer hackle: Brown saddle hackle *(alternatively, red game hackle)*, clipped to a stubble

C. K. NYMPH

Someone—probably Jerry Stercho—mentioned this "old time nymph pattern" as a footnote to Mary Kuss's article in the *Mid Atlantic Fly Fishing Guide*. Jere Haas, of Easton, Pennsylvania, listed the pattern on the Fly Tying World site (www.flytying-world.com), and I have merged the two listings in the recipe below.

When I contacted Haas, he replied that he was introduced to the pattern by his friend Barry Hoskins. Neither could recall who developed the pattern, but they agreed it was introduced in the late 1940s or early 1950s on a part of the Bushkill Creek the local "trout bums" always referred to as "the C. K. Williams stretch," after the pigment-producing plant that owned the property. Even after the property was acquired by the Pfizer pharmaceutical company, it remained the C.K. Williams stretch to trout fishers.

C. K. Nymph

Hook: 2X-long nymph or wet-fly, sizes 4 and 6
Thread: Black Danville Monocord or similar
Underbody: *Optionally, lead wire wrapped around the shank*
Tail: (1) Wood-duck flank, half as long as the hook; or (2) a grizzly hackle tip, a gap-width long, plus hackle fluff from the base of the same feather
Body: Black wool or poly yarn, wrapped in a taper
Palmer hackle: Grizzly saddle, clipped short (1/8 to 3/16 in), optionally, with 2 turns of soft, webby barbs near the base of the feather left long as a wet-fly collar

Tying Tip

On the FTW site, Haas noted that the fly can be tied in a variety of colors, and that brown and olive are also good. In his e-mail to me he reported that Hoskins said he also tied a yellow-bodied version on a size 10, 3X-long hook.

Fishing Note

All agree that this fly can be fished as a stonefly nymph, although Haas adds that fish also might take it for a cranefly larva or small crayfish.

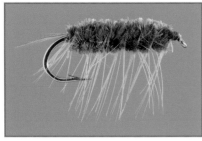

This pattern by Gil Nyerges, of Clinton, Washington, is representative of numerous fly patterns that are palmered, then the hackle is clipped short on top and sides, to simulate the legs of scuds and other crustaceans. Given the size of their brains, fish might also mistake it for a stonefly nymph. More productive than most such patterns, however, the Nyerges Nymph can be fished in riffles, pocket water, pools, and still water. It can also be fished in warm as well as cold water, and in salt water as well as fresh. This classic is a real keeper.

In a recent e-mail, Nyerges wrote, "The original was first tied in 1952 at Jameson Lake in central Washington, using a size-10, 3X-long hook. I tie it in sizes 6 down to 16 for rainbow, brook, cutthroat, and brown trout, grayling, bass, bluegills, sunfish, carp, and other warmwater species such as walleye and great northern pike (some tied on larger hooks).

I also tie it on saltwater hooks for bonefish, dorado, snook, mackerel, and baby tarpon."

Besides the pattern's versatility, Nyerges also points to its elegant simplicity: "It is tied with just two pieces of material—a single, long, brown hackle with fibers just a little longer than the gap of the hook and medium, moss-green cheni" the body."

Nyerges Nymph

Hook: Mustad 9672, a 3X-long streamer, sizes 6 to 16
Thread: Brown or olive 6/0
Tail: Brown rooster saddle hackle tip, thin and short—no more than half again as long hook gap is wide
Body: Moss-green medium chenille
Palmer hackle: Brown rooster saddle, palmered to the e approximately 6 turns; top and sides are clipped flush after palmering, leaving hackle-barb legs only on the underside
Head: Tying thread

Tying Tip

After tying in the body chenille, take the thread to the eye. Begin forming the body by taking one wrap of chenille over the hackle tie-in wraps, then lift the hackle feather out of the way and continue wrapping forward.

They just don't come much simpler than this, when it comes to imitating the so-called "freshwater shrimp" (scuds and such, actually).

Simple Shrimp

Hook: Straight- or curved-shank nymph, sizes 8 to 16
Thread: Orange, brown, or olive, a long tag end left dangling at the bend
Back: Single-strand light-gray wool yarn, pulled over the body before palmering the hackle
Body: Pale-green, gray, tan, or salmon-pink wool yarn, wrapped
Palmer hackle: Ginger hen, clipped almost flush on top and sides

This pattern was listed by Keith Perrault.

Gray Sow Bug

Hook: Standard or 1X-short wet-fly, sizes 10 to 14
Thread: Gray
Body: Light-gray and olive fur, mixed and dubbed
Palmer hackle: Blue-gray [blue dun] hen, trimmed almost flush with the body on top and bottom

The name of this Bill Beardsley creation suggests that it's a leech imitation.

Lacking the undulating suppleness of a swimming leech, it looks to me more like a hellgrammite (albeit the wrong color) or some other many-legged, blood-engorged, creepy-crawly thing. Nor would I be afraid to fish it when damsel or dragonfly nymphs were about.

Bloodsucker

Hook: 4X- to 6X-long streamer, sizes 2 to 8
Thread: Black 6/0, or 3/0 Monocord (I often use red thread when I want a pattern to suggest a blood-engorged leech, mosquito, or biting fly.)
Underbody: *Optionally, lead wire wrapped around the shank*
Tail: Short, thick tuft of scarlet or hot-red wool, extending just to the back of the bend
Body: Red or dark-red chenille; *some listings call for black*
Palmer hackle: Fiery-brown or red-dyed saddle hackle, palmered rather closely and clipped short—less than a gap-width long; *alternatively, use a dry-fly saddle that is long enough, but short-barbed*
Head: Tying thread, rather large, gloss-coated

Tying Tip

When you get to the front of the body, wrap several touching turns of the hackle, forming a hackle collar. In forming the thread head, pull back on the front hackles with your fingers and wrap over the butts to cause the front hackle barbs to sweep back. In trimming the palmer hackle, you needn't clip these front barbs so short.

This pattern comes from *Perrault's*, where it is listed twice: once, unweighted, as a Canadian pattern with this name; again, weighted, as a western fly called the **Bloody Butcher.** (To confuse things even further, but hardly his fault, Perrault lists five other, different patterns under the name Bloody Butcher.)

Blood Sucker

Hook: 1X- or 2X-long wet-fly, sizes 2 to 8
Thread: Black, dark-brown, or red
Underbody: *Optionally, lead wire*
Tail: Bright-red yarn or hackle fibers, about a gap-width long
Body: Black chenille
Palmer hackle: Brown or fiery-brown (natural-red) saddle, clipped to about 1/4 inch

Breathes there a Midwestern or Deep South crappie fisherman who doesn't like catalpa trees and catalpa worms? Actually, few warmwater fish will pass up a catalpa worm, particularly bluegills and the other sunfishes, including large- and smallmouth basses. The larvae of certain species of sphinx moths (the ones that look something like hummingbirds with antennae, also known as hawk moths), catalpa worms "hatch" in August. More-or-less-related, more-or-less-look-alike caterpillar larvae of other species that inhabit other streamside trees and fall into the water also spice up the summertime menus of warmwater fish. This pattern is by the erstwhile Texas panfish master Jack Ellis who now has bigger fish to fry (having become a Baptist missionary). The recipe below is based on the one presented in his book *The Sunfishes: A Fly Fishing Journey of Discovery* (1993).

Catalpa Worm

Hook: Mustad 79580, a 4X-long streamer, slightly bent down *(alternatively, a hook with a long, slightly curved shank)*, size 6

Thread: Black 6/0

Tail: 2 black goose biots, forked—more or less a gap-width long

Back: Fine black chenille, pulled over the back before the hackle is palmered

Body: Cream or pale creamy-yellow wool, lamb's wool, or chenille, and black permanent marker to add a string of small spots down the sides

Palmer hackle: Black or well-marked grizzly saddle, stripped on one side and clipped very short (almost flush) on all sides after palmering

Head: Tying thread, fairly large, and reinforced with cement or lacquer

Another of Jack Ellis's creations, sometimes called **Walnut Worm**, this one imitates the colorful, striped caterpillars that plop into the water not only from walnut trees, but also from the high branches of the related hickories and unrelated oaks—both of which are a lot more common than walnuts at water's edge. Late September is the season.

Walnut Caterpillar

Hook: Mustad 79580, a 4X-long streamer, slightly bent down *(alternatively, a hook with a long, slightly curved shank)*, size 6

Thread: Black

Tail: 2 goose biots (dark or light, as required to match the "hatch"), forked, a gap-width to half again as long

Back: Yellow chenille or yarn, pulled over the back (before the hackle is palmered), then a line is drawn down the center with a black permanent marker

Belly: The same yellow chenille or yarn as for the back, but tied in under the shank and pulled forward over the bottom of the body before the hackle is palmered

Body: Black chenille (which will show only a "stripe" down each side after the back and belly are pulled forward)

Palmer hackle: Black, grizzly, ginger, cree, or badger saddle (depending on the general look of the walnut caterpillars in your area), stripped on one side, palmered fairly closely over the body, and clipped closely on the finished fly

Head: Dark-red chenille, 1 turn; finish with a fairly substantial thread head, which should be gloss-coated with clear lacquer or nail polish

I don't know a thing about this pattern's provenance, and can't remember where I picked it up. True to its name, this pattern sure has me wondering.

Wonder Nymph

Hook: Mustad 9671 or equivalent 2X-long streamer, sizes 6 to 12
Thread: Black
Tail: 3 porcupine quill tips, a gap-and-a-half long
Body: Muskrat, dubbed
Palmer hackle: Blue-dun and brown saddles palmered together in 4 turns, then clipped short
Head: Black ostrich herl

I think this fly is named for the vegetable it resembles, not for any creepy-crawly it imitates. Fish it when long, green, wormy things are dropping from overhanging trees into the water.

Cucumber Worm

Hook: 3X- to 6X-long streamer, sizes 4 to 16
Thread: Dark-green or dark-olive 3/0, 6/0, or 8/0
Tail: Gap-length stubs of peacock herl, dark-green or olive yarn (sparse), or dark-green Krystal Flash
Body: Peacock herl, dark-green wool yarn or dubbing, or green, olive, or peacock chenille
Palmer hackle: Green, dark-green, or olive saddle, clipped to bristle length or, on the larger sizes, the same colors of ostrich herl, palmered closely

A key to this Al Troth pattern's effectiveness lies in the trimming of the marabou. Don't use scissors; pinch the marabou against your index finger with your thumbnail. Pinched marabou produces livelier, shaggier-looking tips. The resulting fly can be made to "swim" like a leech writhing in the current.

This sort of looks like a flattened, tailed, collar-less big brother to Jack Gartside's **Wet Mouse** (page 46).

Troth Leech

Hook: Mustad 79580 or similar 4X-long streamer, size 4
Thread: Black
Tail: Dark-brown marabou, pinched to a gap-width in length
Body: Tying thread
Palmer hackle: Dark-brown marabou, palmered very closely (2 to 4 feathers will probably be required), then clipped flush on top and bottom (so the hackle looks like a narrow bow tie when viewed, dry, from the front), and the sides pinched to a wedge shape, narrowing toward the tail

Tying Note

Saltwater fly fishers can make just minor adjustments to this pattern to tie Don Avondolo's **Motion Fly**, a marabou-palmered Bugger listed in Lefty Kreh's *Salt Water Fly Patterns*: saltwater-fly hook in sizes 1 or 1/0, white thread, white marabou for both the tail (full and at least a hook-length long) and palmered body and "hackle."

Reduced-hackle Woolly Worms

CDC Caterpillar

The minimalist nature of this pattern's twisted peacock-herl-and-CDC palmer hackle almost gives it a clipped-hackle appearance. This Gerhard Laible pattern is listed as a nymph by Randall Kaufmann in *Fly Patterns of Umpqua Feather Merchants* (1995), but that fine-wire hook and water-repellent body material suggest it's fished as an emerger. I think you'd need a heavier hook and a weighted underbody to efficiently sink a poly-bodied, CDC-palmered fly. If you don't like heavy flies or split shot and want to fish it deep, substitute wool yarn to make the body water-absorbent. Personally, I'd also use an Airflo sinking leader to take it to the bottom.

CDC Caterpillar

Hook: TMC 5212, a 2X-long, 2X-fine nymph or dry-fly, size 8
Thread: Black or olive
Rib: Peacock herl, a few turns wrapped behind the body as a butt
Body: Yellow poly yarn *(or wool)*
Palmer hackle: CDC feather, twisted together with the peacock herl and wrapped forward in 5 open spirals
Head: The fifth spiral wrap of CDC and peacock, finished with a small thread head

Ray Charles   *Courtesy of Cabela's; tied by Montana Fly Company*

No, not *that* Ray Charles! The Montana Fly Company categorizes this fly as a sow bug. The Cabela's catalog calls it the **R. C. Scud**. Besides the listed pink, this fly also comes in orange, tan, white, and gray; just substitute those colors for pink in the recipe. There's also a gray/tan pattern in the Montana Flies catalog, and I don't think it much matters to the fish which materials are gray and which are tan.

Ray Charles

Hook: Standard streamer or nymph, sizes 14 to 18
Thread: Fluorescent fire-orange 6/0 UNI
Shellback: Pearl flat Mylar tinsel, tied in at the bend and pulled over the top before ribbing
Palmer hackle: Pink-dyed ostrich herl, tied in at the front and reverse-palmered over the dubbed body in touching turns
Body: Pink Wabbit (a rabbit–Antron blend) dubbing, dubbed from front to rear, after the ostrich herl has been tied in
Rib: Tying thread, ribbed forward in open spirals, after the shellback has been pulled over
Head: Tying thread

Tying Tips

After tying in the shellback at the bend, take the thread forward and tie in the ostrich herl. Dub the body to the bend. Now, reverse-palmer the ostrich herl over the dubbed body and use the thread to tie it off; clip the excess herl. Pull the shellback over the top, hold it in place at the eye, and take the thread forward in open, spiral turns, tie down the shellback and clip the excess tinsel. Finally, wrap a neat head, whip-finish, and varnish the head if you wish. I like to use hard, clear or pink-pearl nail polish.

Creeper

A minimalist pattern, the Creeper can be surprisingly effective when the fish are being picky.

Creeper

Hook: Standard to 3X-long, straight- or curved-shank nymph, sizes 10 to 18
Thread: Black, brown, or dark-olive, to suit the rest of the pattern
Underbody: *Optionally, .010- to .015-in lead wire*
Body: Black, brown, olive, green, tan, pink, or yellow medium or small (to suit the hook size) chenille
Palmer hackle: Ostrich herl, in a color to suit the body and the local creepy crawlies, wrapped so the stem gets buried between the turns of chenille

Pick your hooks and glass beads carefully, or spend a lot of time finding a bead that will slip around the bend.

Herly Nymph

Hook: Barbless or debarbed, fine-wire hook with a straight or slightly curved shank, sizes 10 to 20

Head: Amber glass bead, as small as will slip around the bend

Thread: Orange or tan 8/0, tied on at the bend

Rib: Fine gold or copper wire through the abdomen

Abdomen: Bronze peacock herl, twisted as a chenille rope

around the tying thread and wrapped to a point about 1/4 to 1/3 the shank length behind the bead head

Palmer hackle: A single brown ostrich herl, tied in just ahead of the peacock body and reverse-palmered in 5 or 6 open spirals back to the bend where it will be caught by the wire rib

Thorax: 4 or 5 brown ostrich herls with dense, long flues, tied in just ahead of the peacock herl at the same time as the palmer hackle and palmered in touching turns to the bead head after the thread is taken forward

Tying Tip

Try this color variant: dark-green bead, chartreuse or light-olive thread, green peacock herl, olive ostrich herl, and either gold or silver rib.

This Paul Canning creation could almost be called a reduced-hackle, reverse-bivisible nymph, the body materials virtually serving as palmered hackles. Depending on the length of your ostrich herls and the thickness of their flues, you may have to palmer two or three of them together to cover the hook thickly enough.

Canning's Caenis Nymph

Hook: Standard nymph, size 14

Thread: Black

Tail: Grizzly or badger rooster hackle fibers

Rib: Fine oval silver tinsel or silver wire, used to catch the abdomen herl and to both dress up and reinforce the body

Thorax: Brown or golden-olive ostrich herl, palmered tightly from mid shank forward

Abdomen: White ostrich herl, reverse-palmered tightly from mid shank to bend

This pattern imitates a true freshwater shrimp, *Mysis relicta*, which survived the Ice Ages. It also can pass for a scud or other freshwater crustacean. Many *Mysis relicta* patterns exist, because they will take everything from stream trout to Great Lakes steelhead. Most use fur dubbing and burnt mono eyes. Use either component, or both, if you wish. I like the simplicity of this pattern.

Mysis Shrimp

Hook: 1X- or 2X-long nymph, straight or curved shank, sizes 16 to 20 *(sample tied slightly larger)*

Thread: White 8/0

Body: White poly floss (the kind used to make spinner wings) or Antron yarn—a short frayed stub end left exposed over the bend as part of the "tail"

Rib: 2 or 3 strands of pearl Krystal flash, twisted together and spiraled through the palmered herl—the nearly shank-length ends left untrimmed over the bend as part of the "tail"

Palmer hackle: 2 or 3 white ostrich herls, the tips trimmed, then tied in behind the hook eye by their trimmed tips and reverse-palmered to the bend

Tying Tip

When you tie in the body floss/yarn, leave the short, frayed end sticking out over the bend as feelers. Next, tie in the 6 strands of Krystal Flash ribbing, leaving nearly shank-length ends extending to the rear as antennae.

HACKLE-FREE WOOLLY WORMS

Strictly speaking, a fly without a palmer hackle shouldn't be called a Woolly Worm. However, some tiers, apparently having taken their clue from those who tie Woolly Buggers without palmer hackle (see the second half of the book for a more detailed discussion of that issue), have started using Estaz and other long-fibered tinsel chenilles for the body and eschewing the palmer hackle altogether. I'll list a single pattern, to stand for all of them (but see also the **Floating Cactus Woolly Worm** on page 91 and **Dixon's Devil Worm** on page 191.)

HESTER'S SPARKLE GRUB *Tied by Jim Hester*

This easy-as-pie panfish pattern is the creation of "Big Jim" Hester, proprietor of the Chesapeake Fly & Bait Company (www.chesapeakefly.com) of Arnold, Maryland. His web pages were being redone when I last looked, so I don't know how many colors he offers. Use the color or colors you are used to fishing in your panfish ponds, lakes, and streams.

Hester's Sparkle Grub

Hook: Standard or 1X-long wet-fly or nymph, izes 8 to 12

Thread: 6/0 in a color to match, complement, or contrast with the body

Body: Chenille

Palmer "hackle": Micro tinsel chenille, wound forward in 4 or 5 open spirals

Now let's look at some special-purpose Woolly Worms.

Time was, flies tied for Atlantic salmon were distinctly different from those tied for Pacific salmon and steelhead. A few decades ago, Atlantic salmon patterns such as the misnamed General Practitioner (Major Esmond Drury called it G.P., for golden pheasant) began seeing duty on Pacific salmon and steelhead streams. More recently, West Coast patterns have been used with success in Eastern Canada and Europe. The introduction of steelhead and all kinds of salmon to the Great Lakes have made the categorical waters even murkier. You could probably tie and fish any of the patterns in this chapter for any of the salmonids, or tie them on corrosion-resistant hooks and fish them in salt water.

SALMON & STEELHEAD WOOLLY WORMS

In a note accompanying his **Vancouver Island Woolly Bugger** (see page 130), the British Columbia illustrator and fly tier Loucas Raptis wrote, "According to the British Columbian angling historian Art Lingren, in the mid 1960s Bob Taylor of Vancouver introduced the Woolly Worm in large sizes for steelhead fishing in the Pacific Northwest with remarkable success. The pattern is now used regularly on the Thompson and the Dean and is tied and sold commercially in sizes as large as 2/0." He also mentioned **Haig-Brown's Caterpillars**—Woolly Worms without tails—which we included in an earlier chapter, on page 28. Since those halcyon days, anadromous-salmonid fishers have taken the Woolly Worm concept farther along the conceptual road.

WOOLLY BRAHAN

This mongrel fly is a bit of a cross between the Woolly Worm (or Woolly Bugger; see Tying Tips below) and a British hairwing salmon fly called the Black Brahan. Here, we have replaced the black (bear, calf, or similar) wing with a palmer hackle.

Woolly Brahan

Hook: Salmon/steelhead wet-fly, sizes 2 to 10
Thread: Black 6/0
Body: Flat Mylar tinsel—red or green is traditional, but you can use orange, blue, purple, pink, or whatever color suits your fancy
Rib: Silver or gold fine flat tinsel *(alternatively, gold or silver wire)*, spiraled forward *between* the wraps of palmer hackle
Palmer hackle: Glossy-black hen saddle, palmered forward in open spirals with the barbs angled forward

Tying Tips

The Brits use a body material called Lurex, but any good, strong Mylar tinsel will do.

If you wish, use a streamer hook of appropriate size for trout.

For a Woolly Bugger version—the **Buggered Brahan**, just add a black marabou tail and palmer the hackle conventionally, with the barbs angled to the rear.

FEATHERDUSTER

Many flies go by this name: big bass flies, midges down to size 20 or smaller, gaudy steelhead patterns. A series rather than a single pattern, these British Featherdusters traditionally are used for Atlantic salmon.

Featherduster

Hook: Salmon wet-fly, sizes 2 to 10
Thread: Black
Tail: Optionally, golden pheasant tippets, or hackle fibers in the color(s) used in the hackling
Body: Variously, none, tying thread, flat silver or gold tinsel, or fluorescent green, orange, or red floss
Palmer hackle: 2 folded saddle hackles, one inside the other or tied in side by side, palmered together in touching turns; usually a combination of light and dark, e.g., orange and grizzly, orange-dyed grizzly and black, yellow and black, ginger and badger, etc.
Face hackle: Orange- or yellow-dyed guinea hen (other colors may be used), wrapped as a wet-fly collar

KRILL

Krill are those tiny marine crustaceans that are the principal food of baleen whales, particularly in the Antarctic Ocean. Because this fly is tied on a size 6 bronzed nymph hook, it can't be a saltwater pattern. I'm guessing it's a salmon fly, for fish freshly returned from the sea (where they feed heavily on shrimp and other crustaceans) but it wouldn't take much imagination to figure out how to tie it for steelhead, trout, bass, bluefish, or whatever else you think might take a shiny jig or spoon. I am listing this Rich Henry fly as it was tied by John Edwards on Hans Weilenmann's Flytier's Page (www.danica.com/flytier/). You can figure out how to tie it to suit your own purposes.

Krill

Hook:	TMC 5263, a 3X
Thread:	Black 6/0
Tail:	2 strands of pea[rl] length long
Rib:	Fine gold or silve[r] palmer hackle be[hind] through the hackl[e]
Body:	4 strands of pearl together before w
Palmer hackle:	Brown saddle, the long, tied in at the to the bend in ab[out]
Head:	Tying thread, rela[ted]

Tying Tip

Someone, probably Edwards, wrote that the color of the Krystal Flash should be changed to match the krill in the area being fished. Indeed, the world's oceans support some 85 species of krill. But I haven't noticed any krill in the waters I fish, so I suppose it's all right to try to match the local shrimp, crayfish, scuds, or whatever. This pattern should do an excellent job of that.

SHRIMP

This Norwegian salmon pattern comes from *Perrault's Standard Dictionary of Fishing Flies* (1984).

Shrimp

Hook:	Standard salmon/steelhead, sizes 4 to 8
Thread:	Red or black
Palmer hackle:	Hot-orange saddle, tied in behind the eye by the butt and reverse-palmered from front to rear, wrapped very closely at the front
Tail:	Hot-orange hackle point, "tied upright"
Body:	Red wool, wrapped thickly
Rib:	Flat gold tinsel

SALT AND PEPPER

Also known as **Scotch and Soda** (named for the brand of Scotch?), this Canadian pattern also comes from *Perrault's*. Fish this one as a surface-disturbing skater or waking fly. Or, if you prefer, cast it upstream and across, dead-drift it dry, and pull it back wet—the way you might fish a Hornberg Special for trout.

Salt and Pepper

Hook:	Salmon/steelhead, sizes 4 to 1/0
Thread:	Black 6/0 or 3/0
Tail:	Black and white hackle points
Body:	Tying thread
Palmer hackle:	Black and white saddles, palmered together or one through the other, very thickly

PAINT BRUSH

Yet another listed by Perrault, and as gaudy as the previous pattern is subtle, call this one a salmon or steelhead Tricolore. My guess is, closely palmered stiff hackle would let you fish this one on top as a skating, or waking, fly.

Paint Brush

Hook: Standard salmon/steelhead, sizes 2 to 8
Thread: Black
Body: Flat gold tinsel
Palmer hackle: In thirds, from rear to front: orange, purple, and turquoise saddle or schlappen

BADGER PALMER *Tied by R. G. Balogh*

Not quite as bright as the preceding pattern, this one uses a yellow body for its chiaroscuro effect.

Badger Palmer

Hook: Standard salmon/steelhead, sizes 2 to 8
Thread: Brown or black
Body: Yellow wool
Palmer hackle: Badger saddle

MEAD

Still another from *Perrault's* (are you beginning to get the idea this somewhat obscure book is a major tying resource?), this one has a bright-yellow "girdle."

Mead

Hook: Standard salmon/steelhead, sizes 4 and 6
Thread: Black or dark brown
Body: Black, yellow, and black chenille, in thirds
Palmer hackle: Brown saddle

SPRING WIGGLER *Tied by R. G. Balogh*

Robert D. Farrand, of RDF's Steelhead Flies, says he ties and sells "more of this fly than all the rest of my steelhead fly patterns combined. It is without a doubt the most popular steelhead fly in Michigan." I found his pattern on the Fly Tying World web site (http://flytyingworld.com/). Except for the squirrel, all colors are specified "to suit." I listed the colors Farrand showed in his fly on the FTW site. Essentially the same pattern appeared under the same name, using a brown hen hackle and sometimes tied on up-eyed salmon hooks, in a *Wild Steelhead & Salmon* article on nymphing for steelhead by Ralph F. Quinn.

Spring Wiggler

Hook: Mustad 3399, a standard nymph or wet-fly, sizes 4 to 10
Thread: White or cream 6/0, *or other color of choice*
Tail/Back: Red or gray squirrel, the untrimmed butts pulled all the way over the body before palmering the hackle
Body: Yellow chenille, *or other color of choice*
Palmer hackle: Grizzly saddle, *or other color to suit*
Head: Thread

Tying Tip

Substitute a marabou blood feather for the squirrel (the tail should be less than twice the gap width in length), and you've got the **Marabou Wiggler**. Both versions are tied in a variety of body colors, including chartreuse, neon red, orange, hot pink.

According to Randall Scott Stetzer, in *Flies: The Best One Thousand*, this steelhead pattern by Bill McMillan is based on Roderick Haig-Brown's **Carpenter Ant**.

Black Palmer

Hook:	Black, up-eyed salmon/steelhead, sizes 6 to 1/0
Thread:	Black
Palmer hackle:	Iron-blue dun, reverse-palmered from front to rear
Tag:	Fine copper wire—opposite the hook point
Rib:	Fine copper wire from the tag
Body:	Black seal (or substitute) or goat fur, dubbed
Head:	Tying thread, lacquered

GENERAL MONEY'S PRAWN FLY *Tied by Ian Ricketson*

General Noel Money, who fished the waters of Vancouver Island from 1913 until his death in 1941, called this simply **Prawn Fly**. "As well as an accomplished fisherman," Ian Ricketson wrote on Robin Pike's Vancouver Fly Fisherman site (www.coastnet.com/~rpike/), "Money was also a mentor to an individual who was to become perhaps the all-time master of fly fishing in British Columbia: Roderick Haig-Brown." Haig-Brown dedicated *The Western Angler* (1941) to "General Money of Qualicum Beach, finest of western anglers, and to his own Stamp River, loveliest and most generous of western streams." To this day, a pool on the Stamp bears General Money's name.

"The Prawn Fly is perhaps the most forgotten of all Money's fly patterns," Ricketson says, "most likely due to the introduction of the General Practitioner to the West Coast."

The Prawn Fly enjoys one advantage over the GP: simplicity. "So simple in fact that three or four of these patterns can usually be made in the time it takes to tie one General Practitioner."

General Money's Prawn Fly

Hook:	Salmon wet-fly, sizes 3 to 4/0
Thread:	Unspecified, but black 6/0 will suffice
Tag:	Flat silver tinsel
Body:	Orange wool
Rib:	Flat silver tinsel
Palmer hackle:	Red-dyed hen

PRAWN FLY (1)

This is another pattern from *Perrault's*. I suspect it's a variation on General Money's fly.

PRAWN FLY (1)

Hook:	Standard salmon/steelhead, sizes 4 to 1/0
Thread:	Fluorescent hot-orange
Palmer hackle:	Hot-orange saddle, reverse-palmered from front to rear
Tag:	Flat gold tinsel
Body:	Fluorescent hot-orange wool
Rib:	Embossed gold tinsel
Head:	Tying thread, lacquered

Prawn Fly (2)

Yet another steelhead Woolly Worm listed by Keith Perrault. It's roughly the same as the previous two patterns, but sports a flashy tail.

Prawn Fly (2)

Hook: Standard salmon/steelhead, size 4/0; *sample tied smaller, for photographic consistency*
Thread: Red or orange 3/0 Monocord
Tail: Several strands of silver Mylar tinsel, Flashabou, or Krystal Flash
Body: Orange wool
Rib: Silver wire or tinsel
Palmer hackle: Scarlet saddle, reverse-palmered from front to rear

Steelhead Soft-Hackle Woolly Worm (1)

Whoever wrote the copy for the Salmon River/Lake Ontario Sportfishing Home Page (www.salmon-river.com)—where I picked up the pattern—comments that other color combinations also work well.

Steelhead Soft-Hackle Woolly Worm (1)

Hook: Mustad 36890 or similar up-eyed steelhead/salmon, sizes 6 to 10
Thread: Black or fluorescent-red 6/0
Tail: Grizzly hackle fibers
Palmer hackle: Grizzly hen
Body: Fluorescent chenille, in 2 sections: rear half, green; front half, red
Hackle collar: Grizzly soft-hackle collar

Steelhead Soft-Hackle Woolly Worm (2)

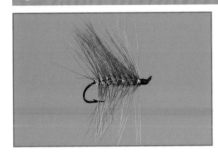

Same name, but different pattern. I don't know the origin of this particular pattern, but it has been popular with steelheaders in New York State.

Steelhead Soft-Hackle Woolly Worm (2)

Hook: 3X-long streamer, sizes 2 to 6
Thread: Black
Palmer hackle: Black, extra-long, soft hen saddle, palmered from front to rear, with the barbs angled toward the rear
Tail: *Optionally, grizzly hackle fibers*
Butt: Fluorescent-green floss or wool
Rib: Oval silver tinsel, medium
Body: Black wool

Red-Butt Woolly

This one is from the virtually legendary Ontario fly tier Jay Passmore. I found it on the Rodworks web site (www.rodworks.on.ca), where it is described as "deadly in coloured water, both spring and fall." I've also seen it listed as the **Orange-Butt Woolly**, with the appropriate adjustment in tail and butt colors. (See also the **Hot-Butt Woolly Worm** on page 42.)

Red-Butt Woolly

Hook: Mustad 79580, a 4X-long streamer, sizes 8 and 10
Thread: Fire-orange 6/0 UNI
Tail: Hot-pink or -red hackle fibers or yarn
Butt: Neon-red chenille, opposite and as long as the point (from barb to tip)
Back: 3-4 strands of peacock herl, pulled over the body before palmering the hackle
Palmer hackle: Grizzly hen, webby
Body: Chartreuse chenille
Head: Tying thread

NIX'S WOOLLY SPECIAL

Fran Verdoliva, the guru of New York steelheading, listed this pattern in his *Guide to Flies and Fishing New York's Salmon River Region* (1994; difficult to find, but the entire text is online at www.salmon-river.com/fran-pg.htm). It bears the name of New York State steelheader Ron Nix, and combines the colors of Verdoliva's Frammus fly [*body of fluorescent-green chenille and a wing of cerise Glo-Bug yarn*] with the palmered hackle's action. Fished in spring and fall, Nix's Woolly S[...] brown trout, steelhead, and chinook[...]

Nix's Woolly Special

Hook:	Standard steelhead[...]
Thread:	Black 6/0 or 3/0
Body:	Fluorescent chenille[...] cerise; front half, ch[...]
Palmer hackle:	Grizzly saddle

WORM

Other color combinations are used by steelheaders on New York's Salmon River, but this Fran Verdoliva pattern is perhaps the most popular. Similar to the above, but body colors are reversed.

Salmon River Woolly W[...]

Hook:	Standard salmon wet[...]
Thread:	Black or fluorescent r[...]
Tail:	Grizzly hackle fibers
Palmer hackle:	Grizzly saddle
Body:	Fluorescent chenille, in halves: rear, green; front, red
Hackle collar:	*Optionally, 2 or 3 turns of a larger grizzly hen hackle in front of the body*

SALMON RIVER HELLGRAMMITE

In early spring and fall, you will find fly fishers using this Fran Verdoliva pattern for steelhead and lake-run browns in New York's Salmon River watershed.

Salmon River Hellgrammite

Hook:	Mustad 1510, a 3X-long, curved-shank nymph, sizes 2 to 6
Thread:	Black
Tail:	4 strands of black Krystal Flash
Shellback:	Black Swiss straw or Diamond Braid, pulled over the body and hackle
Body:	Tinsel chenille in 2 sections: rear 2/3, black Crystal Chenille; front 1/3, red Estaz
Palmer hackle:	Black saddle, clipped flush on top and fairly short on bottom and sides
Pincers:	*Optionally, black goose biots, forked over the eye*

EGG-FARTING LEECH *Tied by Steve Schweitzer*

This variation of the regionally infamous steelhead pattern is the one tied by Steve Schweitzer, of Schweitzer's Fly Boxes and The Global Fly Fisher web site (www.globalflyfisher. com). Steve says the pattern was revealed to him by Marcos Vergara, of Hareline Dubbin.

Egg-Farting Leech

Hook:	Mustad 36890 or similar salmon/steelhead wet-fly, size 6
Thread:	Black 6/0 or 8/0
Palmer hackle:	Black schlappen, palmered head to tail
Tail:	Golden McFly Foam, tied in egg-yarn style at the back of the hook bend
Rib:	Fine copper wire
Body:	Chartreuse floss
Head:	Black, varnished

Tying Note

Schweitzer—a far more experienced steelheader than I—insists that the mid-bend position of the McFly Foam "egg" does not interfere with hook-ups. Call me a worry wart, but I might be tempted to put the egg in standard butt position—at the rear of the shank, where the bend begins.

Salmon fisher Ralph Shaw, of Courtenay, British Columbia, developed this pattern during a drought summer a few years back to fish for large (average, 12 pounds, with some more than 25) chum salmon in Vancouver Island's Puntledge River. He used a 9-weight rod, a sink-tip line, and short, 10-pound-test or heavier leaders to cast his fly upstream and let it dead-drift down, experiencing "a hook-up on most casts." I am listing the **Puntledge Blue**, the most productive pattern, but Shaw used a variety of bright bodies and either white or yellow hackle.

Puntledge Chum

Hook: Eagle Claw 67DT Billy Pate Tarpon (but any heavy-wire, short-shank or wide-gap hook might do), sizes 1 to 4
Thread: Black 3/0
Body: Electric-blue Mylar tinsel
Palmer hackle: White saddle or schlappen

SEA-TROUT WOOLLY WORMS

In some parts of Europe, sea trout (sea-run browns) rival Atlantic salmon in fly-fishing popularity and esteem. In many places around the globe, anglers fish for anadromous trout in their natal streams. But around the Baltic, fly fishers pursue sea trout in salt water, often at night. These saltwater Woollies usually are tied on stainless-steel or other corrosion-resistant hooks. However, if you tie them on standard steelhead, salmon, or streamer hooks and fish them in fresh water, you will find them effective for steelhead, nonmigratory trout, and other game fish. Martin Jørgensen—the Danish editor, webmaster, consultant, fly designer, fly tier, and sea-trout expert who tied many of the flies in this section—says he also has successfully fished several of the patterns in fresh water for brownies, perch, and pike. (If you'd like to learn how to fish for sea trout, or to see all the many other patterns that aren't variations on the Woolly Worm theme, check out the Global Flyfisher web site (www.globalflyfisher.com), of which Jørgensen is a founding partner.

Admittedly, these sea-trout patterns—and particularly the last four shrimp patterns—push the Woolly Worm concept out to the horizon and perhaps a bit beyond.

MAGNUS *Tied by Martin Jørgensen.*

This sea-trout fly from the Danish fly fisher and tier Magnus Ting Mortensen has spawned a whole host of related patterns, some of which follow. On the Danish coast, the Magnus is especially popular for fishing clear waters in the Baltic. Mortensen's original pattern was pretty much a grizzly Woolly Worm (grizzly rooster hackle palmered over a body of gray hare dubbing) tied with tan thread, with two half-a-body-length grizzly-hackle points for tails, an oval silver-tinsel rib, a grizzly wet-fly hackle in front of the body, bead-chain or pearl eyes tied atop the shank, and the head varnished red. What follows is a modernization by Martin Jørgensen, who has a son named Magnus.

Magnus

Hook: Stainless-steel saltwater fly (*for fresh water, a 4X-long streamer*), sizes 4 to 10
Thread: Tan
Eyes: Bead-chain, tied in *under* the shank behind the eye, covered with the tying thread and the wraps varnished or head-cemented
Tail: A pair of shank-length strands of clear, white, or pearl Flashabou or similar material, covered by the shorter tip (a shank-length or less) of the feather you will use to palmer the body
Body: Natural rabbit-fur dubbing
Palmer hackle: Grizzly, ginger, or cree rooster saddle, the barbs constantly stroked back with wet fingers as it's palmered forward
Head: Thread or thin dubbing over the eyes

Tying Note

To increase the pattern's visibility at night (to both fish and fisherman), Martin Jørgensen also ties an eyeless, spun-deer-hair–headed **Magnus Muddler**: orange deer hair, orange-dyed grizzly hackle, and natural rabbit dubbing "with a bit of orange flash mixed in." For fishing deep, he ties a cone-headed version he calls the **Bullet Head Magnus** (same dressing as his regular Magnus; just substitute a cone head for the bead-chain eyes). He says all of the Magnus-based patterns that follow can also be Muddlerized or cone-headed.

This souped-up Magnus was designed by Jørgensen "primarily to make use of those very webby feathers that always seem to be left over on the necks and saddles after all the 'good' feathers have been used." This thrifty pattern turned out to be a real winner for sea trout. "Today," says Jørgensen, "I would guess that it's responsible for almost 75 percent of my fish." He fishes it in the salt water of the Baltic Sea, hence the stainless-steel hook. The Bjarke is based on the Magnus, so Jørgensen decided to name this sibling pattern for his youngest son.

Bjarke

Hook: Stainless-steel saltwater fly (for fresh water, a 4X-long streamer), sizes 2 to 10

Thread: Tan or olive

Eyes: Bead-chain, tied in under the shank behind the hook eye

Tail: The tip of the hackle feather, about 2 gap-widths long, plus 4 longer strands of clear, white, or pearl Flashabou or similar material

Body: Natural rabbit-fur or similar tan dubbing, with a bit of red crystal dubbing at the very front, leaving about 2 eye-widths of shank bare; *optionally, dub the front third in olive-dyed fur or synthetic*

Gills: 2 or 3 turns of bright-red synthetic dubbing immediately behind the bead-chain eyes

Palmer hackle: A very webby grizzly hen saddle, steeply tapered, with the barbs at the base at least half again as long as the hook gap is wide

Head: Tying thread over the eyes, varnished

Nils Mogensen, writing in Mats Sjöstrand's on-line *Rackelhanen Flyfishing Magazine* (www. rackelhanen.com/eng/), says the pattern he simply calls **Chilimps** or **Chilimpsi** was invented at the Valhalla Hotel on the banks of the Mörrum, Sweden's most famous salmon and sea-trout river, in April 1942 by three Swedes: Sven O. Hallman, Rolf Vilhelmsson, and Olle Törnblom. Be that as it may, but most European tiers I know say the Chillimps is a Danish pattern.

As listed by Mogensen, the Chillimps is not ribbed and everything wrapped on the 2/0, extended-shank salmon hook is fiery red-orange: tying thread, two not-quite shank-length hackle points for the tail, wool yarn for the body, and rooster hackle palmered over the body and wrapped up front as a hackle collar. (If you use a long, sharply tapered saddle hackle, you can use the same feather for both hackles; otherwise, use a collar hackle that is a size larger.)

Some consider this a sea-trout pattern, but Martin Jørgensen fishes the Orange Chillimps mainly for "garfish" (needlefish). A hook simply wound with orange yarn works nearly as well, he admits, "but the Chillimps looks so much better." Tied in larger sizes, expect this pattern to appeal to a variety of anadromous and saltwater species.

Orange Chillimps

Hook: Saltwater streamer with turned-down eye, sizes 12 to 16

Thread: Red or black

Palmer hackle: Orange saddle, palmered from head to tail

Tail: Orange hackle fibers or points, 2/3 as long as the hook

Rib: Thin oval gold tinsel

Body: Orange wool yarn or dubbing

Hackle collar: Orange, a size larger than the palmer hackle

Tying Tips

Across the Baltic, in Malmö, Sweden, Paul Milstam ties virtually the same fly and uses it for both sea trout and salmon. Only Milstam sometimes ties it larger and uses it for Atlantic salmon. Here are the changes to make in tying his **Chillimps Flash**: Use a size-10 to 2/0 salmon wet-fly hook and two orange hackle points for the tail, reverse-palmer an oversize orange hackle over a body of red wool yarn (wrapping a virtual wet-fly collar at front), rib forward with flat gold tinsel, then add 6 to 8 long strands of gold Flashabou to that front collar as a flashy, but minimalist, wing.

BORSTEN *Tied by Paul Milstam*

On his web site, Paul Milstam's Flyspot (fly-spot.members.easy-space.com/home.html), the Swedish tier describes Göran Cederberg's sea trout pattern as "a sovereign saltwater fly from the Swedish west coast." I'm not certain, but I think the name means "brushes." Milstam goes on to describe the Borsten as "a good impersonation of both chaetopods and small shrimps. Perfect spring and autumn fly."

Borsten

Hook: 3X-long nymph or streamer *(alternatively, a heavy salmon double)*, sizes 6 and 8
Thread: Black 6/0
Underbody: Lead wire wrapped on the shank; *alternatively, a bead head or dumbbell or beadchain eyes*
Palmer hackle: Fiery-brown (natural red) saddle, in 6 open spirals through the body, then 2 or 3 tight turns up front, as a wet-fly collar
Body: Brown chenille

MESSING HOVED NYMFE *Tied by Jens Larsen*

The name is Danish for **Brass Head Nymph**. Jens Larsen, of Dronninglund, Denmark, says it's really a brown trout fly he ties larger for sea trout. So, scale it down if saltwater fishing for sea-run browns is not in your cards. It ought to work, wherever you live: "I think it's an American pattern," Larsen says, giving the lie to its superficial similarity to Martin Jørgensen's **Bjarke**, above.

"I use this fly in the springtime, when the weather is very cold and the water temperature stays at almost 0 degrees Celcius [32°F]," Jens explains. "The sea trout stay on the bottom and feed on small shrimps. This fly imitates them well, and the heavy head keeps it on the bottom."

Messing Hoved Nymfe

Hook: Kamasan B170, a 1X-heavy nymph or wet-fly, sizes 4 to 8
Thread: Black or brown, tied on twice
Head: Brass bead (3- to 4.5-mm) or cone, slipped over a wet, glue-soaked base of tying thread
Palmer hackle: Grizzly rooster, tied in behind the bead and reverse-palmered
Tail: 2 grizzly hackle points, as long as the hook, tied in back to back, and rainbow LureFlash
Rib: Fine gold or copper tinsel or wire
Body: Hare's ear, dubbed after twisting it in a dubbing loop

GRÅ SANDRÄKA *Tied by Paul Milstam*

The name is Swedish (in English, **Gray Sand Shrimp**), but the pattern is Danish. In both countries, the pattern is fished chiefly in the Baltic for sea trout. This is one of many sea-trout patterns from the Swedish fly tier Paul Milstam.

Grå Sandräka

Hook: Streamer, size 6 to 12
Thread: Black
Tail: 2 grizzly hackle points, back to back
Palmer hackle: 2 to 3 grizzly saddles, tied in at the front and reverse-palmered
Body: Tying thread
Rib: Tying thread, spiraled forward through the palmer hackle
Head: Tying thread, rather large
Eyes: *Optionally, yellow, with black pupils, painted on the head*

The "n" makes it plural—dead giveaway that we're dealing with a *series* of shrimp flies. Swedish sea-trout fishers use a variety of these patterns when fishing in the Baltic for sea-run browns. "With these shrimps," Milstam advises, "it's very important to follow the bottom color." Shrimp populations tend to take on the color of their habitat. Milstam, who lives in Malmö, Sweden, offers three patterns: *Stenräka* (Stone Shrimp), for fishing over rocky bottoms; *Tångräka* (Seaweed Shrimp), for fishing grassy bottoms; and *Sandräka* (Sand Shrimp) for fishing sandy bottoms. But for color, they are identical.

RÄKAN

Hook:	Streamer, size 8 to 12
Thread:	6/0, the color to match the body
Tail:	Gap-width tuft of fiery-brown Partridge SLF dubbing material
Antennae:	2 hook-length (or slightly longer) stripped brown hackle stems
Eyes:	2 gap-width pieces of monofilament, the ends burnt, black-varnished
Rib:	Oval tinsel or fine wire (see Tying Tips), tied in at the bend and counter-wound
Body:	Fly Rite or similar poly dubbing of appropriate color (see Tying Tips), tapered so that it gets narrower as you proceed
Palmer hackle:	Large saddle hackle, reverse-palmered over the rear 2/3 of the body (see Tying Tips)

Tying Tips

After dubbing two-thirds of the way up the shank, tie in the hackle feather, then continue dubbing the tapered body the rest of the way. When the body is finished, reverse-palmer the hackle to the bend, secure it with the rib, and wind the rib in open spirals to the front of the body.

Stenräka: Silver rib, dark-gray (Fly Rite #7) body, grizzly hackle
Tångräka: Gold rib, caddis-pupa green (#40) body, brown hackle
Sandräka: Fine copper rib (doubled and twisted "for more reflection"), Cahill tan (#22) body, badger hackle

That's **Gremlin**, in English, according to Jens Larsen, the Danish creator of this pattern, which seems like a larger, more ostentatious version of the Räkan patterns just listed. But Larsen says the pattern is based on the Finnish Sunk Bomber, which worked so well on salmon for a group of Finns that Larsen was watching one day. Larsen's adaptation was an instant success when he tried it on sea trout that enter Danish rivers in early spring. He fishes the Smølfen on a fast-sinking line.

"Often, I just 'park' the fly over a spot I know holds a good fish, then wait for a minute or two," Jens says. "When those 'whiskers' get working in the current, the fish can't resist and usually take the fly very hard."

This may well be a sea-trout pattern, but I can't see steelhead or salmon giving it a cold shoulder. I also can't see myself tying such an elegant, exhibition-quality fly onto a tippet and casting out into cold, turbulent waters where large fish are going to savage it. Then again, I probably wouldn't mind drowning a sacrificial Smølfen impersonator from *my* vise.

Smølfen

Hook:	Sprite Double Low Water, a 2X-long, 1X-heavy salmon double, sizes 2 to 6
Thread:	Red or orange
Palmer hackle:	Orange rooster saddle, tied in by its tip at the front and reverse-palmered Woolly Worm style with the convex, shiny side facing toward the tail, so the barbs angle forward
Tail:	Golden pheasant tippets, about a gap-width long
Whiskers:	4 orange hackle stems, about 2-1/2 times as long as the hook, splayed 2 to each side (see Tying Tip)
Body:	Orange Antron yarn; *alternatively, 2 layers of orange floss or 3 of orange thread*
Rib:	Oval gold tinsel, medium, counter-wound

Tying Tip

To prepare the "whiskers" (antennae), clip the tips flat on 4 long, orange-dyed saddle hackles. Leaving a small triangle of barbs at the tip, strip off all the rest of the barbs. Tie in the hackle stems in pairs, back to back, so they will splay out, 2 on each side.

Saltwater Woolly Worms

Not many patterns based on the Woolly Worm have been devised specifically for saltwater fishing in the ocean and its briny bays and gulfs. But that should not stop you from tying Woolly Worms on corrosion-resistant hooks and fishing them in the salt chuck. Many a snapper and other saltwater panfish has taken a **Miller Woolly Worm** (page 32), so tied by yours truly, for a shrimp. Some of the saltwater Buggers can be tied with shorter tails and fished effectively; for a perfect example, see **Dixon's Devil Worm** on page 191.

Joe Brooks Shrimp

The Blonde series of saltwater streamers are perhaps Joe Brooks' best-known fly patterns. Before Lefty Kreh introduced his Deceivers, Blondes were *the* all-around saltwater flies.

But too few contemporary salty fly fishers recall this bonefish pattern Brooks introduced in the late 1940s. From the few pictures I've seen, it seems Brooks might have used a short-shank or wide-gap hook, but I think you could safely use a standard saltwater-fly hook, such as a Mustad 34007.

Joe Brooks Shrimp

Hook: Saltwater fly, sizes 2 to 1/0
Thread: Red 3/0
Tail: 2 pink saddle tips, a hook-length long
Body: Flat silver tinsel
Palmer hackle: Pink saddle hackle, the barbs slightly longer than the gap width, but clipped short on top and sides
Head: Tying thread, gloss-coated

Orange Annelid

Also known as the **Bristle Worm**, this pattern is one of the simplest, yet no less effective, creations of Jack Gartside. I found it in Dick Brown's *Fly Fishing for Bonefish* (1993), where Brown says, "Effective blend of color, sparkle, and long-shank shape make this a good pattern for suggesting many polychaetes." Amen.

Orange Annelid

Hook: Mustad 34011, a long-shank stainless-steel fly, size 4
Thread: Orange 6/0
Body: Orange Mylar chenille
Palmer hackle: Grizzle saddle

Pink Polly

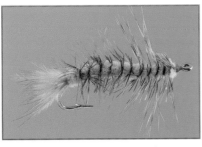

This Dick Brown bonefish pattern is from the same book as the Jack Gartside pattern above. This is what Brown has to say about his fly: "Suggestive of many polychaetes, including clam worms and fire worms *[striper fishermen, take note—GS]*, this is a good shallow-water pattern to use along sandy shores. These species live and feed on invertebrates, including other worms."

Pink Polly

Hook: Mustad 34011 *(as above)* or Partridge CS 11GRS (a 4X-long streamer with a Grey Shadow finish), "bent slightly at one-third segments along shank to give it the shape of a wiggling sea worm," size 4
Thread: Fluorescent-orange 3/0 Monocord
Tail: Tan or white marabou, short
Body: Pink chenille
Palmer hackle: Brown grizzly or white, "trim top and bottom" *(however, the white-hackled fly illustrated in the book does not appear to be trimmed)*

SILVER THORN *Tied by Barry Thornton*

This saltwater pattern, which *just* squeaks in as a reduced-hackle Woolly Worm (much to its originator's amusement), is from Barry Thornton, Vancouver Island's acknowledged master when it comes to fishing for salmon in salt water.

Other colors should also turn on predatory instincts. An orange version, for example, might do wonders during one of those East Coast worm "hatches." I might even be tempted to add a white or grizzly palmer hackle on occasion. Tied in smaller sizes, and perhaps in other colors, I think it might make a pretty good facsimile of peeking caddis larvae as well as other sweetwater creepie-crawlies. And I can see this baby working on a lot of briny predators, too. In fact, Barry Thornton tells me his Thorns (and there are several variations, some of them winged) "have been used very effectively for northern pike in Alberta and Saskatchewan and for many saltwater fish species in New Zealand."

Silver Thorn

Hook: Mustad 34007SS or 34011SS, stainless-steel saltwater-fly, sizes 6 to 5/0
Thread: Silver 6/0
Tail: Silver Krystal Flash; *other B.C. tiers sometimes add or substitute holographic tinsel, Flashabou, or a combination thereof*
Body: Silver tinsel chenille, short-fibered

Tying Tips

If you'd like to turn it into a **Silver Thorn Flashtail**, tie a piece of silver Mylar tubing onto the hook at the bend, and fray the rest so the strands form the tail.

Add silver bead-chain eyes to the basic pattern, and you've got the **Silver Thorn Optic**. Although winged flies are beyond the purview of this book, two winged versions have proved to be real killers in the South Pacific and may be interesting to saltwater fly fishers in the audience: the Hakai Thorn (pink bucktail or polar bear wing) and the Tonquin Thorn (chartreuse Krystal Flash underwing covered with chartreuse polar bear).

Thornton writes: "Sleek, silver, and simple—that is what has worked so very well in the Pacific. The wonderful thing about fly tying today is that there are materials that, when combined, will work for such non-traditional species as Pacific salmon in the salt. Over the years I have found that once a pattern has been found for the target species, almost all other predatory species in the same environment will also take that fly. One good example are the dogfish (mud sharks) of the Pacific coast that I have caught with the Silver Thorn. So they don't cut off the fly, I use a wire leader much like that used for pike. Other Pacific species like lings, rockfish, kelp greenling—even seals!—take the fly when it is retrieved near them."

PLUM-CRAZY WOOLLY SHRIMP

I don't recall where I picked up this saltwater pattern. (I haven't yet tied it smaller and tried it in fresh water, but I see no reason not to, other than a serious shortage of fishing time.) If the purple body bothers you, substitute pink, gray, brown, tan, olive, or whatever color will make you comfortable. I like the purple. Some days, fish want purple. And when they want purple, you'd better be fishing purple.

Plum-Crazy Woolly Shrimp

Hook: Mustad 34007, or equivalent saltwater-fly, sizes 4 to 1/0
Thread: Brown 6/0 or 3/0
Palmer hackle: Brown or brown-dyed grizzly, tied in behind the eye and reverse-palmered to the bend; optionally, clipped almost flush on top and sides
Tail: A tuft of squirrel, woodchuck, or other multicolored hair, about half as long as the shank; *optionally, 2 to 4 long bucktail hairs or hackle stems for antennae*
Body: Purple chenille, yarn, or dubbing
Rib: Clear monofilament or thin gold or silver wire, depending upon the toothiness of your prey
Head: Tying thread, coated with clear, glossy finger nail polish
Eyes: *Optionally, painted on the head; for those who like slinging heavy flies (I don't), bead-chain or dumbbell eyes tied in first*

Time to go topside.

It takes little ingenuity or effort to turn a wet Woolly Worm into a dry fly, or a dry Woolly Worm into a Bivisible. Add a third color of palmer hackle and you get—you guessed it!—a Tricolore. It probably has already occurred to you pioneering sorts that a "Quadricolor" is the logical, if piscatorially unproven, next step.

Dry Woolly Worms

You can turn almost any Woolly Worm pattern into a dry fly, just by tying it on a dry-fly hook and palmering stiff rooster hackle very closely from stem to stern. Unsatisfied by such simplicity, however, some tiers have taken the conversion process a bit further.

Dry Woolly Worm   *Tied by Peter Frailey*

Randall Scott Stetzer includes this generically named pattern as one of his *Best One Thousand* flies, but he doesn't attribute it to anyone.

Dry Woolly Worm

Hook: TMC 5212 or Mustad 94831 (both, 2X-long, fine-wire dry-fly), sizes 8 to 12
Thread: Olive 6/0, a long tag end left dangling at the bend, as a rib
Palmer hackle: Grizzly rooster hackle, reverse-palmered to the rear, a V clipped out of the bottom
Body: Olive rabbit fur, dubbed

Palmer Dry Fly   *Orange Asher tied by Wayne Mones; Bloody Butcher tied by R. G. Balogh*

Writing in their "Beginner's Corner" column in the Summer 1986 issue of *American Fly Tyer*, Paul Fling and Don Puterbaugh said this is the first dry fly they have their beginning students tie. Why? "First, it is an effective fly and one that is commonly used in our area *[Pennsylvania]*.... Second, it is about the easiest type of dry-fly pattern to tie...."

Fling and Puterbaugh stress technique over pattern in fishing this fly, so didn't list a materials recipe. Here's what I use, varying the colors to suit whim or conditions.

Palmer Dry Fly

Hook: Standard or light-wire dry-fly, sizes 10 to 16
Thread: Black (or other suitable color)
Body: Floss, an 8- to 10-inch piece tied in behind the eye and wrapped down the shank and back up, forming a slightly tapered body
Palmer hackle: Rooster hackle, tied in by the stripped butt, the barbs about 1-1/2 times the gap width

Tying Tips

Fling and Puterbaugh offered these two tips in handling the floss:

"The trick to handling floss so that you get a nice smooth body without separating and fraying is to keep the floss wet while wrapping, and keeping the fingers close to the hook." I'll add this: Use a nice hand lotion and an emery board to keep your hands and fingers smooth and free of burrs.

"Increase the amount of overlap of the wraps as you move forward so that the floss forms [a] tapered shape...."

They also pointed out that a neater-looking fly results from tying the feather in by the tip, but that produces a fly in which "the hackle size gets larger from back to front" and that "doesn't

float quite as effectively because the bend (the heaviest part of the hook) rides lower in the water and the fly isn't supported as well." Fishermen as well as tiers, they go on to observe, "The trout don't seem to care so try it both ways and then use the one you prefer."

They give three color combinations popular in their waters: an unnamed version with green floss and grizzly hackle; the **Orange Asher** (burnt-orange floss and ginger hackle); and the **Bloody Butcher** (dark-red floss and black hackle). That last name is used for entirely different flies out West and over in Britain, and I've seen it hung on other patterns as well.

ROMAR

The name is Slovenian for "Palmer," or Pilgrim," after the fly-naming fashion of Thomas Barker and Charles Cotton. When I fished Slovenia some years ago, the Romar was one of the most effective flies we used, especially in such "milky" rivers as the Sora. The flies we bought in Ljubljana sporting-goods stores showed a lot of variability in hackle color and body material; what remained fairly constant was the way grayling, brown trout, and even rainbows responded to this pattern.

But for my personal experience with this fly, I would be

tempted to call it just another version of the **Brown Palmer** (page 108) or, gold tinsel-ribbed, **Golden Palmer** (page 83). But the Romar it was, is, and ever will be in my memory and heart of hearts.

Romar

Hook: Standard or light-w
Thread: Black or brown 6/
Palmer hackle: Brown or ginger ro closely
Rib: Usually none; optio or fine flat tinsel
Body: Variably, none, a th tinsel, or thin peacock herl

ORANGE PALMER *Tied by R. G. Balogh*

Charlie Garwood, of Linwood, North Carolina, says of this autumn pattern, "It's simple to tie, a good floater, and a favorite in the Great Smoky Mountains National Park." Garwood also says his creation "imitates the large, pale-orange caddis that emerge in fall, and golden-brown mayflies as well. Harvey Wall of High Country Outdoors in Lowgap, North Carolina (see the next pattern), also ties, fishes, and sells a black-bodied, white-calf-winged version called the Smoky Mountain Rattler.

Orange Palmer

Hook: Fine-wire dry-fly (Garwood uses Tiemco's TMC 531, a 2X-short, 2X-fine, slightly wide-gap, black dry-fly), sizes 12 to 18
Thread: Orange or brown 6/0 or 8/0
Tail: Golden pheasant tippets, optionally, light deer hair
Body: Pale-orange dubbing
Palmer hackle: Brown and grizzly rooster, palmered together

YELLOW PALMER *Tied by Harvey Wall*

Essentially similar to the preceding pattern, this traditional South-ern Appalachian favorite has just enough differences to merit a separate listing. I found it on the High Country Outdoors web site (www.high-countryoutdoors.net) in Lowgap, North Carolina, where Harvey Wall is the proprietor and head guide. Harvey says he likes to fish it on the small freestoners in North Carolina and Tennessee. "It floats very well and does exactly what an attrac-

tor pattern should," Harvey reports: "it imitates a little of everything, but no one thing in particular. And it catches fish."

Yellow Palmer

Hook: Mustad 94840, or equivalent dry-fly, usually sizes 14 and 16, *but adjusted according to the season and conditions*
Thread: Orange 12/0 Benecchi
Tail: Grizzly hackle fibers
Body: Yellow dubbing of choice
Palmer hackle: Grizzly rooster

Tying & Fishing Tips

Sometimes Harvey adds a brown hackle to the Yellow Palmer and substitutes golden pheasant tippets for the tail, as in the Orange Palmer. Actually, Harvey considers the Yellow and Orange Palmers as virtually one pattern, a continuum, and says, "I fish this pattern all year long and adjust the size to the season. I also change the body color with the season. I like to

fish smaller, darker flies in the winter and then gradually lighten the color and make the flies larger until a peak right before the dead of summer, and then start scaling back down in size and color. Also, I seem to do better with rainbows and browns on the Yellow Palmer and have more luck with brookies on the Orange Palmer."

George Griffith's wonderful creation is nothing but a tiny, tailless dry Woolly Worm with a peacock-herl body. Unless you are seriously into hatch-matching and like to fool around with itty-bitty emergers, this is all you really need to fish during a midge emergence. In its smallest incarnations, Griffith's Gnat might well be taken for a midge that's still a bit messed up from its recent shedding of the nymphal shuck. More likely, and certainly in its larger sizes, the Gnat looks like a hungry trout's delight: a cluster of adult midges. Why trout slam such tiny morsels so hard is anyone's guess, but don't expect many sippers when you fish a Griffith's Gnat during a hatch.

Griffith's Gnat

Hook:	Fine-wire dry-fly, sizes 18 to 28
Thread:	Olive or black 8/0
Body:	1 to 3 peacock herls, tied sparsely
Palmer hackle:	Grizzly rooster, palmered very closely through the body; *reverse-palmered head to tail, if a rib is used*
Rib:	*Optionally, very-fine gold wire (Tiers who wire-rib their Gnats must be expecting to catch much bigger trout than I usually do during a midge hatch.)*

Tying Tips

If you palmer the hackle Woolly Worm-style, with the glossy side of the feather facing aft and the barbs angled fore, you might find a slight improvement in the fly's floating ability and in its fish-appeal.

This good advice comes from Steve Skulpa of Knoxville, Tennessee: "Wind the peacock herl sparsely, leaving a gap between each wrap. This will make it much easier to palmer the hackle so it falls between the herl, instead of laying it on top of the herl and mashing it down. If you wiggle the hackle pliers back and forth while you palmer the hackle, you'll have better luck getting it to fall between the windings of herl." Tie your Griffith's Gnats this way, and you will have no need of a reinforcing rib.

If you omit the peacock herl and palmer the grizzly hackle over a thread base, you will wind up with the **Cluster Midge**, usually tied no larger than size 20. *If* we permitted winged flies, you could add a small, white CDC feather to the Griffith's Gnat and get René Harrop's **CDC Cluster Midge**.

A tier named Jerry L. Case submitted a **Light Griffith's Gnat** to the Killroy's Flytying web site (www.killroys.com). He uses 8/0 or 12/0 light-tan or cream thread and tightly palmers in 5 turns a light-ginger grizzly hackle over a body made from either bleached peacock herl or light, creamy ostrich herl. He says it's an excellent representation of lighter-colored midges and "micro caddis adults." He says this fly and the tradition Griffith's Gnat are all he needs to cover all the adult-midge bases.

Fishing Tip

"Never hit the stream with just a single Gnat in your box," Skulpa adds, "'cuz they tend to get slimed after a couple of fish and will need some time on the drying patch before they're ready to get back to it."

The English company Fulling Mill lists seven Grayling Gnats in their fly catalog, apparently differing only in the body color. As you can see, Brits tend to use somewhat larger midge drys than we usually do.

Grayling Gnat

Hook:	Standard to 2X-long, fine-wire dry-fly, sizes 12 to 16
Thread:	Black 8/0
Body:	Black, green, olive, orange, purple, or pink floss, or pearl Mylar tinsel
Palmer hackle:	Grizzly rooster saddle, palmered closely, with the barbs angled forward, Woolly Worm-style (*not* the way it came out in my hands)

This Franz Grimley pattern—which I lifted from Stan Headley's *Trout & Salmon Flies of Scotland* (1997)—is unusual among British palmer flies for two things. First, it's a river fly rather than a loch or reservoir pattern. Second, the palmer hackle is clipped flush on the bottom, so this dry fly rides *in* the film. A pattern that has been kicking around for at least 35 years, it is both a midsummer prospecting pattern as well as a hatch-matcher during large olive and March brown emergences.

I had to deviate from the recipe in tying the sample, because I had no hope of finding the specified hook. I just used what I had on hand.

Big Grey

Hook:	Partridge L4A Captain Hamilton Featherweight, a *6X-fine* dry-fly, size 12
Thread:	Black
Body:	Dubbed dark hare's ear or black Super Poly
Palmer hackle:	"Smokey grey" grizzly rooster saddle, clipped flush underneath

Tying Tips

You might also want to try the lighter-bodied version. Use primrose (yellow) tying thread and either primrose or light-olive dubbing for the body.

This pattern's little cousin, the **Wee Grey**, is pretty much the same, except tied on a size-16, 4X-fine, 1X-short hook, using the black poly dubbing, and a "well-marked" grizzly saddle. Because the palmer hackle is *not* clipped on this version, the wee one rides higher and is fished in faster, more tumultuous water.

I found this Luis Antúnez pattern on the Fly Tying World web site (http://flytying-world.com) where it was submitted by his friend Paco Soria, the fly tier, veterinarian, and Coq de Leon breeder from Gerona, Spain, who corrected the listing below. The full name of the pattern is *Chochín de Peralejos*; *chochín* means "wren" and Peralejos is the name of a place. If you aren't comfortable with Spanish pronunciation (in my mouth, it always comes out sounding like Italian or Spanglish), I won't tell anyone if you decide just to call it just plain **Wren**.

Chochin

Hook:	TMC 100, or equivalent 1X-fine dry-fly, size 18 *(sample tied larger)*
Thread:	Brown 8/0
Underbody:	Gold Mylar tinsel
Body:	Green Swannundaze or similar translucent ribbing (D-Rib, V-Rib, Jelly-Rope, etc.), fine
Palmer hackle:	Light dun rooster
Head:	Chocolate-brown fur dubbing

This one is by Frank Cutler, one of the UK's stillwater trout-fishing aces; I found it in *Bob Church's Guide to New Fly Patterns*. Using a light floating line, Cutler fishes this midge imitation very slowly or even without any sort of manipulation at all.

Cutler's Midge

Hook:	1X- or 2X-short, fine-wire dry-fly, sizes 12 to 14 (smaller, in our waters)
Thread:	Black 6/0 or 8/0
Palmer hackle:	Sparse honey hen hackle, reverse-palmered head to tail
Tail:	3 or 4 tail-feather fibers from a cock ring-necked pheasant
Rib:	Fine gold metallic thread
Body:	Several bronze peacock herls, twisted together with the tying thread and wrapped up the shank
Head:	Tying thread, lacquered or varnished

I based this one on an Australian pattern I picked up somewhere and whose original name I have since forgotten. It works, but I confess I rarely think "grasshopper" when I look at it in a fly box.

Woolly Hopper

Hook: 2X- to 3X-long, fine-wire, sizes 4 to 12
Thread: Brown or orange
Tail: Wine-colored hackle fibers
Body: Cream or tan poly yarn over an underbody of thin, closed-cell foam; *the original pattern called for natural raffia*
Palmer hackle: Brown or speckled hen *(the original pattern called for partridge, practically impossible to palmer)* and orange-dyed grizzly, palmered together, or one through the other

PACKING WORM

This dry Woolly Worm is doubly buoyant. Its stiff palmer hackle will keep it riding high. And when the hackle tips break the surface tension, the body foam will help keep it afloat in the film.

The body uses polyethylene packing foam. You know, the kind that comes in thin (usually 1/16- or 1/8-inch-thick) sheets or rolls for packing crystal, china, and delicate instruments. It's semitransparent, white, "bubbly," and usually has long, parallel ripples in its surface. In his book *Tying Foam Flies* (1994), Skip Morris calls it Ethafoam, a Dow Chemical Company brand name. Be careful when tying it in and when wrapping it. Too much tension makes it less buoyant and way too much can break it; too little tension, and the fly will come undone. Go for the Goldilocks compromise.

Packing Worm

Hook: 1X- or 2X-long dry-fly, sizes 12 to 16
Thread: Black 8/0
Palmer hackle: Grizzly, furnace, or badger rooster (I used grizzly, tied in by the tip at the rear of the shank and palmered forward over the body in fairly close turns with the dull, concave, underside of the feather facing forward
Underbody: *Optionally, flat Mylar tinsel in gold, silver, or a bright color—even the brightest colors will barely show (I used red)*
Body: Polyethylene packing foam (1/16-in thick, cut in a strip about 1/8-in wide), tied in behind the hook eye and wrapped to the bend and back, taking a single wrap behind the tied-in hackle feather before reversing direction

Keith Perrault didn't say whose pattern this is, but you can bet he or she hailed from Pennsylvania.

Little Lehigh Special

Hook: Standard or 1X-long dry-fly, sizes 12 and 14
Thread: Brown or black
Tail: Badger hackle fibers
Rib: Gold *(wire or tinsel; Perrault didn't specify)*
Body: Olive floss
Palmer hackle: Golden badger rooster saddle, tied in at the front and reverse-palmered

Nixon's Caterpillar *Tied by Alberto Jimeno*

It's modestly listed in *Perrault's* simply as **Caterpillar**. This one comes from the late warmwater specialist Tom Nixon. To me, the hook size seems smallish for bass, so Nixon probably fished this one for panfish or perhaps even trout.

Alberto Jimeno has kindly tied two versions for us, one subtle and one not so subtle, to prime your creative pump.

Nixon's Caterpillar

Hook: Long-shank streamer, sizes 8 to 14
Thread: Black
Body: Natural or dyed deer hair, spun, packed, and clipped to shape.
Palmer hackle: Grizzly or other saddle hackle

Tying Tip

If you tie this on up-eyed salmon and steelhead hooks, sizes 4 to 10, add a squirrel tail, and clip to a bullet taper, you wind up with a **Buck Bug**, one of the best Atlantic salmon flies I've ever fished. It casts easier than the longer, more popular Bomber. Traditional colors are natural deer hair, red squirrel, and brown hackle, but I've seen them in dead white, solid black, and every color in between. Fish the Buck Bug as a waking fly and hold on!

McKenzie

Here's an easier use of deer hair in a floating Woolly Worm. Although this pattern hails from the Eugene, Oregon, area, it ought to work well almost anywhere, sized to fit the local insect fauna.

McKenzie

Hook: Standard dry-fly, sizes 8 to 12
Thread: Black
Tail: Coastal blacktail-deer body hair
Body: Light-green floss
Palmer hackle: Grizzly rooster saddle, palmered only moderately full over most of the body, but wrapped tightly as a dry-fly collar up front

Mole Hackle *Tied by Wayne Mones*

Call this one a Moley Worm, if you wish. Mole fur used to be a popular dubbing material. Now, it's getting hard to find.

Mole Hackle

Hook: Standard dry-fly, sizes 10 to 14
Thread: Black, brown, or dark gray
Rib: Gold wire or tinsel
Body: Brown mole fur, dubbed
Palmer hackle: Grizzly and brown rooster saddles, tied in up front and reverse-palmered together, or one through the other

Super Pupa *Tied by Alberto Jimeno*

In his native Swedish, Lennart Bergqvist named this fly *Superpuppan*. Fished dry, or just below the surface as a hatching sedge, this pattern is dynamite in caddis country. The colors may be varied to approximate local caddis species, but this is the most popular color combination in Sweden.

Super Pupa

Hook: Standard dry- or wet-fly, size 12
Thread: Black
Body: Fly-Rite, dubbed in 2 sections: golden yellow over the rear two-thirds of the shank and dark gray or dun over the front third
Palmer hackle: Dark dun high-quality dry-fly saddle, palmered forward in about 9 or 10 evenly spaced open turns, then clipped top and bottom so that when viewed from head-on the hackle looks like a bow tie
Head: Tying thread, varnished

NETOPIR FLY

Although its inventor is convinced that his "monster fly" (also known as the **Netopir Dry Fly**) resembles nothing that lives in or near the water, it looks as much like fish food as a lot of fly patterns that claim resemblance to this organism or that. The inventor is Marjan Fratnik, whose F Fly series launched the current worldwide fascination with CDC (*cul de canard*) feathers.

Writing of this pattern in John Roberts's *The World's Best Trout Flies*, Fratnik said, "After each catch, wash it and dry it with a few false casts. It floats like nothing else, it rides the waves and is visible as far as you can cast it. I wouldn't like to guess what fish take it for, but I know only that especially in the late afternoon and in the evenings they grab it constantly and without hesitation."

Netopir Fly

Hook: Standard or 1X-long dry-fly, sizes 12 and 14
Thread: Black
Palmer hackle: 5 to 8 CDC feathers (or however many it takes to cover the shank), "tied in tightly one after the other and wound to the eye without being overlapped"

WHISKEY AND SODA

I should think that tan or light-brown thread and either barred-ginger or light brown-dyed grizzly hackle would better fit the name of this dry fly. But apparently steelhead and salmon prefer black and grizzly on the rocks.

Whiskey and Soda

Hook: Steelhead/salmon dry-fly, sizes 6 to 10
Thread: Black
Tail: 2 grizzly hackle points
Body: Tying thread
Palmer hackle: Grizzly rooster saddle, palmered very closely

Tying Tip
Can also be tied wet, using webbier hackle.

GOLDEN PALMER

This couldn't-be-much-simpler pattern came from John Harrington Keene, a New York fly tier whose book *Fly Fishing and Fly Making* (1857) included not only ink and paper but also some samples of tying materials.

Golden Palmer

Hook: Standard dry-fly, size to suit
Thread: Brown or black
Body: unspecified; *none, or thread base*
Rib: Gold tinsel
Palmer hackle: Brown rooster, tied in at the front and reverse-palmered

BLACK MOTH

I discovered this Commonwealth palmer pattern on the same anonymous New Zealander's web site that yielded the **Terrestrial** (page 91) and **Red Setter Woolly** (page 43). "A black moth imitation dappled along the surface at night in calm back waters," wrote the Kiwi tier, "often will coax a fish lurking in the shadow of the bank or weed to strike."

Black Moth

Hook: Standard or 1X-long dry-fly, sizes 8 and 10
Thread: Black 6/0
Body: 1/8-in-wide strip of thin, black closed-cell foam wrapped around shank in one or two layers, depending on the length of the hook and the thickness of the foam
Palmer hackle: Black rooster saddle, palmered very closely

Fishing Tip
"Unlike a dry fly during the day, when any drag will spook a fish," our unknown benefactor advised, "a moth imitation at night needs to be dragged across the surface and is most effective on dark, non-moonlit nights."

ORANGE-BELLIED WOOLLY WORM *Tied by Alberto Jimeno*

Jimmy Darren, the colorful proprietor of the legendary Angler's Roost, listed this dry-fly pattern in the *Noll Guide to Trout Flies and How to Tie Them*. He simply called it **Woolly Worm**, but it needed a more descriptive name. "Gaudy Buck Buck" might also suit it.

Orange-Bellied Woolly Worm

Hook: Unspecified, but a 2X- or 3X-long nymph or streamer will suffice

Thread: Black

Tail: Grizzly or mallard-breast hackle fibers or points

Body: Black deer hair, spun, packed, and clipped to a caterpillar shape, orange-lacquered on the bottom *(craft paint works well)*

Rib: Silver tinsel; *Darren specified flat tinsel, but oval tinsel may hold better on a clipped deer hair body*

Palmer hackle: 4 or 5 turns of grizzly ("barred Plymouth Rock") rooster saddle

P. B. SKATER YELLOW

I found this stubby, yellow-bellied Woolly Worm on the Kraig Matlock Flies web site (www.flydealer.com/). Given the name (and I have no idea who or what "P. B." is—unless it's "peacock Back") and word order, I suspect this is fished as a waking fly, and tied in other colors as well. If you haven't tried waking surface flies (using a Portland Creek riffling hitch helps, although it isn't necessary), you are missing out on a major source of excitement in fly fishing. No recipe was listed, so I'm winging it.

P. B. Skater Yellow

Hook: Standard or 1X-short dry-fly, size 10

Thread: Black 6/0

Belly: Yellow floss, tied in at the bend on the underside of the hook and pulled forward over the body before the hackle is palmered

Body: Peacock herl

Palmer hackle: Orange-dyed, stiff rooster hackle, the barbs about a gap-width long, spiraled forward in 5 turns over the body and belly, the barbs angled toward the eye; alternatively, use a larger hackle and clip it to size after the fly is finished

Tying Tip

You might want to experiment with different belly colors: orange, chartreuse, pale olive, pale gray, white. If you are an adventurous soul, you might even try pink, purple, light blue, or other shocking shades.

THREE-HACKLE DRY FLY *Tied by Peter Frailey*

Imitative of nothing in particular, this traditional pattern works during and between hatches—of caddises, stoneflies, mayflies, midges. It probably comes closest to matching caddises or even small, ovipositing stoneflies. Designed as a trout fly (by Jeff Mottern of Harrisburg, Pennsylvania, according to the University of Maryland's Charlie Gelso), it will also take panfish and bass. The density of its hackle floats the fly well, but it fishes well drowned, and can be fished, like the Hornberg, dry and wet on the same cast. (Cast it upstream, dead drift it down, pull it under, and twitch-retrieve it back.) One or two brisk false casts will dry it out.

Grizzly–brown–dun and grizzly–brown–cream are traditional combinations, but many other combinations will produce. I like ginger, badger, furnace, and dyed-grizzly hackles in the mix,

depending on mood, whim, or whatever. Often, the "whatever" is whatever is lying at hand on the tying table.

Use the Three-Hackle as a searching pattern, or during a hatch when fussy fish won't take the usual imitations. You may be surprised, how often fish will refuse a more closely imitative pattern but accept the incredibly buggy impressionism of the Three-Hackle.

Three-Hackle Dry Fly

Hook: Light-wire dry fly, from 1X-short to 1X-long, sizes 12 to 24

Thread: Black, brown, or gray 6/0 or 8/0

Body: Tying thread, wrapped down the shank to a point opposite the hook point

Tail: Hackle barbs (a few selected from each hackle feather, mixed, and aligned), tied in opposite the point or barb, the tips extending about half a shank length beyond the bend

Palmer hackle: 3 dry-fly hackles, each palmered forward in sequence, through the previously palmered hackle or hackles, "interweaving" them

In Missouri, this version of the Woolly Worm (sometimes called the **Crackle-back Dry Woolly**) has achieved virtual cult status over the past 50 years. The creation of Ed Story, of Feather-Craft Fly Fishing in St. Louis (www.feather-craft.com), the Crackleback is a difficult fly to pigeonhole. Somewhat resembling the much bulkier Miller Woolly Worm—but *sans* the tinsel rib and with an oversize furnace palmer hackle replacing the grizzly—the Crackleback, like the preceding pattern, can be fished wet *and* dry, often both ways on the same cast. According to Dr. Scott D. Blystone of the Washington University School of Medicine in St. Louis, trout hit Cracklebacks so hard, the flies seldom survive more than four or five fish.

Crackleback

Hook: Mustad 94840, Dai-Riki 300, Daiichi 1170, TMC 100, or similar dry-fly, sizes 12 to 16
Thread: Black or olive 6/0 or 8/0
Back: 2 strands of peacock herl pulled over the body before palmering the hackle
Palmer hackle: Furnace saddle, slightly oversize and sparse, tied in at the bend with the dull side facing you and palmered forward in 4 1/2 to 5 evenly spaced turns (see Tying Tips below)
Body: Pale-olive synthetic dubbing, thin

Tying Tips

Here's what Ed Story says: "I tie them with a special neck hackle with a thin stem and a more 'sparse' dry-fly hackle than is normally found. The reason for the sparse hackle is to allow the size, shape, and color of the fly body to show through the hackle. I want just enough hackle to float the fly body. I use 4 1/2 evenly spaced hackle wraps on a size 12. A few years ago, we had Whiting Farms grow us 500 furnace 'saddles' with these features. They sold out in no time. The reason for the thin stem and sparse hackle is that I designed the pattern to float on top as a dry-fly terrestrial. No need to wait for a hatch."

Feather-Craft also sells Cracklebacks in pale-yellow, brown-spider, lime, and sulphur-orange versions (www.feather-craft.com). Preston Larimer, of Elsah, Illinois, reports successful trials with a chartreuse version. "I spin-dub Glo-Bug Yarn."

Fishing Tips

To fish the Crackleback as a dry fly, dress the hackle with floatant and fish it dead-drift or skitter it across the surface in the manner of an emerging caddis. Most anglers prefer to fish it both ways, as well as wet, on a single cast. As Ed Story explains, "Allow the fly to dead drift on top. If no hit on top after a few yards of drift, *pull the fly under*. Then 'skip' it with your rod tip as it goes downstream: a steady skip–skip–skip with your rod tip. To go really deep in off-color water, use a full-sinking line, a four-foot 4X or 5X tippet, and again skip–skip–skip the fly really deep for great success."

Dr. Blystone adds, "Cast across the current and let it drag. When the fly starts into the bend of the drag, give a sharp tug and pull the fly under the surface. Let the line hang below you in the current for a count of 20 or so. Fish hit most often on the swing and when the fly is hanging in the current below you."

If you want a purely wet Crackleback, fish it with a full-sinking line or sinking leader, pinch a split shot on the tippet 5 inches above the fly, or weight it with a bit of lead wire or a bead head and use softer hackle when you tie.

Ed Story has the last word: "This is a year-around, all-season fly, and if I had only one fly to fish every trout stream, this would be it, in size 12."

CATALONIA

This is my adaptation of **Catalana**, a Juan Lorite pattern submitted to the Fly Tying World web site (http://flytyingworld.com) by the Spanish veterinarian, Coq de Leon breeder, and fly tier Paco Soria. I had to adapt it because the original sported hackle-tip wings, a no-no in Woolly Worm protocol, and it called for two kinds of Coq de Leon hackle, of which I have none. (If you happen to have some dark-dun *indio* and some *aconchado* or *corzuna* Coq de Leon in your tying kit and are dying of curiosity, see the original on Soria's web site http://coqdeleonfeathers.homestead.com/indioflies.html.) I adapted it for inclusion, because I like the way it looks, and because I think Soria's method of preparing the palmer hackle in advance of tying in is a good idea you might want to adopt for other palmered and clipped-hackle patterns. You can probably tie it better than I did.

Catalonia

Hook:	1X- or 2X-short, fine-wire dry-fly, sizes 12 to 16
Thread:	Dark-red, 6/0 or 8/0
Tail:	Cree or ginger rooster hackle fibers, hook-length
Rib:	Yellow thread, 3/0 or larger, tied in at the bend
Body:	Tying thread
Palmer hackle:	Dark blue-dun rooster, prepared before tying it in (see Tying Tips below) by the base up front and reverse-palmering to the bend

Tying Tips

Select a hackle whose barbs are about half again as long as the gap width near the tip of the feather. Before tying in the hackle, stroke the barbs back until they stand perpendicular to the quill. Clip the barbs at a continuous taper, so that the longest barbs (near the base) are at least one and a quarter times the gap width and the barbs at the rear are about a gap-width long.

After tying in the hackle by its tip, leave the tying thread hanging at the hook eye, palmer the hackle to the bend, and secure it with the yellow thread. Carefully spiral the yellow thread through the palmered hackle, wriggling as you go, trying not to trap the barbs. Tie it off at the eye, clip the excess materials, build a neat head with the tying thread, and whip-finish.

Place a drop of cement on the thread head and on the thread wraps at the rear of the fly.

WISCONSIN FANCY *Tied by R. G. Balogh*

Eric Leiser attributes this caddis pattern to the Little Dixie Flies catalog.

Wisconsin Fancy

Hook:	Mustad 94840, or other standard dry-fly, sizes 12 to 18
Thread:	Black
Tail:	Brown hackle fibers
Palmer hackles:	Brown and grizzly rooster saddles, palmered together or one through the other
Body:	Cream- or ginger-colored red-fox dubbing

George Vosmik tells me that he "stumbled across" this pattern back in the 1950s while fishing the Little Manistee River: "Toward evening, tiny Royal Wulffs and Adamses worked great, but in the middle of the day it was difficult to get a trout to rise. Then I noticed that whenever a little tan or green caterpillar would fall off one of the bushes, the place would erupt!" Thus was born the High-Noon Caterpillar, which should be fished anywhere vegetation hangs over the banks.

George advises using a slightly shorter-than-normal hackle. The barbs should not be longer than the hook gap is wide. Use a really good dry-fly hackle ("perhaps one-fourth to one-half of a Hoffman saddle feather") and palmer it fully in very close turns. "These flies float!" he exclaims.

High-Noon Caterpillar

Hook: Mustad 79580, a 4X-long streamer, sizes 8 to 14
Thread: Color to match the body
Body: Dubbing to match the natural
Palmer hackle: Hoffman dry-fly saddle, the barbs no longer than the gap is wide; color to match the natural

Tying Tips

Vosmik says he varies the pattern as the season progresses and the local caterpillar fauna changes. Some of the fall caterpillars are too long for the 4X-long hook, so he will go to a longer shank to better match the naturals. Here are some of his favorites.

Inchworm: Bright-green thread, chartreuse body, and grizzly or light-tan hackle
Horned Caterpillar: Black thread and body, furnace hackle, size 8
Midsummer Caterpillar: Light-green or tan thread, medium-olive body, tan hackle (closely palmered), sizes 10 and 12

This pattern, adapted from several different sources, imitates the larval caterpillars of certain tiger moths of the family Arctiidae. (Other tiger-moth species produce the familiar fuzzy, black-and-brown larvae we call woolly bears.) In late summer (early fall, if it was a dry year), these webworms fall out of streamside trees (particularly sweetgums) and are promptly gobbled up by sunfish and other warmwater species. Earlier in summer, look for streamside trees infested by tent caterpillars, and plan your return accordingly. (Incidentally, most other tent caterpillars are less hairy than the webworm and sink when they hit the water, so are best imitated by clipped, wet Woolly Worms.) Don't worry if you miss the "hatch" by a few days; once locked onto this manna from heaven, the greedy sunnies linger awhile in their fixation.

Fall Webworm

Hook: 2X- or 3X-long, standard to 2X-fine dry-fly or terrestrial, sizes 10 to 14, 12 being most often used
Thread: White or pale-gray 6/0
Body: Fine, creamy-yellow or light pale-olive chenille, or cream (62031) Purr-fect Punch craft yarn, plus a gray or black waterproof marker
Palmer hackle: Barred-ginger, ginger, or light-dun grizzly rooster, the barbs about a gap-width long

Tying Tips

After wrapping either plain color yarn or chenille, use a permanent marker to mark a line right up the center of the back and to lightly speckle the sides and underside. If you can find it, a fine or extra-fine variegated chenille would be ideal for the body, as webworms are sort of a gray-speckled yellow.

A chenille body can be single-ply, wrapped from the bend to the eye; Purr-fect Punch yarn is thinner, so should be tied in behind the eye and wrapped down to the bend and back. If you like, give the finished fly a waterproof treatment, either a spray or a dip; both chenille and Purr-fect Punch yarn absorb water.

Another pattern cadged from Hans Weilenmann's fine web site (www.danica.com/flytier/), this Wally Lutz pattern preserves the palmer hackle but otherwise tosses Woolly tradition to the winds. In the words of its originator, "It's a skinny Bomber-style pattern without the hassle of clipping a hair body."

No-Brainer

Hook: Very long-shank, down-eyed dry-fly, sizes 10 to 14

Thread: Brown Kevlar

Palmer hackle: Coachman brown or ginger rooster hackle, to match the body, slightly undersized for the hook; tied in at the shank and palmered over the body after it has been secured to the hook

Tail: Tips of a bundle of 20 to 30 strands of elk or deer body hair, tied in tightly to flare out about a gap-width past the bottom of the bend

Body: The same bundle of elk or deer hair, laid atop and alongside the thread-wrapped hook shank

Head: The clipped butts of the body hair, extending above and slightly forward of the eye

Tying Tips

Lutz says you can use "any colour, but I like the natural elk—especially the urine-stained stuff off the belly of a bull." Almost makes it the Tup's Indispensible of the Woolly world.

When you tie in the hair, don't let it spin freely, but do let it roll around the hook shank. Lutz then winds the thread forward on the shank and binds the hair bundle only at bend and eye; my gut instinct is to wrap a thread base before tying the bundle in and then secure it to the shank with open spirals of thread. Suit yourself.

Fishing Tip

"It doesn't matter how you present this one," says Lutz, "hence its name." He uses it as a searching pattern for trout. I'd be tempted to tie it on larger hooks and fish it as a waking fly for Atlantic salmon, the way I use Bombers, Buck Bugs, and Muddlers.

Another topwater Woolly that uses a deer-hair body, this one is actually based on a streamer, Keith Fulsher's famous Thunder Creek bucktail. It's a waking fly rather than a dead-drift dry.

Bullethead Woolly Worm

Hook: Long-shank, light-wire popper or terrestrial, sizes 8 to 12

Thread: Black or brown 6/0

Tail: Bright red, orange, or yellow hackle points, which will be surrounded by the tips of the deer hair

Palmer hackle: Fiery-brown or furnace hackle, palmered over the body to where the bullet head will be formed

Head: Tan deer hair, laid atop the shank with the tips extending a bit more than a shank-length forward of the eye, the butts short of the shank, allowed to roll about the shank (without spinning freely) when tied in, then lashed down before being folded back to the rear to form a bullet head, which will be cemented

Body: The folded-back tips of the head hair, secured by open spirals of tying thread to the rear, then lashed securely so the tips flare out around the tail, before the thread is open-spiraled to the rear of the head where it will tie down the palmered hackle

Eyes: Optionally, painted or glued-on eyes over the head cement—the former after the cement has dried, the latter while it is still tacky

Gills: Optionally, tie on with red thread or floss at the rear of the head after the hackle has been palmered and tied off, wrap a few turns, and whip-finish

BREAD FLY

This is my Woolly take on Oliver Edwards's Breadfly, which uses a standard-length hook palmered just halfway down the shank. He designed it for tench, an Old World "rough" fish, but just think of all those bluegills and other warmwater species you've seen fighting over crumbs of bread tossed in the water.

Bread Fly

Hook: 1X-short, fine-wire dry-fly, sizes 12 to 16
Thread: White or tan, tied on at the eye and wrapped to the bend and back to the front after tying in the hackle, forming a thread base
Palmer hackle: 3 or 4 strands of white marabou or CDC, tied in at the rear and palmered forward together

SODA BUTTE SPECIAL   *Tied by Alberto Jimeno*

The Vermonter Peter Burton, who submitted the pattern to Eric Leiser for his *Book of Fly Patterns*, said he found it in the "junk box" at Dan Bailey's Fly Shop in Livingston, Montana. An unusual pattern, it has a palmer hackle over a clipped palmer hackle. Otherwise, it resembles a Buck Bug.

Soda Butte Special

Hook: Mustad 94831, a 2X-long, 2X-fine dry-fly, sizes 8 to 12
Thread: Gray
Tail: 12 to 14 woodchuck guard hairs, a gap-width long
Body: Blue-dun rooster hackle or hackles, palmered *very* tightly, then clipped to a bullet shape, almost as if it were spun deer hair
Palmer hackle: Brown rooster saddle, palmered in open spirals over the clipped-hackle body

COLONEL MONELL

Devised by George M. L. La Branche in honor of Colonel Ambrose Monell, this venerable dry-fly still sees a lot of service on eastern Canadian salmon rivers.

Colonel Monell

Hook: Salmon dry-fly, sizes 4 to 10
Thread: Black
Palmer hackle: Grizzly rooster saddle, very thick
Tail: Grizzly hackle fibers—thick, stiff, and long
Body: Peacock herl
Rib: Red floss or flat Mylar tinsel

NEVASINK SKATER   *Tied by R. G. Balogh*

Not a single pattern, but a design, E. R. Hewitt's Nevasink (sometimes listed as Neversink) Skaters are a fully palmered version of his Nevasink (Neversink) Spiders. Like his Spiders, Hewitt's Skaters have the aft hackles tied Woolly-Worm–style (with the hackle barbs angled forward) and the fore hackles tied palmer-style (with the barbs angled rearward). Hewitt used several neck hackles to palmer the whole length of the shank. Today's tier can use just one or two long saddle hackles.

Nevasink Skater

Hook: 1X- or 2X-long dry-fly, sizes 12 to 18
Thread: Black 6/0 or 8/0; alternatively, use a color that suits the hackle or your fancy
Body: *None, or a thread* ....
Palmer hackle: As man....
cree, o....
hackles ....
the rear ....
underside ....
the front h.... .....pside of
the feather .... ..rward

Tying Note

In Scandinavia, fly fishers tie a similar **Black Skater**, using very stiff rooster saddle, the barbs twice as long as the hook's gap, for the palmer hackle. The hackle is palmered with the barbs upright or facing forward—more like a Woolly Worm.

GUL FLYTANE

Obviously a European pattern (I think the name means "floating yellow" or "yellow floater" in Swedish), this bivisible-bodied dry Woolly Worm comes from the Kraig Matlock Flies web site (www.flydealer.com/). I am frankly guessing at the recipe, based on the picture. (Answering e-mail queries is apparently not a Kraig Matlock forte.)

Gul Flytane

Hook: 1X- or 2X-long dry-fly, size 12
Thread: Black 6/0
Palmer hackle: Blue-dun rooster saddle, tied in by the tip at the bend and palmered forward in 5 or 6 turns so that the barbs angle rather sharply forward; after the fly is finished, trim the hackle palmered *over the abdomen only:* clip the top and sides of the hackle so it is less than a gap-width long, and thin out the long bottom hackles by carefully snipping out some of the barbs
Abdomen: Yellow dubbing, tapered, over the rear half of the shank
Thorax: Black dubbing, thicker than the abdomen, over the front half of the shank

GEEHI BEETLE *Tied by Peter Frailey*

Back around 1947, Dr. Keith Zwar came up with this variation on the WW theme, apparently to imitate the beetles prevalent on the Geehi River and elsewhere in the Snowy Mountains of Australia, where the pattern remains hugely popular. It is used to suggest or imitate everything from iridescent green Christmas beetles to grasshoppers, cicadas, and other bankside terrestrials. According to Stephen Welsh (from whose Flyflickers web site—www. flyflickers.com.au—I first learned of the pattern) says that the late John Sautelle, author of *Fishing for the Educated Trout,* "was so taken with the Geehi, that he would choose it over all others if he were restricted to just one dry fly pattern."

Geehi Beetle

Hook: Mustad 94840, TMC 100, or similar standard or 1X-long dry-fly, sizes 8 to 18
Thread: Black or brown 6/0 or 8/0
Tail: Several golden pheasant tippets, about as long as the shank—*angled a bit below the horizontal, in some listings*
Palmer hackle: Natural red (fiery brown), Coachman brown, or ginger rooster—tied in at the front and reverse-palmered to the rear
Body: Peacock herl—4 herls alternated tip to butt before trimming and tying in, suggests one lister
Rib: Fine gold wire

Tying Tips

Although the gold rib is apparently standard, some listings omit it—in which case, the hackle can be tied in at the bend and palmered forward.

According to Stephen Welsh, the original pattern called for a ginger hackle, but most contemporary listings call for Coachman brown or natural red. In his listing on an Australian fly swap (www. fishnet.com.au), Barry Jacobson used two hackles, Bivisible-style: a brown or furnace palmer hackle behind fronted by 3 or 4 turns of ginger face hackle. "Don't leave out the gold ribbing!" he urged.

Welsh also quotes an angler and tier named Cliff Wintel, who has a different way of wrapping and securing the palmer hackle: "[T]ie in a length of gold metallic thread at the tail together with the palmering hackle, twist both together to make a rope, wind forward over the body in the opposite direction of the peacock herl, tie off at the head. ... Try 'em with 10–12 turns, they float like corks on the fastest of streams." Rather than wrap either the peacock herl or the palmer rib the wrong direction, setting yourself up for an unraveling fly, I'd tie in the peacock herl at the front and wrap the body to the rear.

Be sure to see also **Frailey's Geehi Bivisible,** on page 94.

Fishing Tip

Generally considered a searching fly, "The Geehi Beetle comes into its own in late spring or summer," according to Welsh, "when it is warm and there is a deal of insect activity. It is especially effective the fish the first warm, sunny day after a few cold, drizzly days when insect life has gone somewhat dormant." He also recommends fishing the Geehi in the rain (when "all sorts of landborne bankside terrestrials can end up washed into a stream") and on into the twilight ("when fish can become picky").

STYX SPECIAL

Geoff Hall, of the Goulburn Valley Fly Fishing Centre in Thornton, Victoria (www.golburn-vlyflyfishing.com.au), suggests this "more subtle and therefore realistic" variation of the Geehi "for searching slower waters rather than the rougher stuff you would float a Geehi in." He adds, "Windy days are best, and a slight ripple on the water seems to help."

Named after the Styx River in the New England district of New South Wales, this fly imitates a small scarab-type beetle common in the area. Although the palmer hackle is partially clipped, it certainly isn't a hackle-*challenged* pattern. Nor is it quite a Bivisible, because the body palmer is so much smaller than the collar hackle, which suggests the beetle's legs.

Styx Special

Hook:	Standard or 1X-long dry-fly, sizes 8 and 10, usually, but Geoff Hall prefers to tie and fish it in sizes 14 and 16
Thread:	Black 6/0
Tail:	3 dark furnace hackle tips
Rib:	Fine gold wire
Body/Palmer hackle:	Black rooster saddle, tied in by the butt far enough behind the eye to accommodate the collar hackles, palmered thickly, then clipped to shape
Hackle collar:	2 furnace hackles, tied quite thickly

FLOATING CACTUS WOOLLY WORM *Tied by "Big Jim" Hester*

I found this foam-bodied panfish fly on the web site of the Chesapeake Fly & Bait Company (www.chesa-peakefly.com), of which "Big Jim" Hester is proprietor. "The Floating Cactus Woolly Worm is a very simple fly," Hester says. "I tie it in several colors, but either all-black or green-and-black have been the best producers for me. I'm not certain, but I think it works because fish mistake it for either a terrestrial, or a large aquatic struggling to break through the surface film, in which case the light-reflecting Cactus Chenille may look like air bubbles." Use whatever colors suit your mood, or those of the fish you seek.

Floating Cactus Woolly Worm

Hook:	3X- or 4X-long streamer, sizes 6 to 12
Thread:	6/0
Palmer "hackle":	Pearlescent micro-size Cactus Chenille or similar short-fibered tinsel chenille, wound forward over the body in open spirals
Body:	Closed-cell foam, a strip 2-mm–thick, tied on at the front and wrapped to the bend and back

TERRESTRIAL

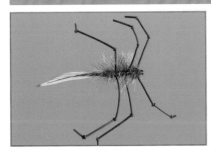

I found a picture of this generic terrestrial (cranefly? daddy long-leg? crippled hopper?) on an unidentified New Zealander's web site. Every time I tried to get to his or her home page, it crashed my computer. I have guessed at the recipe and have in fact made a few changes from the fly in the photograph. So, whoever you are, thanks for the idea; I hope you don't mind my using it.

Feel free to tie the Terrestrial in whatever color, or colors you think will work for you.

Terrestrial

Hook:	1X-long dry-fly, sizes 8 and 10
Thread:	Black 6/0
Tail:	Light furnace or other two-tone, brown, hook-length saddle
Legs:	3 pairs of black rubber legs, evenly spaced along the shank, oriented at different angles to the shank, and knotted twice
Body:	Brown polyester "sparkle yarn" (a single strand of Aunt Lydia's Rug & Craft Yarn from a craft shop or dime store will save you a lot of money)
Palmer hackle:	Brown rooster, the barbs about a gap-width long, clipped short on top

Tying Tip

Don't leave those legs too long, or their weight will sink the fly.

Be careful, when clipping those top hackle barbs, not to cut off any of the rubber legs.

Fishing Tip

The anonymous Kiwi advised that "terrestrials are useful below overhanging vegetation, or on windy days when insects get blown onto the water."

BIVISIBLES

Bivisibles are nothing but heavily palmered dry Woolly Worms with two colors of hackle—one, dark, the other, white or very light. This makes the flies easier to see—for both fish and fly fisher. Traditionally, the white (or light) hackle goes up front; depending on the tier, the high-visibility front hackle may be as short as five or six turns or as long as the front half of the shank. Some angling historians think two-color palmer flies date all the way back to the Macedonian beginning of fly fishing. But most credit E. R. Hewitt, who started tying and fishing Bivisibles, especially the Black Bivisible, back in the 1920s. In his *Illustrated Encyclopedia of Fly-Fishing* (1993), Silvio Calabi notes that Hewitt's Bivisible was "soon adopted by everyone as the great advance that it was. Lee Wulff called it the most popular single pattern of the 1930s." The Bivisible isn't nearly as popular today, and it's high time for fly fishers to rediscover the effectiveness of a pattern that will dance on waters that are too torrential even for the Elk Hair Caddis or the Wulff series.

I discovered the effectiveness of the Brown Bivisible fishing the great trout and grayling streams of Slovenia and Croatia in the mid 1980s. (It was the closest thing I had in my box to the **Romar**—see page 78.) A decade later, when I lived in Maryland, I used to love a certain rock in the Big Gunpowder River. Standing on it, I could virtually predict what I would catch, depending on which direction I cast my Bivisible: upstream, rainbow trout; downstream, brown trout; across to the rock on the other side, bluegill.

The Bivisible has had two great vocal champions: Ray Bergman and Gary LaFontaine. Bergman devoted most of a long chapter in *Just Fishing* (1932) to singing the praises of this "fluffy bit of a fly which one cannot help but drop softly on the water." Bergman first called it the Bivisible Spider, somewhat confusing it with Hewitt's other great dry-fly innovation, the Nevasink, or Neversink, Spider. (In a true Spider, the hackles are concentrated in the center of the shank. Rather than being truly palmered, the Spider's two hackles are tied so the dull, concave undersides of the feathers are facing one another.)

Bergman said he carried the "Brown Bivisible Spider" for two years before fishing it. Finally, one day, at the end of eight hours without even a rise, he decided to try the Bivisible on a likely looking run over which he "had floated various flies … at least fifty times without interesting a fish." On its first drift, the Bivisible took an 18-inch, 2-pound, 4-ounce brown. On the next cast, to another place he had fished "faithfully" but fruitlessly with other flies, Bergman rose but missed another fish. On each of the next seven casts, brown trout rose to the fly.

I won't repeat Bergman's other anecdotes, some of which bordered on scientific experiments, the way he kept repeating and recording his trials. He discovered that Bivisibles often could move fish that were otherwise inclined to sulk. He also observed that, "With them one may fish fast water on which it is impossible to float an ordinary dry fly. This alone is enough to recommend their place in any angler's box." He concluded that Bivisibles were "quite essential and necessary to my assortment. Without them I could not get the most out of my fishing." In the 1978 third edition of *Trout*, he wrote of his "crush" on Bivisibles: "I was so sold on Bivisibles for one complete season that if the trout wouldn't take one, I figured they wouldn't take anything, and I was perfectly satisfied with that decision." During a period when he figured he could get by with just six dry flies, three of them were Bivisibles: Badger, Blue (dun), and Brown.

More recently (notably in his 1990 *The Dry Fly: New Angles*), the late Gary LaFontaine waxed ecstatic over the Bivisible. "The Bivisible sits up on the numerous hackle points, never presenting a solid picture to the fish," he observes. "It is my favorite 'exciter' for a dead-drift presentation…." But he also fished Bivisibles actively, "skipping them across current lanes and down runs. This is a very exaggerated motion, not meant so much to imitate as excite. I can't do that with flies designed to pique curiosity."

LaFontaine said his "favorite colors for the rear hackle are black, grizzly, cree, golden badger, brown, blue dun, and pink."

BROWN BIVISIBLE *Tied by Wayne Mones*

Let's take a look at the basic Bivisible pattern. I've chosen to list my sentimental favorite, but the **Black Bivisible** is equally popular and perhaps even more nearly universally effective. It's an easy switch.

Brown Bivisible

Hook: Standard or 1X-long, fine-wire dry-fly, sizes 6 to 18 (for salmon and steelhead, use a salmon dry-fly in sizes 6 to 10)

Thread: Black or brown

Face hackle: At least 5 or 6 close, touching turns (dry-fly collar style) of white or cream rooster neck or saddle *(alternatively, palmer the front quarter of the shank or more)*; the barbs should be more than a gap-width long

Tail: Brown hackle fibers, extending a shank-length past the bend

Palmer hackle: Brown dry-fly saddle, palmered *(reverse-palmered, if the fly is ribbed)* very closely; if you use neck hackles or short saddle hackles, be prepared to use 2, 3, or more feathers to cover the shank

Body: *Almost anything: bare shank, tying thread, colored thread, flat gold or silver tinsel, brown floss or dubbing.*

Rib: *Optionally, fine silver wire or flat tinsel; if a rib is used, tie the main hackle in behind the face hackle and reverse-palmer to the rear*

These days, when you see Bivisibles in the shops and catalogs, if you see them at all, you usually see just two: Black and Brown. These flies are among the effective in any fly fisher's arsenal, but the Bivisible offers numerous other opportunities to beguile and seduce trout and other fish (bluegills love them). But over the years, a lot of Bivisible dressings have been listed, particularly by J. Edson Leonard (in *Flies*, 1950) and Keith Perrault (in *Perrault's Standard Dictionary of Fishing Flies*, 1984).

Bivisibles Listed by Leonard (1950), Perrault (1984), and Others

Abbreviations used: BV = Bivisible; FT = flat tinsel, HF = hackle fibers, HP(s) = hackle point(s), OT = oval tinsel

Pattern Name	Tail	Body	Rib	Palmer Hackle	Face Hackle
A. C. Allen's Mayfly	3 cock pheasant-tail fibers	Yellow floss	Gold FT, fine	Badger	Yellow-dyed guinea
Aggie Bivisible	Dark-brown HP			Dark brown	Ginger
Ashey BV	Gray dun HF	Gray floss	Silver	Gray dun	White
Badger Bivisible (1)	Light badger HPs			Dark badger	Light badger
Badger BV (2)	Badger HPs			Badger	White
Bang Bivisible	Scarlet HP			Scarlet	White
Barred BV	Grizzly HF			Grizzly	White
Black Bivisible	Black HF	Black floss	Gold wire/OT	Black	White
Blue BV (1)	Blue HF	Gray floss	Gold rib, opt.	Blue-gray	White
Blue BV (2)	Grizzly HPs			Blue-gray	White
Blue Dun Bivisible		Gray-blue fur dubbing		Dark-gray	Grizzly
Brown Dun Bivisible	Wood-duck flank HF	Red floss		Brown	White
Brown-and-Gray BV	Brown and gray HF, mixed			Brown and gray	White
Brown-and-Grizzly BV				Grizzly (2/3)	Golden ginger (1/3)
Brown-and-Grizzly BV (Art Lee)	Brown and grizzly HPs			Brown and grizzly, one through the other	White
Candy Bivisible	Scarlet and white HF			Scarlet and white, mixed	none
Coachman Bivisible	Brown HF	Peacock herl	Gold tip	Brown	White
Dancer Bivisible	Blue dun HP			Blue dun	White
Devil Bivisible	Scarlet-dyed grizzly HP			Scarlet	White
Fiery Brown Bivisible	2 white deer hairs	Fiery-brown wool or fur dub		Pale yellow	White
Furnace Bivisible		Scarlet floss or dubbing		Furnace	White
Gray Bivisible	Grizzly HPs	Gray dubbing	Silver	Grizzly	White
Gray-and-White BV	Long white HF	Gray fur dubbing		Gray	White
Gray Palmer Bivisible		Gray dubbing/scarlet tip	Gold	Grizzly	White
Grayling Bivisible	Brown HF	Gray dubbing/gold tip opt.	Gold	Blue dun	White
Green Bivisible	Green HF	Olive or olive-and-green dub	Gold	Green	White
Grouse Bivisible	Grouse HF	Black thread		Grouse	White
Guinea Bivisible	Guinea HF			Guinea	White
Irish Bivisible	Light-green HP			Light-green	White
Martinez (Don Martinez)	Red breast-feather HF from golden pheasant	Blue-and-yellow wing quill, stripped		Furnace	Blue-dyed grizzly
Orange Bivisible	Orange HPs			Light-orange	White
Pale Yellow Bivisible		Cream fur		Pale-brown or ginger	White
Partridge Spider	Partridge HF	Gray floss	Black thread	Badger	Partridge
Phil Armstrong (Peter Schwab)	Brown HF + 2 grizzly HPs			Grizzly	Ginger
Sand Bivisible	Brown HF			Brown	Blue Dun
Sedge Bivisible		Peacock herl		Grouse	Cream
Sid Gordon Bivisible	Long golden pheasant tippets	Orange dubbing or yarn		Orange	White
Skunk	White over black, HF or hairs	Black thread		Grizzly, thick	White
Skunk Bivisible	Black HPs	Black thread		Black	White
Toil and Moil	Red goose quill slip	Yellow floss		Brown	Scarlet
Yellow Bivisible		Yellow dubbing		Yellow	White

TIPS FOR TYING BETTER BIVISIBLES

Not all tiers agree on how a Bivisible should be tied. Latitude is allowed, but you ought to know how various approaches affect the fly's performance on the water.

Hackles

Bivisible hackles should be stiff, long, and very closely palmered. Use top-quality rooster hackle, and wrap it almost as tightly as you pack deer hair. The finished fly ought to look like a bristly fuzz ball. In the old days, it took two to four feathers in the rear and one or two up front to get the fly palmered fully enough. Thanks to today's hackle breeders, you can use a single top-grade saddle hackle and still have enough left over to hackle a few conventional dry flies.

Most tiers tie in the front hackle first, a bit behind the hook eye, and palmer the body hackle up to the front hackle's tie-in point. It helps prevent your crowding the eye. Eric Leiser suggests that the palmer hackle be taken a turn or two in front of the light hackle before tying it off. That way, when the light hackle is wound forward, the color transition is more graduated. Suit yourself.

The acuity of your eyesight and your hunch about what the fish want can determine the balance between the dark and light hackles. I sometimes tie my Bivisibles half-and-half, but more often use a 3:1 ratio. Five or six tight turns should be considered minimum for the face hackle, unless the pattern specifies otherwise.

Tails

Some tiers tail their Bivisibles, others don't. Does it make a difference? It depends on how you hackle them. Bivisibles palmered with hackles of the same barb-length from rear to front don't need tails. If you use a longer face hackle, you should tail your Bivisibles. Tails should be dry-fly long (as long as the hook shank) and stiff. Use good dry-fly rooster-hackle fibers. If you want to get fancy, you can use exotic pheasant tippets. Or I suppose you could use a thick hair tail similar to the tails on Wulffs.

Most tiers use tails that are the color of the main palmer hackle. However, some like the effect of tailing the fly with the face hackle's fibers. Taff Price shows a **Red Bi-visible** bass fly (his spelling) that has a white hackle-fiber tail and a white face hackle flanking a bright-red hackle palmered over a red thread base.

Bodies

Leonard specified no body for several of the Bivisible patterns he listed. When I tie them, I usually wrap the shank with a base of tying thread—typically of a color that matches or complements the hackle. As for Leonard's gold bodies, I'd probably use flat tinsel or metallic thread, depending on how flashy I wanted to get. I also use floss, dubbing, and fine synthetic yarn for bodies. If dark furnace is your main hackle, all you really need is a thread base on the shank; the fly will appear to have a fairly thick, dark, translucent body—very buggy looking.

In truth, the body probably matters little. It's all those hackle tips denting the water and refracting light that give the Bivisible its fish-catching allure. That, and the way it dances on fast water.

Whatever else the Bivisible may be, an exact imitation of an insect species it isn't. So you can afford to be creative in designing yours. To help prime the creative pump, here are a few more patterns.

FRAILEY'S GEEHI BIVISIBLE *Tied by Peter Frailey*

"After tying my first Geehi Beetle" (page 90), Peter Frailey said in a note accompanying his flies, "it occurred to me that an effective variation could be created using the tying technique I employ in one of my favorite dry flies of American origin, the Katterman" (see next). "In fact, several of the variations out of Australia employ two hackles of different colors applied to the hook just as in a Katterman. The colors and tailing materials are different, but it is nevertheless fascinating how two such similar flies evolved independently on two opposite ends of the world. Change the front hackle to cream, and you have a Katterman with a golden pheasant tippet tail. Would that be a Katterman Beetle? Or, perhaps a Geehi Bivisible?"

Frailey's Geehi Bivisible

Hook: Mustad 94840, TMC 100, or similar standard or 1X-long dry-fly, sizes 8 to 18

Thread: Orange 6/0 or 8/0

Tail: Several golden pheasant tippets, about as long as the shank

Palmer hackle: Coachman brown rooster, palmered over the body

Face hackle: Ginger rooster, wrapped forward from the front of the body to the eye in 3 open turns, then 3 turns back to the body, then 3 turns forward again

Body: Peacock herl, counter-wrapped over the rear 2/3 of the shank

Tying Tip

To increase the visibility of this fly, Frailey suggests, tie the face hackle in so the underside (lighter, concave side) of the ginger hackle faces forward on the forward wraps.

One could call this Walt Dette pattern simply a peacock-bodied Brown Bivisible. Peter Frailey calls it "one of the most simply elegant flies ever designed—a winner." I heartily agree. The combination of the iridescent body and chiaroscuro hackle gives the Katterman just about everything a trout could want. All the trout fisher has to provide is a proper presentation. Pennsylvania's Hiram Brobst (almost Dette's peer in dry-fly dressing) substituted light-ginger hackle points for the tail.

Katterman

Hook:	Dry fly, sizes 12 to 18
Thread:	Cream 8/0
Face hackle:	5 or 6 turns of white rooster
Tail:	Brown hackle fibers
Rib:	Fine gold wire
Palmer hackle:	Dark-brown ("mahogany," according to Brobst) rooster
Body:	Peacock herl

Tying Tips

In *The Book of Fly Patterns*, Eric Leiser counseled, "This pattern…is constructed more easily if you first tie in the white hackle which is to become the front collar and then proceed with tail, rib, palmer, and body." He also advised forcing the white face hackle out of the way with "a turn or two of thread," because the brown hackle is palmered first. "It's not a bad idea," Leiser wrote, to wind the brown hackle "one or two turns beyond the white hackle. This will result in a gradual blend from brown to all-white after the white hackle has been wound forward to the eye."

Peter Frailey tied two versions of this pattern: as described above and with the following changes: "Orange thread, because I believe it is a great attractor color. No rib. I counterwrap the peacock herl over

the rear two-thirds of the shank, then palmer the brown hackle forward, creating a reinforcing cross-rib over the herl. The cream face hackle is tied in conventionally, then I use a technique borrowed from Gary Borger: Wrap the hackle forward in 3 slightly open turns; then reverse-wrap it to the rear for 3 more turns; finally, forward-wrap 3 more turns and tie off. This lays down a greater number of barbs over a short space and splays the barbs forward and backward, creating a more aggressive 'footprint.'"

This slightly different pattern was listed in the *Noll Guide to Trout Flies and How to Tie Them* (1965), which presented patterns selected by the late James Darren of the now legendary Angler's Roost fly shop in New York City.

Badger Bivisible Spider

Hook:	Unspecified, but from the picture, a short-shank *(perhaps even wide-gap)* dry-fly, with a turned-up eye; size not specified, but of a size to accommodate your dry-fly saddles
Thread:	Cream or gray
Tail:	Long (half again as long as the hook) badger hackle barbs
Palmer hackle:	Extra-large badger rooster hackle, at least twice as long as the hook gap
Face hackle:	White rooster hackle

CHAUNCEY

This pattern departs from Bivisible tradition in using a short-shanked hook and grizzly rather than white or other plain pale hackle up front.

Chauncey

Hook:	1X-short, 1X-fine dry-fly (Mustad 94838 or similar), sizes 6 to 14
Thread:	Brown
Body:	Tying thread
Palmer hackle:	Brown rooster
Face hackle:	Grizzly rooster

LOCH ORDIE DAPPING FLY

Palmered dapping flies used in the British Isles resemble big overgrown Woolly Worms, with grossly oversize hackle palmered in touching turns. Most use a single hackle color: furnace, badger, black, and so on. A few are Bivisibles. This is one of the best and most popular. (Works even better if you can keep the face hackle from sloping so much to the rear.)

Loch Ordie Dapping Fly

Hook:	Standard or fine-wire dry-fly, sizes 6 to 10
Thread:	Brown or black 6/0
Tail:	*Optionally, hackle fibers, at least half again as long as the hook gap*
Palmer hackle:	Brown rooster saddle, oversize, on rear 2/3 of shank, *optionally, over a thread base*
Face hackle:	Light-ginger rooster saddle, slightly larger than the palmer hackle, palmered forward of the main hackle

Tying Note

Another interesting Bivisible dapping fly is the **Badger-and-Yellow Dapping Fly**. The badger is the palmer hackle, and yellow, the face hackle. Unless you use steeply tapered saddle hackles, you will have to clip the hackles to shape, so that the fly resembles a cork stopper from the side, tapering from a gap-width or less in the rear to nearly two gap-widths in front.

FRENCH-PARTRIDGE MAYFLY *Tied by R. G. Balogh*

This dry fly, which Taff Price calls one of his favorites, uses the barred hackle from a French partridge up front. Go ahead and substitute Hungarian partridge or grouse, guinea fowl, or even extra-large rooster, if you aren't likely to run into Taff Price or a French *pêcheur à la mouche* on the stream. Because of the dominance of that soft-hackle collar, this isn't really a Bivisible, but I've included it anyway, it's such a nice fly.

This falls into an old category of French dry flies that use stiff rooster palmer hackles merely to support long, soft shoulder hackles of game-bird feathers. The flies actually float on top of the surface film on the "knuckles" of the soft game hackles as they bend over the stiff palmer hackles. Datus Proper in *What the Trout Said* (1982) categorized them as bent-hackle flies. They should be dressed with floatant, but even then they are good only for a few casts as dry flies. But they are very good indeed while they float.

French-Partridge Mayfly

Hook:	2X-long, light-wire dry-fly, size 12
Thread:	Black or brown
Shoulder hackle:	French-partridge barred hackle
Palmer hackle:	Olive rooster
Tail:	Cock-pheasant tail fibers, as long as the hook
Rib:	Fine gold wire
Body:	Natural raffia

BLACK-AND-YELLOW BIVISIBLE

Bivisibles traditionally are tied with the light hackle up front and the main hackle in the rear, but nothing prevents your hackling them the other way around. Some tiers think the impressionistic Bivisible more resembles the natural insect if the light hackle is in the rear, where the wing would be. Who knows what the fish think? This particular color combination is often tied in reverse order, with the dark hackle up front.

Black-and-Yellow Bivisible

Hook: Fine or standard dry-fly, sizes 10 to 16
Thread: Crimson or yellow 6/0 or 8/0
Tail: Black or yellow hackle fibers, *sometimes mixed together*
Palmer hackle: Bright yellow-dyed rooster hackle
Face hackle: Black rooster
Body: *Variably, black or yellow floss, tying thread, or flat gold tinsel*

TASMANIAN CAENIS *Tied by Peter Frailey*

Another Bivisible pattern that was designed "backwards." Bob Church, from whose *Guide to New Fly Patterns* I borrowed this recipe, says he used this backwards Bivisible to catch trout that were tailing at lakeside in the early morning in such shallow water their backs were out of the water when their bellies touched bottom.

Tasmanian Caenis

Hook: Standard dry-fly, sizes 12 to 14
Thread: White
Tail: White rooster-hackle fibers
Body: White seal fur or substitute, dubbed
Palmer hackle: Rear half, white rooster; front half, badger rooster

Tying Note

The English tier and fly fisher Paul Canning has a similar, but simpler, pattern for trout during a *Caenis* hatch: the **Caenis Nymph** (see page 63).

ASSASSINE *Tied by Alberto Jimeno*

Alberto Jimeno found this pattern for me, in a George Wentzel article ("A Long Cast from Home") in an old issue of *Fly Tyer*. Thanks, Alberto and George. Wentzel discovered the pattern in a German book, *Zwanzig Fliegenmuster Reichen Aus (Twenty Fly Patterns Reach Out!)*, by Dr. Jean-Paul Metz, Horst Kretschmer, and Rudi Rubel. According to the three authors, the Assassine is a mayfly imitation. Wentzel, who was dubious at first ("A palmered, wingless mayfly imitation with a clipped partridge hackle at the head? Nah."), now concurs because "it always seems to work for me." I certainly would not hesitate to fish this fly during a sulphur hatch.

Later, I found the pattern attributed to Dr. Jean-Paul Pequegnot of France in *Perrault's Standard Dictionary of Fishing Flies*. And I looked it up in Pequegnot's *French Fishing Flies* (Nick Lyons, 1987). I have merged the Wentzel and Pequegnot recipes.

Assassine

Hook: Standard dry-fly, sizes 10 to 14, sometimes smaller
Thread: Light-yellow, yellow, or olive 6/0 or 8/0
Body: Tying thread
Face hackle: Two turns of gray or brown French partridge, *trimmed to the same diameter as the palmer hackle according to Wentzel, untrimmed and larger according to Pequegnot*
Palmer hackle: Pale blue dun or natural gray rooster— palmered tightly behind the partridge a few turns and then reverse-palmered sparsely to the bend according to Pequegnot
Tail: *Optionally, if desired, according to Pequegnot, the untrimmed tip of the gray hackle*

Tying Tip

According to Pequegnot, the fly should be finished off at the bend. The illustration in his book shows what looks like a small knot of tying thread at the bend.

Even among the most traditional Atlantic salmon fishers, the Bivisible has made for itself a comfortable and honorable place with this pattern, also known as **Pink Lady Palmer** and **Pink Lady Bivisible**.

I have seen listings that use flat gold tinsel for the body, but that leaves me wondering where the "Pink" comes in. In fact, I think a tinsel rib covers up an awful lot of that pink body; I prefer wire or very narrow tinsel.

Pink Lady

> *Hook:* Salmon dry-fly, sizes 4 to 10
> *Thread:* Black 6/0
> *Tail:* Light-ginger rooster hackle fibers, almost as long as the shank; *alternatively, some tiers omit the tail*
> *Body:* Pink floss
> *Rib:* Gold or silver wire or tinsel
> *Palmer hackle:* Light-ginger rooster saddle, very stiff, closely palmered
> *Face hackle:* Traditionally, chartreuse or pale-olive rooster saddle (or two neck hackles), wound over the front fourth of the shank; *alternatively, white*

Tying Tips

Because of that rib, I would tie in the saddle for the palmer hackle about three-fourths of the way up the shank, then wrap the floss to that point, secure the floss temporarily with a wrap of thread, reverse-palmer the ginger hackle, secure it with the rib, wind the rib through the hackle, tie down the rib and clip the excess. Now, tie in the face hackle and continue wrapping the floss body forward prior to palmering the face hackle.

Some listers specify using as many as four hackles to palmer the body. I think you will find that today's saddle hackles are large and long enough to do the job with just two feathers, one for the main palmer and one for the face hackle. If you have to use neck hackle for the face hackle, you might have to use more than one feather.

Again, try no to slope the face hackle as much as I did.

Call this John Hazel variation on the well-known Atlantic-salmon fly a grizzly-faced, big-fish Bivisible with an exaggerated tail. Like the regular MacIntosh, the steelhead version can be skated as a waking fly (often tied to the tippet with a Portland Creek riffling hitch) or dead-drifted as a dry fly.

Steelhead MacIntosh

> *Hook:* Salmon dry-fly, sizes 4 to 10
> *Thread:* Black
> *Tail:* Black squirrel tail, tied in opposite the point, and as long as the shank
> *Body:* Thread base
> *Palmer hackle:* Black rooster saddle, the barbs slightly shorter than the hook gap
> *Face hackle:* Orange-dyed grizzly rooster saddle, the barbs at least a gap-width long, palmered over the front fourth (or even third) of the shank

In case you are wondering, Tricolore flies aren't usually tied in red-white-and-blue or other tricolor-flag colors. I guess fish don't often take out of patriotism.

Taff Price says the Tricolore is a French pattern that is widely used across Europe for both trout and grayling. Despite its French name, the Tricolore may be as popular in Germany and the U. K. as it is in countries that have tricolor flags, maybe even more.

Of the many color combinations tied, Price lists this one in *Fly Patterns: An International Guide* (1986).

Tricolore

> *Hook:* Standard or 1X-long, light-wire dry-fly, sizes 12 and 14; *Price shows an up-eyed hook, but I doubt it matters*
> *Thread:* Black
> *Tail:* Light-ginger rooster hackle fibers, about as long as the hook
> *Palmer hackle:* In 3 equal parts; from bend to eye, black, ginger, and blue dun

TRICOLORE NO. 2 *Tied by Alberto Jimeno*

Writing in the German magazine *Fliegen-Fischen*, Ingo Karwath reports how he discovered Tricolores by reading a book by Charles Ritz, and how Ritz discovered the Tricolore in 1951. According to Ritz, it was one André Ragot who put the Tricolore on the map. Ragot's fly came in three sizes—13, 15, and 17—and just one color combination: black, brown, and grizzly. Ritz said his 50 years of fly fishing had converted him from the "2,000-fly man" of his youth to maturity as a committed "Cahillist." But after fishing Ragot's pattern, he became for a few months a "Tricolorist."

Tricolore No. 2

Hook: Standard dry-fly, sizes 10 to 18
Thread: Black
Tail: Brown hackle fibers
Body: Tying thread, varnished, beginning at the bend
Palmer hackle: Hen hackles of medium stiffness, in thirds: dun, tied in opposite the hook point, brown in the middle, and black up front

Tying Tip

If you want a fly that's easier to see, try Karwath's Nos. 3 and 4: just substitute bright yellow or white hackles, respectively, for the black.

Semi-palmered over the front half of the body only, and tied in a single color—black, dun, brown, or yellow—it is called a **Paysanne**, *Peasant Woman*.

FLUE BRUSH *Tied by R. G. Balogh*

In Merrie Olde England, the series of patterns known collectively as Flue Brushes might be considered reverse-tied Tricolores. Whereas Bivisibles and true Tricolores are dry flies, Flue Brushes usually are tied and fished as wet flies, but wet flies that can also be greased and fished dry. Here is the late Lynn Francis's original pattern as tied by Mick Huffer, who knew Francis and is arguably the foremost Flue Brusher alive.

Flue Brush

Hook: Standard wet-fly, sizes 8 to 14, or long-shanked wet-fly, sizes 8 and 10
Thread: Black
Tag: *Optionally, a few turns of pearl Mylar tinsel*
Tail: Usually none, but one of the Francis-tied Flue Brushes illustrating Huffer's article in *Fly-Fishing & Fly-Tying* clearly sports a tail of white hackle fibers; *some contemporary tiers add 2 strands of Krystal Flash—4 on the larger, long-shank versions*
Palmer hackle: Rooster hackle, in thirds; from bend to eye, white, olive, brown

Tying Tips

Writing in *Fly-Fishing & Fly-Tying*, Mick Huffer says you shouldn't use hackles that are too stiff, because you want them to be mobile. (So, save those Hoffman No. 1 Super Saddles for flies that need them.) Huffer also says, "The length of the hackle barbs can be up to twice the hook gape, but should not cover the hook point," because that can hinder the point's penetration or the hook's holding.

As for color variations, use your imagination. Huffer cites white-orange-and-brown and the "Italian job" in white-green-and-red. "I have even seen one tied (and catch fish!) in red, white, and blue."

Fishing Tips

"What the trout actually take the Flue Brush for, I have no idea," Huffer admits. "All I do know is that they do, and the original dressing in particular is a very good summer pattern (July, August, and into September)."

Most Brits fish wet flies three at a time, so their advice may need to be tweaked a bit for our tradition of fishing single flies. Huffer says he usually starts off by fishing Flue Brushes as high in the film as possible, "and this means greasing them up." If that doesn't produce, he fishes untreated flies deeper in the water column until he finds the feeding depth. Retrieve rates vary all the way from medium-speed hand-twist retrieves to fast, 2- or 3-foot strips. Experiment until you discover what the trout want that day.

Huffer's favorite way of fishing the Flue Brush in still water is sight-casting to moving fish in a flat calm. Under such conditions it's important that the tippet, leader, and floating fly line be undressed, so they float *in* the film, not on top of it. Once you spot a cruising fish and cast well ahead of it, "straighten the fly line and leader out and then wait—do nothing at all," Huffer advises. "When the trout shows again within a few yards of where your flies are, start to retrieve using steady, 2- to 3-foot pulls. You'll be surprised to see how far a trout will come to take a Flue Brush fished just below the surface in those conditions...."

This isn't exactly a Tricolore, or even exactly a Woolly Worm, either, but I thought it worthy of your attention and didn't know where else to pigeonhole it. I discovered this Tasmanian pattern—which looks nothing like any dragonfly pattern I've ever fished—on the Fly Anglers OnLine website (www.flyanglers online.com). The Woodard's Dragonfly on the FAOL site, as well as all the tying-sequence step models, were tied by Richard Komar, of Plano, Texas, who also graciously tied the fly shown here.

Apparently in response to some FAOL bulletin-board postings by bass fishermen on dragonflies, Alan Shepherd, of Launceston, Tasmania, responded with some trout-fishing dragonfly observations of his own, including submission of this pattern by the late Dick Woodard, who had given the pattern to David Scholes for inclusion in his book *Ripples, Runs, and Rises* (1988).

After describing a meticulous dragonfly imitation he had spent hours perfecting—which attracted another dragonfly, but not a trout—Shepherd explained the conundrum: "Dragonflies and damsels can't actually land on the water like smaller insects such as mayflies or caddis without becoming trapped." And as every waterside observer knows, trout often ignore adult dragonflies trapped in the surface film. So, how to fish dragonfly patterns?

Dick Woodard, "a creative trout angler and fly dresser in Tasmania in the 1970s," explains Shepherd, who has done extensive research into Tasmanian fly patterns, "approached the problem from an entirely different perspective. Dick concentrated on presenting his fly as an egg-laying female. He would cast it again and again to an area where a trout worked a regular beat. He would only leave the fly on the water for four or five seconds before lifting it and casting again. Dick's concept was that the arrival of his enormous fly got the trout's attention, much the same as with grasshopper fishing, although in this case there is no need to thump it down—just the size of the fly alone will announce its arrival to any trout in the area."

Woodard's Dragonfly

Hook: Standard dry-fly, size 4

Thread: Black 6/0

Tail: 2 dark green-dyed rooster saddles, hook length, cemented together at the tip

Rib: Yellow Pearsall's silk floss, half a strand, to rib the palmer hackle only

Body: 3 peacock herls, covering the rear two-thirds of the shank

Palmer hackle: Dark green-dyed rooster hackle, the barbs a gap-width long, reverse-palmered from the front of the body with the concave underside of the feather facing forward

Main hackles: 3 dry-fly rooster hackles, the barbs a gap-width-and-a-half long, in this order over the front third of the shank: dark green-dyed and red-dyed, the dull, concave side facing forward, and dark blue-dyed, the shiny, convex side facing forward

Head: Tying thread

Tying Tip

As Alan Shepherd observes, "Depending on the color of particular species in your part of the world, you may wish to change or experiment with the cock feathers used in making the Woodard's Dragonfly." There are, he notes, some 6,500 species of dragonflies in the world, including 500 or so in North America.

To help support that long tail, take two wraps of thread around the hook shank beneath the tail feathers, and put a drop of head cement on the thread wraps.

Fishing Tip

"Because trout stalk dragonflies flying erratically close to the surface," Shepherd says, "where possible, cast near a natural dragonfly. A trout may actually be lurking underneath, stalking that very fly. When your imitation fly lands, the trout may react on impulse and, before it knows what it has done, whoops!"

Now, let's meet that distinguished old British family named Palmer.

Palmer flies have been used in Britain since before the time of Izaak Walton. Classifying them isn't easy. They resemble Woolly Worms in most particulars, save for their generally shorter shank lengths and the non-requirement of palmering the hackle so the barbs angle forward. They can be and are fished singly as wet flies. But palmer flies are much more commonly fished in tandem with one or more other flies—more often in lakes, lochs, loughs, reservoirs, and concrete bowls than in streams. In the typical three-fly "cast" (that's Anglish for "leader"), palmer flies often occupy the "bob" (uppermost) or "point" (lowermost) position, or both. (The intermediate position, the "dropper," in such rigs usually is occupied by a collar-hackled wet pattern—winged or wingless.)

A palmer pattern fished as the point fly would qualify as a typical, wet Woolly Worm. Bob flies usually are drifted or skittered on the surface, so a palmered bob fly would functionally more resemble a dry or waking Woolly Worm. Tied extra large and bushy, many palmer patterns also see service as dapping flies. (Dapping, in case you don't know, is a curiously Irish and British form of fly fishing in which the conventional fly line is replaced by a 6- to 15-foot-long piece of poly floss so the wind can blow it about and keep the fly skating and dancing across the surface.)

As you may not intend to go dapping or to fish a multi-fly reservoir rig, you can always tie these British patterns American Woolly Worm-style, with the hackle barbs angled forward, and fish them in still or moving water. Some fly fishers, myself among them, think the forward-angled barbs give a pulsating action in the current and on a stripping retrieve. And no matter the specs listed in the recipes or tables, you can tie them dry or wet, to suit yourself and the way you like to fish.

CHARLES COTTON'S GREEN GRASSHOPPER

In his Part II of *The Compleat Angler*, which was added to the fifth edition of 1676, Cotton recommends for June fly fishing "also a green grasshopper; the dubbing of green and yellow wool mixed, ribbed over with green silk, and a red capon's feather over all." This doesn't much resemble the hopper patterns tied today, nor does it closely resemble the grasshoppers I usually see. Given the color and the month, I'd guess this might be a leafhopper, which it still doesn't come truly close to imitating. Nevertheless, this Grasshopper still sees some service in the British Isles, and it deserves our attention for its place in history alone.

Charles Cotton's Green Grasshopper

Hook: Light-wire dry-fly of a size appropriate to the fish
Thread: Bright green floss or thread
Body: Green and yellow dubbing, mixed
Palmer hackle: Fiery-brown (natural-red) or brown rooster
Rib: Tying thread—either leave a long tag end at the rear for ribbing, or dub and reverse-palmer from the front to the bend and rib the fly forward with the working thread

BEWL GREEN NYMPH

This creation of the British fly fisher Chris Ogbourn was listed in Taff Price's authoritative *Tying and Fishing the Nymph* (1995), where it is described as a "killing pattern...[that] works well during a hatch of green chironomids."

Bewl Green Nymph

Hook: Wide-gap wet-fly or nymph, sizes 8 and 10
Thread: Olive 6/0
Underbody: *Optionally, for weight, copper wire wrapped the full length of the shank or less*
Tail: Olive-dyed hackle fibers
Body: Dark-olive seal fur, dubbed
Palmer hackle: Olive-dyed saddle

ZULU

Of all British palmer-fly patterns, the Zulu is perhaps the one most often tied—for trout, grayling, and sea trout it can be fished wet, bobbed, or dapped. It seems to be directly derived from Thomas Barker's "black Palmer, ribbed with silver" from the mid 17th century.

Zulu

Hook: Standard wet- or dry-fly, sizes 8 to 16
Thread: Black
Tail: Red yarn, a gap-width long, or shorter
Palmer hackle: Black hen
Body: Black floss or tying thread
Rib: Oval silver tinsel

Tying Tip

Omit the tail and use a steeply tapered hackle (or tie a longer wet-fly collar up front), and the Zulu becomes the famous Irish lough pattern **Bibio**—which is actually imitative of black gnats, hawthorn flies, and other dark midges.

SOLDIER PALMER *Tied by R. G. Balogh*

But of all the British flies that are actually *named* Palmer, the Soldier Palmer is virtually ubiquitous in British fly boxes. In *Favorite Flies and Their Histories* (1892), Mary Orvis Marbury wrote that the Soldier Palmer "can boast the longest record of any fly known and used today." That is not quite true, as some other Woolly Worms and palmer flies also hark back to those described by Charles Cotton in the fifth edition (1676) of Walton's *Compleat Angler* and even back to Thomas Barker's *The Art of Angling* (1651).

Soldier Palmer

Hook: Standard wet- or dry-fly, sizes 8 to 14
Thread: Black
Tail: *Optionally, red wool*
Body: Red or orange wool
Rib: Fine gold or silver wire
Palmer hackle: Medium fiery-brown (natural red) rooster

SINGLE-STRAND SOLDIER PALMER *Tied by R. G. Balogh*

Martin Introna introduced this simplified tying of the classic Soldier Palmer in the pages of *Fly-Fishing & Fly-Tying*. It shouldn't give you much of a headache, figuring out how to adapt this fast and easy method to a lot of your Woolly Worms and other flies.

Single-Strand Soldier Palmer

Hook: Standard, 1X- or 2X-long wet- or dry-fly, sized to suit your purposes
Thread: White, black, or orange
Rib: Silver wire, tied in at the eye and lashed atop the shank—down to a point opposite the hook point or barb—then wound forward
Palmer hackle: Fiery-brown (natural red) saddle, reverse-palmered closely over the yarn from front to rear, stopping just above the hook point or barb
Body and Tail: A single strand of orange, red-orange, or red wool or other yarn, tied in at the front then laid and held atop the shank while the hackle is palmered; trim the end so the frayed tail extends to the back of the bend or slightly beyond

Tying Tips

After lashing the ribbing wire to the top of the shank, take the thread back to the eye and tie in the hackle (by the butt end) and the yarn.

After closely reverse-palmering the hackle, let the unused hackle tip dangle with hackle pliers attached while you rib the silver wire forward; tie down and clip the wire, form a head, and whip-finish. Finally, closely clip the excess hackle at the rear.

SOLDIER PALMER VARIANT *Tied by R. G. Balogh*

This even more simplified take-off on the Soldier Palmer was created by the late Phil Gee. I found the pattern as well as a good description by Gordon Watson on the web site of the Grafham Water Fly Fishing Association (www.gwffa-grafham. co.uk). In Watson's words, it san be fished "wet, dry, or damp" in still waters, usually on a short dropper in front of a Mini Muddler or other wet point fly.

Soldier Palmer Variant

Hook: Light-wire, short-shank dry-fly, sizes 10 to 22
Thread: Fluorescent-red (no. 5 in the Glo-Brite brand) floss

Tail: Separated strands of the tying floss
Body: Tying floss
Palmer hackle: Badger, "preferably from a genetic cape"
Rib: Tying floss
Head: Tying floss, clear-varnished

Tying Tips

Begin by clipping a few short lengths of floss to be used in tailing. From here on out, I am modifying the procedure outlined by Gordon Watson. Tie on at the bend and tie in the tail fibers. When dressing the body, spin the bobbin to spread and flatten the floss. Just behind the eye, tie in a palmer hackle by the butt; then take the floss back to the bend, spinning and flattening as you go. Reverse-palmer the badger hackle, beginning with two touching turns at the front. Secure the hackle at the bend with the floss and wind the floss forward (without spreading it) through the hackle in open, spiral turns. Form a neat, but "slightly bulbous" head, whip-finish, and varnish the head after picking out any trapped hackle fibers.

DOOBRY *Tied by Stan Headley*

This face-hackled palmer fly is the creation of Stan Headley, who is one of the best-known fly tiers, fishers, and guides in Scotland's Highlands and Islands. I once had the great pleasure of fishing the Orkney trout lochs with Stan Headley some 20 years ago. I distinctly recall his making me use a 16-foot leader and cast from a seated position (SOP on British waters), but I don't recall fishing this pattern. Perhaps it is a more recent creation. In any event, it has become one of the most popular palmer flies in Britain. "Dooby" is British Army slang for "thingumbob" or "thinga-majig."

Here's "Deadly Headley" on his fly: "The Doobry was an attempt to produce a fly for the brackish water of Loch Stenness in Orkney in the early 80s. At the time, good patterns for that water were Dunkeld and Zulu, and the Doobry contains elements of both. Unfortunately, it failed in its original task of becoming an essential for Stenness, but it fast became indispensable for Orcadian peat-water lochs and on almost every water in the U.K. mainland for browns and rainbows. Almost every commercial catalogue [in the U.K.] offers it for sale. A Muddler-headed version now has more followers than the original."

Doobry

Hook: Standard wet-fly, sizes 8 to 14
Thread: Black
Tail: Fluorescent fire-red wool
Body: Flat brassy-gold tinsel
Rib: Fine oval gold tinsel
Palmer hackle: Black rooster, tied in at front and reverse-palmered to the bend
Hackle collar: 2 turns of hot-orange hen, with 2 turns of slightly longer black hen in front

PEARLY GREEN PALMER

I purloined this pattern from "deadly" Stan Headley's *Trout & Salmon Flies of Scotland* (1997), an excellent book available here from Amazon.com. This one's particularly effective in waters stained by green algae or when trout are feeding on *Daphnia* "or, obviously, insect species of similar colouration." Headley usually fishes this one on intermediate or sinking lines although he reports that once, while checking to see whether his leader was tangled and his flies fouled, a 2-pound brown trout leaped out of Loch Leven and took a Pearly Green Palmer "as it hung at least 18 inches above the surface!"

Pearly Green Palmer

Hook: 1X-long, 1X-heavy nymph, sizes 10 and 12
Thread: Fluorescent lime green
Tail: Fluorescent phosphor-yellow and lime-green floss (Glo-Brite nos. 11 and 12), mixed, the tuft a gap-width long
Rib: Silver wire or very fine oval tinsel
Body: Flat pearl Mylar tinsel
Underbody: Tying thread, 2 layers
Palmer hackle: Light olive-green hen, tied in behind the eye, 2 turns wrapped in front of the body, then reverse-palmered to the bend

PADDY'S FANCY

This pattern by the late Rodger Wooley was once very popular for brown trout in Scotland, but it is not so widely known these days. However, those in the know still recognize it as a "taking" fly early and late in the season. Brits usually fish it as the bob fly (on the top dropper in a multifly rig), but I'd rather fish it as a solo wet fly.

Paddy's Fancy

Hook: Standard wet-fly, sizes 8 to 14
Thread: Black 6/0 or olive-green silk
Rib: Fine gold wire tied in at the bend
Body: Olive-green floss or (the way Wooley tied it) tying silk
Palmer hackle: Furnace, tied in by the butt at the front and reverse-palmered to the bend

Tying Tips

Select a steeply tapered hackle so the fly has a longer hackle "collar" up front.

Use the gold ribbing wire to secure the hackle at the bend and create a small tag or tip before spiraling the wire forward through the hackle, wriggling as you go to trap as few barbs as possible.

GRENADIER

Dr. Howard A. Bell, an English physician who fished and studied the insect fauna of the Blagdon and other local-area reservoirs every Friday and Saturday for more than 40 years, is considered the Skues of stillwater fly fishing. He created a number of imitative nymph patterns as well as this impressionistic nymph. Taff Price has written, "I have seen this pattern used successfully when fish were feeding on *Daphnia*. It works well at dusk during a rise to caddis and has also proved its worth when red midges were emerging." Charles Jardine, who lists it as a soft-hackle wet, says, "It can also be dressed dry." This is the palmered version shown by Robert Atkinson.

Grenadier

Hook: Standard nymph, sizes 12 to 16
Thread: White, red, or orange
Palmer hackle: Soft, webby, light-furnace hen saddle, reverse-palmered head to tail
Rib: Fine oval gold tinsel
Body: Hot-orange seal fur, seal substitute, or floss

SATSUMA SPARKLER

This Julian Davies pattern from England is representative of a host of hot, colorful, high-contrast palmer flies. Davies fishes this pattern both fast and slow, always on a floating line, and usually as the top-dropper waking fly in a multifly stillwater rig.

Satsuma Sparkler

Hook: Standard-length, up-eyed dry-fly, sizes 10 and 12; standard salmon dry-fly, in larger sizes, for larger fish
Thread: Black
Tail: Mixed snow-white and hot-orange rooster-hackle fibers, with 2 strands of bronze Krystal Flash
Body: Bronze Krystal Flash, twisted together and wrapped around the shank
Palmer hackle: Snow-white and hot-orange rooster saddles, palmered together

PEACOCK PALMER

Another pattern from Stan Headley's *Trout & Salmon Flies of Scotland*, it is by the ghillie Norman Irvine—with whom I also had the pleasure of fishing the Orkney lochs one day on my first fishing trip abroad. It is similar to, and perhaps based on, an early 20th century pattern called the Red Palmer, which risks confusion with the still-popular **Soldier Palmer** (page 102-103). Headley thinks wild trout take it for a shrimp or cased caddis. Like most British palmer flies, this is a stillwater pattern usually fished in a multifly cast, but don't be afraid to fish it singly in flowing water.

Peacock Palmer

Hook: Partridge L2A (a 1X-fine, wide-gap wet-fly), sizes 10 and 12, or SH2 (a 1X-heavy, 1X-long nymph), sizes 12 and 14
Thread: Brown
Rib: Fine flat gold tinsel, tied in at the bend and wound thround the palmer hackle in about 4 spirals
Body: One long peacock herl, tied in behind the eye and wrapped down the shank in butting turns to the bend, then back up to the eye in open turns
Palmer hackle: Medium red-brown rooster, tied in up front, 2 turns wrapped in front of the body as a collar, then reverse-palmered to the bend in about 5 or 6 turns

Tying Notes

Headley also lists a somewhat similar pattern, the **Hot-Spot Peacock Palmer**, which uses black thread, a ginger palmer hackle, a copper wire rib, and a joint of fluorescent fire-red wool separating the front and rear sections of the peacock herl body. It apparently imitates a *Gammarus* freshwater "shrimp" (amphipod) that has been parasitized by an organism that may need to attract trout or other predators to complete its life cycle.

VIC'S FAVOURITE

I don't know who Vic is or was, but you can guess he was a Brit by that "u." This pattern uses the black-edged brown body feathers from a ring-necked pheasant cock.

Vic's Favourite

Hook: Heavy-wire wet-fly or nymph, sizes 10 and 12
Thread: Black 6/0
Tail: Fairly thick bunch of fibers from a black-edged cock pheasant body feathers
Palmer hackle: Fiery-brown rooster, tied in behind the eye (leaving room for the face hackle and thread head), and reverse-palmered over the dubbed body to the bend
Rib: Gold wire, used to tie down the palmer hackle and to rib the fly
Body: Medium- or dark-olive seal's fur or substitute, dubbed
Face hackle: 2 turns of black-edged brown body feather from a cock pheasant, tied in after ribbing through the palmer hackle

ALLIE HARDY

I found this Alastair Jamieson pattern in Headley's pattern book. Although "Shetland patterns generally tend towards the brash side of garish," Headley says, he notes that this pattern "is distinctly understated." Like many patterns featuring olive, green, or yellow, it is taken well by trout feeding on *Daphnia*.

Allie Hardy

Hook: Standard or heavy wet-fly, sizes 10 and 12
Thread: Olive 6/0
Tail: Fluorescent phosphor-yellow floss (no. 11 Glo-Brite, if you can find it), the tuft a gap-width long
Palmer hackle: Fiery-brown and olive rooster hackles, tied in behind the eye—2 turns each in front of the body and then reverse-palmered back to the bend
Rib: Gold wire
Body: Fiery-brown and dark-olive seal, mixed and dubbed

SNATCHER *Tied by Sir Kevin Moss*

This is a relatively new pattern from Sir Kevin Moss, and is commercially available from just a few places in the U.K., principally his own Glen of Rothes Trout Fishery (www.morayflyfishing.co.uk). Sir Kevin, a fulltime fly-fishing instructor, guide, and professional fly tier, lives in Lossiemouth, Morayshire, Scotland, beside the River Spey and Findhorn Bay.

A series rather than a single pattern, the Snatcher is identified by dominant color (red, black, claret) or by the traditional British pattern (Soldier Palmer, Kate McLaren, and so on) on which it's based. Only the colors vary with the pattern. Below, I have listed the **Claret Snatcher**. Substitute red for claret and fiery brown (natural red) for black to tie a **Soldier Palmer Snatcher**. The **Black Snatcher** has a black body and brown or fiery-brown palmer hackle; the **Kat** Snatcher is all black, but for the pearl rib.

Snatcher

Hook:	Kamasan B100G (a 1X-short, wide plated scud) or B110 (a 1X-short, gape, scud/grub/larva; *rough eq Daiichi 1130, Mustad 80250, TM 2487; sizes 10 to 14*
Thread:	Black 6/0
Rib:	Pearl Lurex, a flat Mylar tinsel, 1/:
Body:	Claret yarn or dubbing
Palmer hackle:	Black saddle, tied in by the butt be and reverse-palmered to the rear
Horns:	2 jungle cock nails, more than a gap-width long, splayed in a Vee; *when Sir Kevin ties Snatchers for sale, he uses red goose biots*
Head:	Tying thread, rather large, coated with head cement or clear nail polish

Fishing Note

Designed for all "game fish" (meaning trout, sea trout, salmon, and grayling), Snatchers are usually fished subsurface, "as the point fly or on the dropper in a team of two or three flies. A lot would depend on the weather as to which way to fish to fish them." On our side of the pond, we'd probably fish them as single wet flies, on the swing, or on a twitching retrieve, come rain or come shine.

WICKHAM'S SPIDER

I found this palmered bead-headed adaptation of Wickham's Fancy on the Diptera web site (www.diptera.co.uk). Also known as the **Wingless Wickham's**, the fly can be tied in a variety of colors, by varying the tail fibers and palmer hackle: grizzly, red-dyed game bird, and so on. I am listing the "natural" pattern

Wickham's Spider

Hook:	Kamasan B170, a 1X-strong wet-fly or nymph, sizes 10 and 12
Head:	2- or 3-mm gold bead
Thread:	Black 6/0
Tail:	Ginger hackle fibers, as long as the hook
Palmer hackle:	Brown hen or brown-dyed grizzly saddle, tied in up front and reverse-palmered from front to rear
Rib:	Fine gold wire
Body:	Gold holographic or flat tinsel

CACTUS CLUSTER

The English company Fulling Mill makes a series of dry flies/emergers it calls Cactus Clusters. The last catalog I saw listed four colors (oops, "colours")—black, olive, orange, and red—but in my mind's eye I can also see green, pearly white, purple, and a variety of other colors and color combinations. Here's the near-nothing recipe for the **Orange Cactus Cluster**.

Cactus Cluster

Hook:	Standard or 1X-long dry fly, sizes 10 or 12
Thread:	Orange or red
Body:	Orange Cactus Chenille or other tinsel chenille
Palmer hackle:	Orange, or orange-dyed grizzly, hackle

NIGHTINGALE FLY

I found this pattern in *Bob Church's Guide to New Fly Patterns* (1993), where it was selected by the professional fly-tier (and first captain of the English Ladies' International Fly-fishing Team) Jeanette Taylor, who got it from a Mr. Nightingale of Southport, England.

Nightingale Fly

Hook: Kamasan B175 or other 1X-long dry-fly, sizes 10 to 14
Thread: Black
Palmer hackle: Badger rooster, tied in up front and reverse-palmered to the bend
Tail: Fluorescent-yellow or lime-green yarn
Body: Fluorescent-yellow or lime-green yarn, to match the tail
Rib: Fine oval silver tinsel, spiraled through the palmer hackle
Collar: Badger rooster hackle, a size larger than the palmer hackle
Head: Tying thread, clear-varnished

BRUISER

This Irish trout and sea-trout pattern is one of the few blue flies you are likely to see anywhere. It is from the late T. C. Kingsmill Moore (1893–1979) who served for many years as a justice on the Irish High Court and Supreme Court. Far less well known than his popular Bumble series of flies, the Bruiser is still fished in Ireland and far northern and western parts of Scotland. I found it in Stan Headley's *Trout & Salmon Flies of Scotland* (1997). Although I have listed the blue hues precisely as specified, I had to make some chromatic substitutions, approximations, or outright guesses to tie the sample.

Bruiser

Hook: 2X-fine or 3X-strong (*I compromised and used a standard*) wet-fly, sizes 8 to 12
Thread: Black
Tail: Flax-blue wool tag
Rib: Fine oval silver tinsel
Body: Gentian-blue wool
Palmer hackle: Gentian-blue and natural-black rooster hackles, tied in behind the eye and reverse-palmered together back to the bend

REDDISH PALMER

While not of British pedigree, this dry fly is very much in the British tradition of palmer flies. This Soldier-like pattern from the 30th-anniversary edition of *FFF's Patterns of the Masters* is by Lucie Simanova, the then-10-year-old daughter of Jan Siman, whose innovative Dubbing Brushes and Softdubs (the former twisted on fine wire; the latter, on tying thread) ought to be much better known in North America. (www.siman.cz)

Reddish Palmer

Hook: Standard or 1X-fine dry-fly, sizes 8 to 14
Thread: Brown or red
Body: Reddish Brown (05) squirrel Softdub, standard size
Palmer hackle: Brown or orange-brown Hoffman grizzly saddle

Fishing Tip

Lucie and her dad say you should cast this fly onto bankside grasses and then hop it into the water. Or you can lightly drop it "right on the head" of a sighted fish.

Some British and Other Palmer-Fly Patterns to Prime the Creative Pump

D, dry; W, wet; HF, hackle fibers; HP(s), hackle point(s)

Name of Pattern	Hook	Thread	Tail	Body	Palmer Hackle	Other
Annabelle (Charles Jardine)	W: 10-16	Yellow	Fluorescent-chartreuse floss	Flat gold tinsel	Fiery-brown rooster	*Rib:* Fine gold wire; *Hackle collar:* Grizzly
Badger Hackle (1) (T. J. Hanna)	D: 10-16	Black	Ginger rooster HF	Flat silver tinsel	Badger rooster	*Face hackle, optional:* White rooster
Badger Hackle (2) (T. J. Hanna)	D: 14-16	Black	Badger or black HF	Black floss	Badger rooster	none
Badger Hackle (3)	D: 10-16	Black	Badger HF	Peacock herl	Badger rooster	none
Badger Hackle (4)	D: 12-18	Black	Badger hackle points	Light-gray wool	Badger rooster	*Rib:* Silver
Badger Hackle (5)	D: 10-14	Black	Scarlet or badger HF	Red or yellow wool or floss	Badger rooster	none
Black Robin (H. Westmoreland)	D: 6-8	Black	none	Thread	Black rooster, thick, & trimmed to a cylindrical, "bottle brush" shape	*Tag:* Fine flat gold tinsel
Black-Hackled Dry Fly	D: 15	Black	none	Black ostrich herl	Black rooster, clipped short except at collar	*Rib:* Fine gold wire
Blue Badger [also Black, Red, etc., Badger]	D: 14-16	Black	none	Blue [black, red, etc.] floss; or flat silver or gold tinsel	Badger rooster	*Rib:* Fine silver or gold wire
Blue-Tag Red Palmer (Stan Headley)	W: 10-12	Scarlet	Cambridge-blue [aka Carolina- or Columbia-blue] floss or yarn	Red seal fur or substitute	Ginger	*Rib:* Oval gold tinsel
Blue Upright (R. S. Austin)	D: 15-17	Purple or cream	Dark-blue dun rooster HF, long	Stripped peacock herl, dyed or naturally brown	Dark-blue dun rooster	none
Bostwick	W: 10-12	Black	Barred mandarin HF	Flat silver tinsel	Brown & grizzly hen, mixed	none
Bottle Brush	W: 4-10	Black	none	Brown fur dubbing	Stiff brown rooster; or brown & grizzly rooster, mixed	none
Brown Palmer (A. Ronalds)	D: 6 (XL Terrestr.)	Brown	none	Mulberry wool, dubbed	Brown hen, soft	none
Brunton's Fancy (Dr. J. Brunton)	D: 12-14	Black	Scarlet HF	Peacock herl	Badger rooster	none
Clan Chief (Capt. John Kennedy)	W: 10-12	Black	Red & yellow floss	Black fur dubbing	Crimson & black rooster, together	*Rib:* Oval silver tinsel
Claret Bumble Ireland (T.C. Kingsmill Moore)	W: 10-12	Claret	Golden-pheasant tippets	Claret seal fur or substitute	Claret & black rooster, together	*Rib:* Oval gold tinsel
Claret Hackle Australia (Howard Joseland)	D or W			Claret fur	Badger	
Dyson	D: 12-14	Black	Red HF	Peacock herl	Furnace or badger rooster	*Rib:* Silver
Eildon Shrimp Australia	W: 10-12	Black or brown	none	Flat gold tinsel (rear half) & claret wool (front)	Brown over rear, black over front—both oversize, soft hen	none
Eric's Beetle (Eric H. Turner)	W: 10-12	Brown or black	none	Peacock herl over yellow wool	Blackbird feather, soft, from base of wing	*Tag:* Yellow wool *Rib:* Tying thread
Feather Duster	D: 12-14	Black	none	Dubbing blend: light-blue seal or substitute blue-gray rabbit	Blue dun rooster, very heavy	none
Fiery Grenadier (Dr. Howard Bell)	W: 10-14	White	Fluorescent hot-orange floss or yarn	Hot-orange seal or substitute dubbing	Natural red game rooster	*Rib:* Gold wire
Fluorescent-Red Palmer	W: 10-14	Red	Fluorescent red-dyed hair	Fluorescent-red seal or substitute	Furnace rooster	*Rib:* Fine gold wire

Name of Pattern	Hook	Thread	Tail	Body	Palmer Hackle	Other
Furnace and Copper Canada	W: 8-14	Black or brown	Furnace HF	Copper tinsel	Furnace hen	none
Furnace Hackle	D: 12-14	Black	none	Orange floss	Furnace rooster	*Tag:* Flat gold tinsel
Golden Badger	D: 8-14	Black or brown	2 long golden-badger hackle points	none	Golden-badger rooster, heavy	none
Grey Palmer	D: 10-16	Black	none	Any: *peacock herl; gray, orange, or red fur dubbing; blue, gray, green, red, or yellow floss; black thread; flat or embossed gold or silver tinsel; green or purple wool; etc.*	Dark or light grizzly rooster	none
Grizzly Palmer	D: 12-14	Black	Scarlet HF	Blue floss or yarn	Grizzly rooster	*Rib:* Oval or flat gold tinsel
Hackle Olive Quill (F. M. Halford)	D: 15-16	Black or olive	Olive-dyed HF	Yellow-dyed peacock quill	Pale silvery-dun rooster, sparse	*Tag:* Silver
Hill's Floater (C. A. Hill)	D: 12-14	Black	Scarlet HF	Yellow chenille	Grizzly rooster	none
Honey Dun Bumble (T. C. Kingsmill Moore)	W: 12-14	Black or brown	none	Orange or salmon floss	Honey dun	none
Loch Ordie J. Yorsten & W. S. Sinclair	W: 10-12	Black	none	Tying thread	Brown or furnace hen hackles (or both), or game bird body feathers	none
Machair Claret (Capt. John Kennedy)	W: 10-12	Black	Golden-pheasant tippets	2 sections: black & claret floss	Black rooster	*Rib:* Gold wire
Maxwell Reel	D: 12-14	Brown	Rusty-dun HF	Rust-brown wool	Rusty-dun rooster	*Rib:* Gold fine tinsel
Mills's Ripple (William Mills)	D: 12-14	Red or black	Red HF	Gray wool	Grizzly	*Rib:* Red floss or thread
Oakham Orange	W: 10-14	Hot-orange	Fluorescent-orange floss	Flat gold tinsel	Hot-orange rooster	*Rib:* Fine gold wire
Oakham Orange (Pearl) (Dave Shipman)	W: 10-14	Hot-orange	Fluorescent-orange floss	Pearl Lurex or Mylar tinsel	Hot-orange rooster	*Rib:* Fine gold wire
Olive Bumble (T. C. Kingsmill Moore)	W: 10-12	Yellow	Golden-pheasant tippets	Golden-olive seal fur or substitute	Olive hen	*Rib:* Gold Lurex or Mylar tinsel
Orange and Gold	D: 12-14	Brown or orange	none	Flat gold Lurex or Mylar tinsel	Orange-dyed rooster	none
Palmer Grey	D: 12-14	Black	none	Gray wool	Badger rooster	*Rib:* Gold tinsel
Palmer Grizzle	D: 10-14	Black	none	Black or brown wool	Brown & grizzly rooster, mixed	*Rib:* Gold tinsel
Paul Lake Canada	W: 8-10	Black or brown	Long pheasant rump HF	Fluorescent-green wool	Brown hen	*Back:* Pheasant fibers from tail, pulled over the body; *Rib:* Copper wire over all, 5 turns
Pearly Wickham (Steve Parton & Steve Newsome)	W: 10-14	White	Red game-rooster HF	Pearl Flashabou or similar	Light-red game bird	*Rib:* Fine silver wire
Pool Hackle	W: 16	Black or brown	Soft brown HF	Thread	Soft, bright-brown hen	none
Rash Worm	W: 10-12	Black	Gray HF	Wool: white over aft 3/4, brown over front 1/4	Gray hen	*Rib:* Black thread
Red and White Canada	W: 6-8	Red or black	Red wool tag	Red wool	Red & white hen, mixed; heavy in the collar	*Rib:* Oval silver tinsel
Red-Arsed Wickham	W: 10-14	Brown	Fluorescent-red floss	Flat gold tinsel	Light-red game bird	*Rib:* Fine gold wire
Red-bodied Ashy	D: 12-16	Brown or red	none	Red yarn	Brown rooster	none

Name of Pattern	Hook	Thread	Tail	Body	Palmer Hackle	Other
Red Fly (R. S. Austin)	D: 15-17	Brown	none	Olive floss over thread base	Brown hen	*Rib:* Peacock quill
Red Tag	W: 8-12	Black	Scarlet wool tag	Peacock herl	Brown hen	none
Red Tag Palmer	D: 12-14	Black or red	none	Bronze peacock herl	Red (fiery-brown) rooster	*Tag:* Gold or silver tinsel
Relish New Zealand	D:10-14	Black	none	Dark-claret seal fur, dubbed	Brown rooster	*Rib:* Gold wire
Rough Bumble [grayling]	D/W: 12-20	Black	none	Yellow floss	Blue hen	Peacock herl & red floss or thread
Ruby Bumble [grayling]	D/W: 12-20	Black	none	Claret floss	Pale blue dun	*Rib:* Peacock herl
Scarlet Butcher	D: 10-12	Red or black	Red HF	Peacock herl	Red rooster	none
Sedge Fly (Maj. Oliver Kite)	D: 12-14	Dark-brown	none	Pheasant tail fibers, twisted & wrapped around thread	Dark-brown rooster	none
Sgt. James	D: 12-14	Brown	3 olive-brown HF	Peacock herl, green	Brown hen, with a grouse face	*Tag:* Gold
Silver Twist	D: 12-14	Black	none	Blueish fur dubbing	Medium blue-dun hen	*Rib:* Silver twist (like Krystal Flash)
Silver Twist [grayling]	D/W: 12-20	Black	none	Mole fur dubbing	Blue dun	*Rib:* Round silver twist
Spencer	D: 12-14	Black	Yellow wool tag	Gray fur dubbing	Gray badger hen	*Tag & Rib:* Gold tinsel
Steel Blue (Rodger Wooley)	W: 12-14 D: 13-14 D/W:12-20, for grayling	Black	none	Peacock herl; thin on dry fly; *alternatively,* peach or salmon floss	W: Grizzly or badger hen; D: Bluish-tinged grizzly rooster, sparse	*Tag:* 3 turns of orange floss or tying thread *Rib:* Gold wire
Straddle Bug (G. E. M. Skues)	D: 11	Black or brown	Brown mallard HF	Raffia	Ginger rooster	*Rib:* Fine gold wire
Toffee-Paper Wickham (John Ielden)	W: 10-14	Brown	none	Green Mylar tinsel	Red game bird	*Rib:* Fine green wire
Vindaloo	10-14	Hot-orange	Hot orange-dyed golden pheasant tippets	Fluorescent-scarlet seal-fur substitute	Orange-dyed partridge breast	*Rib:* Fine gold wire
Welsh Blue Palmer [sea trout]	W: 2-12	Black	Golden pheasant crest	Peacock herl	Blue dun hen	*Tag & Rib:* Flat silver tinsel
Whiskers	D: 12-14	Black or brown	Coch-y-bonddhu HF	Peacock herl	Coch-y-bonddhu	*Tag:* Gold
White Witch	W: 10-12	White or black	none	Peacock herl	White	*Tag & Rib:* Silver wire; *Tip:* Red floss
White Witch [grayling]	D/W: 12-20	White or black	none	Peacock herl	White	*Tag & Rib:* Silver wire
Yates's Standby Africa	W: 10-16	Black	none	Peacock herl	Furnace hen	*Rib:* Gold wire or tinsel
Yellow Palmer	D: 12-14	Black	Yellow HF	Yellow fur dubbing	Yellow-dyed badger	none
Yellow Peril Canada	D: 6-8	Black or red	Red & yellow HF	Yellow wool or fur dubbing	Red & yellow, mixed, with a full collar	*Rib:* Gold tinsel
Zwars Geni Africa	D: 12-18	Std/1XS Black	Golden pheasant tippets	Peacock Herl	Brown or furnace rooster	*Rib, optional:* Gold wire or fine flat tinsel
Zulu Red	W: 10-14	Black	Scarlet wool tag	Peacock herl	Black hen, sparse	*Rib:* Scarlet floss

WOOLLY BUGGERS

Rocky Mountain fly fishers have always had their favorite big-fish flies—think of "the Bunyan Bug No. 2 Yellow Stone Fly," the Norman Means pattern immortalized by Norman Maclean in *A River Runs Through It*. However individual and varied such choices may be, in the second half of the 20th century, and into the 21st, three big-fish patterns have predominated out West: first, the **Woolly Worm**, thanks to Don Martinez's championing of a contemporary modification of an ancient pattern; next, the **Muddler Minnow**, Don Gapen's versatile sculpin imitation that could also pass for a grasshopper or a *Pteronarcys* nymph; and now, the **Woolly Bugger**, thanks in part to the catchy name given it by a seven-year-old named Julie Blessing and to Barry Beck's and Doug Swisher's steadfast promotion of the pattern.

Oddly, none of these patterns is native to the West, each having migrated to Rocky Mountain streams and lakes from outside the region: the Ozarks, the North Woods, and Pennsylvania, respectively. No matter, because each has become ubiquitous across North America and most of the continents of the world (Antarctica notably excepted).

The Woolly Bugger has become so omnipresent a pattern, it seems that it has been around forever. In some respects, it has been. In *Fish Flies, Volume Two* (1995), Terry Hellekson wrote, "The Woolly Bugger has been like a person without a country, left wandering around for years. In this case, without a name—but a good one was finally found and stuck. As you can see, the Woolly Bugger is simply a variation of the Woolly Worm...."

Countless tiers have been playing around with variations for many generations and no one or one hundred fly tiers can begin to take credit for it.

As Kevin Tracewski noted in the March/April 1995 issue of *Flytying*, "'Woolly Bugger' better defines a style of fly than a specific pattern."

That hasn't stopped people from trying to establish the Woolly Bugger's paternity. On his web site (www.eflytying.com), Mike Hogue insists the Bugger is a Missouri pattern that "dates back at least to the 1920s and perhaps even to the

Russell Blessing at the vise, tying a Woolly Bugger.
Russell W. Blessing photo

1890s," confusing it, I think, with the Woolly Worm. On its web pages, the Raging River Hook and Feather Company erroneously attributes the Bugger to Doug Swisher, a Montanan who was an early devotee of the pattern. Because of all his magazine articles and memorable photos featuring a Woolly Bugger in the company of big fish and his wife, Cathy, Barry Beck is mistakenly thought by many to be the Bugger's daddy. But like Don Martinez with the Woolly Worm, Beck is only the Woolly Bugger's godfather.

Credit the Woolly Bugger as we know it today to the account of Russell C. Blessing, of Harrisburg, Pennsylvania, who devised the Woolly Bugger not as the leech imitation so many consider it to be, but to imitate the hellgrammite, the larva of the dobsonfly. Blessing says that he had spent years, experimenting with hellgrammite patterns.

Russell Blessing told the whole story in "The Birth of the Bugger," in the March/April 1989 issue of *Flyfishing* magazine. According to Blessing, the Woolly Bugger is rooted in his youthful fascination with hellgrammites. "Considering the effectiveness of the hellgrammite, particularly for smallmouth bass and rock bass, or 'redeyes,'" he wrote, "it was little wonder that I attempted to imitate these larvae shortly after I started tying flies in the winter of 1962–63." Those first hellgrammites had bodies of muskrat fur or variegated chenille, with a palmered black hackle trimmed to stubble length. "These imitations caught trout and bass," he remembered, "as well as other species."

The real turning point came in the mid 1960s, when Blessing read a magazine article about a chenille-bodied, marabou-tailed bass pattern called the **Blossom Fly**.[1] He didn't save the magazine article and couldn't remember who first tied or popularized the Blossom.[2] He wrote that he recalled "names like Lemon Blossom and Blackberry Blossom, etc. My favorite one was black." He then quoted an entry from his fishing diary, made on March 31, 1967, on the Little Lehigh River:

"Lemon and Blackberry Blossom flies saved the day. Expected short hits on these huge flies, but was amazed at how even 9-inch and 10-inch trout can engulf these huge lures. Natural downstream drift worked best except when an across-stream retrieve at footbridge produced a 15-inch brown and a 16-inch rainbow. Natural type nymphs non-productive today."

By summer's end, his experiments to develop a hellgrammite pattern with "more action or breathing effect" had produced the fly we all now know as the Woolly Bugger. "I hackled a Blossom or put a marabou tail on a Woolly Worm and came up with something that was not at all complicated." Although he had intended to trim the hackle as he had with his earlier hellgrammite imitations, Blessing said the fly "looked so ugly and undulating when breathed on that I decided to leave it alone." Blessing admits he never fished his new pattern in the presence of one of his Pennsylvania fishing partners, the imperious Vince Marinaro, "who called the flies 'Woolly Boogers.'"

"I give Barry Beck all the credit for remembering where he first saw this fly, and also for promoting it," Blessing wrote. He introduced Barry Beck to the Woolly Bugger early one August morning in 1967 on Pennsylvania's Little Lehigh River. When shown his first Woolly Bugger, Beck wrote many years later (*The Fly Fisherman*, May 1984), "I strained to keep from laughing." After he saw the way the Bugger caught fish, Barry Beck was never again tempted to laugh at Russ Blessing's "ugly" fly. Beck took the Woolly Bugger into the western frontier on his first trip to Montana. "I tied several dozen for him in exchange for an old 8-foot Paul Young bamboo rod," Blessing wrote. "This rod was the only material benefit I've ever received from the Bugger."

So much for fly-fishing fame and fortune.

Despite Russell Blessing's having tied it as a hellgrammite, most fly fishers consider the Woolly Bugger to be a leech, and it *is* is one heck of a leech pattern. I suppose it even passes muster as a hellgrammite, despite the presence of that long marabou tail (hellgrammites don't have tails). But neither leeches nor hellgrammites swim the way most anglers fish it, streamer-style. And those who fish Woolly Buggers like streamers have plenty of evidence that fish take them for minnows and other baitfish. I suspect a tadpole-hunting fish might take a Bugger, too. In salt water, a large, rapidly-fished Woolly Bugger of appropriate color probably fools more than a few fish into thinking it's a squid.

To imitate baitfish, light colors are the ticket. When he wants to imitate baitfish, the aforementioned Kevin Tracewski says, "White or gold flies tied with a body of Antron instead of the standard chenille seem to work best; particularly when a soft red, black, or yellow hackle is palmered over the body." He says that baitfish Buggers work almost anywhere, "from a small brook to the ocean. In my area, landlocked salmon in the tail waters of hydroelectric dams are particularly vulnerable to these flies fished down and across with a strip-tease retrieve." He also notes that he often uses grizzly-palmered yellow Buggers, "particularly in salt water when fishing for mackerel or striped bass."

Still, I have a suspicion—one almost strong enough to be called a theory—that trout, bass, and other fish often take the Woolly Bugger for a fleeing crayfish. Notwithstanding such reddish-brown patterns as the Henrys Lake Leech, and even paler patterns, most leech-imitating anglers tie their Woolly Buggers in dark colors. To imitate crayfish, brown, olive, gray, orange, and dark red are your best bets.

Whether the Bugger should be called a realistic or impressionistic imitation, a suggestive pattern, or a broad-spectrum attractor, I'm not sure. That it's an almost universally effective fish-catching pattern is certain. The Woolly Bugger has become to fly fishing what the red-and-white striped Daredevle spoon is to plug casting and spin fishing: a lure that can be fished almost anywhere, for almost anything, almost any way. However and wherever you fish it, it will usually catch fish. More often than not, more and bigger fish.

---

[1] Substitute a thick clump of long hackle fibers for marabou in the tail and you get a **Panfish Tube Fly** as featured in "Big Jim" Hester's Chesapeake Fly & Bait Company's catalog (www.chesapeakefly.com).

[2] Since then, Blessing has assigned paternity of the Blossom Fly to Mark Sosin, as do Lefty Kreh and others in good position to know. (Fly fishers from Oklahoma to Missouri fished a similar pattern, the **Ozark Leech**—a marabou-tailed, chenille-bodied, tinsel-ribbed fly tied in black, brown, olive, or gray.)

8. Tying Woolly Buggers

These days, as we shall soon see, tiers use many different materials and techniques in tying Woolly Buggers. Wanting to confirm the point of departure, I decided to contact Russell Blessing, to find out how he ties Woolly Buggers. Here's the gist of what he told me.

Russell Blessing's Original Woolly Bugger *Tied by Russell Blessing*

Except for that long, full marabou tail, the Woolly Bugger looks much like a Woolly Worm. The only other differences are, the Bugger's hackle is palmered more closely and the barbs need not angle forward. On this last point, Buggers can be, and are, tied both ways, but they are more often hackled conventionally, with the barbs angled toward the rear.

A grade 2 rooster saddle has become pretty standard, but I know tiers who use the stiffest dry-fly hackle they can find, and others who use hen saddles that are webby enough for soft-hackle wet flies. Which feather to use depends on how you fish, where you fish, and what you fish for.

Russ Blessing told me he also ties brown and gray Buggers, and, "I've fooled around a bit with white." He also admitted to using fluorescent chartreuse chenille on occasion. When I asked whether he ever used tinsel chenille, he said, "Not much."

Russ Blessing says that when he isn't fishing his standard Woolly Buggers, he likes to fish Woolly Worms to imitate caterpillars and cased caddis larvae and Gary LaFontaine's partridge-bodied Cased Caddis and Sparkle Pupa, but mostly he fishes hatch-matching patterns: Quill Gordon, Iron Quill, Gray Fox, March Brown, and all the other insects found along Pennsylvania's trout and smallmouth streams. Remember, the Woolly Bugger was born out of assiduous experimentation and field testing to develop a hellgrammite imitation.

Russell Blessing's Original Woolly Bugger

Hook: 4X-long streamer, sizes 4 to 14; "In smaller sizes," Blessing says, "I sometimes use standard-length hooks to imitate caddis and fish fly larvae"
Thread: Black 6/0
Tail: Black marabou, tied full and as long as the shank
Body: Dark-olive chenille, size to suit the hook
Hackle: Black grade 2 or lesser rooster saddle hackle, palmered over the entire length of the body
Head: Tying thread, waxed

Tying Steps   *(Photos by Peter Frailey)*

Because some of the steps are similar or identical, you might want to review the Woolly Worm tying steps on pages 13-14. In the photo sequence that follows, Peter Frailey substituted white thread to make the various materials easier to see. In the last step, he used black thread to build up the head.

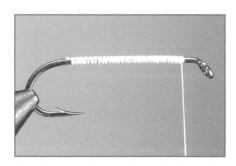

Step 1: Tie on behind the eye.[1] *Optionally, wrap a thread base to the bend and return the thread to the eye in open spirals.*

[1] *(Note: If I want to use a wire underbody for weight—something neither Blessing nor I do very often, but most tiers do—I next wrap a thread base down to the rear or about the midpoint of the shank, depending on where I want the weight. I then tie in lead or, more likely, nontoxic lead-substitute wire. After wrapping the wire forward, I overwrap the wire by taking the thread to the front and back again, building a sloping ramp of thread aft of the wire, finish up front, and sometimes even coat the thread-wrapped wire with cement before proceeding to what would otherwise be the second step.)*

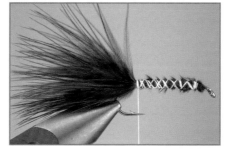

Step 2: Lay the marabou along the top of the hook shank and trap the end. Clip the marabou butt or butts just behind the eye. *(If the shank has been wrapped with lead wire, tie in the marabou behind the wire, using the thickness of the thread-wrapped tail butt to keep the underbody reasonably uniform in diameter.)* Hook-length is about right for the tail, but I sometimes make them a bit longer; on the water, I can always shorten a long tail by pinching—not cutting—the marabou to the length I want, which some days may be a stubby bobtail. Wind the thread down the shank to the bend, securing the marabou to the hook as a smooth underbody.

Step 3: As with the Woolly Worm, strip at least a quarter-inch of fuzz off the string core from one end of the chenille by pinching and pulling with the nails of your thumb and forefinger.

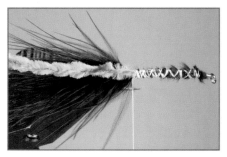

Step 4: Tie in the chenille by the stripped core immediately ahead of the tail, leaving the rest of the chenille dangling over the marabou tail.

Step 5: Prepare a long saddle hackle by stroking the barbs perpendicular to the central rib and clipping the tip square across, leaving a small triangle of barbs for tying in.

Step 6: Tie in the saddle hackle by the tip, glossy, convex side up. Take the thread back up the shank to the eye.

Step 7: Take the first wrap of chenille behind the hackle.

Step 8: Wrap the chenille body all the way forward, tie down, and clip the excess.

Step 9: Wind the hackle forward over the body in close, evenly spaced turns. Tie down the hackle and clip the excess.

Step 10: Wax the thread well (unless it's already prewaxed) and build a neat, smooth head with the tying thread, whip-finish, and clip the thread close. When Blessing hopes for larger fish, or is fishing in waters where the Bugger is going to take a beating, he will coat the head—more often with cheap, hard-finish fingernail polish than head cement.

These days, tiers are apt to use other colors, wrap lead wire on the shank, and add flash materials, bead or cone heads, or beadchain or dumbbell eyes. One writer erroneously reported that Russell Blessing "adds a bead head to almost all of his Woolly Buggers today." Blessing recently told me that, "although I use bead heads, I still prefer the original unweighted fly. I either fish it unweighted or with various sizes of shot on the leader at the fly's head. I've also carried some beads in the 1/8-, 5/32-, and 5/16-inch sizes and slipped them onto the tippet." (It cheered me to hear that Russell

Blessing fishes his Buggers the way I often fish mine.) "It works fine," he added, "and you do not need to carry as many different-size beadhead Buggers. In other words, the fly is more versatile."

Although he doesn't use the original Blessing dressing, Skip Morris has a particularly lucid step-by-step guide to tying a **White-and-Grizzly Woolly Bugger** (thanks in great part to his photos and to Richard Bunse's illustrations) in his *Fly Tying Made Clear and Simple: An Easy-to-Follow All-Color Guide* (Portland, OR: Frank Amato, 1992).

WOOLLY BUGGER BASICS

(Photos by Peter Frailey)

So we won't have to keep repeating dimensions and specifications in the tying recipes that follow, let's agree on some standards.

Hook

Shank lengths run from standard to more than 6X-long. Most tiers use heavy-wire hooks, but some use standard-diameter hooks, and a few even use fine-wire hooks for easier penetration. Turned-down eyes are fairly standard, but several patterns call for straight-eye streamer or saltwater hooks, and steelhead and salmon Buggers usually are tied on salmon hooks with turned-up looped eyes. Sizes from 2 to 10 are most common, but you will find larger and smaller Buggers.

The Woolly Bugger offers creative tiers even more hook options than the Woolly Worm. Some patterns require certain hooks, but most give you creative leeway in selecting different lengths, weights, and styles.

If you want to imitate the vertical, undulating swimming action of a leech, you should probably tie your Buggers on those bent-up-shank swimming-nymph hooks. On the other hand, some tiers like to use stonefly-nymph hooks whose shanks are bent down toward the point. In truth, hook selection seldom is critical in Woolly Buggers.

Let me repeat what I said in the first part of this book: "When the recipe I found specified a particular hook, I listed it. But don't waste your tying and fishing time, running all over the county, trying to find something like a Kamasan 170. Use a close equivalent. Quite a few hook-equivalent charts are posted on tiers' web sites; find them by doing a search using Google (www.google.com) or another Internet search engine. What they lack in comprehensiveness they make up for by being free. But if you tie a lot of flies, you should invest in a copy of Bill Schmidt's excellent *Hooks for the Fly: A Tier's Reference Guide* (Stackpole Books, 2000). In a pinch, use your imagination."

Thread

Unless the pattern requires, or the originator calls for, a different size, we'll assume 6/0 thread, waxed or unwaxed as you prefer. Colors pretty much run the gamut, so will usually be specified.

Tail

Marabou is the gold standard. Some tiers use whole plumes; others build up the tail by tying in small clumps of fluffy marabou barbs. Suit yourself. Some tiers prefer full, heavy tails that look like old-fashioned shaving brushes when they are dry; others go for a leaner look. *Rule of thumb:* Wet the marabou a little before or as you tie it in; it's a lot easier to handle when wet, and you can better see how the fly will look in the water.

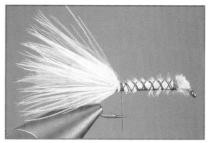

This is the way a Woolly Bugger's dry marabou tail looks in the vise—big and fluffy, like a featherduster.

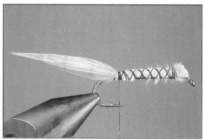

But, wetted down, this is the way it looks to a fish. It's more manageable in the tying as well.

The Bugger's tail is usually about as long as the hook. Marabou tails that are much longer tend to foul the hook when cast. If you want a very long tail, you can minimize if not altogether prevent the fouling by (1) First, tie in a "support platform: for the limp marabou (either a short loop of monofilament that sticks out over the bend or, as A. K. Best recommends, a small, slightly shorter, color-matching clump of bucktail, bear, or squirrel hair). Also you can tie a strand or two of Flashabou or Krystal Flash on either side of the marabou, which helps keep the wet marabou atop that platform. (2) take the first wrap of the body material under the tail. (3) Cut down on the number of false casts you make. (4) Slow down your casting stroke and make sure you deliver the power gradually and smoothly. (5) Use two or more of the above in combination.

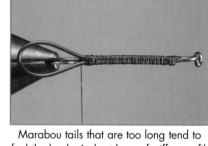

Marabou tails that are too long tend to foul the hook. A short loop of stiff monofilament can help solve the problem.

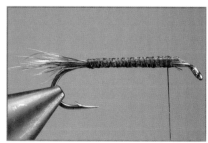

Another tail-support option for extra-long tails is a short, color-matching clump of bucktail or other hair.

You can adjust the length of the marabou when you are tying it in, or you can tie it long and adjust the length when you are done; the result will be pretty much the same. Just don't cut marabou to length; *pinch* it off with your thumb nail. Pinched marabou looks and moves better than cut marabou. More drastic solution for ultra-long-tailed Buggers: Substitute another tailing material for the marabou (eg, ostrich herl, natural or artificial hair, or stiffer feathers).

Extra material—usually peacock sword or herl, Flashabou, Krystal Flash, or similar stuff—can be added to the tail for extra flash. Peacock usually should be tied so it lies atop the marabou, or fans out from the top of the shank. The flashy stuff may be added in a number of ways. Like peacock, it can be laid on top of the marabou; more commonly, tiers put one or more strands on either side of the tail. When the pattern calls for the flash filaments to be "mixed in," build the tail in three steps: a bottom clump of marabou, a bunch of flashy filaments, and a top clump of marabou. The flashy filaments typically extend as far back as the marabou—except in crayfish- or shrimp-imitating patterns, where they may be longer to imitate antennae.

Body
Chenille is standard, the size (diameter) mostly dependent on the size of the hook. Wrap the chenille fairly tight, without bunching it together. The Woolly Bugger can, like the Woolly Worm, be tied with a nontapered, cylindrical body; frequently, however the body may be tapered at either or both ends.

Standard method is to strip the fluff off the last 1/8- to 1/4-inch of the chenille and tie it in by the exposed core of string. That will keep your bodies from lumping up unattractively. A single ply of wraps from bend to behind the eye produces a relatively slim Bugger. For a thicker body, tie in the chenille up front, lash it to the top of the shank all the way back to the bend, and wrap the chenille forward. For a really thick fly, tie in the chenille up front and wrap it down to the bend and back.

Unless otherwise specified, always tie in the body before the hackle or any rib, and take the body material behind the hackle or rib when you make your first wrap at the bend. This method produces the strongest, smoothest flies.

Hackle
Woolly Buggers typically are more closely palmered than are Woolly Worms, so long saddle hackles are standard. If the fly is fairly small, you might get by with a really long neck hackle. Otherwise, you might have to use two or more neck hackles to get the job done. In that case, you will get a neater-looking fly if you wrap and hackle the body bit by bit.

If the fly isn't ribbed, tie in the hackle at the bend—usually by its tip, so the barbs get longer as you work your way up to the eye. The old standard was to end the palmer right at the front of the body. Nowadays, it's more common to see Buggers with a virtual collar in front, the hackle having been wrapped two or three times in tight, touching turns in front of the body. Suit yourself, unless the pattern calls for the "collar."

Barbs slanting to the rear are standard, so tie in and wind the hackle with the shiny, convex side facing forward. If the pattern calls for, or if you want, barbs slanting forward, tie in and wind them Woolly Worm style, with the dull, concave side of the feather facing forward. If you prefer an erect hackle, wind the feather with the shiny side down, and embed the stem or quill in the grooves between the wraps of chenille. (The method is illustrated on page 16.) No matter which technique you use, if you are having trouble with trapping barbs as you wrap, or a general unruliness, try folding the feather or stripping the barbs from one side of the quill.

Oversize hackles are standard—at least one size large, and sometimes two. The barb length should be a quarter to half again as long as the hook gap is wide. Some Bugger patterns call for a hackle that is twice as long as the gap is wide. The length of hackle barbs and how closely the hackle is palmered affects the performance of the fly.

Hen or rooster, soft or stiff hackle? Almost anything goes, according to the effect you want. If the originator specified hen or rooster, I have followed his or her wish. But you won't be jailed for making your own decision. You won't even incur purist wrath, because purists and Woolly Buggers seldom hang out together.

Head
The standard Woolly Bugger has a thread head. The head may be wrapped small and neat or large and bulky. It may or may not be coated with head cement, epoxy or cyanoacrylate cement (superglue), fingernail polish, lacquer, or varnish. The coating may be dull or shiny. It's pretty much tier's choice. As we shall see later, other materials may be and often are used to head Woolly Buggers.

Tying Variations & Fishing Consequences
Today's tiers make all sorts of variations in Russell Blessing's patterns, changing the colors, adding or substituting materials, tampering with the tying steps. Most of them seem to work. But so does the original. While Woolly Buggers of every size, color, and variation can be and are fished successfully in just about any kind of water for any kind of fish, some choices are better, under certain conditions, than others.

Color counts—sometimes

All other things being equal, color matters more to fishermen than to fish. But sometimes color counts. Steelheaders and Pacific-salmon fishers know this, and their fly boxes would put many a painter's palette to shame. But even trout fishermen have discovered that color can make a difference. And we're not talking about subtle earth tones and insect greens.

Writing of the Woolly Bugger on Ralph and Lisa Cutter's California School of Flyfishing web site (www.flyline.com/, formerly called Adventure West On-Line), Ralph Cutter says that "for whatever reason, bright purple ones will work when nothing else does." Out in steelhead country, fly fishers know about the deadliness of purple. Elsewhere, purple shows up in fly boxes far too seldom.

In *The American Masters Fly Fishing Symposium, Part Two—Tackle* (1992), part of the series called Lefty's Little Library of Fly Fishing, Lefty Kreh calls purple one of the two best all-around colors to use in fly design (the other being chartreuse), neither of which shows up in all that many fly patterns. More specifically, Lefty also said, "If I could only pick two Woolly Buggers, one of them would have to be purple."

The English authority Charles Jardine has written, "Atlantic-salmon anglers tend to agree that purple will either catch or clear the pool. If the same is true of steelhead, the color should be changed immediately" if you suspect you are spooking fish.

In my own experience, admittedly more limited than Kreh's or Jardine's, purple has hooked more often than it has spooked fish. I've seen purple take Spanish mackerel, largemouth bass, and Atlantic salmon when other colors were being ignored. While catching nothing but a cold, test-fishing the Kharlovka River on the Barents Sea coast of Russia's Kola Peninsula in the pre-season, I watched Ehor Boyanowski catch several salmon on Purple Peril steelhead flies (and the superior fishing skill) he'd brought with him from British Columbia. The water was just above freezing—2 degrees Celcius, about 35 or 36 degrees Fahrenheit—and the fish weren't exactly playful or plentiful just yet. For some reason, purple seemed to warm up those frigid pools. Purple Woolly Buggers probably would have worked as well as the Perils, had anyone thought to carry any.

Lest you think purple flies are garish, newfangled notions, remember that Charles Cotton, in Part II of *The Compleat Angler* (Part II first appeared in the fifth edition of 1676), listed for June fishing two purple-bodied palmer flies—ancestral Woolly Worms, if you will:

"3. We have also a hackle with a purple body, whipt about with a red capon's feather.

"4. As also a gold-twist hackle with a purple body, whipt about with a red capon's feather."

Stick a marabou tail on either of those three-centuries-old flies and you have a Purple Woolly Bugger, although today's anglers are more likely to use a black or grizzly palmered hackle.

Writing in *Pennsylvania Angler* a few years back, Dave Wonderlich observed that, "It is possible to fish a section, catch trout, and believe you've moved most of the fish in that stretch. If you change colors and fish back through, you may be surprised at how many more trout you see, particularly on limestone water." (Not to mention changing colors after having been skunked on a stretch.) Wonderlich continued, "The brighter patterns do tend to do better on limestone and the more subdued, on freestone streams, although they will take trout on either type of water." Wonderlich thoughtfully included a list of the better Bugger color patterns, with the "hottest" ones in bold face.

These Woolly Buggers from the Orvis catalog illustrate just a few of the many variations you will see in fly boxes today: *left to right,* Salmon Bugger (colors suited to target species), Krystal Bugger (tinsel-chenille body), Beadhead Woolly Bugger (chromed bead head), Tunghead Woolly Bugger (tungsten bead head), Conehead Woolly Bugger (brass cone head), Travis Bead-a-Bugger (brass bead head, rubber legs).

Limestone streams

Marabou tail	Chenille body	Palmer hackle
Black	**Orange**	**Black**
Smoky gray	**Orange**	**Dun**
Yellow	**Yellow**	**Yellow-dyed grizzly, or yellow**
Orange	**Brown seal**	**Badger**
Red	**Brown seal**	**Badger**
Red	Orange	Brown
Yellow	Black	Yellow-dyed grizzly, or yellow
Orange	Red	Badger
Yellow	Red	Yellow-dyed grizzly, or yellow

Freestone streams

Marabou tail	Chenille body	Palmer hackle
Black	**Black**	**Black**
White	**White, or cream**	**Badger, or grizzly**
Black	**Olive**	**Black**
White	White	White
Black	Brown	Black
Brown	Brown	Brown

Whether you would arrive at Wonderlich's formulas on your home waters is anyone's guess. Fly fishing isn't exactly an empirical science with results that can be replicated by another experimenter. But the general principle makes sense: Fish that live in relatively barren freestone streams can't waste time tasting things that don't look like food; trout in limestoners and spring creeks often are so well fed, the angler's best bet may be playing to their curiosity. Call it the Dessert Theory of hatch-matching.

Some tiers change the Bugger's colors and give the pattern a whole new name; for example, an Icelandic pattern called **Yogi Bear**: very full brown tail, bright-red body, bright-yellow palmer hackle, large black tying-thread head.

The original black-and-olive Bugger is still very popular, and so are all-black, all-white, all-olive, and all-brown versions.

But today's fly fishers tie and fish Woolly Buggers in just about every color or color combination imaginable. White, pink, purple, yellow, green, maroon, chartreuse—you name it, a Bugger of that color will catch fish somewhere, sometime.

Lately, some tiers have been adding copper to their otherwise all-black Woolly Buggers: ribbing them with copper wire, adding some copper Krystal Flash in the tail, running a strip of copper Flashabou down each side to the tip of the tail, or heading it with a copper bead or cone. Adding copper to basic black is a nice cosmetic touch, and fish seem to approve.

Here are just a *few* of the other color combinations rattling around in my head as I write this, most of them plucked from contemporary tying books, magazine articles, and web pages. As you can probably guess, many of the gaudier combinations are designed for steelhead or coho salmon.

A Few of the Popular Color Variations for the Woolly Bugger

Pattern Name	Marabou Tail	Body	Palmer Hackle
Black WB (Iceland)	Black	Yellow	Black
Black-and-Blue WB	Black	Black, or very dark blue	Bright blue
Black-and-Brown WB	Brown	Dark brown, w/copper-wire rib	Black
Black-and-Chartreuse WB	Chartreuse	Black	Black, or grizzly
Black-and-Orange WB	Orange	Black	Black, or grizzly
Black-and-Yellow WB	Black	Black, w/ pearl Flashabou sides	Yellow, or yellow-dyed grizzly
Blood Leech	Black, w/maroon flash	Black	Black and maroon, palmered together
Bloody Bugger (1)	Red; or black, w/ red flash	Black	Red
Bloody Bugger (2)	Black, w/ red or black flash	Red floss or tinsel	Black
Brown-and-Tan WB	Brown	Tan	Brown
Burning Bugger	Hot red-orange	Red, or red-orange	Red-dyed, or orange-dyed, grizzly
Chartreuse-and-Pink WB	Chartreuse, w/orange flash	Pink	Chartreuse
Creamy Bugger	Creamy white	Cream	Cream, or light ginger
Ghostly Bugger	White	White, or pearl	Bleached grizzly
Green-Butt Black Bugger (similarly, for **Red-Butt**)	Black	Black, w/a bright-green butt	Black, or dark grizzly
Green-and-Yellow WB	Yellow	Green	Badger, or grizzly
Grizzled Old Bugger	Gray or mottled gray	Gray, or black-and-gray variegated	Grizzly
Maroon Woolly Bugger	Maroon	Black	Grizzly, or maroon-dyed grizzly
Motley Bugger (aka Brindled Bugger) (colors to suit)	Barred, or mottled	Variegated	Grizzly (natural or dyed) badger, cree, or furnace
Olive-and-Green WB (1)	Lime green	Olive	Olive-dyed grizzly
Olive-and-Green WB (2)	Olive	Olive	Green, or green-dyed grizzly
Perilous Purple WB	Purple	Black	Brown, brown-dyed grizzly, or furnace
Pink-and-Purple WB	Purple	Hot-pink	Purple
Purple Woolly Bugger (1)	Black	Purple	Black, or grizzly
Purple Woolly Bugger (2)	Purple	Black	Purple
Purple Woolly Bugger (3) (aka Lake Leech)	Purple	Purple	Purple—saddle or marabou
Red-and-White WB	White	White	Red
Ugly Bugger	Black	Chartreuse	Grizzly
White Woolly Bugger	White	White	White, grizzly, or bleached grizzly
Woolly Bruiser	Black	Blue	Olive-dyed grizzly
Woolly Weasel	Purple, w/ lots of rainbow flash	Black	Grizzly

Let's face it, Ralph Cutter pretty much said it all by specifying "any color" for the Bugger's marabou tail, chenille body, and palmer hackle. It would take a pretty twisted tier to come up with a color combination that wouldn't catch something, somewhere, and probably sooner than later.

Material matters

Beyond esthetics (which is too often the reason behind the choices that tiers make), the nature of the materials used can affect a fly's performance in the way it reflects light or changes color, whether it absorbs or repels water, how it behaves in the current or on the retrieve.

Weighty considerations

Although weighted Woolly Buggers probably dominate in today's fly boxes, I often tie mine unweighted and use weighted leaders to get them down. Weighted flies fish like jigs; unweighted flies drift and swim more like the menu items fish are accustomed to, and the range of their actions is limited only by the skill of the fly fisher on the other end of the line.

The standard weighting practice is to wrap lead or nontoxic lead-substitute wire around the hook. To save space, I'll specify "lead," but our wildlife and waterways will be healthier if you use a nontoxic substitute instead. In general, tiers use "lead" wire that is roughly the same diameter as the hook wire, but everything from .010- to .035-inch can be used. Unless the originator specified a size and number of turns of wire, I'm leaving it up to you to decide how heavy a fly you want or need. Some tiers wrap the shanks almost from bend to eye, others use less weighting wire and center the wraps along the shank or, more often, concentrate the weight in the front half or third of the shank. Again, I'll mostly leave it up to you when the pattern permits.

Most tiers cover or at least spiral-bind the wire wraps with thread. Some cement the thread-covered wire, others don't. Many good tiers "ramp" their weighted flies by building thread ramps at either or both ends of the wire wraps, particularly when the pattern calls for a tapered body. For marabou-tailed Buggers, you seldom need to ramp the rear end of the lead wraps.

Taff Price, the English fly tier and fisher,

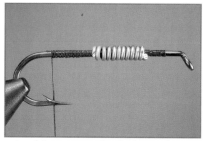

Lead (or nontoxic lead-substitute) wire often is wrapped only on the front half or third of the shank.

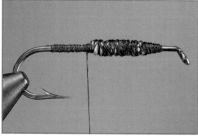

Thread is used to "ramp" up to and cover the wire underbody to make smoother bodies that won't be stained by lead corrosion.

wrote this in his *Tying and Fishing the Nymph*: "Woolly Buggers are generally pre-weighted with lead wire but, for best effect, the fly should be tied unweighted with a lead shot or 2 crimped onto the leader, 6–8 in (15–20 cm) from the fly. This shotting of the leader helps to activate the tail[ing] fly when it is retrieved with a figure-of-8 retrieve." Some others, including Russell Blessing, think the shot should be crimped on immediately ahead of the fly, which almost turns the unweighted fly into a lead-head pattern.

Weight-forward flies swim differently from flies that are center-weighted with wire wraps. I'm not alone in thinking the difference is all positive for weight-forward flies. Unweighted flies swim even better than weight-forward flies, which is one reason I prefer to fish unweighted or lightly-weighted flies on sinking leaders.

Two reasons tiers add eyes to flies: weight and attraction. (Bead heads can accomplish both. So can cone heads and dumbbell eyes, but weight probably predominates in the decision to use these heavyweights.) When fishing for bass, especially, eyed flies have a distinct advantage. Bass direct their strikes at eyes, as do many other slab-sided fish with lots of fin area, and so do many of the predators that hang out around coral reefs. To them, eyes mean food. When you want the attraction of eyes, but not the weight, use the plastic "bead chain" you can find in fabric and sewing shops; it's faster (not to mention safer) than melting knobs on the ends of a piece of monofilament.

Some tiers specify sizes for their head-weighted or metal-eyed Bugger components, while others don't. Bead and cone heads are simply slipped onto the hook (and sometimes barbs will have to be pinched down or filed away to allow the beads to slip past), while bead-chain and dumbbell eyes are lashed to the shank with crisscrossing, figure-8 thread wraps, which usually are cemented for security. In some patterns, the body material is wrapped only to the rear of the metal eyes, and the head is finished with thread, dubbing, herl, or something else. In other patterns, the body chenille is continued over and beyond the eyes, using the same figure-8 wraps.

Metal heads and eyes add weight more efficiently than wrapping wire under the body. It takes a lot of wire wraps to match the weight of metal heads and eyes.[2]

Use figure-8 thread wraps to tie in and secure dumbbell eyes. A drop of cement on the wraps is a good idea.

Typically, body material is also wrapped over, under, and ahead of the dumbbells, using figure-8 wraps.

WOOLLY WISDOM

The simple-Simon, cheap-Charlie alternative to dumbbell eyes is a split shot crimped to the front of the shank. Because crimped shot tends to work loose during the back-and-forth stresses of fly casting, you should crimp the shot over a thread base that has been coated with glue. Paint the shot or not, as you wish. Unpainted lead will corrode when wet, spreading white "dust" in your fly box.

Brits have a series of Buggerish, lead-headed flies called **Nobblers**, or **Dog Nobblers** (page 161). ("Dog" is Brit slang for big brown trout.) And I notice in the pages of the Bob Church & Co. Ltd. catalog that a Woolly Bugger with a bit of Flashabou in the tail and bead-chain eyes up front is called a **Pretty Dog**—shown in four colors: yellow, orange, white, and green-butted black.

When I weight my Buggers, which isn't as often as most people do, I prefer to use metal or glass beads, either slipped onto the shank before clamping the hook in the vise, or slipped onto the tippet before tying on the fly. Either way, the front-weighted fly casts easier, swims better, and even sinks faster than most wire-underbodied flies. And the bead head can add a bit of contrast and flash that may attract an otherwise jaded fish's attention. (In the U.K., fly fishers have a pattern they call **Bead Head Cat's Whisker**—essentially a bead-head Bugger using a gold bead, fluorescent-green thread and body, white palmer hackle, and a few strands of pearl Krystal Flash in the white marabou tail.)

I use glass, and sometimes even plastic, beads as often as metal beads. Obviously, their attractive qualities are paramount. Glass and plastic beads don't have the density of brass, tungsten, or the other metals used to make beads, but they come in so many attractive colors and finishes, I can't resist them.

Muddler-type heads of spun, packed, and trimmed deer hair also are showing up on Woolly Buggers (pages 192–194). Until they become waterlogged, deer-hair heads are buoyant. For fishing around submerged weed beds, try using a shot load or a weighted leader with a Bugger that has an even more buoyant head of foam (pages 167–168), cork, or balsa. That way, you can hug the bottom and fish the fly just along the top of the weeds.

Chenille, ostrich herl, peacock herl, yarn, or dubbed heads add attraction without changing the fly's density. Stick a head of bright red, orange, yellow, or pink chenille ahead of that palmered body and you get the famous (infamous, to some) **Egg Sucking Leech** (page 162) that has become one of the Alaska fly-fishing guide's main bread-and-butter flies. (See also many other Egghead, Headstrong, and other patterns.)

Tails, you win

Woolly Bugger purists (if such a term isn't an oxymoron) would insist that a proper Bugger needs a *marabou* tail. Tie it with anything else, they say—ostrich or peacock herl, bear hair, whatever—and it needs another name. They have a point, but we'll ignore it for now. For reasons laid out in the next chapter, "Fishing Woolly Buggers," there are sometimes good reasons to use other materials in the tail.

Marabou works its fish-catching magic because of the way it "breathes" and pulsates in the water. But 'tain't so in really fast water—not unless you are fishing your Bugger yo-yo fashion, using fast, stop-and-start strips in the retrieve. Marabou slicks back in rapid currents like the greaser hairdos of the late fifties and early sixties. If you will be fishing your Woolly Buggers in heavy currents, better use a thick clump of wiry hair or ostrich herl instead of a marabou plume for the tail. A few iconoclasts tie all their Woolly Buggers with ostrich-herl tails because the ostrich is almost as lively as marabou in slow and still waters and much livelier in fast water.

Whether marabou plumes or ostrich herls are used, tails may show considerable variation in both length and density. Quite a few Great Lakes steelheaders like marabou tails that are a shank-length long or shorter, and of only moderate fullness; some of their Buggers are so slightly tailed, they could as well be called marabou-tailed Woolly Worms. Other anglers couldn't imagine fishing a Woolly Bugger whose tail wasn't twice the length of the body, and so full that the fly resembles a short-handled feather duster for some little girl's doll house.

Various animal hairs or kinky yarns make fine, Bugger-look tails. But before tying a great many such hairy-Bugger variations, give them a trial. The fish may not like them as much as you do. At the very least, tie one and give it the Water Test: Fill a basin full of water, sink the fly, and see how the tail looks underwater. Swish it around to see how the tail behaves. If you like it, fish may well agree.

Ribbing & teasing

Ribs on flies serve two purposes: attraction and reinforcement. If a Bugger pattern specifies a rib, you have three methods at your disposal. You can (1) rib the body before palmering the hackle, (2) wind the rib between the turns of hackle, or (3) cross-rib the fly by winding over and through the hackle in the opposite rotational direction. The first two methods add visual contrast, but not much physical strength. Cross-ribbing reinforces the fly against sharp teeth. Because the Woolly Bugger is considered a big-fish fly, cross-ribbing is the method most often used.

By far the best way to cross-rib a palmered fly is to tie in the hackle at the front (usually by its butt) and tie in the rib

---

2 According to Jim Cramer, a California fly fisher and retired engineer, you'd have to wrap approximately this many turns of .020-inch diameter lead wire around the shank of a Mustad 9671 2X-long, standard-wire streamer hook to match the weights of the other weighting options listed:

4-mm (Spirit River "large") glass bead: 7 to 8 wraps • 1/8-in brass bead: 12 wraps • 1/8-in tungsten bead: 32 wraps • 1/8-in Orvis faceted tungsten bead: 35 wraps • 1/8-in steel bead-chain eyes: 20 wraps • Small (4.5-mm) glass eyes: 21 wraps • 1/8-in Spirit River brass dumbbell Dazl Eyes: 34 wraps • 1/8-in lead dumbbell eyes: 61 wraps • 5/32-in Spirit River brass cone head: 18 wraps • Small Orvis tungsten cone head: 76 wraps

These figures were calculated from tables in an article I commissioned from Jim, and which appeared in the November/December 1998 issue of *American Angler*. In the article he points out that nontoxic, lead-free wire "weighs about 60 percent as much as lead wire of the same diameter."

at the bend. Palmer the hackle to the rear (reverse-palmering), catch in the hackle with ribbing material, and rib the fly forward. As you rib through the hackle, wriggle the rib back and forth as you wind, to trap as few hackle fibers as possible. Starting both the rib and the hackle at the rear of the fly and winding them in opposite directions around the body usually results in a loose rib and a clunky-looking, nondurable fly.

Wire-ribbed flies are the most durable and Krystal Flash-ribbed flies, the least. Oval tinsels and thread usually are stronger than flat tinsels. Floss ribs may be stronger or weaker than flat-tinsel ribs, depending upon their material and construction.

A good many tiers today always incorporate some Flashabou or Krystal Flash or similarly reflective materials in the tail (an innovation variously credited to Angus Cameron, Travis Duddles, Taff Price, and Dave Whitlock) or add them as side stripes or shellbacks. Using tinsel or tinsel-blend chenille for the body raises the fly's reflective quotient even higher. But flash and glitter aren't piscatorial panaceas. The flashy fly that drives fish wild today may drive them *away* tomorrow. To be on the safe side, tie your Buggers both ways.

Some fly fishers like to use tinsel and other flash materials for fishing early and late in the day, under overcast skies, or in murky waters. They say the bright glare of the midday sun on reflective materials frightens fish. Others prefer to use drab flies under low-light conditions and say that reflective materials won't work unless there's some light to reflect. Being a Gemini, I see the logic in both arguments. I really have no idea which works better. Fish are unpredictable.

In deciding whether to fish a plain or flashy fly, you will have to rely on theories, gut hunches, or good old trial and error.

Atlantic salmon fishers seem to have a theory for everything, including the use of tinsel. Joseph Hubert—a fine fly fisher who originated the acclaimed Black Sheep pattern (in fact, the whole Sheep series of flies) without which no respectable fly fisher would be caught on a salmon river in Iceland—has developed a Tinsel Theory. According to Hubert, silver is for mornings and gold, for afternoons, and the effectiveness of either color varies inversely with the amount of sunlight. You should start fishing early in the morning with silver-tinsel bodied flies, but by high noon you'd better not have more than 10 percent of the pattern in tinsel. As the afternoon drags on, you can fish flies with more and more tinsel, but gold rather than silver. This approach to fly selection works about as well as anything else in Atlantic salmon fishing (that is, very well to not at all, depending on the whims of those notoriously moody fish).

The use of fluorescent materials requires the same thoughtfulness and care. Fluorescence is caused by ultraviolet light, which must reach the fluorescent material for it to work. At high noon of a summer's day along the equator, UV light will penetrate gin-clear water to a depth of about 45 feet. In mid morning, mid afternoon, or colored water, UV penetration is only about 4 or 5 feet. Earlier or later or murkier, it's much less than that.

Used much less often than either reflective or fluorescent materials, phosphorescent (glow-in-the-dark) threads, braids, tapes, paints, and other materials actually emit light and can be used in total darkness. They must be charged by exposure to strong light: either sunlight or a photoflash. Flashlights generally aren't strong enough to cause phosphorescent materials to glow very brightly or for very long, which causes some fly fishers to carry a small photoflash unit. Like many another curious angler, I have experimented a bit with phosphorescent materials, but I don't yet have enough experience to make sweeping judgments. In saltwater fishing, it makes sense: Squid often "light up" when being chased or otherwise excited. In freshwater fly fishing, the jury is still out. Orvis's Tom Rosenbauer, one of the best fly fishers I know, insists that phosphorescent fly materials simply drive trout into hiding.

Body counts

While chenille may be traditional, other materials may be substituted without doing much harm to the Bugger's performance. The body is fairly obscured by the palmer hackle, anyway. Like many another angler these days, I often use peacock herl for the body. I like the shaggy iridescence of peacock, and so do fish. Because herl is so fragile, compared to chenille, I sometimes rib my peacock Buggers with fine wire—silver, gold, or bright copper when I want the flash; black, brown, or dull copper when I don't. On the other hand, I sometimes wrap a more somber body of wool yarn, because it soaks up water and sinks better than most chenilles.

Many other materials show up in Bugger bodies: tinsel, dubbing, braids, piping or tubing, you name it. If you can wrap it around or slip it over a hook shank, somebody probably uses it in his or her quest for a better Bugger.

Tinsel chenille (Cactus Chenille, Estaz, Ice Chenille, and so on) and tinsel-blend chenilles (New Age Chenille, Sparkle Chenille, and others that blend textile and tinsel fibers) are especially popular Bugger-body materials. Some tiers apparently think tinsel chenilles are shaggy and attractive enough to allow doing away altogether with the palmer hackle. Whether a marabou-plumed fly without a palmer hackle should properly be called a Woolly Bugger is a good question. I prefer to call them **Cactus Blossoms**, because that's what they are: Blossom Flies tied with Cactus Chenille or similar tinseled material. The California watercolorist and fly fisher Mark Vinsel calls his **Shortcut Sparkle Buggers** (page 203). In England, Bob Church & Co. Ltd., calls their version the **Fritz Lure**, after the brand of tinsel chenille used. Fulling Mill, another English outfit, adds bead heads and calls them **Cactus Flies**—in black, white, olive, orange, Montana (black, with a little yellow in the thorax), Cat's Whiskers (white, with a chartreuse soft-hackle collar in lieu of the bead), and Viva (same front end, but with a black body and tail) manifestations. Use a short-fibered tinsel chenille for the body and Estaz or other long-fibered tinsel chenille in a contrasting color for a collar "hackle," and you've got **Jim's Gem**, the creation of "Big Jim" Hester of the Chesapeake Fly & Bait Company.

Now, Cactus Blossoms by whatever name are very good flies, but if it's a real *Bugger* you want, you should palmer hackle through those shaggy, shiny bodies as well.

Many different materials can be used for Bugger bodies. Here are just a few (clockwise from upper left): short-fibered tinsel chenille; Estaz, a long-fibered tinsel chenille, Vernille, peacock herl, yarn, chenille. Naturally, these and other materials can also be used to make Woolly Worm bodies.

Hackles & hackling

As mentioned in the first half of this book, the Woolly Worm should be palmered so the hackle barbs angle forward. Some tiers also hackle their Woolly Buggers this way, although it isn't necessary. More commonly, tiers palmer the hackles so the barbs angle backward. I use both methods as well as the Merwin–Leiser method (see page 16), forcing the top (shiny) side of the feather down into the body between the turns of chenille.

Hackle selection also varies widely from tier to tier. Because of the length of the Bugger's body, most tiers use saddle rather than neck hackles. Soft hen or stiff rooster hackles? Some tiers prefer one, other tiers, the other. Most of us use both, soft-hackling some of our Buggers and stiff-hackling others. Big-fish anglers, especially saltwater fly fishers, often use schlappen feathers to palmer their big Buggers. Panfishers, small-stream trout fishers, and even a few steelheaders (notably Hal Janssen) sometimes palmer game-bird feathers, ostrich herl, even emu or CDC feathers over their Bugger bodies. Each different type produces a different effect in the water.

Some tiers heavily hackle their Woolly Buggers by palmering in close turns for that fuzzy caterpillar look; others like the more raggedy look of a sparsely palmered fly. Barbs may angle forward or backward or stand straight up, depending on the look and action you want.

I discovered a really terrific and different palmering technique in the course of writing this book. It involves tying in two saddle hackles, twisting them together, and palmering the resultant hackle "rope." The result is wonderful and could be adapted to many a Bugger pattern. For specific patterns employing the technique, see the **Twisted Woolly** and **Cased Caddis** (pages 30 and 54).

Many tiers effectively add a hackle collar in front of the body by taking two or three extra turns of the palmered saddle feather around the front of the shank. For best effect, they like to use steeply tapered saddle hackles, tying them in by the tip so the longest, softest hackles wind up in front. Others go all-out and use a second, longer-barbed feather to add a wet-

fly or soft-hackle collar, the color of which may match, complement, or contrast with the palmer hackle.

I hackle my Buggers every which way, and still haven't come to any firm conclusions about which hackle feathers and palmering techniques work best under which conditions. Too many variables and vagaries in fly fishing for that. Every time I think I have something figured out, the fish will prove me wrong the next time out. I hope I never solve all the mysteries.

A few flies bearing the Bugger moniker are only semipalmered—usually up front, in the "thorax" region; in the case of backward-facing crayfish patterns, toward the rear of the shank. I have included a few of these. But I draw the line when it comes to

When a pattern calls for two hackle feathers palmered one through the other, tie them in as usual, then try a twisted palmer hackle.

After both hackles have been tied in, twist them together. A dubbing twister, swiveled hackle pliers, or similar tool makes it easier.

Palmer the twisted hackles together, stroking back the barbs with each wrap, and see the striking effect you get.

patterns with fore-and-aft and other separated hackle sections; I think such flies ought to carry other names.

Some tiers retain the Bugger name when they abandon hackle altogether and wrap the body or palmer over it with mohair, fur strips, marabou, or long, natural or synthetic fibers (or a blend of both) in dubbing loops. Others recognize the radical departure from tradition by calling their creations leeches or something else. Later in the book, I'll give examples of each. You can decide whether they should be called Buggers.

For such a simple pattern—really just three materials (marabou, chenille, hackle) in addition to hook and thread—the Woolly Bugger lends itself to an astonishing range of variation and adaptation.

9. Fishing Woolly Buggers

Everything I said earlier about fishing the Woolly Worm applies here. If anything, the Bugger is even more adaptable to piscatorial whim.

Russell Blessing, who invented the pattern, says he usually starts out dead-drifting the Bugger, "to see what happens." If that doesn't produce, he will add jigging motions on the strip, jig it back at the end of the drift as Barry Beck described *[see several paragraphs below]*, cast up and across the current and let it swing, use hand-strip retrieves. "Sometimes," he says, "it takes fast strips. Some of the guys around here will strip it as fast as they can. Almost everything works, some of the time." Amen to that.

Al Rockwood, the Michigan steelhead guru and steelhead fly tier, says, "In my opinion, the Woolly Bugger is the most effective wet fly for trout in Michigan. It works for steelhead and salmon in bigger sizes. I have found it deadly for brookies in Labrador, steelhead in Michigan, and browns in New Zealand. Dead-drifted or stripped, down deep or on the surface, the Woolly Bugger is a sure attractor pattern." California's Ralph Cutter has written, "The Woolly Bugger is an intern's fly: It can't be fished wrong." The Lake Taneycomo guide Brian Schaffer, of Branson, Missouri, calls the Bugger the "Fly of the Century." He says he does 90 percent of his night fishing with a black Woolly Bugger (often tied with fluorescent lime green thread and three strands of Krystal Flash added to the tail), working his way to lighter colors as necessary. "The best thing about having a Woolly tied to your leader," he says, "is you almost can't fish it wrong."

Although the Woolly Bugger can be fished anywhere in the water column, it probably is more often fished close to or down on the bottom. That's why most people tie them weighted. How much you weight a fly determines how quickly it will sink and how well it will stay down in a current. The aforementioned Brian Schaffer ties them both ways, in sizes 4 to 12, using 10 to 24 wraps of 0.10- to 0.30-inch-diameter lead wire on his weighted Woollies.

Where you place the weight affects the way it will swim. Lead wire that's centered on the shank creates a Woolly Bugger that's better for bottom-bouncing than for swimming higher in the water column; it just won't produce an enticing action when twitched or stripped in midwater. Slide those wire wraps forward or backward along the shank, and the Bugger fishes altogether differently. Mount a split shot, a bead, or a cone head at the front of the shank, and your Woolly Bugger will have a rising–diving, yo-yo action on a stop-and-go retrieve.

Unweighted Woolly Buggers have, I believe, a more seductively sinuous action than heavily weighted ones. The problem is getting them down where the fish are. If you want a yo-yo action, crimp a split shot onto the tippet immediately ahead of the fly. If you prefer a fly that will respond better to your manipulations of the line and rod, crimp the shot farther up the tippet, or use a sinking leader, a sinking-tip line, or a full-sinking line. Weighted leaders and crimped shot will keep a sunken fly swimming closer to the bottom than either a sinking or sinking-tip line. It's a simple matter of geometry: When the *line* is weighted, you will be pulling it toward you, off the bottom. Keeping the weight closer to the fly (in or on the leader or the fly itself) keeps it deeper, longer. Sinking-tip lines offer a compromise.

You can dead-drift, swing, bottom-bounce, crawl, or fast-strip a Woolly Bugger. Given the right time and place, each of those techniques will take fish. If one doesn't work, try another. Or combine two or more on the same retrieve.

Barry Beck, writing in *The Fly Fisherman*, said, "[T]he most productive technique is to pump [the Woolly Bugger] back with a slow, patient retrieve." (The retrieve is preceded by pinching a B or BB shot immediately ahead of the fly and casting it up and across the current.) He defined the winning retrieve as a combination of 3- to 5-inch, hand-over-hand strips accompanied by a 4- to 5-inch, up-and-down rod motion. That combination gives the Bugger's marabou tail the proper "breathing" action that turns fish on.

For trout, Barry Beck likes to fish Woolly Buggers in low-light times of day—the first two or three and the last two hours of daylight—or at night. For bass, he concentrates on deep channels and runs during the afternoon and on the flats and shore areas and the edges of lilypad beds early in the morning and as night approaches. For bluegills and crappies, Beck likes an all-white Bugger. For pike and pickerel, he fishes yellow or red-and-yellow Buggers over weedbeds with a fast, hand-strip retrieve.

Whether you weight your Woolly Buggers or not, you can fish them as baitfish, as leeches, hellgrammites, aquatic worms, nymphs, crayfish, or who-knows-what-else.

Fishing Woolly Buggers to Imitate Different Fish Foods

Although a Woolly Bugger will probably catch fish no matter how you fish it, you can move the odds in your favor by fishing it to resemble whatever forage species may be about.

Baitfish

Think of the Woolly Bugger as a streamer. Use a stop-and-go retrieve to give the Bugger the darting motion of a nervous baitfish. From time to time, insert a long, fast strip into the retrieve, as if the baitfish had spotted a predator and decided to scram. Twitching an unweighted Bugger just below the surface sometimes makes fish mistake it for a wounded minnow.

To imitate darters, keep the fly on the bottom and use fast, short strips. Sculpins swim a bit more deliberately, so you can also fish the Bugger along the bottom a bit more slowly. If the stream you are fishing has both darters and sculpins, fish your bugger like a sculpin: They're slower and easier to catch, and fatter besides, and predatory fish have figured that out.

Leeches

To imitate leeches, your fly must be long and supple and swim with vertical undulations. In midwater, leeches don't swim as much as they writhe and struggle while the current carries them along. When leeches are hugging the bottom or being bruited about in fast water, they aren't nearly so long and thin and supple. However you fish your Woolly Buggers, they might be taken for leeches. Then again, they might be taken for something else. You never know.

Nymphs

Although most anglers think of the Woolly Bugger as a general-purpose streamer or leech imitation, Russell Blessing had the hellgrammite in mind and he ties them short and small to imitate caddis and fishfly larvae. In different sizes and colors, the Bugger probably also passably imitates or strongly suggests the nymphal forms of dragonflies, damselflies, craneflies, stoneflies, and the larger mayflies. Fish a Woolly Bugger the way you would any other nymph: dead-drift, in Leisenring lifts, or twitched along the bottom. Or high-stick an upstream nymph presentation (what Brits call long-tumble nymphing).

Minnesotan Reed Munson, usually fishes his Buggers where runs or riffles tail out into pools, casting across the stream and letting the current drift the fly down into the head of the pool. But if the water is low or very clear, he says, "most likely the trout will see you." That's when he switches to upstream nymphing techniques. "You can sneak up on the fish with less likelihood of being seen," he says. "Look for a good run. I like heads of pools, large submerged rocks, or undercut banks. Cast the Woolly Bugger upstream of the fishy-looking spot. Watch the strike indicator. Hopefully, as the Bugger passes the likely-looking area, you'll see your indicator jump."

Crayfish

I am convinced that trout, bass, and panfish often take the Woolly Bugger for a fleeing crayfish. When I want to present a crayfish imitation, I will often fish a Bugger or some variation thereof. Many so-called crayfish patterns are designed to look more like crayfish in the vise than in the water, are a bear to cast, and often twist the leader. The few patterns that don't suffer from these afflictions—the Clouser Crayfish being a notable exception—are a lot more difficult or time-consuming to tie than Woolly Buggers. (My love of fishing Clouser Crayfish is offset by my fear of losing the expensive-to-buy and tedious-to-tie critters, which too often keeps them in the safety of my flybox.)

Many fly fishers use medium-length, medium-speed strip retrieves to fish crayfish patterns. It works, but it doesn't mimic the way crayfish move. When crayfish aren't being threatened, they crawl along very slowly. When threatened, they may rapidly scoot several yards at a clip. So don't be afraid to mix in both slow, steady, hand-twist retrieves and long, fast strips.

Saltwater prey

In salt water—from which leeches, hellgrammites, and crayfish are absent—anglers often fish their Woolly Buggers in midwater and near the surface. Salty Buggers tend to be gaudier than freshwater Buggers (steelhead and Pacific-salmon Buggers excepted), as well as bigger. What do saltwater fish take them for? I don't know—lighted-up squid? Tropical reef fish? Royal

Wulffs? But they sure do take them. A long-tailed, silvery-green Bugger, tied on a 6X-long hook and stripped fast, can probably pass for a needlefish or sand eel in salt water. In *Fly Fishing for Bonefish* (1993), Dick Brown writes of the Woolly Bugger, "This ubiquitous freshwater pattern, in its original olive and black colors, is a good goby imitation for shoreline and tidepool areas. In tan or flesh colors, it is also effective as a polychaete worm pattern." (Later in the book he clarifies the polychaete pattern as having an "orange or flesh-colored body and white marabou and saddle hackle….")

Although I haven't fully field-tested it, a large, pale tan or gray Bugger with short or clipped hackle just might pass muster as a squid.

Denmark's Martin Jørgensen, who probably knows as much about taking sea-run brown trout in salt water as any man alive, has written (in *Saltwater Flyfishing—Britain & Northern Europe* by Paul Morgan and Friends, 1998), "If you have the choice of one single fly, choose a black or grey Woolly Bugger, size 6. This fly represents the stem of many of the most successful flies for sea trout in salt water." This, from a man who has designed many of the best-known and most successful flies used to fish for brown trout in the Baltic Sea.

No matter how or where you fish your Woolly Buggers, don't be in a hurry to snatch the fly out of the water for another cast. Because of the way marabou "breathes" in water (even—no, especially—when the fly is motionless in the slightest bit of current), you should always give the tail a chance to do its thing. Lift the fly in the water column, then let it fall slowly without any input from you. Let it dangle in the current at the end of a drift or retrieve for a few moments, enticing a following fish to grab it before it gets away.

You won't live long enough to experiment with all the different ways Woolly Buggers can be fished, to take advantage of the myriad variations in materials and tying methodologies currently in use on waters and vises around the world. It's hard to go wrong, fishing Woolly Buggers. Whenever the fishing slows down, try them even when experience dictates that you fish a wildly different fly.

Mark R. Tompkins, of Sacramento, California (whose fishing photographs grace several of the pages herein), related an eye-opening home-water experience while photographing for this book. In describing three of the photos, he wrote:

"The rainbow in the slides was one of the most beautiful I have ever caught. And he was one of the strongest, too. He jumped at least half a dozen times before I could bring him in. And I don't think I would have caught him if it weren't for you. You see, I normally fish two tiny caddis nymphs in the Calaveras River. But I decided to give one of my dumbbell-eyed Olive Woolly Buggers a try. On the first cast, my line went tight. You just never know!"

I can't promise you a trophy rainbow on your first cast with a Woolly Bugger, but I can safely promise you will over time catch a variety of fish under a variety of conditions, often when nothing else is working.

10. A Boggle of Buggers

To save time, so we needn't go into detail on each pattern, let's lay out our rules of thumb.

Tie in the ingredients in the order listed. In some cases, a given material may be the first thing added to the hook, but one of the last things that gets wrapped.

Barbed or barbless, use the hook you want. On bead-head patterns, you may need to pinch down or file off the barb to allow the bead to be slipped onto the shank. Whenever possible, use special fly-tying beads that are drilled with conical holes to allow the bead to slip around the hook's bend. Unless otherwise specified, the small hole should face forward, toward the eye of the hook.

Generally, use 6/0 thread. If the pattern's originator specifies a thread size, I'll list it. Otherwise, assume that 6/0 is a happy medium. If you like tying with finer thread, especially on smaller flies, go to 8/0 or even finer. But don't go heavier than 6/0 unless the pattern calls for it. Otherwise, your flies will be too bulky. Waxed or unwaxed? Tier's choice. Kevlar or polyfilament? Don't wrap too tightly, or you will cut through your materials.

Unless otherwise specified, use lead or nontoxic wire that is about the same diameter as the hook shank. Some tiers specify the wire size. When they do, I'll list it. As for the number of wraps, I'll list the pattern originator's specs, if any. Otherwise, use as few or as many wraps as you need to fish the water you will be fishing. To keep words to a minimum, I'll use "lead" as shorthand for "lead or a nontoxic lead substitute."

Wrap the wire as you see fit—unless specified otherwise. Many tiers like to wrap a thread base first, and some also soak the thread in cement. Others prefer to bind the wire in place by wrapping over it with a thread layer or two. Either way, some tiers lock the wire wraps in place by wrapping thread around the shank fore and aft of the wire, then spiral-wrapping back and forth across the wire a few times. As for positioning the wire wraps on the shank, most tiers either center the wire wraps or, perhaps more frequently, position them closer to the eye than the bend. See Dennis Potter's **Rivergod Bugger** (page 129) for a contrary viewpoint.

If no head is specified, use the tying thread. Except when otherwise specified, wrap neat, conical, standard-size heads on Woolly Buggers. When the pattern I list specifies a head coat, I'll repeat the specification. It's up to you whether to follow the directions slavishly. If a high-gloss head is called for—as on saltwater or some salmon patterns—I like to use cheap, high-gloss fingernail polish. It's tough and readily available, and it costs less than most other head coats.

Unless otherwise specified, make your marabou tails full and about as long as the shank. Some patterns call for short-er tails and some, for longer. If they do, I'll state it. Otherwise, use your own judgment and please yourself. Remember, marabou tails that are much longer than the hook tend to foul the bend; long ostrich-herl tails generally don't foul the hook. One worthwhile trick is to make your Woolly Bugger tails as long as you conceivably might ever need them; shorten them to match fishing conditions when you tie them onto your tippet. To shorten marabou plumes or ostrich herls, pinch or twist them with your fingernails; scissors don't do a good job. On wire-weighted flies, lash the marabou butts to the shank *aft* of the weighting wire (or, conversely, wrap the wire on the shank above the tail butts), to help smooth the transition to the wire-wrapped portion.

Reverse-palmer (wrap from front to rear) the hackle on patterns that call for a reinforcing rib. If the rib is wire, consider it a reinforcing rib. If it's floss or flat tinsel, consider it decorative, which means you could palmer the body from the bend forward and lay the rib down between the hackle turns. Thread, monofilament, and oval-tinsel ribs may be decorative, reinforcing, or both, so you can decide how you want to tie the fly. When in doubt, I reverse-palmer the hackle from front to rear. After reverse-palmering the hackle, use the ribbing to catch the hackle in place at the rear of the shank. Because I like to reinforce palmer-hackled flies, I often specified reverse-palmering whenever the originator or listing I consulted failed to describe the procedures on a ribbed fly. However, Hal Janssen, Erling Olsen, and a few other, far more gifted tiers than I don't like cross-ribbed flies. They prefer to lay the rib down between the spirals of palmer hackle, usually right at the base of the hackle stem.

Rooster or hen hackle? If the pattern doesn't specify, suit yourself. When in doubt, go for Grade 2, or 3, rooster hackles that are webby in the center and soft on the edges. Because of shank length, I like to use nothing but saddle hackles on my Buggers. Whenever I try to use a large neck hackle, I invariably run into trouble somewhere along the way. Some of the patterns call for quite specific hackles, but most don't. If I specify a particular hackle, it's because my source did. Most patterns should be palmered with the longer, butt-end barbs up front; a few specify the reverse. The standard Woolly Bugger palmer hackle should have barbs that are longer than the hook gap is wide—1 1/2 times the gap width isn't too long for most patterns.

Let's tie some Woolly Buggers! And, lest you forget, go back to page 114 and review **Russell Blessing's Original Woolly Bugger**. No matter where you fish, you will need some of those black-and-olive woolly wonders in your fly boxes.

BLACK WOOLLY BUGGER

Patterns with this name abound. Many are all-black; others are mostly black with maybe one or two highlights of another color. Despite its name, this Bugger from Al Rockwood of Flies for Michigan in North Muskegon, Michigan, carries the same general colors as Blessing's original. The important difference is that it has copper Flashabou in the tail, "which increases its effectiveness a great deal," says Rockwood, who credits Angus Cameron with introducing Flashabou to the Bugger's basic recipe. "This pattern can be fished in many different ways," Rockwood says, "and is often very effective dead-drifted because even the slowest current will cause the Flashabou to sparkle and attract a hit."

If you haven't yet tried combining metallic copper (Flashabou, Krystal Flash, wire, Antron yarn, thread, braid, whatever) with black in a pattern, you're missing a good thing. I don't know why, but a bit of copper on a black field often seems to excite fish.

Black Woolly Bugger

Hook: Mustad 9672, a 3X-long streamer, sizes 4 to 12
Thread: Black 3/0
Underbody: Lead wire, from bend to eye, overwrapped with thread
Tail: Black marabou, 2 plumes "at least 1-1/2 hook lengths beyond the bend, with 10 strands of even longer copper Flashabou in between" (see Tying Tip)
Body: Olive chenille
Palmer hackle: Black saddle, tied in at the bend by its tip and palmered forward in 6 turns; "carefully pick out any stray hackle barbules with a bodkin"
Head: Tying thread, coated with head cement

Tying Tips

Tie that tail in three steps. First, tie in a long, black marabou plume. Next, tie in ten strands of copper Flashabou that are slightly longer than the marabou. Finally, tie in another plume or clump of black marabou. The tail should be half again as long as the hook and, when dry, very full.

As mentioned earlier, to keep such a long tail from fouling the hook, you might want to tie a small loop of monofilament jutting out over the bend, beneath the marabou.

NORTH WOODS WOOLLY BUGGER *Tied by Dave Smallwood*

Dave Smallwood hails from northern Saskatchewan and what he doesn't know about catching lake trout and pike probably isn't worth knowing. So, when he says this is his favorite Bugger pattern, I sit up and pay attention. Differences needn't be large, if they are telling. Like Al Rockwood's Bugger, immediately preceding, Smallwood's also incorporates a bit of metallic flash, this time as a gold rib.

North Woods Woolly Bugger

Hook: Standard or long-shank streamer, sizes 4 to 8
Thread: Black
Tail: Dark-green *(alternatively, dark-olive)* marabou
Body: Light-olive chenille
Palmer hackle: Black saddle, in about 5 to 7 open spirals
Rib: Oval gold tinsel, wound between the turns of hackle

PEACOCK WOOLLY BUGGER

Except for the use of a bead head or flash materiel, the addition or substitution of peacock herl is the fillip most often employed by tiers who want to dress up Blessing's Bugger. I've included just a small sampling of peacock-bodied Buggers.

Peacock Woolly Bugger

Hook: Your favorite Woolly Bugger hook, sized to suit your purposes
Thread: Black, olive, red, lime-green, whatever
Tail: Black marabou plume
Underbody: *Optionally, lead wire, covered by tying thread, Purr-fect Punch yarn, or other single-strand yarn*
Body: Peacock herl—several strands, twisted together; around the tying thread as well, if you want a more durable body
Palmer hackle: Black or grizzly saddle (reverse-palmered, if you use a rib)
Rib: *Optionally, silver wire, oval tinsel, or heavy thread to reinforce the hackle and perhaps add an attractive lagniappe*

MIKE'S PEACOCK WOOLLY BUGGER *Tied by Mike Hogue*

Mike Hogue, of Badger Creek Fly Tying (www.e-flytyer.com), explains the effectiveness of his Woolly Buggers this way: "I use the best materials I can find! For tails, I use Hareline's Woolly Marabou, or strung marabou. No broken tips! For hackle, I use Ewing saddles, Whiting Bugger Packs, or Chinese necks. The grade 2 rooster saddles I used to use don't come wide or webby enough these days." The Ewing saddle feather he uses for this pattern—grizzly that is bleached, then dyed olive, a color he suggested to them—is a wonderfully subtle chiaroscuro that carries hints of blue and maroon. Although this pattern has plenty of originality, Hogue credits Dave Whitlock's **Lectric Leech** (see page 134) as his original inspiration.

Mike's Peacock Woolly Bugger

Hook:	Mustad 9672, a 3X-long streamer, size 8
Head:	Large (5/32-inch) gold bead
Thread:	Black
Palmer hackle:	Bleached-grizzly Ewing saddle, dyed olive, tied in up front and reverse-palmered
Tail:	Olive strung marabou, with several strands of bronze Flashabou over the top
Back:	7 strands of peacock herl, pulled over the body before hackling and ribbing
Body:	Olive-and-black variegated chenille
Rib:	Gold Danville oval tinsel, medium

Tying Tip

That Danville ribbing tinsel is "*very* hard to find, but worth the effort," says Hogue.

PURPLE WOOLLY BUGGER

Don't let the Plain-Jane name fool you; this Australian pattern by Rick Zieger isn't just any old Purple Woolly Bugger. For one thing, it's tied on a bent-up-shank swimming-nymph hook which gives the fly a sinuous motion when strip-fished. For another, Zieger specifies using a twisted-wire-core chenille *stick* (first cousin to a pipe cleaner) for the body, which obviates the need for a weighted underbody, eyes, or head to get it down, but makes the fly a slow sinker.

However, in tying the above sample, I didn't use a chenille stick because (1) I didn't have any and (2) I don't like wrapping the things, especially not around such relatively fine-wire hooks. But I had plenty of copper wire in a couple diameters and some ultrafine (.008-inch diameter) lead wire I could use to wrap an underbody, which would give me more flexibility in building in a sink rate. If you want to follow the original pattern, Zieger offers this advice to make the wrapping of that chenille stick easier: Bend the end that you will tie onto the hook back and forth several times to soften the wire. And be

sure to use wire cutters to clip the excess; the twisted wire will ruin your tying scissors.

I found this interesting Bugger on the Aussie Fishnet (www.fishnet.com.au). If you don't know that site, check it out; it's a wonderful source of patterns.

Purple Woolly Bugger

Hook:	Swimming nymph (Mustad 80150BR, Daiichi 1770, Orvis 1512, TMC 400T, etc.), sizes 8 and 10
Thread:	Black 6/0
Tail:	Purple marabou, shank-length
Palmer hackle:	Purple hen saddle, oversize
Body:	Purple chenille stick, weakened by bending prior to tying in; *alternatively, purple chenille (or tinsel chenille) over an underbody of copper or very fine lead wire*

Fishing Tips

Zieger, who mainly fishes his Purple Woolly Bugger in ponds, varies leader length with the depth of the water and uses a range of relatively slow-speed retrieves. He has caught "bass, bluegills, and a few catfish" on the pattern.

Dennis Potter, a fly designer for Umpqua Feather Merchants and a Whiting Farms Pro Team tier, says he palmers his Bugger variation with stiff dry-fly hackle—specifically, Metz Microbarb Saddle—because, "being so stiff, the hackle makes more 'noise' going through the water." Potter also wraps the hackle so the soft, marabou-like barbs toward the butt (the "junk" most tiers reflexively remove from the feather) form a collar that "opens and closes like an umbrella" just behind the eye. Now you know what to do with the webby butt sections of those expensive super-grade saddles!

Contrary to most tiers' practice, Potter likes to tie his Bugger rear-weighted: "If I am going to fish this fly in still or slow water, I really like to weight only the back half of the hook. When it is fished in those conditions with a slow strip and pause, the weight pulls the fly down butt-first in the water and the collar opens all the way over the eye. Deadly action! I am convinced that it really pisses fish off."

Potter lives in Grand Rapids, Michigan, but also has a home on the storied Ausable main stream, where he has been fishing for more than 25 years. This fly used to be called the **Ausable Bugger**, but lately Potter has come to be known among Ausable anglers as the River God, hence the recent name change for the pattern.

Rivergod Bugger

Hook: TMC 9395, a 4X-long, 3X-heavy, straight-eyed streamer ("very stout!"), size 6 (but you can suit the size to your prey)

Thread: Black

Underbody: Optionally, none, .025-in lead wire wrapped the length of the shank, or .030-inch lead wire wrapped on the rear half of the shank

Tail: Black or olive marabou, not longer than the hook, with strands of pearl Crystal Hair or Krystal Flash from the sides

Palmer hackle: Black Metz Microbarb Saddle, or equivalent, with the hackle fluff forming a soft collar

Body: Several long, thick strands of peacock herl

Sides: 3 to 5 strands Pearl Crystal Hair or Krystal Flash on each side, tied in at the hook eye, pulled to the rear, and held in place while the hackle is palmered; trim flush with the end of the tail

Tying Tips

Potter likes the "very manly" TMC 9395 hook, but says, "I don't use this hook larger than a size 6 without lead eyes or lots of lead wraps because it has a tendency to ride with the eye angled up, it is so heavy."

After trimming the tips of peacock herl and tying them in by their trimmed tips, make a "peacock chenille" rope by twisting the herl around the tying thread before wrapping forward. "Do not crowd the eye," Potter warns, either with the peacock body or the lead underbody. "The fluffy collar takes a lot of space."

To tie this fly properly, you must select a saddle hackle of appropriate length: On a size-6, 4X-long hook, Potter says, "You will need about 2 inches of the good hackle above the

fluffy stuff." (Don't be surprised if you don't get it exactly right the first time.) Prior to palmering the hackle, pull the side strands of flash material all the way back and hold them in place as you wrap the hackle forward. "As soon as the soft part of the feather hits the end of the body, moisten it with a little saliva, fold it wet-fly style, then wrap it all the way to the eye and tie it off."

Potter lists the tying sequence as follows: "Tie on thread, wrap weight, tie in tail, tie in hackle, tie in peacock, wrap peacock around thread, wrap body, trim excess body, tie in flash, wrap hackle holding flash in place along each side, fold fluffy part of hack wet-fly style to create a heavy collar, finish fly."

Just glancing at the fly or its photograph, this looks like a pretty ordinary peacock-and-grizzly Woolly Bugger. But it isn't. It is the result of several years of experimentation with various patterns by Loucas Raptis, of Victoria, British Columbia, to, in his words, "address the problem of difficult trout during early-season blooms of aquatic copepods such as *Daphnia* and *Cyclops* as well as tiny chironomids and bloodworms." Why such a mismatching of the hatch of such tiny creatures? Because dragonfly and damselfly nymphs often join trout in feeding during such blizzards, and are taken by trout while they gorge on the tiny creatures. But Raptis and others discovered that the trout in each Vancouver Island lake responded to different patterns at different times, making fly selection almost a guessing game. That is, until Raptis discovered this universally effective pattern: "a hybrid of a peacock-bodied Woolly Worm, tied thin, with the tail of a traditional Woolly Bugger."

Raptis, a natural-history illustrator and formerly editor of *Fly Lines*, the publication of the British Columbia Federation of Fly Fishers, says this is one Bugger that can't be varied in size, color, or material—at least not if you are fishing for fussy trout on Vancouver Island. "From head to tail," he writes, "the fly should not be longer than 1.5 inches." That means a 3X-long streamer hook in size 8 or a 4X-long in size 10.

Vancouver Island Woolly Bugger

Hook: TMC 5263, a 3X-long, 2X-heavy, bronzed streamer, size 8, for trout in fresh water; TMC 9394, a 4X-long, 3X-heavy, nickel-plated streamer, size 10, for searun coastal cutthroat trout on the beach

Thread: Green 3/0 Monocord

Tail: Black hackle fluff from the base of a webby feather

Rib: Fine green wire, counter-wrapped through the hackle without trapping too many hackle barbs (pick them out with a needle, as necessary)

Palmer hackle: Grizzly rooster, dry-fly-quality with stiff barbs not much longer than the hook gap, spiraled forward in 6 or 7 turns

Body: 4 or 5 peacock herls, twisted around the tying thread before being wrapped forward

Head: Fine green wire used to rib the fly, double-coated with head cement

Tying Tips

Raptis does not reverse-palmer the fly (although I would be tempted to do so): "All the body materials are tied in at the base of the tail and then brought forward."

After ribbing through the hackle (in counter-clockwise windings as viewed from the front), form a neat head with the wire "and then twist the wire around the tying Monocord and tie off with a few half hitches (the tying thread is barely visible). The fly is surprisingly durable and I have yet to have the ribbing come apart on me. I usually retire them because the tail becomes too frayed and sparse after about 25 fish." We should all be so lucky as to have such "problems" with our flies.

Fishing Tips

"The pattern is most effectively fished with a full sinking line, slowly and with no action (either dead drift or with very slow trolling) right off the bottom."

Raptis describes his Vancouver Island Bugger as a searching pattern, but says it also "acts as a diagnostic tool of the trout's mood and behaviour. If the trout are actively feeding, the pattern is taken with decisive strikes, almost always hooking the fish right at the corner of the mouth. When the trout are not feeding, they pull it in the most uncanny way without getting hooked; and when they do get hooked, the fly always holds at the front tip of the upper or lower jaw."

The black-and-olive colors here are about the same as in several of the patterns listed earlier—including the original Woolly Bugger, but the material used for the body is different. Chenille, wool, Crystal Dub, and other synthetics all reflect light and are affected by water differently, so similarly colored flies can produce strikingly different effects. Note, too, the difference in the weighting wire: copper, rather than the lead so often used. North Dakotan Bob Morenski developed this pattern in July 1995 to fish Tokaruk Lake in western Manitoba. It turned out be a killer pattern for rainbows in the 24- to 30-inch range.

Tokaruk Special

Hook:	1X-long, 1X-heavy streamer, sizes 8 and 10
Thread:	Black
Underbody:	28-ga copper wire
Tail:	Black marabou
Body:	Dark-olive Crystal Dub (I used a Siman Antron-blend Dubbing Brush)
Palmer hackle:	Black saddle
Head:	Tying thread, large

Tying Tips

Morenski is adamant about wrapping copper rather than lead wire around the shank. "Lead wire is too heavy," he says. "It ruins the action. And once the fly has been shredded by a few trout, the lead is a turn-off to the fish. On the other hand, copper wire adds weight without killing the action, is easier to wrap, and attracts fish once they've 'ventilated' the body."

If you can't find Crystal Dub for the body, use Antron, SLF, Crystal Seal, Sparkle Yarn [Aunt Lydia's Rug & Craft Yarn], Fly Rite Poly, or similar synthetic dubbing, or try a blend such as Haretron or Spectrablend; or use a synthetic Softdub. Whatever you use, just don't wrap it over *lead* wire.

Later that same fall, Morenski discovered that, while rainbows fell for the Tokaruk Special, brown trout preferred the **Tokaruk Brown**: same materials as above, just change all the colors to brown (tobacco-brown marabou for the tail and medium-brown Crystal Dub for the body). Use hot orange 3/0 UNI-Thread and tie the head extra-large for the brown version he calls the **Psychedelic Tokaruk Special**.

Psychedelic Tokaruk Special.

"I got this pattern from Ray Sapp at the Colorado Angler fly shop," John Gierach writes. "The story he told was that a woman in a beginning fly-tying class tied it because she thought it was 'pretty.' Then she took it fishing and cleaned up. Soon, other tiers picked it up. Fire Butts were sort of a craze around here for a while, then began to die out. But I still do well with them, usually in trout lakes. I think it's the flash of red or orange behind an otherwise nondescript, muddy-looking bug."

Fire Butt

Hook:	TMC 200R, a 3X-long, straight-eyed, curved-shank nymph, sizes to suit your purposes
Thread:	Red (or orange) 6/0
Underbody:	Fine lead wire, "lightly weighted"
Tail:	Red (or orange) marabou, covered by brown marabou
Body:	Brown fine wool yarn, tied very sparse
Palmer hackle:	Furnace saddle

YELLOW-BELLIED BUGGER *Tied by Steve Probasco*

According to its originator, Steve Probasco, "The yellow belly and silver ribbing give the fly a bit more 'zing'" than the standard Woolly Bugger." In lake or stream, from top to bottom, this Bugger will take take fish of several species. Probasco suggests you might want to experiment with different belly colors.

Yellow-Bellied Bugger

Hook:	Daiichi X220, 4X-long, X-point streamer, size 6
Thread:	Black
Palmer hackle:	Black saddle, reverse-palmered from front to rear
Tail:	Black marabou
Belly:	Yellow chenille, tied in on the underside of the shank, at the bend, and pulled forward over the bottom of the body before palmering the hackle and winding the rib
Rib:	Oval silver tinsel
Body:	Dark-olive chenille

GULLY BUGGER *Tied by Steve Schweitzer*

Jack Madden, of Northern Illinois Fly Tiers, brought this trout pattern north from his native Missouri. Steve Schweitzer calls it "absolutely one of the best-fishing Woolly Buggers I've ever used," and says it has become his go-to Bugger pattern.

Gully Bugger

Hook:	TMC 300, a 6X-long, 1X-strong streamer, sizes 4 to 10
Thread:	Olive 6/0 or 8/0
Palmer hackle:	Grizzly saddle, reverse-palmered from head to tail
Tail:	Golden-olive marabou
Sides:	Pearl Mylar tinsel, medium; tie 1 strip on each side, facing to the rear, then pull alongside body and tie in at front before palmering the hackle
Rib:	Fine copper wire
Body:	Rabbit fur, dubbed and picked out; *Madden uses golden-olive yarn*
Head:	Olive, varnished

HUDSON'S BEADED CRYSTAL BUGGER *Tied by Dave Hudson for The Fly Shop*

The Fly Shop's catalog copy says of this Dave Hudson's pattern: "Remarkably effective," and, "incredible in both hemispheres." Hudson is a commercial tier from Sacramento, California. The Fly Shop also sells this pattern in olive (the brown version is listed here, and both are shown), as well as a beadless Crystal Bugger in two different colors: gray and brown.

Hudson's Beaded Crystal Bugger

Hook:	TMC 5263, or equivalent 3X-long, 2X-heavy nymph or streamer, size 8
Head:	Brass bead
Thread:	Brown
Underbody:	Lead wire wrapped on shank
Tail:	Rusty-brown marabou
Body:	Rusty-brown Crystal Chenille
Palmer hackle:	Furnace, or brown-dyed grizzly, saddle
Face hackle:	*Optionally, a couple turns of a darker hen hackle*

Tying Note

The **Deep Leech**, from Umpqua Feather Merchants, is essentially similar except that all the soft materials are black and the fly is ribbed with silver wire. Reverse-palmer the Deep Leech from front to back.

DELAWARE WOOLLY BUGGER

Some years back, the editors of the *Mid Atlantic Fly Fishing Guide* asked several Delaware River guides to submit favorite patterns. Anthony Ritter submitted this pattern. It's still a winner.

Delaware Woolly Bugger

Hook: Streamer, sizes 8 and 10
Head: Copper bead
Thread: Black
Tail: Brown marabou, sparse, with 2 to 3 strands of copper Flashabou on each side
Body: Brown or maroon chenille
Palmer hackle: Maroon saddle, folded, and heavy at the front to form a wet-fly "collar"

HEX BUGGER *Tied by Kelly Galloup*

I found this Kelly Galloup pattern in Matt Supinski's fine book *Steelhead Dreams*, where it is listed as the **Troutsman Turkey Bugger**. Galloup, owner of the Slide Inn, on the Madison River in Ennis, Montana (and formerly proprietor of Troutsman Outfitters in Traverse City, Michigan), says that, although "it is one of my all-time favorite steelhead flies," this pattern also works well for trout when *Hexagenia* mayflies are emerging. Hence, the name change, now that Galloup lives away from those steelhead streams. Fishing it as a *Hex* imitation, Galloup says, you should imitate the original by "giving the fly a little pulse retrieve, going from bottom to top." He uses the same pattern for either trout or steelhead.

Hex Bugger

Hook: TMC 7989, a 1X-fine steelhead/salmon dry, sizes 4 to 8, with 6 used most often
Thread: Wine 6/0 Danville
Tail: Mottled amber turkey-butt marabou, tied in at the shank and not trimmed
Palmer hackle: Brown-dyed grizzly saddle
Body: The same turkey marabou plume used in the tail, spun gently in a spinning loop, to keep the hackles perpendicular to the thread, and wrapped forward
Collar: Black hare's mask, dubbed
Head: Tying thread

One of many popular patterns from Dave Whitlock, the Lectric Blue Leech is a real winner. "While I seldom fish this fly anymore," Dave recently wrote in a note he included with the fly shown above, "it was one of my favorites—equally for trout, steelhead, and largemouth bass." He once wrote that he considered it especially effective in lakes, but for me it has been a great pattern in Atlantic salmon rivers. You won't believe how effective this fly can be until you try it.

Some tiers and authors prefer to spell it with an "E" at the beginning: **Electric Blue Leech**. I've also seen the pattern listed without the "Blue" and/or with "Dave's," "Whit's," or "Whitlock" appended to the front end of either spelling. The dressing that follows departs from many published versions, but is based on the one Whitlock himself listed in John Roberts's *The World's Best Trout Flies* (1994), modified to reflect the look of the fly Dave sent me.

Lectric Blue Leech

Hook: Partridge low-water salmon-fly (*others specify Tiemco's TMC 7999 or Mustad's 36890*), sizes 10 to 1/0

Thread: Black Danville 6/0

Eyes: Black bead chain, tied under the shank behind the eye

Tail: Black turkey marabou tip

Body: Black African goat and rabbit dubbing, mixed in equal parts

Palmer hackle: Long, webby, soft black saddle

Back: *Optionally, 3 to 6 strands of peacock herl, the tips extending to the back of the tail; for clear water, use "silver" peacock*

Sides: 1 or 2 strands of blue Flashabou down each side, the ends left trailing to the rear of the tail

Head: Tying thread, covered with blue Flashabou from the sides

Tying Notes

I have listed the ingredients in the order in which they appeared in the Roberts book.

Optionally, instead of the bead-chain eyes, weight the fly with 15 to 19 wraps of lead wire on the shank. In this case, wrap a long, bullet-shaped thread head, cover the rear, unsloped portion with blue Flashabou, and coat the entire head with Dave's Flexament. When fishing for salmon, I often coat the thread head with blue-metal-flake nail polish.

Whitlock didn't specify tying instructions, but I should think the peacock herl and Flashabou would be tied in *after* the marabou tail, then pulled back out of the way before being pulled forward and tied down before you palmer the hackle forward.

This fly sometimes appears in fly shops with a monofilament weed guard from the eye to the back of the bend. The first ones I bought were so dressed.

Many tiers use a reinforcing rib of gold or silver wire or oval tinsel—in which case, I think the hackle should be tied in by the butt up front and palmered to the rear.

Like other Bugger-based patterns, the Lectric Leech lends itself to further variations. Blue Flashabou "electrifies" this pattern, but others colors also work well; I also like red and green for bass and other warmwater species, and copper for trout. In fact, try other colors for the tail, body, hackle, or any combination thereof. A brown or burnt-orange Lectric Leech might well be a winning crayfish pattern. In salt water, where you will want to use a stainless-steel or other corrosion-resistant hook, try really bright colors and color combinations.

If you need a light, bright fly, try Whitlock's **White Lectric Leech:** pearl for the Flashabou color, "silver peacock" for the herl, and white for everything else.

I have seen "Electric Leeches" that used chenille or wool yarn for the body. And you may substitute Krystal Flash, holographic tinsel, or fluorescent monofilament for the Flashabou, if you are so inclined.

I sometimes like to use—either at the vise or slipped onto the tippet before tying on the fly—a bead head in lieu of the bead chain or lead wire. I used to use mostly shiny metal beads that matched the Flashabou or ribbing wire, but now I prefer using glass beads in deep or "electric" shades of the Flashabou color, or translucent- or black-pearl beads. A red, orange, pink, or yellow glass or plastic bead turns it into an **Egg-Sucking Lectric Leech**—as would a chenille or yarn head in those colors.

Fishing Tips

In the Roberts book, Whitlock wrote, "I usually tie it about two to three inches in length and let it sink down deep and fish it very slowly, pausing for a moment, then make a slow retrieve with pauses letting the Flashabou do its work against the dark background."

In salmon rivers with roiled or peat-stained waters, I like to fish Whitlock's electrifying fly on a high-density leader with a short tippet, particularly in the deep, turbulent pools beneath cascades and rapids. I make a pile cast (a high lob cast), and let the line pile vertically onto the water behind the fly. That gets the fly down deep where the fish are.

BLACK-AND-BLUE BUGGER

Both conceptually and effectually similar to Whitlock's Lectric Blue Bugger, this one is both simpler and more simplistic. Like the Whitlock pattern, it also lends itself to color-swapping. Try green, or hot colors (red, orange, pink), with black, or use a white base with dark flash. If you change colors, you'll have to change the name accordingly. I based this on **Black and Blue**, a central Oregon lake pattern Linda Foote submitted to Wes Newman's Wes' Virtual Pattern Book—Undiscovered Patterns Only (www.magiclink.com/web/wesn/).

Black-and-Blue Bugger

Hook: 3X- or 4X-long, straight-eyed nymph or streamer, barbless or the barb mashed flat, sizes 6 to 12
Head: Blue glass bead
Thread: Black 6/0
Tail: Black marabou, shank-length, with 2 strands of blue Flashabou (alternatively, 3 to 4 strands of blue Krystal Flash) on each side
Palmer hackle: Black hen saddle, extra long, or schlappen
Rib: Blue Flashabou *(alternatively, 2 to 3 strands of blue Krystal Flash twisted together)*, spiraled forward over the body in open turns before palmering the hackle
Body: Black chenille

BLACK ELECTRIC BUGGER *Tied by Dan Bailey's Fly Shop*

In this pattern, black tinsel chenille is used to catch and reflect light. Dan Bailey's Fly Shop makes the body from Longflash Chenille, a tinsel chenille whose fibers are about 9-mm long. (The strands in Shortflash Chenille are about a third as long.)

Black Electric Bugger

Hook: Dai-Riki 710, a 3X-long, 1X-heavy streamer, sizes 2 to 8
Thread: Black
Underbody: Lead wire over 2/3 the shank length
Palmer hackle: Black saddle, the barbs 1 1/2 times the hook gap, tied in at the front and reverse-palmered
Tail: Black marabou
Body: Black Longflash Chenille
Rib: Fine copper wire

RED-BACKED BLACK-AND-OLIVE BUGGER

Like so many others, I found this fine Bugger, by Michael Butchard, on the fine Fishnet web site (www.fishnet.com.au), a veritable cornucopia of patterns. Butchard designed the fly to target trout, bass, and carp.

Red-Backed Black-and-Olive Bugger

Hook: 4X-long streamer or a swimming-nymph (I used an Orvis 28GT, 3X-long, 2X-strong swimming larva), size 10
Thread: Black 6/0
Underbody: Lead wire wrapped around the middle third of the shank
Tail: Green marabou, hook-length, topped by black marabou, shank-length
Palmer hackle: Olive-dyed grizzly rooster saddle
Back: 2 or 3 strands of red Mylar tinsel, pulled over the body before the hackle is palmered
Body: Black chenille
Head: Thread, cemented

Fishing Tips

Naturally, use a strip–pause retrieve–"slow, if you want it on the bottom," says Butchard, "faster, if you want to target fish higher in the water column."

Butchard advises fishing this Bugger around snags and drop-offs and around the edges of lakes.

ALASKA BUGGER *Tied by The Fly Shop*

Of this pearly black Bugger, The Fly Shop catalog said, "John Hickey's phenomenal fly outperforms every similar fly in the 49th state." Need anything be added? Yes. The often equally effective purple version simply substitutes purple every time black is listed here.

Alaska Bugger

Hook: TMC 300, or similar 6X-long, heavy-wire streamer, size 2
Thread: Black
Underbody: Lead wire wrapped on shank
Tail: Black marabou, flanked on each side by several strands of pearl Flashabou
Body: Black-pearl New Age (tinsel-blend) Chenille
Palmer hackle: Black saddle, palmered as if the fly were a Woolly Worm, with the barbs angled forward

ALASKA WOOLLY BUGGER

The name's nearly the same, but the pattern isn't. According to the Alaska Flyfishers web site (www.akflyfishers. com/alaska.html), this durable pattern is "an excellent steelhead, Dolly Varden, and rainbow trout producer." When the fish aren't turned on by its gaudy glow, the anonymous author recommends all-black and all-brown Woolly Buggers. Alternatively, he/she says, try the equally excellent version with a grizzly hackle palmered over a fluorescent-orange body.

Alaska Woolly Bugger

Hook: Mustad 9672 or similar 3X-long streamer, sizes 2 to 6
Thread: Black
Underbody: Lead wire wrapped around the front 1/3 of the shank
Palmer hackle: Blue dun saddle, reverse-palmered from front to rear
Tail: Black marabou
Rib: Fine stainless-steel wire
Body: Fluorescent-green chenille

BLACK BLOOD BUGGER *Tied by Round Rocks Fly Fishing*

Round Rocks's Jim Lake says this pattern is one of his favorite stillwater flies. Fish Flair is the Hobbs brand of Flashabou-like Mylar tinsel. Angel Hair appears to be a finer version of the same.

Black Blood Bugger

Hook: TMC 5262, a 2X-long, 2X-heavy streamer, sizes 4 to 10
Thread: Black
Tail: Black marabou, topped by 4 or 5 strands of red Fish Flair
Body: Black-and-red tinsel-blend chenille (red Mylar in black chenille); *alternatively, rabbit fur and red Angel Hair, blended and dubbed*
Palmer hackle: Black Ewing saddle

HALLOWEEN *Tied by Round Rocks Fly Fishing*

Jim Lake says the Halloween is one of the best and most favored flies on a couple of southeastern Idaho's trophy-trout lakes. Round Rocks also sells several other bright, brindle-bodied Buggers, including the **Black/Rainbow Bugger**, which uses black-and-rainbow tinsel-blend chenille for the body and black everywhere else.

Halloween

Hook: TMC 2312, a 2X-long, 1X-fine, slightly curved-hump terrestrial, sizes 4 to 10
Head: *Optionally, a 5/32-inch brass bead*
Thread: Black
Tail: Black marabou, with a few strands of Krystal Flash
Body: Black-and-orange tinsel-blend chenille (orange Mylar in black chenille)
Palmer hackle: Black-dyed Ewing saddle

BOB'S BUGGER *Tied by R. G. Balogh*

R. G. (Bob) Balogh, a retired steel worker from Johnstown, Pennsylvania, modestly calls his weighty design just plain **Bugger**. I discovered this color variation on the beaded Bugger theme on the Fly Tying World web site (www.flytyingworld.com). There, Balogh describes the fly as "a r   workhorse" that "accounted for quite a few February ar   " Although the pattern works well "all year, especially effective in high, m

Bob's Bugger

Hook: Mustad 3906B, a 1X-long, 1X-heavy nymph, sizes 8 to 12
Head: Gold, copper, or pearl bead
Thread: Black 6/0
Underbody: .015-in lead-substitute wire wrapped the entire shank length
Tail: Red marabou, half again as long as the shank
Body: Brown chenille
Rib: Fine gold wire
Palmer hackle: Brown rooster saddle, Whiting Hebert grade #1, tied in by the tip at the bend and palmered to the bead

Tying Tips

Bob Balogh uses the Heber   e, he says, "I find the Heber   er than hen, but not too m   my Buggers because the stiff   cre-ates more 'vibration' do'

Similarly, he explains the long tail: "The longer-than-normal tail provides the undulation needed for attraction."

When I asked Balogh if he reverse-palmers the hackle from the front and winds the rib forward from the tail he said, "I tried it, and did not like it, so never used it."

CATSKILL

well in
o. Jerry
tor/pub-lisher of *Mid Atlantic Fly Fishing Guide,* developed this pattern after a summer of frustration and a winter of pondering why black Woolly Buggers worked so well on brown trout to 18 and 20 inches in his Pennsylvania home waters (the Yellow Breeches, Penns and Spring creeks, some others) but were just so–so in the Catskills (the Beaverkill and both branches of the Delaware). After returning with his lighter, brighter pattern

the following spring and taking about a dozen browns, several of them over 14 inches, from Cairns Pool, Stercho wrote, "Since then, I've come to believe that in our algae-tinted Pennsylvania streams, black Buggers outfish white at least five to one. Contrarily, in the crystal-clear Catskill waters, the exact opposite is true."

Catskill Woolly Bugger

Hook: Woolly Bugger hook of appropriate size for the fish and forage
Thread: Black
Tail: White marabou
Body: Yellow chenille
Palmer hackle: Badger saddle

Tying Tip

Mike O'Brien, Jerry's partner and a guide who fishes in the Pine Creek valley region of Pennsylvania, uses bleached grizzly rather than badger for the palmer hackle, with equally gratifying results.

GRAY GHOST WOOLLY BUGGER *Tied by Wes Autio*

When the white marabou in the Catskill Woolly Bugger pattern gets dirty, it looks remarkably like this one. I got this one from Wes Autio, of Pelham, Massachusetts, a professor of pomology (he research-es better ways to grow apples) at the University of Massachusetts. Autio, who says he got it off an Internet tying list, but can't recall the name of the originator, likes this ghostly Bugger because it's considerably easier to tie than Carrie Stevens' streamer of similar name, and is just as effective. He usually fishes it in the early season, casting it toward shore on a sinking-tip line and slowly stripping it out toward deeper water.

Autio ties in the hackle by its tip, at the bend, and palmers it forward, which is the way I have listed it. If you wish to use the rib to reinforce the fly, tie in the hackle by the butt up front, reverse-palmer to the rear, and rib forward.

Gray Ghost Woolly Bugger

Hook:	Mustad 9872, a 3X-long streamer, size 8
Thread:	Black
Underbody:	10 wraps of .025-in lead wire
Tail:	Gray marabou
Body:	Golden-yellow chenille
Rib:	Round silver tinsel
Palmer hackle:	Gray (blue dun) saddle

BASH BUGGER *Tied by Dan Bailey's Fly Shop*

This Bugger variation looks so simple, you wonder why they even bothered with a different name. You can bet on this: If that little bit of blue flash didn't make any fish-catching difference— well, John Bailey wouldn't even bother with the pattern under any name.

Bash Bugger

Hook:	Dai-Riki 710, a 3X-long, 1X-heavy streamer, sizes 4 to 10
Thread:	Black
Underbody:	Lead wire, 2/3 of the hook shank
Palmer hackle:	Light-olive-dyed grizzly saddle, the barbs 1-1/2 times the gap width
Tail:	Brown *(alternatively, olive)* marabou, flanked by 2 or 3 strands of blue Brighton Flash *(a Flashabou-like tinsel)* on each side
Body:	Dark-olive chenille
Rib:	Fine copper wire

WOOLLY NYMPH

This pattern is from Jay Fair, the master angler of Eagle Lake, California. I got it from a Mark Traugott article in *California Fly Fisher.* According to Traugott, this is *the* fly for Eagle Lake rainbows; he says the second-best fly for taking Eagle Lakers is this same pattern in olive.

Woolly Nymph

Hook:	3X-long streamer, si
Thread:	Black
Underbody:	16 wraps of .015-ir
Tail:	Burnt-orange marab
Body:	Orange Shuck, a sh chenille marketed b *pinch, use any orar*
Palmer hackle:	Orange-dyed grizzl

Fishing Tips

Besides sight-casting to rolling fish (always leading them by 25 feet), Fair fishes this fly in the slots among the tule beds— counting the fly down to the desired depth of 3 to 8 feet, then retrieving it slowly, about 2 or 3 inches at a time every 2 to 3 seconds. He says the fish will strike in the first 15 to 20 feet of the retrieve, or not at all.

Because it takes a 3X or 4X leader to properly turn over weighted flies, Fair says the leader must be at least 10 feet long to keep from spooking those Eagle Lakers.

In that same *CFF* article on fishing Eagle Lake, Traugott says Jay Fair often favorably mentions the Seal Bugger of Denny Rickards, the stillwater fly-fishing guru from Crystal Creek Anglers in Fort Klamath, Oregon, widely known for his book *Fly-Fishing Stillwaters for Trophy Trout* (1998). Rickards ties (and sells) his Seal Bugger in 12 color schemes; I have listed the one that Richard Anderson publisher of the late, lamented *California Fly Fisher* recommends. (This fly is listed in the Cabela's and Montana Fly catalogs as **Rickards' Seal Bugger**.)

DENNY'S SEAL BUGGER

Hook: 4X-long streamer, sizes 6 to 10
Thread: Black UNI
Underbody: 20 wraps of .020-in lead wire behind the eye
Palmer hackle: Burnt-orange–dyed grizzly saddle, the barbs about a gap-width long, reverse-palmered from front to rear
Tail: Dark-olive marabou blood quill, somewhat sparse; *optionally, with a few strands of pearl High Voltage or similar flash material*
Rib: Copper wire
Body: Dark-olive seal fur, or a suitable substitute such as angora goat, dubbed and picked out

Tying Tips

Cabela's sells the Seal Bugger in four color combinations, including the one listed. The others substitute: (1) burgundy tail, purple-dyed grizzly hackle, black body ("with a pinch of red mixed in"); (2) same as the preceding, but with a black tail; (3) burnt-orange tail, burnt-orange–dyed grizzly hackle, all-dark-olive body

Other color combinations listed by Rickards (listed in this order: tail—palmer hackle—body) include:

Black—burnt-orange grizzly—black
Burnt orange—burnt-orange grizzly—black
Olive—grizzly—olive
Black—grizzly—black
Black—black—black
Brown—black—brown + red
Dark olive—black—olive + red
Black—black—olive + red

Rich Osthoff developed this soft-hackle pattern (as well as the similar **Soft-Hackle Woolly Worm**, page 37) to catch big brown trout that inhabit the spring creeks of Wisconsin's Driftless Area. As he and myriad other anglers soon discovered, trout (and plenty of other fish) everywhere are suckers when it comes to something this buggy-looking.

Bi-Bugger

Hook: TMC 5263, Dai-Riki 1720XL, or similar long-shank streamer, sizes 8 to 12
Thread: Black
Underbody: 8 to 10 wraps of lead wire, covered after tying in the tail with Black Purr-Fect Punch yarn, to form a tapered foundation
Tail: Olive marabou, covered by black marabou, with a few strands of gold Krystal Flash
Body: Dubbing blend (2 parts rabbit to 1 part Antron or similar synthetic): olive on the rear 2/3 of the shank, black on the front 1/3 (see Tying Tips)
Palmer hackle: 2 webby grizzly hen hackles (see Tying Tips)
Head: Tying thread, lacquered

Tying Tips

The underbody, body, and hackle are all constructed in two parts. As mentioned above, wrap the lead wire first, then tie in the tail before covering the lead and the tail butts with the yarn.

After tying in the first hackle (the barbs a gap-width in length), dub the rear two-thirds of the shank with an olive rabbit–Antron blend. Then palmer the hackle forward, tie it down, and clip the excess. Now tie in the second hackle (barbs 1 1/2 times as long as the gap is wide), dub the rest of the body in black, then palmer the second hackle forward.

Rich also ties an all-black **Soft-Hackle Woolly Bugger**. On this one, he uses silver Krystal Flash in the black tail.

This one came about when I was sitting at the vise one day, pondering a half skin of golden pheasant, marveling at all the different colors and qualities of the various feathers. I couldn't find a G. P. feather that was suitable for the palmer hackle I wanted, so I used a ginger saddle hackle.

G. P. Bugger

Hook: 3X-long streamer, sizes 8 to 12
Thread: Black 6/0
Tail: Red-tipped blood feather (let's call it "pheasabou") from the golden pheasant's rump
Body: Dusky-orange chenille
Palmer hackle: Ginger hen or rooster saddle
Face hackle: Red golden-pheasant body feather, the barbs longer than the hook shank, wound as a wet-fly or soft-hackle collar

Tying Tips

To tie a **G. P. Woolly Worm**, substitute a bunch of barbs from a G. P. nape feather (dark, iridescent green with black tips), a gap-and-a-half long for the "pheasabou" in the tail.

You can change the chromatics of either Woolly by substituting black chenille for the body, fiery brown for the palmer hackle, and a golden-yellow body feather for the soft hackle.

John Abbott, of Lakebay, Washington, calls this Mike Croft creation "one of the most effective flies I've ever used!" This Buggerized version of the Peacock Carey Special, says Abbott, imitates dragonfly nymphs and leeches in larger sizes and darker colors, and damsel fly nymphs in smaller sizes and lighter colors. Even lighter, flashier colors will imitate minnows.

Carey Bugger

Hook: 3X-long streamer (Abbott uses Tiemco's barbless, curved-shank TMC 200RBL), sizes 4 to 12
Thread: 8/0, color to match the tail
Tail: Marabou, color of choice, tied in opposite the hook point, and as long as the shank
Eyes: *Optionally, dumbbell eyes*
Body: Peacock dubbing blend (65% forest-green wool, 25% peacock Angel Hair, 10% clear Antron; *I twisted together a peacock herl and a green Anton-blend dubbing brush*), at least moderately picked-out: thin for damsels, fat for dragons and leeches
Palmer hackle: Large pheasant rump feather, color to match the tail, in 4 to 6 close turns; the barbs (long enough to flow back to the end of the tail) should be folded back toward the rear before palmering; *alternatively, Abbott sometimes uses filoplume or aftershaft feathers (just to be different, I used a rump feather from a silver pheasant)*
Hackle collar: Thick "aftershaft" feather from underneath the pheasant rump (*again, I used one from a silver pheasant*), tied in by the butt, slightly moistened, and wrapped forward 3 or 4 turns, the soft barbs stroked to the rear with each wrap

Under a variety of names, and in almost every imaginable color, this fly is tied and sold by a number of commercial sources. "This striking color combination," to quote the Streamborn catalog, "turns big fish on in hard-fished water. One of Randall's favorite lake patterns."

Maroon Krystal Bugger

Hook: TMC 5263, a 3X-long, 2X-heavy nymph, size 4
Thread: Black
Palmer hackle: Maroon- or claret-dyed grizzly saddle, tied in at the front and reverse-palmered
Underbody: Lead wire
Tail: Maroon or claret marabou, flanked by several strands of red Krystal Flash, which will be carried forward on either side of the body
Body: Black chenille
Rib: Copper wire
Sides: Red Krystal Flash from the tail, pulled forward on either side and tied down at the front, after the body is wrapped, but before the hackle is palmered and ribbed
Head: Tying thread

England's Peter Cockwill is widely known for his nymph patterns and for catching more and bigger fish than most of his peers. Cockwill says he usually fishes this variation on the Woolly Bugger by stripping it fast on a slow-sinking line.

Long-Tailed Damsel

Hook: Mustad 79580, a 4X-long streamer, size 8; *alternatively, standard-length streamer, sizes 6 and 8*
Thread: Olive or black
Underbody: Lead wire, wrapped over 2 inches of the shank
Tail: Olive marabou; *about an inch long in some listings, as long as the shank in others*
Body: Black-and-olive variegated chenille
Rib: *Depending on which lister you consult, none, tying thread, or oval gold tinsel*
Palmer hackle: Olive saddle, steeply tapered, so it's longer up front

This British Bugger is from Taff Price, who has devised several variations on the Woolly Bugger theme. He also ties the two-tone **White Tail**: black body and hackle, white tail. Both bicolored flies were designed for fishing in murky water.

Yellow Tail

Hook: Long-shank streamer, sizes 6 to 10
Thread: Olive
Underbody: Lead wire
Tail: Bright-yellow marabou, plus about 6 strands of Flashabou or Krystal Flash that are a bit longer than the marabou
Body: Olive wool
Palmer hackle: Olive rooster saddle

Tying Tips

Although Price calls for an olive palmer hackle, I think the fly looks better with olive-dyed grizzly, which is the way I have tied it.

When Price ties this in a single color (black, pink, etc.), and adds to the tail a few strands of Shimma (a twisted metallic thread for which Krystal Flash would be an adequate substitute), he calls the fly a **Shimma**.

ORANGE-BELLY BUGGER

On the Fishnet web site (www.fishnet.com.au) where I found this trout pattern, Ezra Bibby says his creation is meant to imitate a frog, but few if any of our frogs have orange bellies and inner legs. Still, I think the pattern will catch Yankee fish anyway. But if you want to imitate frogs, just substitute pale yellow or cream—maybe even pearl SLF in the tail and tinsel chenille in the belly—for the hot orange.

Bibby insists on a demurrer: "I don't think I would be able to put my name on any fly as an originator. The fundamentals for this fly come from a pattern called the **Woolly Bugger Mk. 2** by the Tasmanian tier and guide Ken Orr. The only real difference is the light belly." I think he's being overly modest. The only picture of the Mk. 2 I've seen is of a black Bugger with a hot-orange veil of picked-out wool at the base of the tail.

A baker by trade ("No excitement there," he says), Bibby says he enjoys tying flies as much as casting them. However, when I contacted him, he'd just returned to his home in Sydney, Australia, from two weeks in the Solomon Islands: "WOW!!, what a fishery, bonefish to billfish, and next to no fishermen!" Sounds like plenty of excitement to me.

Orange-Belly Bugger

Hook:	Heavy nymph or wet-fly (Bibby uses a 3X-strong Kamasan B175), sizes 4 to 12
Thread:	Unspecified; but either black or olive 6/0 will do
Tail:	Black marabou, hook-length
Side flashes:	Fiery orange marabou or Glo-Bug yarn, sparse and a gap-width long on each side of the tail
Rib:	*Optionally, copper wire*
Palmer hackle:	Olive-dyed grizzly hen saddle
Belly:	Orange chenille, tied in on the underside of the shank at the bend and pulled forward before the hackle is palmered
Body:	Olive chenille
Head:	Tying thread, varnished

Fishing Tip

Bibby advises fishing this frog imitation along the margins of shallow lakes or to tailing fish that may be chasing frogs. "You want the fly to land fairly gently, if chasing tailers," he cautions, "and then 'hover,' or sink very slowly."

HOLLOWAY WOOLLY BUGGER *Tied by John Cowens*

John Cowens says the shortish, white tail on his Holloway Woolly Bugger works better than other colors and lengths on the panfish near his home on Waubee Lake in Milford, Indiana. "Over the years, this has been a very productive pattern." He counts the fly down to desired depth, then uses short strips in the retrieve to make it swim enticingly. "Sudden, short pulls are also effective," he says, "by causing the tail to flutter, which makes for sudden strikes."

Holloway Woolly Bugger

Hook:	3X-long streamer, size 10
Thread:	Black
Underbody:	10 wraps of .015-in lead wire
Tail:	White marabou, full, and about 1/2- to 3/4-inch long
Rib:	*Optionally, gold wire; in which case, reverse-palmer the hackle*
Body:	Green medium chenille
Palmer hackle:	Brown or fiery-brown saddle, reverse-palmered if a rib is used
Head:	Tying thread, large, football-shaped, with 2 coats of lacquer

Because of his great success with this fly pattern, the Flippin, Arkansas, fly fisher and tier Tony Spezio often is credited as the originator of the Chili Pepper. But Spezio is quick to point out that the fly originally was given to him by his frequent fishing partner, Bob Root, of Yellville, Arkansas. And Root is equally quick to point out that he first tied the fly as a joke.

"Tony wouldn't fish Woolly Buggers under any circumstances," Root says, so he decided he'd present Spezio with this "bright, ugly" tinsel version he called the Chili Pepper. "Little did I know the joke was on me. I had no idea how effective the fly would become." Root admits that, "Most days on the river, Tony would beat me hands down—until I started fishing the Chili Pepper. I guess that's what forced him to use it."

After carrying but not fishing the fly for months, Spezio finally decided to try it one slow day when he and Root were fishing Arkansas' White River. The date was December 26, 1995. In despair, Spezio decided to give the Chili Bugger a shot. "First cast," he reports, "I caught a rainbow." Now, we all have flies of which we are inordinately fond because they caught a fish on the first cast. But he quickly caught a dozen more fish before breaking off on the fourteenth.

"By March of the following year," Spezio reports, "I had taken more than 350 trout on the Chili. The Chili Pepper is my number-one fly. I have had very few days when I could not catch fish on it, but it happens. In less than three years, I have caught more than 900 fish on it, including both small- and largemouth bass, bluegills, crappies, even a couple of suckers."

Bob Root reports similar success with his Chili Pepper, but says, "I've no idea how many trout I have landed [on it]." He also says he hasn't yet caught a brook trout on a Chili Pepper. The body material is a special blend Root had Danville make for him. "I wanted something with a little flash that would blend in with the sand bars and ripples here on the White River. So I had Danville blend a skein of their ginger chenille with a copper Mylar."

Root also uses other chenille-and-Mylar blends for Chili Pepper bodies, so feel free to use what you can find.

Chili Pepper

Hook: 2X- to 4X-long streamer, sizes 8 to 12
Thread: Brown
Weight: 10 wraps of .010- to .015-in lead wire on the forward part of the shank
Tail: Burnt-orange marabou, with "a little brown added to the dye bath"
Body: Ginger-and-copper, special-order Danville Sparkle Chenille, *or a close approximation*
Palmer hackle: Ginger Chinese neck
Head: Tying thread

Despite his early success with Bob Root's original Chili Pepper, Tony Spezio abandoned the pattern for a time. "I finally took it out of my box because of all the razzing I was getting as 'The Chili Pepper King.' For eight months, I didn't fish Chili Peppers at all, though I was tying them for others. Then, one day as I was leaving to fish Buffalo Shoals on the White, I put in my box a reject Chili Pepper that was lying on the bench. We weren't doing very much, so I tied on the Pepper. I quit counting at 50 trout; it was 50-plus that day in four hours on the one Chili Pepper I had with me. My fishing buddy caught eight fish."

"I like eyes on flies," Spezio says. "That is what prompted me to put a bead on the Chili Pepper. My first one used a gold plastic bead. I had fished through a stretch of water with the standard Chili Pepper with no hits. I came back through the same water in 20 minutes with the bead-head and took three rainbows and one brown. I keep a log so I can go back and check these things." Now he uses brass beads. Because he also likes his fly to fish "light in the water column," he uses *tiny* brass beads and just enough lead wire to keep the bead heads from spinning on the shank (see the Tying Tips following the recipe). "For the shops, I tie with more lead on the shank." He also ties them without bead heads, wrapping oversize heads of fire-orange tying thread. The beadless ones he ties both unweighted and with a few wraps of lead wire on the forward part of the shank. Lately, he has added a size 14 to his repertory, and copper Krystal Flash to the tail.

Because it's easier to find, copper tinsel chenille has replaced the special-blend Danville Sparkle Chenille on most of Spezio's Chili Peppers. The darker color works as well. "My downsized copper version—size 14, with a 3-mm brass bead—has been doing really good this summer. Rising fish have taken it with vigor."

Beadhead Chili Pepper

Hook: Mustad 9672, Eagle Claw LO58, or similar 2X- to 4X-long streamer, sizes 8 to 14

Head: 3- to 6-mm brass or gold bead; *alternatively, for fishing near the top of the water column, a gold-colored plastic bead*

Weight: 10 wraps of .010-in lead wire on size 14 flies, 5 wraps of .015-in lead wire on the larger sizes—just enough to keep the bead from spinning; *optionally, a drop of superglue gel squirted into the bead's center hole before the lead is pushed forward* (see Tying Tips)

Thread: Fire-orange 6/0

Tail: Burnt-orange marabou, with a few strands of Copper Krystal Flash

Body: Copper tinsel chenille

Palmer hackle: Brown or furnace saddle

Collar: Fire-orange tying thread, wrapped and whip-finished behind the bead head

Eyes: Yellow, with black pupils, painted on the bead head; Spezio uses Slick fabric paint (available in craft shops)

Tying Tips

After slipping the bead head on the shank, with the small hole facing the eye of the hook, wrap some lead wire on the bare shank. Slide it forward, into the large opening of the conical center hole in the bead, filling the gap between the bead and the shank. It's important that the eyed beads not spin on the shank. To be extra-safe, squirt a drop of superglue gel into the hole of the bead before sliding the lead wire into place.

When tying beadless flies, omit the collar and wrap an oversize head with the fire-orange tying thread. You can tie beadless editions without any weight at all or with varying amounts of lead wire wrapped on the forward part of the shank.

Fishing Tips

Spezio says the pattern "seems to work best on bright, sunny days." Then he complicates the issue by adding that the pattern also "has done very well on overcast, rainy days and at night."

"I take a lot of trout on unweighted Chili Peppers as the flies rise to the surface," he adds.

Important as the pattern is, know that a few of Spezio's buddies apparently haven't mastered the knack of fishing it. One time, fishing Chili Peppers in the same pool, Spezio caught 33 fish to his buddy's one. Yea, verily, I say unto you: Ever has it been and shall be that presentation trumps pattern.

"In fast water," Spezio says, "I cast down and across, twitch the fly during the swing, then put some slack in the line and let it drift back out before twitching it back to the pickup. You need to keep the line light in your hand on the retrieve, otherwise you will lose a lot of flies—as I did at first."

In still or slower waters, he says, "I sometimes strip as fast as I can, and other times so slowly I can hardly stand it. I always add a twitch. I think this triggers the fish."

Spezio refers to his varied repertory of swinging, drifting, twitching, and strip retrieves as the Chili Pepper Stroll.

Lest you think the Chili Pepper is a pattern specific to Arkansas, know that anglers from Utah to Pennsylvania to Canada have reported back to Spezio on their successes with his beadhead version. Here's a brief report offered by Alexander Wagnecz, of Mine Hill, New Jersey, on September 18, 1998: "Fishing at Picatinny [the Picatinny Arsenal, where fishing is permitted only for military types, civilian employees, or retirees like Wagnecz] was excellent this AM until the wind came up. Caught 12 nice browns (12 to 14 inches)." He caught all 12 fish on the Chili Pepper. He tried two other patterns and went hitless on them. Over the next two months, his reports to Spezio were as impressive. One finger-numbingly cold day in late October, he caught a hook-jawed, 22-inch brown. Because he fishes in deep ponds, Wagnecz experimented with heavier tungsten beads, but soon went back to brass beads.

This versatile stillwater pattern is the creation of Gerhard Laubscher, a co-proprietor of The Flyshop, a South African company based in both Johannesburg and Praetoria. It was described on the company's web site (www.flyshop.co.za) by Angelo Komis, who wrote that "this fly has taken a number of double-figure trout in the fertile still waters of the Eastern Cape and the South Drakensburg." Komis also wrote, "My preferred colour combinations are olive/brown, brown/black, chartreuse/black, or orange/black." I have *italicized* the colors I used in tying the fly above.

Junk Food Bugger

Hook: TMC 300, a 6X-long, 2X-heavy streamer, sizes 8 to 14 *(I used an Orvis 28G1 loop-eye streamer)*

Thread: Olive, brown, black, chartreuse, or *fluorescent-orange* Danville 6/0 Flymaster, to suit the fly and/or the tier

Tail: Two colors of marabou, the dark *(black)* atop the light *(orange)*, flanked by the flash material from the side stripe

Side: Flashabou or Krystal Flash in a suitable color *(root beer)*, extending to the tip of the tail, tied in short of the eye and pulled back on either side of the body before the hackle is palmered

Palmer hackle: Dyed *(orange-dyed)* grizzly saddle, to match the lighter color in the tail combination, tied in by the butt at the front of the body and reverse-palmered

Back: 3 to 6 peacock herls, pulled over the top of the body before the hackle is palmered

Rib: Medium copper wire, used to secure the palmer hackle before being wound forward

Body: Natural fur dubbing, in the darker tail color *(black)*, over the rear 2/3 to 3/4 of the shank

Eyes: *Black* or stainless-steel bead chain, tied in mid way between the body and the hook eye

Head: Antron dubbing (chartreuse for the olive/brown and chartreuse/black combinations, *fluorescent orange* for the brown/black and orange/black flies)

Fishing Tips

Komis says the Junk Food Bugger can be fished in still waters on floating lines (with 10- to 15-foot leaders), intermediate lines (9- to 10-foot leaders), and sinking lines (4- to 6-foot leaders). Depending on the size fly, tippets may vary from 1X to 5X. Komis prefers to use either a hand-twist retrieve or alternating short strips and pauses, both of which allow the marabou tail to "breathe and pulsate underwater."

Depending on where, how, and how deep it is fished, the Junk Food Bugger can imitate "damsels, dragons, leeches, tadpoles, and minnows."

WEIRD & WOOLLY

I suppose some of the patterns already described might qualify as weird, but there's no doubt about the ones that follow.

WIRED BUGGER

I owe the inspiration for this weird, wired, woolly critter to two British sources: Peter Cockwill's Leaded Bug nymph and what the Diptera web site (www. diptera.co.uk) calls a Stalking Bug. (To tie a Stalking Bug, just omit the palmer hackle below and wrap over the lead a floss thorax that color-matches the tail.) Cockwill's pattern gave me the idea of using lead wire for the body, and the Stalking Bug gave me the idea of using epoxy over the lead to protect my fly box from the powdery result of lead corrosion.

By using different colors of wire, marabou, and hackle, you can create Wired Buggers to suit your specific needs. Mostly, however, I tie two versions: Lead and Copper (the copper wire need not be epoxy-coated); the idea of using copper wire for the body probably was suggested by Gene Lynch's Platte River Brassie nymph.

Okay, having thoroughly discredited my creativity, I'll just go ahead and list the recipe for the **Copper-Wired Bugger**.

Wired Bugger

Hook: 3X- or 4X-long streamer, sizes 8 to 14
Head: Small bead: amber glass or copper
Thread: Brown 6/0
Tail: Brown marabou, as long as the shank; *optionally, add a few strands of root beer Krystal Flash or copper Flashabou*
Palmer hackle: Brown-dyed grizzly hackle—hen or rooster, to suit; palmered all the way to the bead head, after the body is wrapped
Body: Copper wire, wound in touching turns over a thread base; *optionally, coat thread base with cement and overwrap with wire while still wet*

Tying Tips

To tie the **Lead-Wired Bugger**, just substitute *fine* lead wire (.010-in or smaller), natural grizzly hackle and black everywhere else. After wrapping the lead-wire body, coat it with a *thin* coat of epoxy; you don't want it to drip. Wait until the epoxy coating is dry before palmering the hackle over the coated wire body. Using 5-minute epoxy minimizes the gravity-drip problem and also shortens the waiting time for palmering the hackle.

To keep the body as smooth as possible, I lay the butts of marabou atop the shank and lash them the full length of the shank before overwrapping with thread and then wire.

After tying in the hackle feather by its tip, keep it well out of the way when using those cements.

When tying either version, should you be so moved, try other colors for the tail and palmer hackle.

Imagine this: a Woolly Bugger designed for ice fishing. If you insist on using a fly rod (an ice-fishing or short jig-fishing rod would be more efficient), be sure to keep those casts *short!*

K. G. (Kat) Cruickshank, a fisheries observer and graphic artist now based in British Columbia (whose métier is "Ichthyography—Artistic and Technical Fish Illustration"—see www.danica.com/kat/index.html), says of her pattern, "This fly sinks headfirst, so jig it sharply for that 'dying minnow' action."

As soon as I stumbled upon this fly—developed by Cruickshank for an ice-fishing fly swap she hosted on the Internet—I figured it would work even when the climate is kinder and gentler and the water surface, softer. In fact, Cruickshank says that it does: "I've used the Glassy Bugger for bass, and it works just fine. Several other flies in that swap have proven very effective on panfish, bass, and trout." She goes on

to admit, "I didn't actually go ice fishing that winter, or this past one either, so it still hasn't been fished in the context for which it was intended." Okay, carry a fly rod and leave the ice auger home.

Glassy Bugger

Hook:	Standard nymph or wet-fly, size 6; pinch down the barb so the beads will fit
Thread:	Black
Head:	Silver bead-chain eyes, tied in with figure-8 wraps cemented with super-glue, then tied off and whip-finished
Body:	4 glass beads—a red, followed by 3 silvered—after which the thread is tied on again at the bend
Tail:	White marabou blood feather, longer than the shank; keep the wraps tight and flat so the last bead will slip over the trimmed, tied-in butt
"Palmer" hackle:	Grizzly neck hackles, or sections of a long saddle hackle, wrapped in stages before each of the 4 body beads

Tying Tips

After pushing the rear bead over the tail butts, tie on again in front of the bead and secure it with a few thread wraps. Then tie in the hackle by its tip in front of that bead, wrap 2 or 3 turns, trim and tie off the hackle. Tie on again in front of the next bead, secure it, tie in the hackle, and continue as before until you have wrapped a hackle collar between the front bead and the bead-chain eyes. Whip-finish behind the bead-chain eyes and cement the wraps with superglue.

If you're as lazy as I am, use several of the tiniest beads (seed or rocaille) that will slip onto a barbless hook and palmer a long saddle hackle with a thin, flexible quill over the beaded body. (If your saddle hackle has a thick quill, carefully split it down the middle with a razor blade and wrap one half.) With the hackle wrapped over the beads, the fly won't be as pretty or as durable, but it will still catch fish.

The "D. B." is Dennis Brown, of TFO, Inc. Rick Pope, of Temple Fork Outfitters calls Brown's Bugger "a great fly—works on all species and in all environs." While bass fishing in Texas, Brown and a partner had their best catches with a weed-guarded, 1/0 D. B. Bugger with a Zonker-strip tail and "hackles like a 12-gauge bore brush."

Tying Tips

Push the beads all the way to the eye and wrap a thread base from opposite the barb to opposite the point, tie in the marabou and trim the butts before tying in the MonoFlash. (For those without vested interests in the brand, Krystal Flash will suffice.)

Tie in a hackle feather over the tail butt wraps, wrap 2 or 3 turns, trim the excess hackle, and tie off with a whip-finish. Push the hindmost bead over the hackle wraps. Tie on again and start the next hackle or hackle section in front of that bead and continue until you wrap a hackle in front of the first bead. Build a small thread head between the front hackle and the hook eye, and whip-finish twice.

D. B. Bugger

Hook:	Daiichi 1720, a 3X-long, 1X-heavy streamer, sizes 2 to 6
Body:	4 Gun Metal (019) Killer Caddis glass beads, the smaller opening of the center hole facing forward
Thread:	Olive Flymaster Plus
Tail:	Olive marabou, 2 shank-length tufts, covered by 8 to 12 strands of peacock MonoFlash Tailing Material; *alternatively, a Zonker strip*
"Palmer" hackle:	Olive saddle, tied in 5 individual segments ahead of, between, and behind the beads

Sweden's Erik Andreasson has a similar pattern he calls a **Bead-Body Flashy Bugger**: 6X-long hook, both white and hackle-matching threads, a pearl Mylar tubing body under phosphorescent or luminescent oval beads (the ones used as saltwater attractors—they'll slip over the hook eye). The frayed end of the pearl tubing serves as a shank-length tail. Collars of hen hackle (choose your own color) front each bead, and several ultralong strands of Flashabou Mirage stream back from the front of the fly (they are tied in between the front bead and the front hackle, which is wound over the Flashabou butts).

BEAD-CHAIN BUGGER

The basic idea for this pattern comes from Bill Black via Ted Leeson and Jim Schollmeyer (*The Fly Tier's Benchside Reference to Techniques and Dressing Styles*, 1998). This isn't really so weird a concept, but it seemed to fit best after the beaded-body wonders immediately preceding. Any number of streamer, nymph, or wet-fly bodies can be constructed this way—including Woolly Worms—but it's an ideal way to weight Woolly Buggers. The bead chain provides both weight and a bit of light-reflecting gleam. After you've tied your first one, you will know exactly how many beads it takes for your favorite Bugger hook, but on your first go you will have to start with a piece of bead chain that's too long.

Bead-Chain Bugger

Hook:	2X- to 4X-long streamer, sizes 4 to 10
Thread:	Suit yourself, but cover the shank with a thread base
Tail:	Marabou, shank-length, in a color of choice; *optionally, with a few strands of flash material on either side, on top, or mixed in*
Soft body:	Chenille, tinsel chenille, mohair, long-fibered dubbing or dubbing brush, or similar bushy material in whatever color you think will work, tied in at the bend and wrapped forward between the beads of the bead chain
Palmer hackle:	Hen or rooster saddle in a color to suit, palmered over the body between the beads
Hard body:	Gold, silver, or copper bead chain, shank-length, tied in immediately ahead of the hackle tie-in point and lashed to the shank between the beads (see Tying Tips)
Head:	Tying thread

Tying Tips

After covering the shank with thread and tying in the tail and hackle feather, lay the shank-length bead chain atop the shank and lash it tightly to the hook between the last two beads. At this point, you must decide how close together you want your beads to be. Most bead chains have some "play" between the beads. You can control this by (1) pulling the forward end of the bead chain with the "off" hand (the one not wrapping the thread) to maximize the space between the beads or by (2) pushing the next bead closer to the bead just lashed down. Once you have determined the spacing you want, maintain it the whole length of the shank. Continue lashing between the beads until you get close to the hook eye, leaving room to tie off the body and palmer hackle and build a thread head. Using a wire cutter, snip off the excess bead or beads.

After lashing the bead chain to the shank, wrap the soft body forward between the beads and tie it off in front of the forward bead. Next, palmer the hackle feather forward, tie off, build a head, and whip-finish.

Caveat piscator: If you want to clip or trim the hackle, remember that the weight of the bead chain will cause this fly to swim upside down, with the point up.

FLOATING WOOLLY BUGGER *Tied by Jeff Serena*

In appearance, this is just another Black-and-Grizzly Woolly Bugger. But it floats! Why would a fly fisher want a floating Woolly Bugger? Jeff Serena, a Westerner recently transplanted to the East—Guilford, Connecticut (via Maine)—explains on the Fly Tying World web site (www.flytyingworld.com): "Back in 1992, when I was living near Evergreen, Colorado, I was invited to fish some local trout ponds that were leased by the Blue Quill Angler, a fine fly shop in nearby Bergen Park. One of them had a good population of large rainbow trout. The first time I fished the pond, I put in a float tube at daybreak. As I kicked out into the pond, I tied on a Woolly Bugger—almost a reflex activity for me when fishing new trout water where there isn't any obvious feeding activity. I flipped the fly out to get it wet, but it didn't sink immediately, so I gave it a twitch to pull it under. It didn't have time to sink; a good fish grabbed the fly as soon as it moved and I had my first trout of the day. When the scene virtually repeated itself a couple hours later, after I'd switched to a fresh fly, I began thinking about the possibilities of the Woolly Bugger fished as a dry fly."

After experimenting with dubbed bodies, Serena turned to closed-cell foam. At first, he tried wrapping strips of foam around the shank. But wrapping the foam tended to compress it so much that the flies didn't always float well. Now, he uses Rainy's Float Foam, cylindrical, closed-cell foam you just cut into the body lengths you need. Serena reports, "The medium-size Float Foam is just right for these flies in sizes 6 and 8, which I've found the most useful for trout. I cut the foam a little shorter than the hook shank and taper the ends by cutting them with scissors at about a 45-degree angle. I then make a shallow slit along the length of the foam body with a razor blade or *sharp* knife so that it fits over the hook shank. A little superglue applied to the shank before putting the body in place strengthens the fly and helps to prevent the torque from the thread and palmered hackle from twisting the body around the shank."

Floating Woolly Bugger

Hook: Mustad 79580, or equivalent 4X-long streamer, sizes 6 and 8

Thread: Black 6/0

Tail: Black marabou: "the tip of a turkey marabou blood feather, dyed black, tied about as long as the hook shank and not too heavily"

Body: Black Rainy's Float Foam, size medium, the ends tapered at 45 degrees

Palmer hackle: Grizzly rooster saddle, "dry-fly quality"

Tying Note

Before discovering this Jeff Serena pattern, I used to tie a floater I called a **Woody Bugger**, using shaped balsa-wood or small cork torpedo floats for the body. You had to be careful tying them, getting just enough torque on the palmer hackle to dent the soft bodies without breaking the hackle stems. Also, you first had to paint the balsa bodies and—if you used hard-finish paint—palmer the hackle while the paint was still tacky, which could be messy. Serena's is definitely the better mousetrap, so I have decommissioned my pattern. If you are of a masochistic bent, go ahead and resurrect the Woody Bugger.

Fishing Tips

"I've found the Floating Woolly Bugger especially effective for bank cruisers in trout ponds," Serena writes, "casting the fly a little behind or to the near side of the fish, then inducing a take with little twitches. For bank cruisers, this is my go-to fly."

Serena also fishes the fly on a high-density sinking line. "I let the line sink until it's on the bottom. The fly is buoyed up by the foam. A slow, twitchy retrieve will allow the fly to ride anywhere from a foot to several feet off the bottom—depending on the length of the leader. This technique will catch a lot of fish, especially in weedy ponds."

If this innovative Bugger were an American pattern, I suppose it would be called the **Disco Bugger**. But it's an Aussie pattern and I found it, like several others in this book, on the Fishnet web site (www.fishnet.com.au), a wonderfully fertile source of fly patterns. The fly was presented by Jerry Caruso, who indicated the pattern was originally shown to him without the pinhead eyes or sparkle paint. (I was unable to track down Caruso—who was listed as having a military e-mail address, which returned my messages as undeliverable—to find out who originated the pattern.)

Caruso presented it as a large fly—sizes 1 and 1/0, with a 1-inch-diameter head disk—appropriate to his quarry: Australian bass and golden perch, imported largemouth and pike, and saltwater species. Caruso wrote, "Target species include any that will take a topwater fly, if presented in the proper size and color." I think it can be scaled all the way down to panfish-popper size. Use 6-mm-thick foam and cut large disks for saltwater popper—and tie them on stainless-steel or corrosion-resistant plated hooks. And if I were tying it for salt water, I'd add a wire rib and reverse-palmer the hackle from front to bend.

Although the fly can be tied in a variety of fish-attracting colors, I am presenting the white pattern presented by Caruso.

Fun Foam Popper

Hook: Terrestrial or long-shank dry-fly with a straight or turned-down eye, sizes to suit your target species: perhaps 2 to 12 in fresh water, 4 to 1/0 in salt water (I used a Mustad 37187 wide-gap, bass-bug, size 6)

Thread: White 6/0 or 3/0

Tail: Pearl Flashabou or Krystal Flash covered sparsely by white marabou

Body: Tying thread

Head: Disk die-cut from a sheet of thin, white, closed-cell craft foam in a size suited to the hook (the diameter roughly 1 1/2 times the hook gap); optionally, translucent (or even phosphorescent) sparkle fabric paint may be used to add to the fly's come-hither seductiveness—in this case, I used gold-glitter fabric paint

Eyes: Optionally, yellow or red, round-headed plastic pin heads, secured with epoxy cement, a tiny drop of black paint added for a pupil

Palmer hackle: White rooster saddle

Tying Tips

To die-cut the foam disk, use a grinder, file, or emery paper to bevel the edges on one end of a short piece of copper, brass, aluminum, or other metal tubing of suitable diameter. A rap of the hammer turns the sharpened tubing into a simple die. Alternatively, for smaller flies, use a razor blade or craft knife to slice a disk from a cylinder of fly-body or similar closed-cell foam.

After tying on, lay a short (1/4-in), smooth thread base behind the hook eye. After cutting (and painting, if you wish) the disk head, put a drop of superglue on the thread base. Pinch the bottom of the foam disk around the glued spot on the shank, being careful not to get any of that glue on your skin. Holding the pinched portion in place, wrap it in position with thread. This should produce an upright head that leans slightly forward, its concave-cupped face over the eye.

Wrap a thread base back to the bend and tie in the tail materials. Tie in the hackle by its tip and take the thread back to the head, smoothing out the thread-base body.

Although Caruso listed only the white pattern, don't be afraid to use other colors and color combinations. For night fishing, be sure to try black, because fish can see it so well against the relatively lighter sky.

Fishing Tips

Caruso wrote, "The fly, which represents an injured baitfish, can be popped like a conventional popper, used like a gurgler by making long, slow strips, or used as a darter by using a sinking line. Vary retrieve speed and time at rest to find out what your quarry is interested in that day."

"Fishing top water," he advised, "cast to structure and breaklines, and work thoroughly around weedbeds and stick-ups. Good fly for night fishing or murky waters. If fishing subsurface on a sinking line, fish points and rips. Also works down and across in rivers with a sinking line."

Caruso must know his North American fish species, because he wrote that the fly is "especially good for U. S. species such as black bass and pike species in fresh water and redfish, blues, stripers, and speckled trout in the salt."

I discovered this Ed Weido creation in one of C. Boyd Pfeiffer's "Strange Stuff" columns in *Fly Tyer* (Spring 1997). Weido is a retired coal-miner from Nemacolin, Pennsylvania. A concept rather than a pattern, this oddball fly uses fabric paint for the body. Why? Because it's easy to use, comes in all kinds of colors, including glittery ones, and when applied correctly makes the hackle virtually indestructible. You can use any brand and color fabric paint you choose, but those containing glitter or sparkle may attract fish better, and ones that come in squeeze bottles with tapered spouts are easier to work with.

If you decide to tie up a bunch, do it assembly-line style: After tying in the tail and hackle feather, and applying the body paint, take the unfinished fly out of the vise (without letting the dangling hackle touch the wet paint) and let the body dry for a few hours while you partially tie a bunch more. The key is to let the paint half-set, so the hackle stems will sink into the paint (armoring them) but the paint won't run into the hack-le barbs. If you use glittery paint, it will become translucent when it's ready, and the glitter will show well. That said, let's get on with it.

Painted Fabri-Bugger

Hook: 3X- or 4X-long streamer of choice, sized to suit your angling

Head: *Optionally, a bead or pompom or wrapped chenille*

Thread: 6/0 in a color to match, complement, or con trast with the rest of the fly

Underbody: Thread base; *optionally, wire lead wrapped on the shank*

Tail: Marabou in the color of your choice, the butts lashed along the entire length of the shank; *optionally, flash materials instead of or added to the marabou*

Palmer hackle: Hackle feather in a color to suit, tied in by its tip at the bend, and later palmered forward through the half-cured body paint

Body: Fabric paint squeezed onto the underbody and smoothed out with a toothpick, coffee stirrer, or similar

Tying Tips

Do not let the tail or tied-in hackle feather come into contact with the wet body paint. To help keep the feather from drifting into the paint, use a drinking straw. After tying in the feather and before applying the paint, slip a quarter-inch length of straw (one side of which has been slit lengthwise) over the eye of the hook and down over the hackle and tail feathers.

Wait until the paint is half-cured before palmering the hackle. You want the hackle *stem* to sink into the paint without causing the paint to run into the hackle barbs. Even so, to minimize your chances of making a mess (at least in your first few trials), strip the barbs from one side of the hackle quill or fold the hackle along the quill and wrap it with both sides of the barbs pointing upward.

While palmering the hackle, forming the head, and tying off, be careful not to touch the still-wet body.

Tie it with a shorter tail of hackle tips or fibers, wool, floss, or similar, and call it a **Painted Fabri-Worm**.

If wire-bodied, glass-bodied, ice-fishing, bead-chain-bodied, floating, popping, paint-bodied, and hot-pursuit Woolly Buggers weren't far-out enough for you, consider the Worm Bugger. "This is a fly that will make you cringe," warned the late L. J. DeCuir. But ignore your fine sensibilities, he advised, for the way Gerald Wilt's translucent, soft-bodied, iconoclastic version of the Woolly Bugger catches bass and trout will have you grinning from ear to ear.

About Wilt I know next to nothing except that at the time he unleashed his Worm Bugger on an unsuspecting world, he was on the faculty at Auburn University. DeCuir was a busy fellow; besides tying and fishing flies, he bred and showed English bulldogs, and served the University of Tennessee's Department of Theatre as a lighting designer, teacher, and director of graduate studies.

This pattern also appears in DeCuir's *Southeastern Flies*, published by Menasha Ridge Press.

When fishing this fly, the wearing of a patch-decorated jumpsuit is optional and not necessarily recommended.

Worm Bugger

Hook: Mustad 79580 or similar 4X-long "or longer" streamer, sizes 4 to 10

Head: *Optionally, a metal or glass bead*

Body: A 3/4-shank-length piece of a 6-inch, soft-plastic worm—unflavored, salt-free, translucent, and of a color to suit—skewered on the hook so it is straight and centered on the shank; Wilt favors the color called "motor oil"

Thread: 6/0, color to match the body, tied on and whip-finished 3 times (see Tying Steps)

Rib: Copper wire; *optionally, other colors*

Tail: Marabou, color to suit; DeCuir says, "Black or brown works well with a motor-oil body."

Palmer hackle: Saddle hackle, color to suit

Eyes: *Optionally, bead-chain or dumbbell eyes, if you want a weighted fly that's either lighter or heavier than a bead-head*

Tying Steps

First, *or after slipping on the optional bead*, carefully thread the piece of plastic worm onto the hook (keeping the hook as close to dead-center and the plastic worm as straight as possible) before mounting the hook in the vise. Unless you have plastic-worm–fishing experience or a bit of the Bubba in you, this will take some trial-and-error practice.

Start the thread behind the worm body, tie in the copper wire, and whip-finish.

Spiral the wire over the plastic body, tightly enough to compress it, but not tightly enough to cut into it. Now comes the tricky part: Using a heat source (preferably a heat gun, but a lighter or other open flame will work, *if* you are very, very careful and keep the flame *above* the worm), heat the plastic just enough to soften it, so it will flow around the wire. Too much heat, and it will melt, drip, or burn. A rotary vise helps to distribute the heat evenly; otherwise, hold the hook in a hemostat (forceps) and use forearm and wrist to rotate the fly. As the plastic softens, it will flow around the wire.

After everything has cooled completely, tie on again behind the body, tie in the marabou tail and the tip of the saddle hackle, and whip-finish. It's a good idea to cement this whip-finish. Then, tie on the thread in front of the body.

Palmer the hackle over the body and tie it down well at the front with a few tight wraps. *If you wish to use bead-chain or dumbbell eyes, tie them in at this point.* Whip-finish and cement the head.

Tying Tips

The more transparent or translucent the plastic-worm body, the more visible the wire rib, and the more potentially important its color.

Upon arriving at your local Wal-Mart, Kmart, bait shop, or other hawg heaven and beholding the panoply of plastic-worm colors, "If you don't immediately grasp the unlimited number of variations possible with this fly," said DeCuir, "then you are suffering from a severely impeded imagination." The Worm Bugger's gaudy possibilities can be expanded by tying in some Flashabou or Krystal Flash streamers with the tail or just in front of the body.

This wild creation by the Scotsman Leon Guthrie is difficult to categorize or describe. This picture really *is* worth a thousand words. I suppose it resembles two baitfish fighting over something. The action is quite dynamic, with the main fly trying to sink and the teaser trying to float.

This is such an iconoclastic pattern, you should experiment with different fishing techniques until you find the one that works for you. Of course, you should also experiment with different colors and color combinations.

Leon's Double Bugger

TEASER

Mandrel: A large wooden cocktail toothpick, cut or broken off (if necessary) so that it is about as long as the main fly's hook shank

Thread: Black 6/0

Connector: 10- to 20-lb-test monofilament, lashed to the entire length of the toothpick, leaving a long tag end extending to the front (the long tag end will later be lashed to the shank of the main fly's hook)

Tail: Black marabou, full and about as long as the teaser's body

Body: Black chenille or wool

Palmer hackle: Brown saddle

MAIN FLY

Hook: Salmon/steelhead wet-fly, sizes 4 to 8; 3X- or 4X-long streamer, down to size 14, for trout; larger, stainless-steel hooks for salt water

Thread: Black 6/0

Underbody: *Optionally, lead wire wrapped on the shank*

Teaser: The teaser, tied as above, tied in by its monofilament connector to the shank just behind the main fly's hook eye, the tie-in wraps reinforced by cement

Tail: Black marabou, full and slightly longer than the hook

Body: Black chenille or wool, wrapped to the teaser's connector

Palmer hackle: Brown saddle

Head: Thread, securely covering the teaser connector's tie in, lacquered

Tying Tips

The only tricky part in the tying is finding a way to hold that toothpick for the teaser. I tried several methods, and the one that worked best for me was using a tube-fly tool, inserting the pointed end of the toothpick instead of the tube-holding mandrel. After I finished tying the teaser, I broke off the excess parts of the toothpick.

Before wrapping the body of the main fly, lash the tag end of the teaser's connector to the shank, just behind the hook eye, so that the main fly and the teaser are separated by about a shank-length of monofilament, or less. Wrap the body material and the palmer hackle up to the teaser's connector—and, optionally, one wrap beyond.

Y ou needn't be a Nobel laureate to figure out that putting a bead head on a Woolly Bugger makes it sink faster and adds a bit of extra allure. (We've already listed a bunch of beadhead Buggers in the previous chapter.) This chapter is devoted to Bugger patterns in which heads or eyes play especially important roles.

WEIGHT-FORWARD WOOLLY BUGGERS

Too few anglers realize that by moving the weight forward, the fly swims differently (more alluringly, perhaps), and that beads and heavy eyes sink faster than lead wire. A few tiers have come up with weight-forward patterns that make purposeful use of those advantages. Here are just a few of them.

WOOLLY BOMBER *Tied by Orvis*

This fly has been in the Orvis catalog for quite a few years. I have no idea who originated the pattern.

Woolly Bomber

Hook: Orvis 8808, Daiichi 2220, or similar 4X-long streamer, sizes 4 to 10
Thread: Black
Eyes: Chrome recessed dumbbell eyes, tied atop the shank, with Prismatic Epoxy Eyes (yellow, with black pupils) attached; *alternatively (the way Orvis used to make them), dumbbell eyes, painted black, with yellow pupils*
Tail: Black marabou
Body: Black chenille
Palmer hackle: Grizzly saddle
Head: Black chenille body material, wrapped around eyes and finished off between the dumbbell eyes and the hook eye.

Tying Note

I found an essentially similar Italian pattern of the same name, the principal differences being the use of olive chenille for the body, black saddle for the palmer hackle, and oval gold tinsel for a rib that is wound over the body *before* the hackle is palmered.

JOHN'S WOOLLY BUGGER *Tied by John Gierach*

This dumbbell-eyed Bugger is by today's best-read fly-fishing author, John Gierach, who says, "This one doesn't have its own name; it's just how I tie most of my Buggers. It's tied like a regular Woolly Bugger except for the hook, the eyeballs, and the figure-8 head." And I figure that's difference enough to merit a name. John continues: "I found that, if you tie in lead eyes just behind the hook eye, the hook still swims right side up. (Usually, lead eyes on top of the shank turn the fly over in the water.) I usually tie them in black, but olive and other colors also work." If you

are used to getting a laugh out of John Gierach, sit up and pay attention, because this man knows how to fish! It's also obvious John can tie!

John's Woolly Bugger

Hook: Daiichi 1870 swimming larva, sizes 4 to 10
Thread: Black 6/0
Eyes: Dumbbell eyes (yellow, with black pupils), tied atop the shank immediately behind the hook eye
Tail: Black marabou
Body: Black rabbit, dubbed; "and I try to tie them sparse"
Palmer hackle: Black saddle hackle, palmered almost up to the dumbbell eyes
Head: Black rabbit, dubbed in figure-8 wraps around and between the eyes

SUPER BUGGER *Tied by Barry and Cathy Beck*

Writing in *Fly Fisherman Magazine*, Barry and Cathy Beck say that Cathy's Super Bugger works wonders on big trout. "These streamers sink quickly and look alive in the water," say American's favorite fishing twosome, "even with the slow retrieves that are often necessary when water temperatures drop into the 50s or lower." They tie this in three colors: black (their first choice, as shown above), olive (second choice), and tan (when crayfish are around). I like to fish crayfish patterns, so I'm listing the tan. To tie the others, substitute "black" or "olive" for "tan."

Super Bugger

Hook: TMC 3761, a 1X-long, 2X-heavy wet-fly, sizes 4 to 8
Thread: Tan 6/0
Eyes: Dumbbell eyes, painted yellow, with black pupils
Tail: Tan marabou and pearl Krystal Flash
Palmer hackle: Tan-dyed grizzly body feathers over a thread base
Legs: Tan Sili-Legs, 3 on each side, reaching back to the end of the tail
Head: Tan dubbing brush

PEARL DANCER *Tied by Sir Kevin Moss*

I found this Sir Kevin Moss pattern on his Glen of Rothes Trout Fishery web site (www.morayflyfishing.co.uk). A professional tier, guide, and fly-fishing instructor, Sir Kevin lives beside the River Spey in Lossiemouth, Morayshire, Scotland.

Pearl Dancer

Hook: 3X- or 4X-long streamer, sizes 10 to 14
Head: Brass bead, about 3 or 4 mm
Thread: Black 6/0
Tail: White marabou, more than hook-length, with a few strands of pearl Lureflash—*alternatively, Holographic Flashabou, Krystal Flash, etc.*—mixed in
Rib: Fine gold wire, counterwound through the palmer hackle
Body: Mixed colors of fine Mylar tinsel (*alternatively, twisted Krystal Flash or similar*)
Palmer hackle: Yellow hen saddle, tied in by the butt behind the bead head and reverse-palmered in 5 or 6 open spirals to the bend

BARRY WHITE'S OTHER BUGGER

Although Barry White guides on the Bow River and claims to have "first introduced the Wooly *[sic]* Bugger to the Bow River in 1981," this is not a **Bow River Bugger** (see pages 192-193). Rather, it is a Woolly Bugger for fishing the Bow River. White prefers a conventionally black-hackled, purple-bodied, black-tailed Woolly Bugger, but I am intrigued by the other, unnamed Bugger that is pictured but not listed on his web site (www.bowriver.com). Here's my best guess at the recipe.

Barry White's Other Bugger

Hook: Salmon/steelhead wet-fly, the barb pinched down, size 2; *I think you can safely change hooks and sizes to suit your fishing—I used a 3X-long, size-6 streamer*
Head: Brass or copper cone
Thread: Brown or black 6/0
Tail: Yellow marabou or blood feather, with a strand of pearl Flashabou on either side
Body: Variegated tinsel or tinsel-blend chenille in tan and dark brown or black
Palmer hackle: Grizzly hen or rooster

Tying Tips

"I selected marabou bloods for the tail," White wrote on his site, a choice with which I often concur. White prefers to use neck hackle for his Buggers "because of the action I get while fishing it," but if you don't think your neck hackles will go the shank distance, use a saddle hackle to palmer the Bugger.

D-BUGGER *Tied by Dennis Garrison*

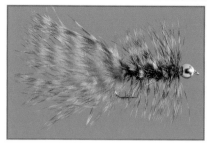

Breathes there a fly-tying angler fisher who hasn't tried to come up with the "perfect" Woolly Bugger? This is the pattern so nominated by Dennis Garrison, a wildlife biologist who is presently based in California. It began life as a beadhead, soft-hackle caddis imitation, tied with the same variegated chenille, and "somewhere along the line" became a stonefly-imitating Bugger with a name to warm the heart of a software programmer.

"I am a fan of basic flies," Garrison writes on the Fly Tying World web site (flytyingworld.com). "Part of this is my belief that trout, even big ones, are inherently stupid. The rest is laziness, which leads me to tie the simplest effective flies I can get away with." He adds however, that this and his other patterns "have been tested thoroughly on some of the best trout waters the West has to offer." Others fishing his D-Bugger have reported great success "from New York to Costa Rica, so far."

D-Bugger

Hook: Dai-Riki 700 or similar 4X-long streamer, size 10
Head: 5/32-in gold or brass bead
Thread: Tan 6/0 UNI
Underbody: .015- or .020-in lead-free wire
Tail: Sand (Wapsi) or tan (Hareline) dyed grizzly marabou
Rib: Fine copper wire, counter-wrapped through the hackle
Body: Brown and yellow variegated chenille (medium)
Palmer hackle: Golden-ginger–dyed grizzly Spencer rooster saddle

Tying Tips

"Changing the length of the hackle fibers and bushiness of the tail changes the way it looks and fishes," Garrison says, "and changing bead color can alter its effectiveness." (*Your author thinks the fly would look and fish great sporting a copper bead.*) "I also tie this pattern in an olive version," he continues, "using New Age Chenille for a bit of sparkle." To tie the **Olive D-Bugger**, substitute a black chrome bead head, olive tying thread, dark-olive–dyed marabou tail, black or green copper wire rib, "Wintergreen" New Age Chenille (medium), and a dark-olive-dyed grizzly hackle.

Although Garrison doesn't specify it, this tier would probably tie in the hackle in by the butt at the front and reverse-palmer it, using the copper wire to secure the hackle at the rear before winding the rib forward.

Fishing Tips

"I usually fish this fly dead-drifted, as a nymph," Garrison writes. "It imitates stoneflies and crayfish, as well as being a generically buggy-looking attractor. Fished as a streamer, it is a fair sculpin imitation. I have used it with great success on fish from trout to bluegill to salmon, in several states."

BEAD-HEAD RUBBER-LEG WOOLLY BUGGER
Tied by Umpqua Feather Merchants for Kaufmann's Streamborn

A Randall Kaufmann pattern, this Bugger comes in three colors: Black, Brown, Olive. Body color matches the name in all three; the Brown version also uses brown tying thread and marabou, while the others use black for both thread and tail. I'm listing Brown.

Kaufmann's Streamborn also sells beadless **Rubber-Leg Woolly Buggers** in Black, Brown (see page 183), White, Olive, Brown/Grizzly, Olive/Black, and Purple. The last three have white legs that contrast with the rest of the pattern; the first four use rubber legs that are identical or similar in hue to the rest of the fly.

Bead-Head Rubber-Leg Woolly Bugger

Hook: TMC 5263, a 3X-l... sizes 4 to 8
Head: Medium gold bead
Thread: Brown
Underbody: Lead wire
Palmer hackle: Black saddle, tied i... bead head; 3 turns... reverse-palmered b...
Tail: Brown marabou, w... Holographic Flasha... carried forward alo...
Legs: Black, round rubber... each side of the bo... upward and back t...
Rib: Fine copper wire
Body: Brown tinsel chenill...
Sides: Silver Holographic Flashabou from the tail, carried forward along both sides and tied down up front before the hackle is palmered and ribbed.

Here's another heavy-headed, rubber-legged Bugger—this one from the red-headed, fly-fishing pharmacist from Edinburgh, Virginia, Harry Murray. I don't have the recipe, so I am basing the listing on the picture in his on-line catalog (www.murraysflyshop.com).

Murray's Road-Kill Nymph

Hook: 3X-long streamer, sizes 6 and 8
Thread: Black or olive 6/0
Eyes: Lead dumbbells, tied below the shank, far enough behind the hook eye to form the head
Tail: Olive marabou, tapered and slightly longer than the hook
Legs: 6 black rubber legs (3 on each side), the first pair immediately in front of and flanking the tail, the third pair at about mid shank—all extending to the tip of the tail or beyond
Body: Black chenille
Palmer hackle: Olive hen saddle, palmered up to and beyond the dumbbell eyes
Head: Black chenille from the body, cross-wrapped between the eyes, finishing with a couple of wraps ahead of the lead eyes and right behind the hook eye

Tying Tip

The catalog also lists a similar **Murray's Magnum Ghost Nymph** intended for fishing slowly "down and across stream in deep pools, between ledges, and below riffles." It looks somewhat similar, but with these differences: 2X-long hook in the same sizes; white thread; the dumbbell eyes painted white with black pupils (probably clear-coated); white tail, body, and legs, the legs more or less evenly distributed along the shank; grizzly palmer hackle. Harry says, "For reasons I can't explain, there are times when this lead-eye, rubber-leg, white nymph will catch more fish than the match-the-hatch patterns."

Fishing Tip

The catalog copy says to fish the Road-Kill Nymph "in deep pools with a spurt–pause–spurt retrieve to mimic the action of dragonfly nymphs and with a slow, crawling action below the riffles."

Another lead-eyed pattern from Harry Murray, this one comes in three colors: Chub, Shiner, and Sunfish. All three are fished slowly and similarly: tight to banks, around grass beds, below riffles, between ledges, in pools, and around the drop-offs of gravel bars. Not surprisingly, considering Harry's renown as a smallmouth master, all three patterns have been proven on smallmouth bass, but the Shiner has been equally effective on trout. "The slower and deeper you fish them," Harry says, "the bigger the fish you'll catch."

I am listing **Murray's Leadeye Sunfish**; changes to make in the other patterns follow.

Murray's Leadeye Streamer

Hook: 3X- or 4X-long streamer, sizes 6 and 8
Thread: Black 6/0
Eyes: Painted lead dumbbells (I used doll's eyes, glued on brass dumbbells), tied a bit behind the hook eye
Tail: Yellow marabou, a bit longer than the hook
Palmer hackle: Olive-dyed saddle, the barbs about a gap-width long, and palmered all the way to the hook eye
Body: Orange chenille, wrapped over and around the lead eyes and finished at the hook eye

Tying Notes

Here are the changes to make to tie the other patterns:
Murray's Leadeye Chub: White marabou and pearl Krystal Flash over blue marabou for the tail; pearl tinsel chenille body; blue-dyed saddle hackle, the barbs half again as long as the hook gap

Murray's Leadeye Shiner: White marabou tail, cream or white chenille body, grizzly palmer hackle, clipped to about half a gap in length

The very name, albeit misspelled, pretty well describes the tail on this fly: humongous. In fact, when tied with a long-fibered tinsel chenille and a big hackle, the whole fly pretty well lives up to its name. The anonymous writer on the Diptera web site (www.diptera.co.uk), where I found this pattern, says, "The Humungus can be tied with large crystal chenille and large hackle, which makes a large lure. I prefer a smaller version using Microbrite leaded sparkle chenille, a 2-mm bead, and a small Whiting cape hackle." The Diptera lister says he or she has taken numerous rainbow and brown trout using "a mixed retrieve of sharp twitches and figure-of-eight [hand-twist] retrieves."

Unable to find the prescribed Microbrite Leaded Glister Chenille, or anything about it, I have had to make minor modifications in my listing. I have listed the **Silver** version; for the Gold, just substitute gold wire and tinsel chenille and brass bead chain

Humungus

Hook: Kamasan B175, a 3X-strong beadhead nymph, size 8; alternatively, Daiichi 1550 or TMC 3769, size 8; or Mustad 3906B, size 6
Thread: Black 6/0
Eyes: 2-mm silver bead chain
Underbody: *Optionally, lead wire wrapped on the shank*
Tail: Black marabou, full and twice as long as the hook
Rib: Fine silver wire
Palmer hackle: Grizzly or cree rooster, the barbs at least half again long as the hook gap, reverse-palmered from behind the eyes to the bend; *alternatively, if you weight the fly with lead wire, a Whiting hackle with barbs about a gap-width long*
Body: Silver tinsel chenille, long-fibered for an unweighted fly; short fibered, if you use the wire underbody, to keep the profile slim
Head: Body material, wrapped between, around, and in front of the eyes

Tying Tips

With such a long, full tail, I'd want to add a loop of monofilament under the tail to prevent its fouling the hook. That, or a "platform" of stiff bucktail at least a gap-width long.

Diptera also lists a **Multicoloured** version. Everything is as listed above except the body, which is in thirds: green in the rear, silver in the middle, and gold up front. Use either color of wire and bead chain.

BEAD HEAD LITE BRITE BUGGER *Tied by Orvis*

Kevin Sloan, who buys flies and develops fly patterns for Orvis, says this is his favorite Woolly Bugger, especially in brown. When I suggested it was taken as a crayfish, Kevin said, "I don't know—I fish it awfully fast." Then I suggested that trout take it as a sculpin, or as a panicked crayfish in full flight. "I don't know—," he said again, "it's an awfully good steelhead fly." Okay, I give up trying to "match the hatch." If trout and steelhead take it well, I don't really care what they take it *for*. Besides Kevin's favorite brown, this pattern also comes in both black and olive. I'm listing the black and showing the olive.

Bead Head Lite Brite Bugger

Hook: Orvis 8808, a 4X-long streamer, sizes 4 to 8
Head: Black metal bead
Thread: Black
Palmer hackle: Dark grizzly, reverse-palmered from front to rear
Tail: Black marabou
Body: Metallic black Lite Brite
Rib: Copper fine wire

Tying Tip

Upon close inspection, it's apparent that Orvis's tiers do not reverse-palmer the hackle on this pattern. I have listed the fly for reverse-palmering, because it will be more durable that way.

If you want to tie Kevin Sloan's favorite version, just substitute a gold-colored brass bead, brown-dyed grizzly, and make the thread, tail, and body brown. For the olive version, just substitute olive for black in the above recipe.

GLASS-HEAD BUGGER

This one is from Erik Andreasson, who hails from Västerås, near Lake Mälaren, in central Sweden. The use of two glass beads in the head is what sets it apart from other bead-head Buggers.

Glass-Head Bugger

Hook: Standard streamer, sizes 8 and 10
Head: 2 green glass beads, the second larger than the first
Thread: Black 6/0
Tail: Chartreuse marabou, at least hook-length
Underbody: The marabou butt(s), lashed to the shank and thread-wrapped to the beads and back
Body: Black medium chenille
Rib: *Optionally, fine wire, in which case the hackle should be tied in behind the beads and reverse-palmered*
Palmer hackle: Black Indian hen or webby saddle

Tying Tips

Other colors can be used. Just match the glass beads to the marabou used for the tail.

"To get a brighter effect from the beads," it says on Rob Knisely's Invicta Flies web site (http://tripod.com/ invicta-flies/id226.htm), "wrap a thin layer of white or yellow thread just behind the eye, tie this off and clip, then slip the beads over this. The white is magnified, producing a brighter color than is produced by the bare hook. Optionally, you can lacquer over the beads to both hold them together and make them more durable. This also 'smoothes' the double-bead head somewhat and makes for a nicer finished product."

CONEY SNOWBUGGER *Tied by Bas Verschoor*

Many tiers and vendors of flies now use cone heads on their buggers, but this was one of the first and is still one of the best. On the world-class Global Fly Fisher web site (www.globalfly-fisher.com), the Dutch tier Bas "Flydutch" Verschoor calls his baitfish-imitating fly an "albino version of the Woolly Bugger." For an extra-heavy fly, Bas says you can also wrap the shank with lead wire; the way I cast, I'd have to wear a hard hat! For a less hefty version, you can replace the cone head with a silver Sparkle Dubbing Brush, wrapping the shank with lead or not. (Like a growing number of master and journeyman tiers in Europe—and far too few adventurous souls on our side of the pond—the Flying Dutchman is fond of Jan Siman's dubbing brushes and Softdubs. So am I.)

Coney Snowbugger

Hook: TMC 5263, or similar 2X- to 6X-long streamer, sizes 2 and 4
Head: 5/32- to 7/32-in, gold-colored cone head; *alternatively, silver Sparkle Dubbing Brush*
Thread: White 10/0 or 12/0, taken back to the bend as a thread base
Gills: Red dubbing brush, tied in behind the head and wrapped ("a few turns") at the end
Palmer hackle: White schlappen feather, tied in by the butt behind the dubbing brush to be reverse-palmered to the bend
Tail: White marabou, half again as long as the hook gap, with a few strands of pearl Krystal Flash on top
Body: Pearl tinsel chenille
Rib: Fine silver wire
Collar hackle: Silver-pheasant body feather, tied in and wrapped as a long wet-fly collar after the body has been palmer-hackled and ribbed

Tying Tip

More recently, Bas has developed the **Black Coneybugger**. To tie it, just substitute a 4X-long streamer hook, black for the color of the cone, thread, palmer hackle, tail, body, and wet-fly collar, and gold for the rib. For a less-weighty version, substitute a *black* Sparkle Dubbing Brush for the cone head. Fish the Black Coneybugger at night or when the water is colored, or whenever your experience or instinct tells you that a dark fly is what's wanted.

SCHILDMEER SPECIAL

This beady-eyed Bugger is the creation of a Dutch flyfisher named Eddie Bouma. I found the pattern on the Global Fly Fisher web site (www.globalfly-fisher.com). Bouma uses this fly for European perch *(Perca fluviatilis)*, which are a good bit bigger and, in my opinion, slightly less succulent than *P. flavescens,* our otherwise similar yellow perch.

Schildmeer Special

Hook: TMC 100, a 1X-fine dry-fly, sizes 8-10
Thread: Black 6/0
Eyes: Large nickel bead chain (oversize for the hook)
Tail: Red marabou, sparse and shank-length, over 2 strands of pearl Krystal Flash
Palmer hackle: Brown saddle
Body: Wine-colored Cactus Chenille or other tinsel chenille
Head: Tying thread, varnished

Tying Tips

To keep the eyes from twisting, secure them to the shank with figure 8 wraps and drop some glue on the wraps. At the end, take the tying thread over the eyes, wrap a neat head, whip-finish, and varnish.

Optionally, give the fly an even bigger head by letting the extra body chenille dangle while you palmer the hackle. After the hackle has been tied off and clipped, take the body chenille over and under the bead eyes, wrap once around the shank in front of the eyes, bring the chenille back over the eyes, and tie off.

I've never had much luck fishing for yellow perch with red flies. My best perch patterns use a chiaroscuro effect of light and dark, the light varying from yellow to cream to light olive and the dark, always shrouding the light, is black, grizzly, or really dark olive. So, here's the way I'd tie the Schildmeer Special for yellow perch: brass bead chain, black marabou over gold or yellow Krystal Flash for the tail, and a black or dark-grizzly saddle hackle palmered over a yellow tinsel-chenille body. Alternatively, use dark-olive marabou and palmer hackle.

AUTUMN SPLENDOR *Tied by Kevin Sloan*

When Kevin Sloan came east from Colorado to work in product development at Orvis headquarters in Manchester, Vermont, he brought this big-fish pattern with him to tempt the Battenkill's wily, outsized browns—fish that have thus far successfully resisted everything I have shown them.

Autumn Splendor

Hook: Orvis 8808, a 4X-long streamer, sizes 2 to 6
Head: Brass or tungsten cone
Thread: Brown
Tail: Marabou, yellow covered by brown
Legs: 6 yellow medium rubber legs (3 pairs); *alternatively, yellow Flexi Floss*
Belly: 2 strands of yellow chenille, pulled over the body beneath the shank
Body: Brown chenille
Palmer hackle: Grizzly

MOTHER-BUGGER *Tied by Chris Del Plato*

Another copperhead Bugger from the Delaware watershed, this one's from Chris Del Plato, a streamer specialist from northern New Jersey: "Here's a Woolly Bugger pattern that, for me, seems to get better results than any other version. Especially with brookies."

Mother-Bugger

Hook: TMC 300, Mustad 3665A, "or any roughly 6X-long streamer," sizes 6 to 8
Head: Large (3/16-in) copper bead
Thread: Black
Tail: Purple marabou, with several strands of Rainbow Flashabou
Body: Black chenille
Palmer hackle: Grizzly

Mike Hogue (alias Badger Creek Fly Tying, www.efly-tyer.com) devised a Bugger pattern (named for the Green River) specifically to take advantage of Danville's then-new purple-and-pearl Sparkle Chenille blend. As always, Mike used a whole feather of strung marabou or Woolly Bugger Marabou to get the full tail he says is key to this Bugger's success.

Mike's G. R. Woolly

Hook: Mustad 9672, a 3X-long nymph or streamer, sizes 6 and 8
Head: Large (5/32-inch) gold bead
Thread: Black
Tail: Claret marabou, very full
Body: Purple-and-pearl Sparkle Chenille, a tinsel-and-textile blend
Palmer hackle: Black saddle; *alternatively, use one feather each of black and claret and palmer them together, or one through the other, for a mixed black-and-claret effect*

Tying Tip

Hogue sometimes reverses the tail and hackle colors: black tail, claret hackle.

DOG NOBBLER

For years British fly fishers have been pinching lead shot onto the front of their shanks and tying Dog Nobblers. Trouble is, the lead weights sometimes fly off during vigorous casts (which is why they should always be secured in place with epoxy or superglue), and British authorities take a very dim view of lead on the bottom of their streams and ponds. Ingested lead has been blamed for the demise of whole populations of swans and other bottom-feeding waterfowl. More recently, British tiers have taken to using painted brass bead heads (the conical holes filled with lead wire and a drop of glue, to keep them from spinning if eyes have been painted on) and Bob Church's innovative Tinhead hooks. If you want to approximate the Tinhead hook, just pinch a tin-alloy split shot onto the front of the shank, over a cement-soaked thread base that will keep it from coming loose during casting or fishing.

Traditionally, Dog Nobblers are tied much like Woolly Buggers, with long—*very* long—marabou tails and hackle palmered over a chenille, wool, or marabou (wrapped or dubbed) body. Lazy as their American counterparts, many Brits now just tie on a marabou tail, wrap the shank with Fritz (a British brand of tinsel chenille), and let it go at that. I've listed the lazy, redheaded, black-and-pearl version, but added the fillip of an optional grizzly palmer hackle. Feel free to us colors you like. Just make the head bright and in cor body.

Dog Nobbler

Hook: 2X-long nymph or streamer, sizes 1
Head: Bright red bead—either a brass be slipped onto the shank before tying split shot, pinched onto wet, ceme thread wraps
Thread: Black or red 6/0
Tail: Black marabou, full and twice as hook; optionally, a monofilament the long tail from fouling the hool
Body: Pearl tinsel chenille
Palmer hackle: Grizzly saddle
Eyes: Optionally, painted or stick-on eyes

EGGHEAD BUGGERS

Because beadhead flies fish deeper and have what many consider a better swimming action than shank-weighted flies, they are effective in many angling situations. But part of their effectiveness may come from the attractive glitz of the metal or glass beads, which might cause fish to see the flies as roe-raiding interlopers. When you want the egg's sizzle, but not the bead's heft, the soft egghead Bugger may be your best bet.

Use any number of materials to fashion your egg heads—yarn, chenille, wool, floss, thread, dubbing, foam, or ready-made pom-poms—as long as the colors are imitate of fish eggs or very bright and eye-catching. One fellow I know, who fishes stocked waters in the East, uses tan and brown eggheads on his Buggers. He says the flies look like small baitfish poaching on pellets of Purina Trout Chow. Lordy, he's probably right.

EGG SUCKING LEECH

Simply a marriage of two big-fish winners—the Woolly Bugger and the Single Egg Fly, or Glo-Bug—the Egg-Sucking Leech seems to have been around for almost as long as the Woolly Bugger. Not so. Writing in the Fall 1986 issue of *American Fly Tyer*, Anthony J. Route described it as a recent invention by Will Bauer, a fly-shop owner in Anchorage. The Alaska Flyfishers concur with this provenance and on their former web site added that the ESL "catches virtually every sport fish in Alaska's lakes, streams, and oceans."

Nowadays, the pattern is tied on a variety of hooks and in a variety of colors: purple, pink, red, orange, yellow, tan, cream, or even white for the Egg head, and black or black-and-purple

for the Woolly Bugger part—often with some Flashabou or Krystal Flash added. The rainbows don't seem to mind the changes. This is the original pattern presented by Route.

Egg Sucking Leech

Hook: Mustad 9672, a 3X-long streamer, sizes 4 to 8, "but any comparable hook will do"
Thread: Dark-brown "heavy-duty" [3/0, perhaps, or Monocord]
Underbody: 10 to 15 wraps of .035-in lead wire
Tail: Black marabou, about the length of the hook
Body: Black chenille, wrapped to a point about 4 eye-lengths short of the hook eye
Palmer hackle: Black saddle
Head: Pink chenille wrapped to form an egg-shaped ball; finished off with a whip-finish of the brown thread, well-lacquered

Tying Tips

Fish eggs vary considerably in color, according to the species, from pale off-white and pearl-gray to dark red-orange. Matching the egg "hatch" doesn't seem to be all that important, except perhaps when rainbow trout are locked onto a particular salmon run's eggs. Then, you might find that a pink egg, say, will result in more pickups than an orange egg. Or vice versa. Brightness and contrast are the keys to success, not color-matching.

Instead of the chenille, slip a bright- or fluorescent-pink, -red-, or -orange glass or plastic bead on the hook before tying on to make a **Hardhead Egg Sucking Leech.**

Tie in a very short "wing" of white calf or similar material (or even white CDC or marabou) just behind the hook eye, so that it lies over the egghead, simulating milt, and you have what I call a **Milty Bugger.**

EGG SUCKING CRYSTAL BUGGER *Tied by Dave Hudson for The Fly Shop*

This is the Egg Sucking Leech gone psychedelic—an Alaska favorite.

Egg Sucking Crystal Bugger

Hook: Tiemco TMC 5263, or equivalent 3X- to 6X-long, heavy-wire nymph or streamer, size 4
Thread: Purple, or black
Underbody: Lead wire wrapped on shank
Tail: Purple marabou, flanked on each side by several strands of purple-pearl Krystal Flash
Body: Purple Crystal Chenille
Palmer hackle: Purple saddle, sharply tapered, to form a long hackle collar at the front
Head: Hot-pink, or hot-orange, chenille

In that same *AFT* article, Tony Route observed that leeches seldom carry off salmon eggs, but that sculpins often do. This Route variation on the Woolly Bugger suggests egg-eating sculpins rather than egg-sucking leeches. Incidentally, even where salmon are absent and when trout aren't spawning, rainbow trout and other fish will avidly take this pattern or the Egg Sucking Leech. Perhaps the bright "egg" just calls their attention to the suggestive pattern which triggers the strike. His listing also included an optional inverted wing (from behind the head to just covering the hook point) of fairly sparse woodchuck or gray squirrel tail; that makes the fly fairly weed-resistant but not very Buggerish.

Egg-Eating Muddled Bugger

Hook: 2X- to 4X-long streamer, sizes 2 to 10, even smaller if you wish
Thread: Dark-brown or black
Egg: Pink (or other roe-colored) medium chenille, tied in at the eye and wrapped as a smallish egg; *alternatively, use a brass or glass bead and omit the weighted underbody*
Head: Brown-and-black variegated or brown chenille, tied in behind the egg and wrapped later
Underbody: Lead wire wrapped around the shank
Tail: Brown-mottled or brown marabou, full and as long as the hook
Body: Brown-and-black variegated or brown chenille
Belly: Several strands of pearl, silver, gold, or yellow Krystal Flash, pulled over the "back," which will be the belly on this inverted pattern
Palmer hackle: Furnace, badger, or brown-died grizzly rooster or hen saddle, tied in at the bend by the tip and palmered through the body, with 3 or 4 tight, hackle-collar turns in front of the body

Tying Notes

When you wrap the sculpin head, be sure to fill the space between the egg and the palmer hackle, and to make the head considerably larger than the egg. Don't worry if it slightly encroaches on the egg, Route says; it may be an even better impression of a sculpin with an egg in its mouth.

Most sculpins vary considerably in color, from tan to brown, red-brown, yellow-brown, gray, and olive; in the case of the Klamath Lake sculpin, even purple! The bellies may be white or yellow, except in the case of breeding male riffle and marbled sculpins, which are dark brown all over. If you know what your local sculpins look like, try to approximate their colors. Otherwise, mottled brown is a happy medium.

If you can't find brown-and-black variegated chenille for the body and head, use brown and speckle it a bit with a black permanent marker. If your local sculpins have dark saddles on the back (e.g., banded, black, Coastrange, deepwater, fourhorn, marbled, margined, mottled, Ozark, Paiute, Potomac, prickly, riffle, shorthead, Shoshone, slender, slimy, spoonhead, torrent, or Wood River sculpins), mark the body accordingly, before you palmer the hackle.

MEG-A-EGG-SUCKING LEECH *Tied by Orvis*

Orvis concentrates the light-reflecting attraction in the egghead and the tail. This is the **Purple/Pink**; it also comes in Black/Chartreuse.

Meg-A-Egg-Sucking Leech

Hook: Standard salmon/steelhead, sizes 2 to 6
Head: Pink crystal egg
Thread: Black 6/0
Tail: Purple marabou, topped by 2 to 4 strands of pearl Krystal Flash
Palmer hackle: Purple saddle hackle
Body: Purple chenille

GRIZ BUGGER *Tied by Steve Schweitzer*

Why the "Griz" in a pattern that incorporates no grizzly hackle? Steve Schweitzer, of Geneva, Illinois, says on the Global Fly Fisher web site (www.globalflyfisher.com) that he named this Olive Woolly Bugger/Egg-Sucking Leech hybrid for Griz Turner, manager of the camp where Schweitzer developed the pattern for Yellowstone cutthroats. Until Schweitzer figured out what the cuts were looking for, he and five other experienced fly fishers had been suffering slow fishing and short takes. The Griz Bugger fixed the problem. Of late, Steve has been calling it The Invincible Griz Bugger.

Griz Bugger

Hook: 2X- to 6X-long streamer, sizes 4 to 10
Thread: Olive
Palmer hackle: Olive schlappen, tied in a bit behind the eye and reverse-palmered
Tail: Black marabou, with 3 strands of pearl Krystal Flash on either side
Body: Olive medium chenille
Head: Fluorescent-orange Glo-Bug yarn, spun and trimmed to shape, "but any bright color will do"

This Doug Brewer extrapolation of the Egg Sucking Leech represents a gluttonous leech that has gobbled more salmon (or trout) eggs than it can handle. It incorporates Brewer's own Hot Head Glue, a hot-melt glue that comes in several colors useful in fly tying. (Your first attempts at making hot-glue eggs probably will not be as neat as Brewer's. But keep trying; you'll soon get the hang of it.) Besides the illustrated purple, the Egg-Regurgitating Leech also comes in black and fuchsia.

Brewer's Egg-Regurgitating Leech

Hook: MFC 7030, or similar 6X-long streamer, size 6
Thread: White Nymo; *alternatively, Danville FlyMaster Flat Waxed Nylon*
Underbody: 0.6-mm lead wire wrapped on the shank
Tail: Purple, black, or fuchsia marabou blood quill
Egg stalks: 2 lengths of clear Wonderwrap *(alternatively, SuperFloss)* tied in behind the eye
Head: Orange or pink Hot Head Glue, on the shank behind the eye and over the tie-in of the egg stalks
Eggs: Orange or pink Hot Head Glue on the ends of the stalks
Palmer hackle: Rooster schlappen to match the tail color, tied in by the butt behind the head and reverse-palmered to the bend
Body: Chenille to match the tail and hackle colors
Rib: Copper wire

Tying Note

Too recently for inclusion of the photo and full description the fly deserves, I found a pattern of somewhat similar concept that doesn't risk burned fingertips. It's called **Greenen's Articulated Egg Leech**, from Ron Greenen, of Columbus, Ohio. (For full tying details, see the photos and tying steps at www.flyanglersonline.com/flytying/fotw2/092004fotw.html.) Here's the gist of it:

Start with a piece of McFly Foam in the color of your choice (Greenen's faves are Grapefruit, McCheese, and chartreuse) and several inches of monofilament (he uses Gamma Deep Blue) in 30- to 50-pound-test strength (the faster the flow you'll be fishing, the heavier the mono). Tie an overhand knot in the mono around the foam and cinch down tight,

using pliers; tie a second overhand knot and cinch. *(Alternatively, use one blood knot, which is just a double overhand.)* Use curved scissors to snip the foam egg to shape and trim the tag end of the mono to about 2 inches.

As for the rest, start by tying a black Woolly Bugger (with flash material added to the tail and a copper wire rib), the shank weighted with lead-wire wraps, but pause after you have tied in (but not wrapped) the body tinsel chenille at the bend and the palmer hackle behind the eye to tie in the egg so that it dangles ahead "no more than 3/4 of an inch from the hook eye, and no less than 3/8 of an inch; this can vary depending on the stream conditions you'll be fishing—shorter for faster flows, longer for slower flows."

The Tennessee tier Ernie Paquette says that his buggy-looking fly is "deadly year 'round," but adds that it "*really* pisses off spawning fish and incites those matriarchal and patriarchal instinctive strikes."

Ernie's Cockle-Bugger

Hook: 2X-long streamer, size 10
Thread: Unspecified
Underbody: Lead wire on shank
Tail: Black marabou
Rib: Fine copper wire
Palmer hackle: Black saddle, tied in a bit behind the eye (leave room for a head) and reverse-palmered to the rear
Body: Peacock herl, tied in up front and wrapped to the bend and back
Head: Yellow floss, "built up to the size of a BB or a trout egg"

I found this pattern by Ray Larson, a guide from Sheboygan, Wisconsin, on the Kreinik Company web site (www.kreinik.com).

Although this beadhead alternative—also known as the **ECL**—can be used all year around, it really excels in the fall, when rivers are running low. Unlike beadhead patterns, which sink fast and tend to snag the bottom, this heady pattern is a slow sinker. The bulbous ribbon head also keeps the fly from splashing down noisily, the way beadheads do, spooking nervous fish in shallow water. Unfortunately, I was unable to contact Larson, either directly or through Kreinik, to get additional information on fishing his leech pattern.

Electric Copper Leech

Hook: 2X- to 4X-long streamer or salmon wet-fly, sizes 2 to 8

Thread: Brown 6/0

Tail: Brown marabou or pheasant-rump marabou, shank-length

Palmer hackle: Brown saddle, palmered over the body

Body: Copper metallic ribbon *(Larson specified Kreinik's Electric Copper 012HL 1/8-in Ribbon—I used Fyre Werks F9B copper Metallic Ribbon; use what you have or can find)*, wrapped to within a quarter to a half inch of the hook eye

Head: Copper ribbon from the body, wrapped tightly to form a round head; tie off and whip-finish behind the hook eye; cement or gloss-finish if desired

I lifted this British pattern (with Bob's permission) from *Bob Church's Guide to New Fly Patterns*. It is the creation of one Ticker Dickens—who ties his Tickerfly by the dozens for his own fishing, it's such a "killing pattern." He fishes it on a sinking line in cold water; in summer's warm waters, he fishes the smaller sizes on a floating line.

Tickerfly

Hook: 2X- to 3X-long, heavy-wire wet-fly or streamer, sizes 8 to 12

Thread: Black

Head: Fluorescent-orange chenille, ball-shaped

Palmer hackle: Long-barbed grizzly, badger, or other variegated rooster feather, reverse-palmered

Body: Flat silver tinsel, tied in at the front and wrapped down to the bend and back, after the tail and rib have been tied in

Tail: White marabou, about a gap and a half long

Rib: Fine silver wire

Tying Tip

Because tinsel-bodied flies show every lump of material on the shank, it's important to lash the marabou butts atop the entire shank to provide a smooth underbody. Spiral the thread over the butts at least twice or, better still, wrap a smooth thread base over the butts. Alternatively, if your marabou isn't long enough to cover the shank, use a single strand of fine yarn to wrap a smooth underbody in front of the marabou butts.

CONCRETE BOWL

This Bob Church pattern, well-known in the U.K. as a reservoir pattern, slightly resembles a miniature Egg Sucking Leech. ("Concrete bowl" is a concrete-lined reservoir in British parlance.)

Concrete Bowl

Hook: Standard wet-fly, size 10
Thread: Black
Tail: Black marabou, full but slightly shorter than the hook
Body: Green or chartreuse fluorescent chenille
Rib: Fine silver wire
Palmer hackle: Black hen, reverse-palmered over the rear 3/4 of the body (see Tying Tips)
Head: The body chenille, wrapped all the way to the eye, then back over the front 1/4 of the shank

Tying Tips

After wrapping the chenille body three-fourths of the way up the shank, tie in the hackle feather by its butt. Continue wrapping the chenille all the way up to the eye, and back to the hackle feather, where you will tie it off and trim. Then palmer the feather down to the tail and use the ribbing wire to secure the hackle before spiraling the wire forward.

To tie Church's gaudier **Concrete Bowl Mk 2** (which resembles our **Egg Sucking Leech**; see page 162), use black chenille for the body and fluorescent-orange chenille for the head; everything else remains the same.

Fishing Tips

Fish this fly the way Church does, in still water on a fast-sinking line.

Early in the season, and again in the fall, Church fishes the bright Mk 2 version, sometimes both versions on the same leader.

PURPLE ULTRA-CHENILLE BUGGER *Tied by Tony Spezio*

Tony Spezio sometimes just calls this pattern **The Purple One**. Here, the bead head is merely attractive; the fly's weight rides on the front part of the shank.

Purple Ultra-Chenille Bugger

Hook: Eagle Claw L058, a 3X-long, 1X-heavy streamer, size 14
Head: 3-mm silver plastic bead
Underbody: 20 wraps of .010-in lead wire, the front wraps pushed into the bead's center hole after a drop of superglue gel
Thread: Purple or black
Tail: Purple marabou, pinched short
Body: Purple Ultra Chenille, a thin, high-density chenille; *alternatively, use Vernille*
Palmer hackle: Purple saddle, undersize (short barbs)
Eyes: Yellow, with a black pupil, painted on the bead (Spezio uses Slick fabric paint)

Tying Tips

To weight the fly and secure the bead, so those painted eyes don't spin, wrap the lead wire on the bare shank, squirt a drop of superglue gel into the bead's hole, and slide the lead wraps forward, jamming them into the gap between bead and shank.

Be sure the paint and glue you use are compatible with the plastic of the bead. Solvent-based paints and cements will destroy the bead.

To protect the painted eyes from abrasion, you can coat the bead with a water-based head cement.

FOAMHEAD BUGGERS

Obviously, the principal reason for adding foam to a fly is to make it buoyant. However, unlike the foam-enhanced Woollies already discussed, these foamhead Buggers are not topwater flies. Instead, they are fished subsurface—the way Lefty Kreh and others often fish saltwater poppers on sinking or sink-tip lines—or way down deep with really high-density lines or shooting heads. Fished deep, the foamhead Bugger can be made to swim just above the weeds or snaggy bottoms. Leader length is critical to properly deep-fishing such foamhead flies.

We have selected very few patterns for this section, but they should be sufficient to improve your catch rate, and inquisitive tiers will see all sorts of ways to devise foamhead Bugger patterns.

ORANGE MUDDLER *Tied by John Gregory*

John Gregory calls this a "Muddler," but actually it's a variation on the Woolly Bugger. (Gregory explains that he thought the Plastazote head made the fly look like a British-style Muddler.) I cadged it from his Heavy Gear Trouting web site (www.heavy-geartrouting.netfirms.com), "one man's personal and extremely opinionated take on reservoir bank lure fishing for trout."

Dissatisfied with the current obsession with light tackle and small flies for trout, Gregory has developed a system of "unashamed retro fishing [that] will strike a chord with anyone who started trouting during the 1970s." He admits this is the trout-fishing equivalent of surf fishing with a fly rod, but says, "With heavy gear, you're in charge."

Gregory says, "Most of the time I fish the Muddler in the lower third of the water column, using an 8-foot, 8-pound-test leader tied to a 36-foot DT-12-S Scientific Anglers WetCel2 fast sinker. This line and the fly's buoyant head allow a slow retrieve without snagging the bottom." This fly fisher would find a lake or reservoir with really *big* trout before spending the day flogging the water with a full-sinking 12-weight! Even then, I might prefer an 8- or 9-weight rod and line. Might even use my 12-foot, two-handed 7-weight.

Orange Muddler

Hook: Your favorite Bugger hook (Gregory uses a Drennan Dropgate lure [streamer] hook), size 8

Thread: Fluorescent-orange UNI 6/0

Tail: 4 slips of tangerine-orange marabou, 1-in wide and 1 1/2 times the hook length

Body: Fluorescent-orange medium chenille

Palmer hackle: Hot-orange rooster hackle, about 5-in long with a barb about 1 1/2 times the width of the hook gap, palmered over the body

Head: A prominent varnished-thread head, over which is pushed a 7.5-mm-long, 9-mm-dia Plastazote (a closed-cell polyethylene foam) cylinder that has already been trimmed to shape

Tying Tip

Before trimming the Plastazote head to shape, Gregory suggests, skewer it onto a round toothpick. This will ease trimming and make a hole that will allow the head to be pushed readily into place over the hook eye.

Fishing Notes

"The retrieve is crucial to consistent success," Gregory says. "Use slow, unhurried, smooth yard-long pulls. Try to make the interval between pulls virtually seamless so that the fly maintains a serene and stately return to the bank. With this silky-smooth retrieve, most takes are felt as a tap–tap followed by a solid take. Sometimes you'll get a succession of taps through four or five pulls. Don't strike; just steel yourself to continue the smooth retrieve and usually you'll get a solid take.

"When fishing deep, wait between 30 seconds and 2 minutes after casting—depending on water depth—before starting the retrieve.

"If you lose a fish on the Orange Muddler, use the **Green and Black Muddler** variant as a 'rest/change fly.'" As above, *except* use black thread, marabou, and hackle, and signal green (aka Viva green) fluorescent chenille.

Another of John Gregory's curiously named patterns. He says this one is designed "specifically for autumn fry feeders but often appeals to wandering bigger fish. Fish it with an 8-foot, 10-pound-test leader tied to a 31-foot WF-13-S Scientific Anglers HiSpeed HiD extra-fast sinker." Because there are several new wrinkles in this pattern, I'm giving it a full listing.

Jack Frost Muddler

Hook: TMC 9394 4X-long, nickel-plated, size 4 (Gregory says the nickel-plated hook consistently outfishes a bronzed hook on this pattern.)

Thread: Black 6/0 UNI *(I think I'd use white or red.—GS)*

Tail: 4 slips of white marabou, 1-in wide and 1-1/2 times the hook length

Underbody: White fluorescent Antron floss; tied in at the head and wound down the shank and back (required to keep the body translucent)

Body: Pearl medium Fritz (British equivalent of Cactus or Ice Chenille, or similar tinsel chenille), tied in *before* winding the underbody; the fibers stroked back after each of the 24 or so closely butting turns

Hackle: Crimson rooster hackle collar, about 5-in long with a barb about twice the width of the hook gape

Head: A prominent varnished-thread head, over which is pushed a 10-mm-long, 10-mm-dia Plastazote cylinder trimmed to shape

BOOBY BUGGER

This is a Buggerized version of the Booby pattern that is so popular in Britain and Down Under. Don't let the use of buoyant foam fool you; this is a *subsurface* fly to be fished with a short leader on a high-density line or shooting head. It is designed for fishing in and around weed beds. The buoyant eyes keep the fly just above the vegetation. Leader length is typically around 3 feet, but if the weeds are tall, use a longer leader to keep the fly working just along the top of the weeds. Although Boobies often are fished in lakes and reservoirs, they have become quite popular for fishing river mouths in New Zealand.

The foam eyes can be placed behind the hook eye (English Booby tradition) or at the bend (as they were shown on an Ashley Morrow Booby Bugger pattern on Australia's www.fish-net.com.au). Either configuration works, but the action is different, so you might want to tie and try them both ways.

Choose matching, contrasting, or complementary colors to suit your waters and target species.

Booby Bugger

Hook: Standard to 3X-long streamer or terrestrial, sizes 4 to 10

Thread: Black 6/0

Eyes: A section of fly-body foam, lashed athwart the top of the shank at either end, or, traditionally, closed-cell foam beads in a 2x2-cm square of hosiery mesh, secured with figure-8 wraps and a drop of glue; *optic   "   the flat ends of the c*

Tail: Marabou, thick and longer; *optionally, w   Flash mixed in*

Palmer hackle: Webby hen or grade   suit

Body: Chenille

Head: Body chenille, wrapped over, under, and ahead of the foam eyes; *normal thread head on the Aussie version with the rear-mounted eyes*

Tying Tip

If you decide to place your eyes at the rear of the shank, tie in the tail first, then tie in the foam eyes on top of the marabou butts.

Fishing Tip

To get a good, fish-enticing action, let the high-density line sink to the bottom and fish the Booby Bugger with fast, short, jerks. The fly will dive on the pull and then rise on the pause, the marabou tail opening and closing in response.

12. SOME SPECIAL-PURPOSE BUGGERS

L̲ike a few of the Woolly Buggers previously listed, these patterns are intended for particular purposes. Most of them have been designed from the get-go to serve that purpose.

Even so, it's easy to modify them to suit your own, different piscatorial purposes.

CRAYFISH BUGGERS

Virtually any Woolly Bugger may be taken as a crayfish, and a lot of Bugger variants probably work because they resemble fleeing crayfish (no matter what their creators had in mind). Still, some tiers have developed Bugger patterns specifically to imitate crayfish.

Too many fly fishers think of crayfish patterns as bass flies, but that is beginning to change. Trout eat crayfish. I have letters from fish biologists all over—Missouri, Ontario, British Columbia, Ireland, etc.—confirming this. As James F. Smith, of Preston, Connecticut, wrote in a letter to *American Angler,* back when I was editor, trout are "a lot more opportunistic in their feeding habits than we care to admit."

To better imitate crayfish, some tiers palmer the hackle only halfway up the body. Others get the same effect by using a steeply tapered feather, tying it in at the bend by the butt (or behind the eye by the tip), so the longer hackle barbs are toward the bend. I've tried crayfish Buggers all three ways—fully palmered, semipalmered, and steeply tapered—and I can't say that it has made a big difference.

Like many another fly fisher, I tend to think "brown" when I think "crayfish pattern." But crayfish come in many colors, and smart fly fishers often use orange or dark-red Buggers rather than the more standard brown and tan patterns. Others, just as smart, use gray or dark olive. Eyeball your local crawdads, and tie accordingly.

As I mentioned in the previous chapter, crayfish patterns may be successfully fished in a variety of ways, from a slow, hand-twist retrieve to long, fast strips. In the October 1988 issue of *Pennsylvania Angler,* Chauncey Lively wrote this about fishing Woolly Buggers to the notoriously finicky fish in Pennsylvania's Letort Spring Run:

"On spring creeks where dense beds of *Elodea* grow along the banks...in late evening crayfish leave their burrows in the banks and crawl out onto the *Elodea* to feed. Anyone who has walked along the Letort at dusk has probably seen faint V-wakes moving slowly over the weedbeds, indicating that big browns are on the prowl for their favorite nocturnal snacks. An unweighted Woolly Bugger cast ahead of the wake sometimes does business, but the presentation should be made quietly because the trout will likely be large and extra wary in such an exposed situation."

Let's begin with a look at Chauncey Lively's own crayfish-imitating Woolly Bugger.

LIVELY CRAYFISH BUGGER

Chauncey Lively, and his wife, Marian, were commercial tiers based in Pittsburgh before they retired to Michigan and the Au Sable River. Despite what he wrote (above) about fishing unweighted Buggers, Lively sometimes weighted his Buggers for fishing waters requiring less "technical" fishing than the Letort.

Lively Crayfish Bugger

Hook: 3X- or 4X-long streamer, sizes 4 to 10
Thread: Brown
Underbody: Lead wire, as long as the shank, folded in half and bound to the shank behind the eye
Tail: Brown marabou, with 3 or 4 strands of "Krystal Hair or Flashabou" [color not specified—I used root beer Krystal Flash] on either side
Body: Dull-orange chenille
Palmer hackle: Brown saddle (or a large neck hackle), the barbs 2 gap-widths long, tied in at the bend with the glossy side of the feather forward

Fishing Tip

"In streams where crayfish are plentiful," Lively wrote in that same *Pennsylvania Angler* article cited above, "I like to cast the Woolly Bugger across-stream to the bank and retrieve it in foot-long spurts. If there is a trout or bass in the vicinity it will often pounce on the fly before it reaches deep water."

Tying Tip

If you want the fly to fish point up, making it a bit less likely to snag a cluttered bottom, lash the folded lead wire to the top of the shank. Otherwise, lash it to the bottom side of the shank.

Also known as the **Delaware River Crayfish**, this pattern is the creation of one Michael W. "Mickey" Maguire, of Hilliard, Ohio, a musician and fly fisher who writes and ties his own. He and Lou Truppi, a G. Loomis rep, caught "a bunch of big fish" on the first day they fished the pattern, and a week later Maguire caught a 30-inch brown trout on the West Branch of the Delaware. "Over the next weekend," he wrote on his Magfly Site (http://home.earthlink.net/~magfly/), "over 20 fish exceeding 20 inches in length were caught on this same pattern by several people." Maguire says his crayfish Bugger also works wonders on smallmouth bass and other gamefish and "has now made its way to Europe, where it has landed big fish wherever it's been dipped into the water."

"The Hare's-Ear Bugger was designed to give the impression of life," Mickey Maguire explains. "That is the secret to its success: It looks alive in the water. I dressed the fly sparsely, much the way you would expect to tie a soft-hackled pattern, but I picked a fairly stiff Hoffman saddle for the palmered hackle. Its fine, delicate tips twitch with even the slightest retrieval of fly line or in the slowest current flow."

Mag's Hare's-Ear Bugger

Hook: 3X-long nymph or streamer, size to suit your quarry
Thread: Brown 6/0
Tail: Hot-orange Secret Streamer Fur, angora goat, or Icelandic sheep, sparse, topped by brown marabou
Palmer hackle: Grizzly Hoffman Super Saddle, palmered over the body to within 1/4 inch of the eye
Body: Hare's ear, dubbed
Head: Hare's ear, dubbed "spikey" (no palmer hackle)
Nose: Brown tying thread

Fishing Tip

"To get the most out of this fly," Maguire wrote, "I use Jim Teeny's T-series fly lines and drag the fly right to the bottom."

CRAWDAD BUGGER

This pattern comes from a tier who identified himself simply as "Elvus" when he posted to one of the several fly-tying bulletin boards on the Internet. He somehow managed not to leave his e-mail address, so I can't give him the credit he deserves. He wisely advised, "Be sure to find some real live crayfish in your local river to match the color. They seem to vary in color from olive to brown to brick-red."

Crawdad Bugger

Hook: 4X- to 6X-long streamer, size 2
Thread: Brown
Tail: Orange marabou, sparse, covered by at least twice as much brown marabou
Body: Brown chenille
Palmer hackle: Brown-dyed grizzly saddle

BUFORD'S CRAWBUGGER *Tied by Montana Fly Company*

This simple, but effective, crayfish pattern—developed by Dave "Buford" Bloom for fishing big browns on the upper Missouri River—is really nothing more than a bead-head Woolly Bugger in crayfish-suggestive colors.

Buford's Crawbugger

Hook: MFC 7008 or similar 4X-long streamer, size 2
Head: 5-mm gold bead
Thread: Black Nymo; *alternatively*, Danville FlyMaster Flat Waxed Nylon
Tail: Light-gray marabou blood quill, with Copper Flashabou Accent (similar to Krystal Flash) on either side
Palmer hackle: Burnt-orange–dyed grizzly saddle, tied in by the butt behind the bead head and reverse-palmered to the bend
Body: Tobacco-brown chenille
Rib: Copper wire

Frank Slider, who fly fishes on the South Branch of the Potomac for smallmouth bass, has written that this crayfish-imitating pattern has been very good to him. "I like to fish it on a dead drift with a tight line through the faster water."

Root Beer Crystal Bugger

Hook: 4X- to 6X-long streamer, sizes 4 to 8

Head: Gold or copper bead

Thread: Brown 6/0

Tail: Brown marabou, with several strands of Krystal Flash mixed in

Body: Root-beer Crystal Chenille

Palmer hackle: Brown or furnace saddle

CRAWBUGGER *Tied by Dan Bailey's Fly Shop*

John Bailey says that Johnny Boyd was the man behind this pattern. Read the recipe carefully because, like most imitative crayfish patterns, this one is anatomically reversed, the tail of the critter being at the eye of the hook, and so on.

Crawbugger

Hook: Dai-Riki 700, a 4X-long, 1X-strong streamer, sizes 2 and 4

Thread: Brown

Underbody: Lead wire over 2/3 of the shank

Tail: Brown marabou, which actually imitates the pincers of a backward-fleeing crayfish

Telson: Brown marabou, less than a gap-width long, tied atop the shank and extending forward above the downturned hook eye; trim it across above the eye to imitate the cr⌐ flipper

Palmer hackle: Brown saddle, 1 1/2 times as l⌐ gap, tied in at the front of the reverse-palmered

Legs: Brown medium rubber, 2 , legs in all) just above and im⌐ of the hook point

Body: Brown chenille (tied in 1/3 of the way ⌐ne shank, then later wrapped to the bend and back, covering just the rear 1/3 of the shank to represent the crayfish's long tail section), plus brown and light-orange chenille (tied in at the same place as the preceding, and later woven Bitch Creek style over the front 2/3 of the shank, representing the crayfish's head and body)

Rib: Fine copper wire, wound through the hackle

Tying Tips

Tie in the telson and "tail" (pincers), then wrap the lead underbody before going any further. Next, tie in all the other materials, and wrap them in this order: brown chenille, hackle, rib, and finally the woven orange-and-brown "body 2" (crayfish tail section).

If you don't know how to make a woven fly body, look up the Bitch Creek Nymph in a good tying book. Better yet, read Section 12, Woven Bodies, in Ted Leeson's and Jim Schollmeyer's monumental *The Fly Tier's Benchside Reference to Techniques and Dressing Styles* (1998). There, you will learn not one way to weave a fly body, but—count 'em—10!

This is my back-to-Bugger-basics variation of the pattern submitted by Robb Nicewonger to the Crawdad Fly Swap on the Virtual Flyshop (www.flyshop.com). Nicewonger's pattern has no hackle and uses thin rabbit strips for the tail pincers. A poster to the page vouched for the original pattern's effectiveness, but said, "I add a copper wire rib to give a segmented look in the thorax/tail."

Cactus Crawdad

Hook:	3X- or 4X-long streamer, size 4
Thread:	Olive
Underbody:	20 "or so" wraps of lead wire
Tail:	2 "thinnish" olive marabou plumes, as pincers
Shellback:	Olive Furry Foam
Rib:	Fine copper wire
Palmer hackle:	*Optionally, furnace saddle*
Body:	Olive Cactus Chenille
Head:	Stub of Furry Foam shellback trimmed square above the eye

Tying Tips

To separate the pincer plumes, I like to wrap a little ball of dubbing or yarn at the rear of the shank.

Because of the Furry Foam back, it is not necessary to reverse-palmer the hackle on this ribbed fly, should you decide to hackle it.

"Mud bug" is slang for baby crayfish in some parts of the country. This is the palmer-hackled version of a fly I call the Near-Nothing Mud Bug, a fly that so far catches nothing but rainbow trout, which it catches with satisfying regularity. I fish it weightless, on sinking leaders, but you can weight it if you wish. At the end of the swing, I let it dangle a few moments, twitch it a couple times, then lift it very slowly into the back cast. I get most of my strikes on the twitching or lifting.

Copper Mud Bugger

Hook:	3X- or 4X-long streamer, sizes 10 and 12
Thread:	Brown
Tail:	Pale-pink, tan, or light-brown marabou or blood-feather fluff, thin and shorter than regulation Bugger tails
Underbody:	*Optionally, lead wire*
Underbody:	Brown or tan single-ply yarn, wrapped back and forth to the desired thickness
Body:	Copper Coats Metallic embroidery thread, a polyester–metallic blend, wrapped back and forth in 3 or more layers sufficient to cover the yarn
Palmer hackle:	Badger, fiery-brown, or brown-dyed grizzly saddle
Head:	A few turns of bronze peacock herl, to suggest the telson

Tying Tips

You may, if you wish, make the tail longer—body- or even hook-length. I find the shorter tail works just fine for me, but you may think or fish differently. Admittedly, the short tail does leave the pattern dangling awkwardly in the never-never land between Woolly Wormness and true Buggerdom.

If you can't find, or don't like to use, that thin metallic thread, substitute a copper ribbon or flat braid, or even a copper tinsel or tinsel-blend chenille.

Although it takes a lot of steps to explain the tying of this pattern, it's actually relatively simple—a lot simpler than some other, hackle-pincered semi-realistic crayfish patterns. And it casts a lot easier and better, too.

When the Beattys first moved to Montana in 1993, they discovered that the Brown Woolly Bugger was the go-to fly on the Madison River below Ennis. While Al guided clients on the Madison and Yellowstone during the day, Gretchen tied flies for the next day's fishing. With each day's fly supply, Gretchen always included a few "idea" flies she thought might improve on the Woolly Bugger as a crayfish pattern. This pattern was what finally evolved.

One day, when Al's clients were catching more fish than any other boat on the Madison, one angler said something along the lines of, "This fly sure makes catching those brown trout easy." Thus was the EZY Crayfish christened. "We feel it is a 'must have' fly, in either warm- or coldwater fishing applications," Al and Gretchen say. I couldn't agree more. If the crayfish in your waters are not brown, just change colors to match them. I also tie them in gray, dark-green, and burnt-orange.

EZY Crayfish

Hook:	Streamer, sizes 4 to 8
Thread:	Brown
Shellback:	Brown poly yarn
Eyes:	Brown or black bead chain, tied on at the bend, under the shank
"Tail"/Pincers:	4 brown Chickabou feathers, 2 on each side
Underbody:	Lead wire, over a thread base
Rib:	Copper wire
Body:	Brown Crystal Chenille
Palmer hackle:	Brown saddle
Head:	Yarn from the shellback, trimmed straight across above the hook eye, tied as the telson, or tail flipper

Tying Steps

After tying on, wrap a thread base that extends slightly into the bend, then wrap forward to the middle of the shank.
Tie in the brown poly yarn on the *underside* of the shank, trim the excess, then tie in the bead-chain eyes at the rear of the shank, also underneath. Take the thread back to the center.

Tie in the Chicakabou feathers, 2 on each side, with the natural curve sweeping away from each other, to form the pincers. Trim the excess.

Wrap several turns of lead wire behind the bead-chain eyes, then tie in the Crystal Chenille body material and the copper-wire rib on the shank immediately above the eyes.

Wrap the chenille around the eyes and bind it in place, leaving the rest of the chenille hanging there. Tie in a brown saddle hackle at that point, then wrap the chenille to the hook eye, tie off, and clip the excess.

Palmer the hackle forward to the eye, tie off, and clip the excess.

Pull the brown poly yarn up and over (an equal number of fibers on either side of the bend, and the whole strand between the pincer feathers) to form a shellback, bind it in place at the hook eye, and clip the excess long and straight across above the eye, forming a telson (tail flipper).

Spiral the copper wire forward, segmenting the shellback and reinforcing the whole fly. Tie if off at the hook eye, trim the excess wire, whip-finish, and apply a drop of head cement to the wraps.

Tying Tips

Note that this fly is tied "upside down" so that it fishes with the point up.

I find that a straight-eyed streamer hook makes it easy for my tired eyes to find the hook eye with the tippet. I haven't yet tried using a hook with a turned-up eye (away from the point), but that might work as well.

No, this isn't a permit pattern for the Florida Keys. It's a crayfish pattern for trout in southern Rocky Mountain streams from Steven J. Meyers, the San Juan Mountains trout guide and fine, fine writer (*Lime Creek Odyssey, San Juan River Chronicles,* etc.). "Bud Collins and I dubbed it the Florida Crab when I first tied it years ago to imitate the crayfish we found in the water and in the bellies of large brown trout in the Florida River just upstream from its confluence with the Animas," Steve says. "For me, it's proven deadly wherever crayfish are found. I bet it would be a great smallmouth fly—if only I had any smallmouth to try it on!"

Florida Crab

Hook: Your favorite nymph or streamer hook, in an appropriate size; Steve ties them on everything from a size-10 TMC 200R to a size-2/0 TMC 7999 steelhead/salmon hook, and he tied the fly pictured above on a Mustad 3665A

Thread: Brown

Underbody: "A ton" of fuse wire

Tail: Brown marabou, sparse and slightly shorter than the shank, flanked by slightly longer dark-tipped feathers from a ring-necked pheasant's breast—1 on each side, nearly as long as the shank, tied with the dull, concave side facing outward

Body: Brown chenille

Palmer hackle: Brown saddle hackle with long, webby barbs

Tying Tips

Steve says, "Sometimes I use the soft, blue-green feathers from the pheasant's rump, instead of the breast feathers with the black triangles in the center of their tips. Whichever feathers I use, I always tie the 'claws' so they curve away from the marabou tail. When you strip the fly, they pulse inward. When the fly is still, they move out again. It's a very lifelike action."

He also comments, "I almost always tie my Woolly Worms and Buggers, and variations thereof, with the concave side of the hackle forward, especially if I'm tying for fast water. On stillwater patterns, I sometimes tie the hackle facing the other way. I have gone back and forth on this for years, but this is the way I tie them now."

BASS BUGGERS

Virtually any Woolly Bugger (or Woolly Worm, for that matter) will catch bass, but some were designed specifically for the purpose. A few other bass Buggers are scattered throughout the book, but belonged in other chapters because of their construction—clipped or reduced hackle, lack of hackle, and so on. Here are four sample bass-specific Buggers.

REDHEAD BASS BUGGER

When I was a kid, the white-bodied redhead plug was a mainstay in our tackle boxes. You simply wouldn't think of leaving home without it. But nowadays, they're hard to come by. I wonder why. Fish haven't changed. Scientific studies show that bass see and key on the color red. Most baitfish flash white when they are feeding, fleeing, or struggling. I no longer own a plug-casting outfit, but this is my redhead bass "plug" now.

Redhead Bass Bugger

Hook: 4X-long streamer, sizes 6 to 1/0
Thread: Red 3/0
Eyes: Large silver bead chain, tied in at least 1/8 in behind the eye—*optionally, for fishing deep, chrome dumbbells, with painted or glued-on iris and pupil*—the eye wraps secured with a drop of epoxy cement
Tail: White marabou, shank-length
Body: White or pearl tinsel chenille, stopping about 1/8 in short of the eyes
Palmer hackle: White or light grizzly saddle palmered through the body
Head: Red tinsel chenille, wrapped around and between the eyes, to form a prominent head

CRYSTAL BASS BUGGER

Here's a bass-fishing version of the Cactus Blossom I based on the Cone Jig offered in The Fly Shop catalog. I am listing a crayfish-suggestive pattern, but many different colors can be used.

Crystal Bass Bugger

Hook: Standard or wide-gap streamer, sizes 6 to 1/0
Weed guard: *Optionally, heavy monofilament tied on behind the hook eye and later lashed to the outside of the bend*
Head: Cone—brass, copper, nickel, or tungsten, to suit
Thread: Brown 6/0
Tail: Brown or black-spotted-brown rubber legs (or spinnerbait skirt), with root beer Krystal Flash in the center
Body: Root beer tinsel chenille
Palmer hackle: Natural or brown-dyed grizzly palmer; *might be considered optional unless the tinsel chenille is short-fibered*

Tying Tips

If you decide to use a weed guard, tie the monofilament to the hook shank behind the eye and leave it dangling until the end. After the body has been wrapped, and any optional hackle palmered, secure the dangling end of the monofilament to the outside bottom of the bend by lashing it with very fine thread or monofilament tippet material.

The ready-made rubber skirts used on spinnerbaits can be used instead of rubber legs for the tail. Select skirts that are very light in weight. The ones made of jelly-worm plastic are very attractive, but are awfully heavy for flies.

The key to this Bugger's personality is its out-sized "egg head". Frankly, I'm loathe to fish it in eastern trout waters, where the fish tend to be smallish and finicky. I prefer instead to use it on bass, which tend to direct their strikes at the heads of baitfish. When stripped rapidly, this baby really plows the waves.

Bighead Bugger

Hook: 3X- or 4X-long streamer, sizes 4 to 1/0
Head: Large plastic bead or pom-pom, color to suit the rest of the fly
Eyes: *Optionally, stick-on eyes—in which case, the head should be cemented in place over a thread base, to keep it from spinning*
Thread: Tier's-choice color 6/0 or 3/0
Tail: Marabou, with Krystal Flash on top or on either side
Rib: *Optionally, fine wire—gold, silver, copper, or colored—to suit*
Body: Chenille or tinsel chenille in a color to complement or contrast with the tail
Palmer hackle: Rooster saddle in a color to suit—grizzly, badger, furnace, dun, black, brown, whatever—tied in behind the bead head and reverse-palmered to the bend

Tying Note

In the fly illustrated, I used a hot salmon-red pom-pom, black 6/0 thread, black marabou tail with copper Krystal Flash on top, black chenille body palmered over with black hackle, and no rib.

HAW RIVER WOOLLY BUGGER *Tied by Gordon Churchill*

Gordon Churchill, a guide from Fuquay-Varina, North Carolina, usually fishes this pattern in the Haw River for white bass and "hybrids," the white bass–striper cross variously known around the country as wiper, sunshine bass, or palmetto bass. (Churchill says the local name is "Bodie bass, named after some dude who used to be director of something or other here.")

Haw River Woolly Bugger

Hook: TMC 5263, or similar 3X-long streamer, sizes 4 and 6
Thread: White
Underbody: 15 wraps of .015-in lead wire; *alternatively, use chromed dumbbell eyes and omit the under body*
Tail: White marabou, sparse, plus 10 to 12 strands of Flashabou, color of your choice (the flies in the photograph use holographic Flashabou)
Body: Yellow medium chenille
Palmer hackle: White soft saddle, tied in by the base and palmered Woolly Worm-style, shiny side facing rearward so the barbs slant forward

Tying Tip

Cap'n Gordon says, "I also like a red chenille body with grizzly hackle and a white tail."

STEELHEAD, SALMON & SEA-TROUT BUGGERS

When Pacific salmon and steelhead fishers tie Woolly Buggers, they tend to use gaudier colors and color combinations. Few Atlantic salmon fishers like to admit that Woolly Buggers also appeal to the "king of fishes and the fish of kings," but Buggers do. You can tie almost any Bugger pattern on a salmon or steelhead hook. Just let the colors of standard salmon patterns help you decide which Buggers to tie for sea-run fish. The following patterns were designed specifically for steelhead, salmon, and anadromous trout, as were a few other patterns listed earlier.

GANNY SPECIAL

This is another Jay Passmore pattern (see also his **Red-Butt Woolly** on page 69) I found on the Rodworks web site (www.rodworks.on.ca), where it is described as "a Woolly Bugger modified for steelhead fishing on the Ganaraska River in Ontario. The fly works great in both clear- and dirty-water conditions. While it was originally tested on the 'Ganny,' it works anywhere you find big migratory fish."

Ganny Special

Hook:	Mustad 79580, a 4X-long streamer, size 8
Thread:	Black 6/0 UNI
Tail:	Black marabou, about 3/4 as long as the body
Palmer hackle:	Black webby saddle or neck hackle, the barbs a gap-width to a gap-width-and-a-half long
Body:	Black chenille, small, covering the rear 3/4 of the shank
Head:	3 or 4 strands of peacock herl, twisted together in a "chenille rope"

TOM'S BEST BET *Tied by Thomas Steele*

Tom Steele, a Chicago steelheader, also fishes this pattern for lake-run king (chinook) salmon and brown trout. But it's a fly you can fish anywhere. After returning from a trip to Arkansas, Steele e-mailed me that "the Best Bet claimed another river: the White." Not many salmon or steelhead in that Ozark stream but, as Steele reported, "many 'bows and browns."

Tom's Best Bet

Hook:	Mustad 3906, or similar standard nymph, sizes 6 and 8
Thread:	6/0, to match the body
Tail:	Red marabou, short—usually less than 2 gap-widths long
Body:	Brown, black, or dark-green chenille
Palmer hackle:	Bright orange

Tying Tips

Identical but for their colors are these patterns from Mike Grandfield, a Great Lakes steelheader from Des Plaines, Illinois. Tom Steele has had such success with the first one listed below, particularly on coho salmon, that he also calls it **Tom's Second Best Bet**.

Chartreuse-and-Purple Woolly Bugger: Chartreuse thread and body, purple tail and hackle

Pink-and-Purple Woolly Bugger: Pink thread and body, purple tail and hackle

Chartreuse-and-Pink Woolly Bugger: Chartreuse thread and body, pink tail and hackle

Peach-and-Brown Woolly Bugger: Peach thread and body, brown tail and hackle.

Also known as the **Kaufmann Dredger**, this Bugger is one of the many patterns that have sprung from the ever-fertile mind of Randall Kaufmann. I have listed the **Purple Dredger**, because, as the Kaufmann's Streamborn catalog copy says, "Purple is always purple, regardless of light conditions. Fish can readily see it."

Dredger

Hook: TMC 700 or similar 1X-heavy streamer, sizes 4 and 6

Thread: Fluorescent-red (really a hot-pink color), single-strand flat nylon floss

Eyes: Nontoxic dumbbell, painted black on the edges and in the middle, with a black pupil on a fluorescent-red iris, on a white background (usually listed as black/white/fluorescent-red/black), with epoxy over the top

Palmer hackle: Purple saddle, tied in behind the eyes and reverse-palmered

Underbody: Optionally, for those who like really heavy flies, lead wire

Tail: Purple marabou, with 2 or 3 strands each of pearl, purple, and wine Krystal Flash

Body: Tying floss, in 2 or more layers

Rib: Gold wire

Tying Notes

The other Dredgers are identical except for the following color substitutions:

Black Dredger: all black, except use the same eyes as above

Green Dredger: fluorescent-green floss body; black/white/fluorescent-green/black eyes; black over fluorescent-green marabou tail with fluorescent-green and black Krystal Flash

Orange Dredger: fluorescent-orange floss body, black/white/fluorescent-orange/black eyes, black over fluorescent-orange marabou tail with fluorescent-green and black Krystal Flash.

"A bottom-dragging fish grabber!" is the way The Fly Shop catalog describes this pattern, which is listed in the Kaufmann's Streamborn catalog as the **Motor Oil Krystal Bugger.**

Dredger Bugger

Hook: TMC 5263 or equivalent 2X-long, 2X-heavy nymph or streamer, size 4

Thread: Olive

Eyes: Nickel-plated dumbbell, tied atop the shank, a bit behind the hook eye

Palmer hackle: Black, tied in a bit behind the eyes and reverse-palmered

Tail: Black marabou, flanked by several strands of black Krystal Flash

Body: "Motor oil" Crystal Chenille or similar olive-hued tinsel chenille

Rib: Silver wire, spiraled through the hackle

Head: The body chenille, wrapped forward of the hackle, behind, over, and in front of the dumbbell eyes

Similar to the preceding two Dredgers, but with beadchain eyes. According to The Fly Shop catalog, it's "A favorite for bottom-hugging steelhead."

Umpqua Dredger

Hook: TMC 5263, or equivalent, size 2
Thread: Black
Eyes: Silver bead chain, tied atop the shank
Underbody: Lead wire
Tail: Purple marabou, flanked by a few strands of purple pearl Krystal Flash, leaving very long butt ends for the sides
Body: Purple chenille
Sides: Purple pearl Krystal Flash—the tail strands pulled forward
Palmer hackle: Purple, or purple-dyed grizzly, saddle

The length of the tail is what sets this fly apart from the crowd. Normally, tiers keep marabou tails down to a shank-length or so, because longer tails tend to foul the hook. Jens Larsen, a sea-trout fisher from Dronninglund, Denmark, says a smooth and gentle casting stroke is the key to fishing a long-tailed Bugger without fouling. "It won't work if you cast as if your rod were a whip," he says.

Jens also explains why he and his fishing buddies tie their Buggers this way: "Sea trout like to feed on worms of different kinds. The worms are generally 10 to 30 cm [4 to 12 inch-es!] in length, and it is difficult to tie a fly to imitate them. Because of its long tail, this fly can."

Black Woolly Bugger (sea trout)

Hook: Kamasan 170, a 1X-strong wet-fly, sizes 2 and 4
Head: *Optionally, for deep fishing in cold water, a brass or tungsten cone*
Thread: Black
Palmer hackle: Black rooster saddle, tied in at the front and reverse-palmered
Tail: Black marabou, very long, 2 to 3 times as long as the hook, with 2 or 3 strands of rainbow LureFlash (Krystal Flash will do.)
Rib: Oval silver tinsel, medium
Body: Black chenille

Fishing Tips

"This long-tailed Woolly Bugger is very effective when fished without weight on a floating line in May and June," Jens says, "because then you can find worms swimming at the surface, and sea trout always take this fly explosively. In spring, I sometimes tie it with a cone head, so I can stay down on the bottom, where the pattern is highly successful on slow, sluggish fish."

Another Danish sea-trout classic, this one is from the Seeland shoreline expert Peter Løvendahl.

Grey Frede

Hook: Partridge SH2 Stronghold Nymph, a 1X-long, 1X-heavy Limerick in the NiFlor Grey Shadow finish, sizes 2 and 4

Thread: Black Kevlar or 3/0 Monocord

Tail: Grizzly marabou or Chickabou, about half a shank-length past the bend (tied so it's vertically flattened, the butt lashed to the shank as an underbody), plus a few strands of light-green Krystal Flash

Rib: Heavy copper thread

Body: Grizzly marabou, the barbs cut from the stem and dubbed

Palmer hackle: Grizzly rooster saddle, palmered from head to tail

Eyes: Bead-chain, tied in under the shank behind the hook eye

Head: Grizzly marabou, dubbed over, between, and in front of the eyes

Tying Tips

Martin Jørgensen also ties a dark version of his own devising, the **Black Frede**. It's virtually identical but for the color (all black or very dark gray) and these few material changes: Martin says Hoffman Chickabou is ideal for the tail (use two feathers, tied in on either side of the shank to make a vertically flattened tail, as well as copper Flashabou) and hackle. Because he ribs the fly with heavy copper thread, he ties in the Chickabou feather by its stem behind the eyes and reverse-palmers it.

Even more recently, Martin has come up with a **Copper Frede** by combining this pattern with a fly called the Copper Bully. The recipe is conceptually similar, but make these changes: Kamasan 175 or similar 3X-strong nymph hook; red thread; chrome bead-chain eyes; thin lead wire underbody; 2 fluffy, dark-red rump golden-pheasant feathers and a few strands of flash material for the tail; copper wire rib; copper SLF, Angel Hair, or similar dubbing for the body; tying thread or, *optionally, rabbit or body material dubbing*, for the head. See both Jørgensen Fredes on the Global Fly Fisher web site he runs with Steve Schweitzer, Bob Raske, and others (www.globalflyfisher.com).

This beady-eyed, seal-bodied black Bugger—which I first picked up from The Norwegian Flyshop web site (www.flyshop.no)—is by Erling Olsen, a professional tier, lecturer, and writer from Frogner, Norway.

Olsen has published 2 books on fly fishing—*Hårfluer for laks og sjøørret (Hairwing Flies for Salmon and Sea Trout)* and *Møte ved elva (A Meeting by the River)*—and was in the midst of finishing a third when we exchanged e-mail messages about Woolly Buggers. Olsen likes his Buggers fur-bodied, with a bit of flash as well.

Besides the black sea-trout pattern listed here, Olsen says that he sometimes ties Buggers in brown and olive—"also good colors, especially during midsummer." He also declares his Seal Bugger to be "a good streamer for trout *[meaning non-anadromous browns—GS]* and grayling" as well.

Erling's Seal Bugger

Hook: Medium-long (3X- or 4X-long) streamer, sizes 2 to 10

Thread: Black

Eyes: Silver bead-chain, tied in an eye's length behind the hook eye on the underside of the shank

Tail: Black marabou, with "a couple" strands of LureFlash Twinkle TW 26; *alternatively, rainbow Krystal Flash might do*

Palmer hackle: Black, soft rooster saddle, grade 1 or 2, tied in by the butt at the bend, with 3 tight turns of hackle collar up front, behind the bead-chain eyes

Rib: Oval silver tinsel

Body: Black seal fur, in a dubbing loop; U.S. tiers, use a seal substitute

Head: Tying thread wrapped around and in front of the bead-chain eyes

Tying Tips

A few comments from Erling Olsen on materials: "For saltwater *[meaning the Baltic, for sea-run brown trout—GS]*, I prefer Tiemco's TMC 9394, sizes 4 to 8; for freshwater, TMC 5263, sizes 4 to 10. As for hackle, go for *quality* hackles like those from Hoffman. I especially like Hoffman #1 natural-black hen hackle. In small sizes, use thin to medium oval tinsel, in wide turns. For size 6 to 10 hooks, I prefer Veniard #14; for bigger flies, 2 or 4, Veniard #16."

After dubbing the seal body, Olsen says, "rough up the fur with a toothbrush (your wife's) and stroke it backwards."

In keeping with classic Atlantic salmon fly tradition, Olsen ribs his Seal Bugger *before* palmering; he says to wrap the hackle forward "following close to the turns of tinsel."

When you palmer the hackle feather, don't let the stem twist as you wrap forward. Stroke as you go, if need be, so the barbs angle back toward the tail at about 45 degrees.

Fishing Tips

"In the spring (in both salt and freshwater)," Erling Olsen says, "very often the water will be heavily stained by the snow melt. At that time the water is cold and the fish are slow. That's where the Seal Bugger comes in." (Much of the season, Olsen is a Muddler maven.) Because of its soft marabou tail, soft palmer hackle, and shiny eyes and rib, "the Seal Bugger can be fished very slowly." He says the soft hackle gives "a living impression" to the fly, and that the bead-chain eyes give the fly "a certain diving movement" that makes fish think the Seal Bugger is a fry, a worm, or an eel.

He likes to fish his Bugger on a floating line or a greased intermediate—"I can't remember when I last used a sinking line"—often with 4 to 6 feet of 25- or 30-lb braided Dacron backing or trolling line between the fly line and a 9- or 10-foot tapered mono leader. He uses loop-to-loop connections at both ends of the Dacron, which will sink slowly, and tapers his mono leader from 30-lb-test at the butt to maybe 8-lb (.009-inch or 2X) at the tippet for sea trout in the Baltic.

Fishing in still water with an intermediate line, Olsen counts to ten before beginning a slow- to intermediate-speed retrieve. "Both cod and sea trout take the Bugger with good appetite," he says. In the medium to fast currents in rivers and

Three of Erling Olsen's Seal Buggers ready to rock and roll, along with the colorful vintage tackle he sometimes likes to use—a restored Montague rod and an old South Bend automatic reel.
Flies and photo by Erling Olsen

streams, he goes to a floating line and fishes the Seal Bugger just beneath the surface, across the current, on the swing—sort of midway between waking a surface fly or swinging a wet fly. "At the end of the swing," he says, "I begin taking the fly home in the same manner I do for still water."

Olsen tells the story of when his brother, Tore, went to visit his son and daughter who were living in the U.S., carrying with him "many Seal Buggers from my vise." Among the places Tore and his son, Anders, fished was the Salmon River at Pulaski, New York, where they found the locals fishing deep with high-density lines, roe sacs, and Glo-Bugs. "Tore and Anders used size 6 Seal Buggers on floating lines," Olsen says, "just adding a 5-foot section of braided Dacron in the leader." To make a long story short, the Norsemen showed the locals a thing or two. "My brother had several takes from king salmon," Olsen writes, "the tippet broke on one huge fish, and they had some nice steelhead up to 5 kilos."

KAUFMANN MISFIT *Tied by Umpqua Feather Merchants for Kaufmann's Streamborn*

"Bead head, egg-head leech, or Woolly Bugger?" the catalog asks. "It attracts steelhead and *all* salmon." Besides the **Cerise Misfit** as listed here ("especially useful for off-color water," says the Kaufmann's Streamborn catalog), the pattern also comes in **Black** (pearl-black body and tail, purple hackle) and **Purple** (purple tail, black body and hackle). "Black and purple are best low-light colors," the catalog says, reminding us of the correlation between "dark days, dark water, dark flies."

Kaufmann Misfit

Hook: Steelhead/salmon wet-fly, sizes 2 to 6
Head: Brass bead
Thread: Red
Egg: Cerise chenille, behind the brass bead
Palmer hackle: Orange saddle, tied in behind the egg and reverse-palmered over the body
Underbody: Lead wire
Tail: Cerise marabou, with several strands of pearl or pink pearl Krystal Flash
Body: Cerise tinsel chenille
Rib: Fine gold wire

Tying Tip

If you can't find cerise chenille or marabou, Randall Kaufmann will permit the use of hot-pink materials (for example, hot-pink, or pearl-pink Estasz, or fluorescent-pink Glo-Brite, Crystal, or similar tinsel chenille for the body) without requiring a name change. If you use a hot-pink egg, body, and tail, use a hot-orange saddle for the palmer hackle.

SOCKEYE WOOLLY BUGGER

Here's a green-and-yellow Bugger for sockeye salmon. That hot-orange head probably represents a salmon egg.

Sockeye Woolly Bugger

Hook: 3X-long streamer, sizes 2 to 8
Thread: Hot-orange 6/0
Tail: Bright green marabou
Palmer hackle: 2 saddle hackles—one yellow, the other bright green—tied in and palmered together, the barbs pulled back after each wrap
Body: Green or chartreuse Crystal Chenille or other tinsel chenille
Head: Tying thread, very large and cemented

BATTLE CREEK BUGGER

This pink-and-white Bugger—originated by John Spencer of Redding, California, according to the Alaska Flyfishers web site (www.akflyfishers. org)—has been used successfully in south-central Alaska for both sockeye salmon and river-resident rainbow trout. Note that it, too, bears an orange head.

Battle Creek Bugger

Hook: 3X-long streamer, sizes 2 to 8
Thread: Orange 6/0
Tail: White marabou
Body: Shell-pink chenille, stopped a bit behind the eye to accommodate the face hackle
Palmer hackle: White saddle hackle palmered over the body
Face hackle: 2 turns of orange hackle between the body and the eye
Head: Tying thread, large and cemented

Like Randall Kaufmann's **Misfit**, a cerise-and-orange Bugger for steelhead and salmon, this time with bead-chain eyes. Formerly a staple in the Orvis catalog, it apparently has given way to trendier patterns. It's still a fish-catcher, though, despite its lack of tungsten weight or holographic flash.

Bead-Eye Salmon Bugger

Hook: Orvis 0167, or similar 4X-long—preferably straight-eyed (I didn't have any left)—streamer, sizes 4 and 6
Thread: Red
Eyes: Silver bead chain
Tail: Cerise marabou
Body: Pink Crystal Chenille
Palmer hackle: Orange
Head: Tying thread, wrapped around and in front of the bead-chain eyes

RUBBER LEG WOOLLY BUGGER

Tied by Umpqua Feather Merchants for Kaufmann's Streamborn

The Streamborn catalog lists this Randall Kaufmann pattern in several colors and combinations, with and without bead heads (see also page 156). But the **Brown/Brown** version is the one they say is "our first pick for Chile and Arentina—sea-runs and resident trout…. A killer!" So, that's the version I'm showing and listing here.

Apparently, fish take the Brown/Brown Rubber Leg Woolly Bugger for a pancora, a crustacean that inhabits many Patagonian lakes and streams. (See also the pancora-imitating Woolly Worms on pages 43-44.)

Rubber Leg Woolly Bugger

Hook: TMC 5263, a 3X-long, 2X-heavy nymph, size 6
Thread: Brown
Underbody: Lead wire
Tail: Brown marabou, flanked by several strands of copper Krystal Flash, the long butt ends of which are carried forward along the sides
Palmer hackle: Brown-dyed grizzly saddle, tied in at the front and reverse-palmered
Legs: Black rubber, 2 evenly spaced pairs on either side (8 legs in all), angled 45 degrees to the rear
Body: Brown chenille
Rib: Fine copper wire
Sides: Copper Krystal Flash from the tail, carried forward and tied down at the front before the hackle is palmered and ribbed
Head: Tying thread, varnished

MERCER'S CHUMBUGGER *Tied by Mike Mercer*

The longtime manager of The Fly Shop—Mike Michalak's Redding, California, emporium of all things fly-fishy—Mike Mercer is also a contract tier for Umpqua Feather Merchants. Mike lists this pattern for Alaska but, tied in smaller sizes, it will work anywhere.

Mercer's Chumbugger

Hook: TMC 5263, or equivalent 3X-long, 2X-heavy nymph or streamer, size 4
Thread: Fluorescent- or hot-orange, glossy
Underbody: Lead wire wrapped on shank
Tail: Wine marabou
Body: Flat silver tinsel, overwrapped with Edge-Glo or similar material
Palmer hackle: Orange-dyed grizzly saddle
Front hackle: Purple-dyed grizzly wet-fly collar
Head: Tying thread

Of the 250-odd varieties of Leon Guthrie's Articulated Combination of Lures, several could be called jointed Woolly Buggers. I discovered them on Salmonfly. Net (www. angelfire.com/wa/ salmonid). I can only imagine the shock and horror as tweedy, tradition-bound salmon fishers stumble upon these flies! (The Montana Fly Company—www.montanafly.com—also makes a small series of rabbit-furred, jointed **Articulated Leeches** you may find, or perhaps special-order, in fly shops.)

The inventive Scotsman's jointed streamers feature modular interchangeability of wings and tails, "to suit any particular color the salmon are going for." I think an equally important advantage is the flexibility and action of the articulated construction. Although Guthrie ties them on salmon hooks, nothing is to prevent your tying them on your favorite trout or bass hooks. Or pike or saltwater hooks, for that matter.

Think of the Articulated Woolly Bugger as a Woolly Worm with a mono loop for a tail (or inside a tail of hackle or yarn fibers) that can be turned into a Woolly Bugger by snapping on a marabou tail. It shouldn't take much imagination to come up with your own assortment of Articulated Woolly Buggers for whatever you like to fish for. The free-swinging tail can be tied on a snap or a hook (single, double, or treble). That trailer hook can even be tied as another Woolly Bugger.

You might even join three sections together to make a sandworm/clamworm/bloodworm pattern for stripers in the surf or a needlefish pattern for barracudas in the brine. I'll show the listing for a fairly conservative **Black Articulated Woolly Bugger** or Leech.

Leon's Articulated Woolly Bugger

Hook:	Salmon/steelhead wet-fly, or 2X- to 4X-long streamer, size to suit
Thread:	Black 6/0
Connector loop:	12- to 15-lb monofilament, doubled and lashed to the shank so the loop extends over the bend
Underbody:	*Optionally, lead wire wrapped on the shank*
Body:	Black Fritz, a tinsel chenille; alternatively, use regular chenille and palmer a saddle hackle over it
Forward tail:	Optionally, none, a tuft of yarn or floss, hackle points or fibers, hackle fluff, blood feathers, or marabou (short), tied on the hook shank at the bend; you will have to adjust the length of the connector loop to suit the tail you choose
Tail:	Black marabou, tied separately, on the smallest, lightest wire snap you can find; *alternatively, tie it on a short-shank hook, as a stinger hook to pick up short-striking fish—in this latter case, use a snap to connect the two modules*

Tying Tips

To make the connector loop, double a long piece of monofilament, tie it in at the bend so that a small loop extends to the rear from the top of the shank, wrap the doubled strands around the shank, and counter-wrap the tying thread over the mono wraps.

To make the tail, tie a clump or plume of marabou onto the smaller end of a tiny, light-wire connector snap. Wrap the thread over the marabou at the "neck" of the snap, and put a drop of cement on the thread wraps to keep everything secure. Tie tails in different lengths and colors, to cover a wide variety of fishing situations. If you wish, tie the tail on a stinger hook, which can be connected to the main fly by a small wire snap or a short length of monofilament. For that matter, you could tie a whole Bugger as a chase fly to the Woolly Worm up front.

Richard Carter's **Black Deep Wriggler** (www.fishnet. com.au) is conceptually similar, except that he uses dumbbell eyes on the main fly and ties a palmered Bugger body with a short marabou tail on a short-shank stinger hook, which rides with its point in the opposite orientation from the main fly's.

The English–German tier Mike Connor (a displaced Liverpuddlian who has been living in Deutschland nearly two decades, and whose fly-fishing wisdom often appears on Paul Arden's Sexy Loops web site, www.sexyloops.com/ index.shtml) suggests a gray-and-grizzly Bugger for brackish or salt water—as in fly fishing for sea trout (sea-run browns) in the Baltic. Baltic shrimp aren't very flashy, and they dwell among the weeds in clear water; hence, the lack of flashy materials in the original and the necessity of built-in weight. Mike says the fly should be fished on the bottom with "a fast, jerky, sink-and-draw motion, which is attractive to the fish." Besides sea trout, the fly also takes "tons of cod and garfish" [*Belone belone*, aka garpike, a needlefish]. The same fly would pass for a grass shrimp on our coasts or, in less somber colors, for pink shrimp down in southern waters.

Grizzly Bugger Shrimp

Hook: Standard or long-shank saltwater-fly, sizes 4 to 12
Thread: Gray 3/0
Underbody: Lead wire—enough wraps of sufficient thickness to keep the fly on the bottom
Palmer hackle: Grizzly saddle, reverse-palmered from front to rear
Tail: Gray marabou; alternatively, for more durability, several gray hackle feathers or gray arctic-fox fur; optionally, a few strands of silver or pearl Flashabou mixed in
Rib: Silver wire or clear monofilament
Body: Gray chenille in the larger sizes, shaggily dubbed gray fur (hare body, or seal, or a substitute) in the smaller sizes

According to Mike, fly fishers who ply the Danish coast for sea trout hold this pattern in high esteem. I see no reason not to tie it on a stainless-steel hook of a larger size and scale everything up for a variety of saltwater species. It closely resembles, or strongly suggests, a grass shrimp.

Baltic Woolly

Hook: Standard salmon wet-fly, sizes 6 to 10
Thread: Black
Palmer hackle: Well-marked, soft grizzly, reverse-palmered from front to rear
Tail: Grizzly marabou, about 2 gap-widths long
Body: Hare body fur, dubbed
Rib: Pearl Flashabou

BRINY BUGGERS

While European anglers who fly fish for sea trout in the Baltic probably have more experience than anyone else with Woolly patterns in salt water, Woolly Buggers have succeeded almost everywhere they've been fished, including oceanic salt water. I don't know whether anyone has taken a big billfish or giant tuna on a magnum Bugger; if not, it's probably just a matter of time.

Tie almost any of the Buggers already described on a stainless-steel or other corrosion-resistant hook, and you can catch fish in estuaries, bays and sounds, the Gulf of Mexico, or either ocean, from the frigid waters of the Arctic to the sun-blasted waters of the tropics. Size them to suit your quarry, whether it be inshore panfish like surfperch or pelagic bruisers like tuna. Just be sure to choose a hook that's up to the task.

In a sense, with their palmer-hackled bodies and saddle- or neck-hackle tails, the **Seducers** (aka **Sea-Ducers**) from Homer Rhode and later Chico Fernandez might be considered distant cousins of the Woolly Bugger. Lefty Kreh's **Marabou Seducer** comes even kissing-cousin closer with its full marabou tail and a body of palmered marabou. Tim Borski offers another, clever half-Bugger compromise in his **Sparky Tarpon Fly**: tan craft fur (barred with a dark-brown permanent marker) for the tail, trailing Bugger-like behind a pear tinsel-chenille body palmered over with furnace hackle, and with the fillip of a chartreuse hackle collar up front, behind a head of dubbed olive Antron. Many of these transgressions against basic Buggerness are more fully explored in the next chapter, Hybrids, Mongrels, and Other Bugger-based Beasties.

Pioneering saltwater fly fishers have so far developed a few Buggers, or near-Buggers, specific to their sport, and many more may be coming down the pike. Here are just a few of them for your consideration.

SALTY BUGGER

Especially popular in southern California, this pattern can be found in one form or another on all our coasts. It might well have been derived from the Lefty Kreh pattern described on the facing page. Bill Kiene, of Kiene's Fly Shop in Sacramento, gave me the recipe. Standard saltwater color combinations include red/white, red/yellow, green/white, and blue/white in addition to the most popular green/yellow. Good solid colors include black, white—even purple at times. The color or color combination used should match your experience with other flies and lures for the species and waters being fished.

Salty Bugger

Hook: Mustad 3407SS or similar saltwater-fly, size to suit (4 to 4/0, say)

Thread: Black 3/0 or 6/0, depending on hook size

Tail: Marabou—light covered by dark, if a two-tone pattern; *optionally, added strands of Krystal Flash or Flashabou*

Body: Tinsel chenille to complement, contrast with, or match the tail—match the lighter color in a two-tone pattern

Rib: Medium-fine wire—gold, silver, or copper will do

Palmer hackle: Webby saddle hackle or schlappen, reverse-palmered from front to rear—match the darker tail color in a two-tone pattern

Head: Tying thread, coated with lacquer, cement, or fingernail polish

Tying Tip

If you need to weight this fly, you can add a bead or cone head, bead-chain or dumbbell eyes, or an underbody of lead wire.

Fishing Tips

Fish the Salty Bugger they way you would fish any saltwater streamer—actively. The proper depth and speed of the retrieve depends on the species. Most saltwater predators like fast-moving prey, and that may require using a two-handed strip: After casting the fly and letting it sink to the required depth, tuck the rod butt and reel under one arm and strip hand-over-hand as fast as you can. A stripping basket helps keep the line out of harm's way.

Sometimes, fish seem to prefer a yo-yo retrieve: Let the Salty Bugger sink, give a sharp pull or two on the line, let it sink again, then repeat the strip. Strikes tend to occur on the drop, or just as you start stripping again. You can accentuate the yo-yo action by adding weighted eyes or a heavy bead or cone head, by slipping a bead or clipping split shot on the leader, or by simultaneously jigging the rod tip.

This Lefty Kreh pattern—a quintessential saltwater Cactus Blossom—is named for the body material he used (Cactus Chenille) and the fish he designed it for (small tarpon), but you can use other tinsel chenille and size and fish it for other quarry.

I am listing the **Cactus Black Baby Tarpon Fly**, but am also showing the **Cactus White Baby Tar-pon Fly** (white marabou tail flanked by 6 to 8 strands of red Krystal Flash on either side, trailing behind

a red Cactus Chenille body) to illustrate the swappability of light and dark colors, the variations in body thickness, and the optional addition of extra flash materials to the basic pattern.

Cactus Baby Tarpon Fly

  Hook: Mustad 34007, sizes 4 to 1/0
  Thread: Black 6/0
  Tail: Black marabou, half again as long as the hook, with 6 strands of gold Krystal Flash on either side
  Body: Yellow Cactus Chenille

Tying Note

In the first edition of his *Salt Water Fly Patterns* (Maral Editions, undated), Lefty also listed a much less Buggerish **Cactus Purple/Black Baby Tarpon Fly**: a body of purple Cactus Chenille and a tail made from 8 black saddle hackles flanked by 8 to 10 tail-length strands of gold Krystal Flash on either side.

I based my fly on the Tarpon Shrimp that was shown on Steve Schweitzer's old Midwest Fly Tyer web site. By simplifying the rear hackles and the "tail" (actually the feeding mouth parts of the shrimp) and palmering the body, I came up with something a little closer to the Woolly Bugger. If you like casting heavy flies, wrap a lead-wire underbody; if you don't, use a sinking-tip or higher-density line, or use a weighted leader. I have suggested colors, but you should try to match the prevailing crustaceans.

Buggered Shrimp

  Hook: Mustad 34007, or similar stainless-steel or corrosion-resistant saltwater-fly, size to suit your prey: e.g., 1/0 to 5/0 for tarpon, 2 to 1/0 for bonefish, 1/0 for seatrout (weakfish)
  Thread: 3/0 Monocord, in a color that matches the body
  Palmer hackle: Brown, tan, grizzly (natural or dyed), badger, furnace, cree, or other steeply tapered saddle, tied in by the tip at front and reverse-palmered, after which it should be clipped rather short on top and sides
  Antennae: A few strands of Krystal Flash of an appropriate color: pearl, silver, gray, copper, gold, green
  Eyes: 2 stalked eyes tied in at the bend: 30-lb. monofilament with the ends melted or with 3- to 5-mm beads epoxied in place
  Tail/Pincers: Marabou to match, complement, or contrast with the body
  Body: Pink, tan, gray, olive, or other "hatch-matching" medium to fine chenille
  Rib: Silver, gold, or copper wire

Tying Tip

Naturally, you could tie this on a size 8 to 1/0 salmon wet-fly hook for anadromous salmonids. Try a basically burnt-orange, copper-brown, or dark, brick-red color scheme (all with some contrasting black) for Atlantic salmon, or gaudier colors for steelhead and coho (silver) salmon.

"Yabby" is Aussie for crayfish (quite similar in appearance to our own), but the name is often loosely applied to saltwater crustaceans as well. I found this Richard Carter estuarine pattern on the Fishnet web site (www.fishnet.com.au). I think it could, with perhaps a tweak here and there, stand in for shrimp, mole crabs, and other coastal crustaceans in our waters.

"I really like this fly for lots of reasons," proud-papa Carter wrote (and I concur): "the work and time that went into its creation, the logical effectiveness of the design, and the fly's features: up-riding hook, egg cluster, swimming action, and defensive posture at rest."

If you don't fish salt water, use a streamer hook and tie the yabby in a crayfish-matching color.

Standing Yabby

Hook: Mustad 34011, or similar long-shank saltwater-fly, size to suit your target species

Thread: White (or other body-matching color) 3/0

Weight: Lead dumbbell eyes tied in on top of the shank right at the hook eye, a drop of super glue added to the wraps for security

Weed guard: 40-lb, or heavier, stiff monofilament, tied in a Vee at mid shank on top of the shank; after the fly is finished, clip the legs so the fly will stand at a 45-degree angle (roughly shank-length)

Antennae: Pearl or rainbow (or a combination thereof) Krystal Flash

Eyes: Black plastic beads super-glued onto 40-lb mono stalks; *alternatively, "balls" melted on the ends of mono stalks*

Feelers: Small bunch of white bucktail; *optionally, with a small clump of white marabou*

Palmer hackle: White saddle, palmered to the mid-shank weed guard; clipped flush on the point side of the fly, opposite the weed guard (the top side of this inverted pattern)

Body: White, pearl, or palest pink chenille or tinsel chenille; *I used a pearlescent-white chenille stick formed around very soft, fine copper wire, which shows through faintly to suggest a crustacean's segmentation*

Egg sac: Fluorescent-orange chenille or egg yarn

Carapace: *Optionally, silicone thinned with mineral turpentine, painted on the back of the fly (the flush-clipped underside of the shank)*

Tying Tips

The chenille body is wrapped in several stages. First, take it from the bend to the weed guard. Then palmer the hackle to the weed guard, tie down and clip the excess feather. Take the chenille forward about 2 more turns. Tie in a short piece of fluorescent-orange chenille. Wrap the body chenille forward 2 more turns. Pull the orange chenille over the body chenille and tie off. If there is any more shank left (there wasn't, on mine), wrap the body chenille to the dumbbells and tie off, clipping any excess. Whip-finish.

Carter wrote that the Standing Yabby was "originally tied with a pre-cut, clear drinking straw as a carapace, [but] I now use thinned silicone if anything at all." Lazy tier that I am, I didn't use either silicone or straw.

Fishing Tips

Carter designed the fly for Australian species not found in our waters: whiting, bream, flathead, trevally. But, as he noted, "What fish don't enjoy a saltwater yabby or two?" Here, I'd fish the fly for almost anything that feeds on crustaceans: stripers, weakfish, pompano, permit, bonefish, jacks, almost anything you can find inshore or on the flats.

Use a floating line and a long leader, Carter advises, because the combination helps to lift the fly on strip-retrieves and twitches and lets it sink slowly to the bottom during the pauses. He likes to sight-cast to traveling fish, casting ahead of and beyond the path of a school, then stripping until the fly is in line with the school's heading. Once the fly sinks in a defensive posture and waves those feelers around, get ready for a strike. Blind-fishing, you should cast up-current, give the fly a few strips, and then let it settle to the bottom. After a few subtle twitches, pause, then repeat.

Because of likely abrasion by bottom sediments on that terminal knot, check your knot and tippet frequently. I think you also should consider using some sort of shock leader.

Carter says the logical location to fish his fly are where yabbies and nippers (the critters the fly imitates) live: along weed beds, sand bars, and mud banks. You know where the crustaceans and other arthropods live in your coastal waters.

KING CREEK WOOLLY BUGGER

Here's another yabby-imitating pattern from Australia I discovered on the Fishnet web site. Its target species is bream (related to our porgies), but it has also caught "small flathead" (distant relatives of our searobins and gurnards), and "the odd whiting" (not at all related to the several unrelated species we call "whiting"). Inquiring minds will figure out how to adjust it for and fish it in our waters.

King Creek Woolly Bugger

Hook: Mustad 34007 or similar stainless-steel saltwater-fly, size 4

Thread: Hot-pink flat waxed 6/0 or 3/0

Tail: Pink marabou, with 6 or so strands of pink Krystal Flash over the top

Body: Pink-and-black variegated chenille, tied in at the bend, and wrapped forward (leaving room for the eyes and head) after the legs have been tied in and the thread base has been cemented

Palmer hackle: Grizzly hackle, tied in at the bend and palmered forward over the chenille body

Horns/Legs: Black-and-red Sili Legs, 2 on each side, tied in just ahead of where the chenille and palmer hackle have been tied in

Underbody: Thread base, coated with head cement

Eyes: Small bead chain, tied in between the chenille body and the hook eye

Head: Tying thread figure-8 wrapped between and in front of the bead-chain eyes, then head-cemented

Fishing Tips

"Over the oyster racks is the only place to fish this pattern," writes Peter Jenkins, who tied the fly illustrated on the web site, but then he adds that it "also works well under overhanging vegetation." (Does that remind you of a spot you know?)

"Best fished in the morning, with a bit of tidal run."

Let the fly sink before retrieving it, we are advised. Jenkins said to use short, slow strips, but you should vary the retrieve according to the taking habits of your quarry.

ALBACORE BUGGER

Henry Ford said his Model T came in any color you wanted, as long as you wanted black. I feel the same way about fishing for Atlantic albacore: Use any color you wish, as long as you wish to fish pink. I haven't fished for Pacific albacore, so West Coasters are free to make their own color choices.

Albacore Bugger

Hook: Standard saltwater-fly, sizes 4 to 1/0

Thread: Red or black 3/0

Palmer hackle: Grizzly, tied in at the front and reverse-palmered to the bend

Tail: Pink marabou

Body: Pink chenille

Rib: Clear monofilament or silver wire

CLAIR'S BONAC BUGGER *Tied by Ira S. Clair*

Ira S. Clair, of Pound Ridge, New York, says he tied this one to imitate the late-season baitfish—white-bellied, but otherwise drab green or olive—on which striped bass, bluefish, and "false albacore" (little tunny) fatten up for their fall migrations. He tends to fish shallow water, so wanted something lighter and easier to cast than the Clouser Deep Minnows that have come to dominate inshore fly fishing on the East Coast. "The white hackle came off more pronounced than I thought it would," Clair says, "but the fly was very buggy and kind of shrimplike." Certainly worth a try.

Clair first fished the fly from a small jetty on Gardiners Bay adjacent to Accabonac Harbor (hence, the name) on a low October tide, in about three feet of clear, calm water over a bottom of mixed sand and small pebbles. As he stripped the slow-sinking fly and let it drift with the current, he noticed lots of baitfish following it. "When the fly was almost at my feet, this round chip of the bottom wound itself up into the water and went after my fly." It was a foot-long flatfish (given the sandy, gravelly bottom, and the ambush attack, probably a fluke, or summer flounder, rather than a winter flounder), the first of several he caught—all on the same fly, in the same sort of water, whether casting from shore or wading 50 to 100 feet out.

To distinguish themselves from the wealthy Manhattanites who litter the place, native East Hamptonians call themselves Bonackers. Having been born and baptized in East Hampton, Claire's pattern qualifies as a worthy and Woolly Bonacker.

Clair's Bonac Bugger

Hook: Orvis 9034 or other stainless-steel saltwater-fly, size 4
Thread: Light-green
Eyes: Small, black dumbbell eyes, tied on the underside of the shank within 1/4 inch of the hook eye
Tail: Olive marabou, with yellow Krystal Flash mixed in
Body: Olive chenille, finished off just ahead of the eyes
Palmer hackle: White schlappen or saltwater saddle
Collar: Red chenille, a single wrap behind the eyes

REDFISH BUGGER *Tied by Doug Sinclair*

Capt. Doug Sinclair, a guide out of Grantsboro, North Carolina (and formerly of New Smyrna Beach, Florida), says his pattern is quite similar to a fly of the same name by Dana Griffith, of Gainesville, Florida, except that it uses a lead underbody rather than dumbbell eyes to get it down fast.

Sinclair, dean of the Saltwater Fly Fishing Academy (www.flyfishacademy.net) faculty, recommends a slow retrieve and fishing the fly on grass flats—in windy conditions or where "white holes" (patches of sand) appear throughout the flat.

Redfish Bugger

Hook: Mustad 34011, or similar long-shank, stainless-steel saltwater-fly (sample tied on Mustad's new C71S SS Circle Streamer), size 1/0
Thread: Rust G Monocord
Underbody: .025-in lead wire wrapped around the shank from 1/8 inch behind the eye to the bend, with a "ramp" of tying thread at the rear and several wraps along the wrapped lead, to secure it
Tail: Orange marabou topped by tan marabou, full and twice the hook length
Sides: 6 strands of gold, silver, or pearl Krystal flash on each side, twisted together in a "rope" and pulled forward before palmering the hackle
Body: Tan Ultra Chenille; *alternatively, pink*
Palmer hackle: Orange-dyed grizzly saddle; *alternatively, natural grizzly*

Tying Note

For tarpon, Sinclair ties a similar **Tarpon Bugger** (shown above, below the Redfish bugger), identical to the above with these changes: purple and blue marabou tail, purple chenille body, and purple-dyed grizzly hackle. The sides of the Tarpon Bugger can use the same Krystal Flash or, alternatively, twisted strands of chartreuse Super Hair, a synthetic hair material used in saltwater flies.

Dixon's Devil Worm *Tied by Paul Dixon*

Paul Dixon, who guides out of the Hamptons and Mon-tauk on New York's Long Island, as well as out of the Ocean Reef Club on Florida's Key Largo, came up with this pattern to match the "hatch" (mating swarm) of cinder worms (errant polychaetes akin to the palolo worms in the Florida Keys) that striped bass gorge on in May, June, and July. He had tied the first ones while "fooling around," dubbing some Lite-Brite at the Orvis store in NYC, where he was working at the time. "As soon as I dubbed some on a hook," Dixon says, "I realized it looked like the body of a cinder worm."

One June night, Dixon was fishing the cinder worm hatch with Mark Sedotti, another Long Island guide. Nothing they tossed at the fish worked. Then Dixon remembered his experimental creation. Dixon promptly lost the first of the three flies in his bag, but the other two took 27 stripers. Sedotti, who said he'd never seen anything like it, promptly named the wondrous fly Dixon's Devil Worm. The rest, as the saying goes, is history.

Dixon's Devil Worm

Hook: Mustad 34007, a stainless-steel saltwater fly, sizes 2 to 1/0

Thread: Red 3/0 flat waxed saltwater

Underbody: Thread base

Tail: Blood-red marabou

Body/"Hackle": Pink Lite-Brite, dubbed rough and bushy on the rear 2/3 of the shank

Head: Dark-green Lite-Brite, dubbed on the front 1/3 of the shank

Tying Tips

When Dixon first started tying his Devil Worms, he tied the tails short—"3/4-inch long, if that," his first description read in *Salt Water Fly Fishing*—which would have pigeonholed the pattern as a Woolly Worm variant. Over the years, the tails got longer. Tie your tails to suit yourself.

"You want to make sure the dubbing is uniform," Dixon says. "You don't want them lumpy, but you don't want them see-through, either."

Fishing Tip

"Use short, erratic strips or dead-drift it in the tidal current."

13. Hybrids, Mongrels, & Other Bugger-based Beasties

Few patterns have swept fly fishing as furiously as the Woolly Bugger. Most fly fishers swear by them. Even those who swear *at* them usually carry something that looks suspiciously like a Woolly Bugger, however it may be named. These days, however, almost anything sporting a marabou tail is likely to be called a Bugger. But some flies bearing "Bugger" in their name really shouldn't be so named, as we have already observed. Phil Stroebel's **Spey-Bugger** (which I found on Steve Schweitzer's old Midwest FlyTyer site) is a case in point. It features a long, white marabou tail with a few strands of pear Krystal Flash and a body that is two-thirds pearl Mylar tubing and one-third natural gray dubbing. So far, so good. But, instead of a palmer hackle, it wears a long Spey shroud formed by two hackle collars: the first, two turns of gray marabou and the second, two turns of natural guinea fowl. A fine fly it is, but a Bugger it isn't.

Having said that, however, I've decided to make exceptions for several patterns that violate one or more Woolly principles, but have something so Woolly Buggerish about them I have included them, even though, strictly speaking, they shouldn't be called or considered Woolly Buggers. Call it authorial privilege.

Hybrids & Mongrels

Just as Russell Blessing created the Woolly Bugger by crossing the venerable Woolly Worm with Mark Sosin's Blossom Fly, other tiers have diluted the blood lines even farther by crossing the Bugger with something else. The first three patterns bear the same name but differ in several respects

BOW RIVER BUGGER (1) *Tied by Alan W. Grombacher*

Up in Alberta's Bow River country, they fish this Muddler– Bugger hybrid in the still and very slow waters of sloughs, ponds, and spring creeks, in slow-flowing streams, and in fast water—in other words, almost everywhere. The slower the water, the slower the retrieve and the smaller the hook.

Credit for the pattern is generally accorded to Peter Chenier, who formerly operated the Bow River Company in Calgary.

"Alberta Al" Grombacher lives not far from the Bow River, in Edmonton, Alberta, and travels and fishes throughout Alberta, Saskatchewan, and the Peace River region of British Columbia. He says he has used this fly to catch rainbow, brown, cutthroat, and bull trout, as well as Dolly Varden, whitefish, burbot, pike, and smallmouth bass. "I find it to be one of my most useful streamers," he says. (Incidentally, in his day job Alberta Al is known as Dr. Alan Wall Grombacher, canola researcher for Pioneer Hi-Bred Production Ltd.)

Bow River Bugger (1)

Hook: Mustad 38941, a 3X-long streamer, sizes 4 to 8, "mostly size 6"

Thread: Black

Underbody: "Lots of lead in a single-wrapped layer; under the chenille only"

Tail: Black marabou, with "blue Krystal Flash added for sparkle"

Body: Olive chenille; "I like a medium-olive color, but I have seen varying shades of olive used, from light to dark"

Palmer hackle: Black saddle

Collar: The unclipped tips of some of the deer hair

Head: Deer hair, spun, packed, and clipped; "Not too tight, because I want the Muddler head shape without the buoyancy"

Tying Tips

Alberta fly fishers also tie their Bow River Buggers with green, brown, and black chenille bodies, and I'm told that Peter Chenier's original Bow River Bugger used two colors of deer hair: natural for the collar and white for the head.

Fishing Tips

Alberta Al—who worked his way north and west from Illinois (where he grew up) and Minnesota (where he was the University of Minnesota's wild rice geneticist)—says he normally fishes this Muddler–Bugger on a floating line with a 9- to 10-foot leader. "A standard Bow River rig is a strike indicator, split shot (if needed to get the flies down), a Bow River Bugger, and a tag fly—usually a San Juan Worm, a Micro Worm, or a soft-hackle." But, he adds, "The BRB is also commonly used by itself on a floating line."

Bill McQuilkin, who tied this version, is a Bow River Bugger aficionado, but he's never fished the Bow or any other western river. Bill is a commercial tier from Stratton, Maine. His fly-fishing haunts are strictly Northeast: from northern Maine to Sachuest Point in Newport, Rhode Island. "My favorite places to fish the Bow River Bugger," he says, "are the North Branch of the Dead River, the Chain of Ponds, and the Upper Dam at Richardson Lake, all located in western Maine."

The keys to tying this pattern, according to some, are *thin* chenille, *soft* hen hackle, and enough *bare* shank (as much as half an inch on a size 2) on which to spin the deer hair. Here's the way the pattern often is listed:

Bow River Bugger (2)

Hook: Mustad 79580, or similar 4X-long streamer, sizes 2 to 10, size 8 being especially popular, I'm told

Thread: Black

Underbody: Lead wire (or flat lead ribbon): a single layer from opposite the hook point to a point well short of the eye (leaving enough room for the bullet-shaped head)

Palmer hackle: Brown (or furnace) soft hen saddle, small (the barbs a gap-width long or shorter), tied in by the stem near the front of the shank and reverse-palmered to the rear

Tail: Black marabou

Body: Peacock-green (or olive) thin chenille

Rib: Oval gold tinsel

Collar: The unclipped tips of some of the deer hair

Head: Medium-dark (or gray) deer hair, spun, packed (not too tightly, if you want the fly to sink), and clipped to the tapered-bullet, Muddler Minnow shape

A fellow named Jim Woolacott listed this conehead BRB on Hans Weilenmann's great Flytier's Page (www.danica.com). Our ace tier, Alberto Jimeno, is another New Englander who ties and fishes Bow River Buggers.

Bow River Bugger (3)

Hook: TMC 300, a 6X-long, 1X-heavy streamer, size 10

Head: Gold cone head, small

Thread: Olive 6/0

Tail: Black marabou, with 3 strands of peacock Krystal Flash on each side

Rib: Copper wire, medium

Body: Olive medium chenille

Palmer hackle: Medium olive-dyed grizzly schlappen, tied in behind the cone and reverse-palmered

Collar: Deer hair, spun, packed, and clipped—the forward hairs clipped even with the cone, the remainder left unclipped, Muddler-style

MONGREL BUGGER *Tied by William G. Tapply*

Like the Bow River Bugger a cross between a Bugger and a Muddler, the Mongrel Bugger was created by the mystery novelist and fishing writer William G. Tapply "one daydreamy Sunday afternoon in February." But Bill also had in mind Jack Gartside's palmered-marabou Soft Hackles while he was discovering what he now considers the perfect streamer. So far, he says, his Mongrels have taken crappies, perch, large- and smallmouth bass, pike, pickerel, bluefish, striped bass, anadromous and landlocked chinook salmon, and tarpon—in addition to scads of big trout.

Mix or match tail, body, and hackle colors at will. Tapply sometimes uses marabou of different colors and palmers two feathers together to achieve an almost mottled effect in the hackle. He suggests such color combos as black and purple, red and white, orange and brown, yellow and green. I'm listing the recipe Bill calls "my favorite, day or night, whatever species."

Mongrel Bugger

Hook: Long-shank, straight-eye streamer, sizes 6 to "as large as you like"

Thread: Black, strong enough to spin deer hair

Eyes: Dumbbell or bead-chain, wrapped behind the eye of the hook and secured with a drop of superglue on the crisscross wraps

Tail: Purple marabou, with 2 or 3 strands of Flashabou or Krystal Flash on each side

Body: Purple chenille, wrapped forward to a point about 1/4-inch behind the eyes

Palmer hackle: Purple marabou, with very long barbs, stroked as the feather is palmered forward

Collar: The unclipped tips of a few strands of the deer-hair head

Head: Black deer hair, spun in 2 or 3 bunches, packed only moderately tight, and clipped to Muddler Minnow shape; *alternatively, lamb's wool, for a faster-sinking fly, or tinsel chenille, for added attraction in off-color water*

TRAVIS SCULPIN BUGGER *Tied by Orvis*

This Bugger–Muddler hybrid is by Tom Travis, of Western Anglers, in Livingston, Montana.

Travis Sculpin Bugger

Hook: Orvis 1526, TMC 5262, Daiichi 1710, or similar 3X-long nymph, sizes 2 to 8

Thread: Brown

Tail: Brown marabou, with 2 strands of pearl Krystal Flash on each side

Body: Golden-yellow chenille

Rib: Copper wire

Palmer hackle: Dark furnace, tied in by the butt about 2/3 to 3/4 of the way up the shank and reverse-palmered to the bend, where it is secured by the wire rib

Hackle collar: Black deer hair

Head: Dark-brown wool, spun, packed, and clipped to shape

Tying Tips

After tying in the chenille and copper wire at the bend, wrap the thread up the shank and tie in the palmer hackle. Then wrap the body, reverse-palmer the hackle, and rib forward.

Spin the deer-hair collar before building the head.

For the olive version, use dark-olive marabou and wool, light-olive chenille, and olive-dyed grizzly.

For those who like fishing deer-hair flies, but don't particularly like the spinning, packing, and clipping part, here's a buggered variation on Keith Fulsher's Thunder Creek bucktails.

Bullethead Bugger

Hook: Long-shank streamer, sizes 6 to 10 (The length will be limited by the length of the deer hair you have.)

Thread: Black or brown 3/0

Tail: Dark-brown marabou; *optionally, with a few strands of flash material mixed in or tied on either side*

Underbody: Lead wire wrapped to the density desired (4 to 12 wraps) over a wet, cement-coated thread base

Palmer hackle: Fiery-brown, furnace, or brown-dyed grizzly, tied in at the bend and palmered over the body to the point where the bullet head will be formed

Head: Tan or brown deer hair, laid atop the shank, the butts a bit short of the bend, the tips extending a shank-length beyond the eye, tied in so the hairs roll around the shank (without spinning freely), then folded back to form a bullet head, which will later be reinforced with head cement or epoxy

Body: The folded-back tips of the head hair, lashed to the shank by open spirals of tying thread to the bend, where a few tight wraps will flare the tips then the thread is spiraled back forward to the rear of the bullet head

Eyes: *Optionally, painted or glued-on eyes, over the cement coat—the former after the cement has dried, the latter while it is still tacky*

Gills: *Optionally, tied on just behind the head with red thread or floss, wrap a few turns, and whip-finish*

Tying Tips

You can use several other colors of marabou and dyed deer hair: olive, black, green, orange. If you like, try a two-tone version, with dark deer hair on top and light or bleached hair on the bottom. Or, a dark body and light tail. The fish will soon enough tell you what works best in your neck of the waters.

Except for the length of the palmer hackle (very, very long, as in a Spey salmon fly) and of the tail (fairly short, verging on Woolly Worm territory), this is an otherwise fairly conventional, flash-bodied Woolly Bugger. Flash Chenille is a tinsel-blend chenille that comes in 2 sizes: Short (fibers, about 3 mm long) and Long (9 mm).

Spey Bugger

Hook: Dai-Riki 899, a black steelhead/salmon, sizes 2 to 6

Thread: Black 6/0

Tail: Black marabou, half as long as the shank

Body: Short Flash Chenille: black over the rear 2/3 to 3/4, red in front

Palmer hackle: Large black schlappen, the longest barbs (up front) slightly longer than the hook shank

Head: Tying thread, varnished

SPARROW BUGGER *Tied by R. G. Balogh*

Evening Star Bugger

This pattern is based on Jack Gartside's Sparrow, a fly design that admittedly needs no improvement. But—*sorry, Jack*—I just couldn't resist Buggering it. (If you want to see how the Sparrow should be tied, and fished, visit www.jackgartside.com.) Like the Sparrow itself, the Sparrow Bugger can be tied in any number of colors, from natural to olive to black to gaudy hues like hot pink, orange, or chartreuse. The squirrel can be gray (natural or dyed), fox, or red (pine) squirrel, depending on the look you want. Also like the Sparrow, this one can be fished upstream or down, with split shot on the leader, or, weightless, as a drowned grasshopper.

Sparrow Bugger

Hook: Mustad 9671, Daiichi 1710, TMC 2312, or similar 2X-long nymph (the second is 1X-heavy and the last has a curved shank), sizes 4 to 14

Thread: Tan, orange, olive, gray, or cream 6/0

Tail: Marabou, roughly half a shank long (almost twice as long as Gartside's original), the butts lashed the length of the shank

Body: Rabbit (2 parts), squirrel (1 part), and a bit of Antron, blended and dubbed "rough, ragged, and 'buggy'"; *alternatively, peacock herl—with black everywhere else, in which case it becomes the* **Evening Star Bugger**

Palmer hackle: Very long, soft, webby schlappen or Spey hackle

Collar: Pheasant aftershaft feather(s), natural or dyed, tied in by the butt and tightly palmered in touching turns, between the body and the hook eye; *alternatively, ostrich or long-flued peacock herl*

Head: Neat, tiny, inconspicuous tying thread

BITCH BUGGER *Tied by Dan Bailey's Fly Shop*

This Woolly Bugger/Bitch Creek Nymph cross was genetically engineered by Johnny Boyd. I have listed the traditional Bitch Creek color combination (black and orange), but John Bailey tells me that a pink-and-purple version "has been a great Alaska fly for rainbows and silvers [coho salmon]." The best way to learn to weave a fly body (there are ten different ways) is to invest in a copy of *The Fly Tier's Benchside Reference to Techniques and Dressing Styles* by Ted Leeson and Jim Schollmeyer (1998).

Bitch Bugger

Hook: Dai-Riki 700, a 4X-long, 1X-strong streamer, sizes 2 to 6

Head: *Optionally, a black cone head, if you want a superheavy* **Conehead Bitch Bugger**

Thread: Black

Palmer hackle: Black saddle, 1-1/2 times the hook gap, tied in up front and reverse-palmered over the black thorax

Underbody: Lead wire, over 2/3 of the hook shank

Tail: Black marabou, with 3 strands of pearl Rainbow Thread (or Krystal Flash) on each side

Abdomen: Black and burnt-orange chenille, woven over the rear 2/3 of the shank

Thorax: Black chenille

Rib: Fine copper wire wrapped through the hackle

Legs: White medium rubber, 2 pairs on each side (8 legs in all) in the front 1/3 of the shank

Tying Tips

After tying in the hackle, the tail, the weighted underbody, and the abdomen materials, weave the abdomen, with the orange chenille on the underside. Then tie in the black chenille, the wire rib, and the rubber legs. Wrap the thorax, reverse-palmer the hackle over the thorax, and catch in the hackle with the wire before ribbing forward through the hackle.

I suppose many tiers have used marabou plumes to turn Montana Stones into something vaguely Bugger-ish. The fly shown here was tied by the Swedish tier Paul Milstam, who does not claim paternity of the pattern: "It was invented at Hökensås, a famous fishing camp a few kilometers west of Sweden's second biggest lake, Vättern." That lake and its big brother, Vänern, are famous for their huge landlocked salmon, which are taken chiefly by downrigger trolling. But the Hökensås Montana is fished in smaller waters for brown trout, rainbows, and landlocked Arctic char.

Hökensås Montana

Hook: 3X- or 4X-long streamer, sizes 6 to 10
Thread: Black
Tail: Black marabou
Abdomen: Black chenille on the rear 2/3 to 3/4 of the shank
Palmer hackle: White rooster hackle *(white, on the version with the red thorax)*, palmed over the thorax
Thorax: Fluorescent-green *(alternatively, bright-red)* chenille on the front 1/3 to 1/4 of the shank
Wing case: Black chenille (the abdomen material pulled over the top of the hackled thorax)

Here's a fly that's tied like a Woolly Bugger, but comes out looking more like a cone-headed Mrs. Simpson or Assam Dragon. Most anglers fish it the same way they fish Woolly Buggers. And like a Bugger, it catches fish however it's used. Tom Rosenbauer, Kevin Sloan, and a bunch of other Orvis aces say it has become their favorite and most productive streamer pattern. Sloan says he devotes an entire box to Moto's Minnows. This winner is Moto Nakamura's first original pattern, which he came up with while "just fooling around" at the vise, experimenting with materials.

Moto's Minnow

Hook: Orvis 8808, a 4X-long streamer, sizes 2 to 6
Head: Brass cone
Thread: Brown
Tail: Brown marabou, with a few strands of peacock herl on top
Body: Tying thread base
Palmer hackle: Hungarian partridge, palmered heavily

Tying Tip

Orvis also has a **Light Moto's Minnow**, which uses white marabou for the tail and sports a white soft-hackle collar up front.

Although this very fishy-looking fly lacks a true palmer hackle, the hackle-barb legs help preserve a lot of the Woolly Bugger's flavor. This pattern—a nice cross between a Woolly Bugger and a generic stonefly nymph—is not an easy one to tie, and will take plenty of practice before you can get it right. I failed utterly in my first few attempts, after which I decided this is a fly I'd rather buy than tie. For you tying-bench diehards, here's the recipe. The tying steps are easy to figure out, but difficult to execute.

Stonefly Bugger

Hook: Orvis 584E, a 3X-long nymph, bent down toward the point just forward of mid shank
Thread: Brown
Tail: Dark-brown marabou
Back: Dark mottled turkey tail, pleat-folded in 7 equally spaced sections from tail to head
Body: Brown, fuzzy leech yarn, combed out long on bottom
Legs: Back feather from a mottled-brown hen, several fibers extending out to each side from under each back section
Head: Tying thread, small and neat

REDUCED-HACKLE & HACKLE-FREE BUGGERS

Some tiers have opted to tie Buggers with a slimmer hackle, perhaps none more effectively than Hal Janssen, who was elected to the Fly Fishing Hall of Fame at quite a tender age.

CHIHUAHUA *Tied by Hal Janssen*

From its origin in 1961 as the **Hairless Dog**, a winter-steelhead pattern designed to imitate tidal shrimp, Hal Janssen's Chihuahua has evolved into four distinct patterns, each with its own steelheading merits. One who finds beauty in utility, Janssen didn't send me fresh-out-of-the-vise photographic models. "Each of these flies," he noted, "has been used and has been in the mouth of a fish. (Note the rust in the eye from use in tidal water.)"

While many tiers avoid ostrich herl because of its fragility, Janssen uses it because it is "thicker and fuzzier than chicken hackle, and has more action and life in the water." He also says, "I don't cross-rib anything, because it traps the fibers." The condition of the tiny, been-there-and-done-that flies Hal sent prove you don't need wire ribs and tougher hackles when your flies are tied carefully.

Because of the Chihuahua's thin bo[...] marabou to offset the greater diamete[...] must be "ramped down" at both ends [...]

Chihuahua

Hook: Mustad 9671, or simi[...] sizes 8 and 10

Thread: Olive, tied on at the [...] left hanging to rib the fly

Tail: Olive-brown marabou, sparse, the butts lashed to the rear portion of the shank to provide a transition to the weighted section in the center

Underbody: 6 to 12 wraps of 1-amp fuse wire, wrapped around the center of the shank; ramped at both ends with tying thread

Body: Pearl Flashabou, tied in at the front and wrapped down to the bend and back

Palmer hackle: Olive-brown ostrich herl, spiraled over the body in 6 to 8 open turns

Rib: The long tag end of tying thread left dangling at the bend, laid down so the thread lies against the front of each spiral of ostrich herl

Tying Tips

Clarifying his preference of ostrich herl over chicken hackle, Hal writes, "I find chicken hackle to be too opaque and lifeless in the water. It masks the shape and color of the body, whereas the ostrich is soft and translucent, letting light reflect and refract from inside the pattern."

Janssen's three other Chihuahua patterns are very much the same, but for the differences noted below.

Red-Butt Chihuahua: Except for the red butt, this pattern is identical to the original Chihuahua. Janssen added the red butt in 1966 "to imitate the egg sac on a female tidal shrimp."

Dark Chihuahua: Tying thread and rib, marabou tail, ostrich-herl palmer, and body are all dark-brown

or black. The rib is copper wire. The tying methods are the same. This 1967 pattern is "best on overcast days and in slightly stained water," Janssen says. "My biggest winter-run steelhead was caught on this fly—20-plus pounds and released."

Green Chihuahua: Borrowing the black tail and "palmer hackle" from the Dark Chihuahua, this one uses clear monofilament for tying and for ribbing and green Flashabou for the body. Hal says this 1967 pattern is "a great mid-morning fly on bright days."

Fishing Tips

Asked how he fishes these diminutive flies for big fish, Janssen replies, "I use long leaders—20 to 25 feet—and light tippets for salmon and steelhead, and fish my fly slowly in the slow-moving tidal currents of our Pacific Coast streams. If you retrieve fast, you are not taking advantage of the combination of fly design and material choice. Not all fish are aggressive or have suicidal tendencies, but all fish are hungry all the time."

Hal Janssen first tied this fly around 1969 to imitate the freshwater shrimp that live in Pyramid Lake and on which the giant Lahontan cutthroats prey. Like other ribbed-and-palmered Janssen patterns, both palmer hackle and rib are spiraled from tail to head. "I don't cross-rib anything," he says, "because it traps the fibers." Janssen doesn't use his customary ostrich-herl palmer here, he uses emu. (Janssen notes that a similarly Bugger-like fly called the **Fluff Butt** was being used in Pyramid Lake in the early 1960s; I don't have a pattern for it.)

Because Janssen didn't send a recipe along with the fly, I am guessing at particulars. Again, this fly has been in the mouth of at least one big fish, so don't blame Janssen for its tattered appearance; yours should have that fresh-as-a-daisy look in the vise. Hope and pray that it soon gets this ratty looking.

Pyramid Lake Special

Hook: 2X- or 3X-long wet-fly or nymph, sizes 6 to 10

Thread: Brown, a long tag end left at the bend for ribbing

Tail: Tan or light-brown marabou, wispy and slightly longer than the hook

Underbody: 6 to 12 wraps of 1-amp fuse wire around the center of the shank; ramped at both ends with tying thread

Body: Gold Flashabou or Mylar tinsel, tied in at the front and wrapped down to the bend and back

Rib: Brown tying thread, spiraled forward to follow the palmer hackle without trapping the hackle fibers

Palmer hackle: Emu feather, tied in by the butt at the bend and spiraled forward

ITTY-BITTY BUGGER

and marabou.

I first tied this little Bugger for small-stream native brook trout, but I soon discovered it works well on panfish, ...ting the ver- I usually tie, ...use a variety of both herl

Itty-Bitty Bugger

Hook: 2X- or 3X-long, heavy-wire streamer or nymph, sizes 8 to 14

Head: *Optionally, a silver, gold, copper, or amber bead*

Thread: Black or brown 6/0 or 8/0

Tail: Naturally mottled marabou

Body: Purr-Fect Punch craft yarn, in a color to suit your whim; *alternatively, twisted Krystal Flash, or silver, gold, or copper tinsel or wire*

Palmer hackle: Black or brown ostrich herl with long, thick flues, palmered in slightly open turns

BLUEG...

its alliterative ...is pattern also ...n other pan- ...well as small- ...trout. If you ...netal or glass bead onto the hook before tying on, it becomes the **Bead-head Bluegill Bugger**. Besides the listed black, I also tie this fly in a variety of colors and color combinations. All in white, or in white and yellow, it's a terrific pattern for crappies.

Bluegill Bugger

Hook: 1X- or 2X-long wet-fly or nymph, sizes 10 to 14

Thread: Black

Tail: Black marabou, full but shorter than the hook; use marabou blood feathers or just pinch it off to length with your thumbnail

Body: Black chenille, wool yarn, or dubbing

Palmer hackle: Black ostrich herl

MINI LEECH

Even simpler is this diminutive Bugger-like lure. The word "leech" makes most anglers think of black or dark brown or olive, but Terry Hellekson says this pattern usually is tied in light colors—tan, gray, even white—"and proves itself best on a very slow retrieve."

Mini Leech

Hook: 3X-long, 2X-heavy nymph, sizes 10 to 14
Thread: Tan, light gray, or white 6/0
Tail: Tan, gray, or white marabou
Body: Tying thread
Palmer hackle: Ostrich herl, in a color that matches the tail, thickly palmered in touching turns

HENRYS LAKE LEECH

Hal Janssen points out that Russell Blessing's Woolly Bugger ("I hate that name!") didn't come along until 1967, and says that this Ruel Stayner pattern was being used in the 1940s. In *The Henry's Fork* (1986), Charles Brooks credited Thom Green as "among the first of the regulars to use a leech pattern" in the lake. Brooks reported the use of chamois and marabou leeches, long, narrow streamers, and Woolly Buggers. This clipped-hackle "Woolly Bugger" finally came to dominate. (See also the Henrys Lake Special on page 53.)

Henrys Lake Leech

Hook: 4X-long, heavy-wire streamer (such as Daiichi 1750 or 2220, and TMC 9395), sizes 6 to 12
Thread: Brown
Tail: Reddish-brown marabou
Body: Reddish-brown chenille
Palmer hackle: Brown saddle, clipped short so the fly has "a pencil-like shape" (straight and relatively lender)

AFTERSHAFT LEECH *Tied by Philip Rowley*

A stillwater expert from British Columbia, Philip Rowley fishes a lot of leech patterns. He considers this one "my ideal leech pattern, both slender and animated." He gives full credit to the late Gene Armstrong's Filoplume Leech for his inspiration. In material selection, the Aftershaft Leech is somewhat similar to Jack Gartside's **Wet Mouse** (page 46-47), but the technique is a bit different. Because of the aftershaft feather's frailty, Rowley likes to use a dubbing loop (see Tying Tips). He says you can expect hits on the drop, so be prepared.

Because of that pheasant wet-fly collar, the Aftershaft Leech isn't exactly hackle-challenged, but it *does* lack a true palmer hackle—perhaps justifying its inclusion in this section.

Aftershaft Leech

Hook: Mustad R74, a 4X-long, 2X-heavy streamer, sizes 6 to 10
Thread: Body-matching 6/0
Underbody: About 15 wraps of .010-in lead-substitute wire wrapped on the front third of the shank, and covered with thread
Tail: Mixed colors of strung marabou *(olive and dark olive in the fly shown here)*, the butts at the rear of the weighting wire
Body: Mixed colors of dyed aftershaft feathers from a ring-necked pheasant rump (olive and yellow, here), in a dubbing loop, wrapped closely and carefully, for a palmered-fly look ("A size-8 fly takes about 5 after-shaft feathers.")
Collar: Dyed pheasant rump feather (in this case, yellow), tied in by the tip and wrapped 2 to 3 times as a wet-fly collar
Head: Tying thread, head-cemented

Prepare the aftershaft feathers by clipping the butts and plucking the fragile tips.

To make the dubbing loop, pull down a 4- to 5-inch length of thread at the base of the tail, apply dubbing wax, and lay the prepared aftershaft feathers longitudinally on the thread, tip to butt. Bring the thread back up to the shank, forming the dubbing loop, wrap around the shank a couple of times, and spin the loop until the aftershaft barbs radiate out perpendicular to the thread. You're ready to wrap.

Prepare the collar hackle by stripping the fluff from the base of the pheasant rump feather, grasp the tip and stroke the barbs back toward the butt. Tie it in by the tip and wrap.

If you carry both weighted and unweighted leeches, Rowley suggests a dab of red fingernail polish on the hook eye to designate weighted patterns. (Other tiers often use red or other color-coded tying thread.)

Speaking of colors, Rowley says, "I prefer to tie this leech pattern in mottled shades of olive/brown, olive/yellow, black/purple, and black/claret, using dyed ringneck pheasant rump. The aftershaft feathers can be challenging to find, as it is a material many tiers neglect and the demand for it is low."

MIKE'S MOHAIR LEECH *Tied by Mike Kruse*

Mike Kruse is a fisheries research biologist who is widely known in Missouri fly-fishing circles for his angling skill, his conservationist ardor, and this fly. "I discovered this fly by accident one day," Kruse admits, "when I substituted some olive mohair yarn in the place of olive chenille on a Woolly Bugger. I decided to omit the hackle entirely after I realized what a fuzzy body the mohair created." Since that happy accident, Kruse has "enjoyed great success" with his creation throughout the U.S. and in New Zealand.

As for the different hues in the flies pictured, Kruse writes, "I've been experimenting lately with a variety of mohair sources and they all vary slightly in color and yarn texture. The lighter one is a very good color, but the yarn is a bit too thin and I had to pick it out a lot to achieve the normal level of fuzziness that I like. The other one is a bit green, but that very same combination absolutely killed 'em last month on Duke's Creek in Georgia. Like many things relating to flies and fishing, *general* size and shape, *approximate* color, and—most important—presentation, are probably the main factors critical to success."

Some of Mike's fishing buddies have also taken to tying the Mohair Leech in brown, in sizes 8 and 10, but Kruse says he still prefers to fish the original olive in size 8.

Mike's Mohair Leech

Hook: Mustad 9672, a 3X-long nymph, size 8
Thread: Olive 6/0
Underbody: 12 turns of .035-in lead wire
Tail: Olive marabou, tied thick, about shank length
Body: Olive mohair yarn, palmered thick and "fuzzy"

Tying Tips

Select marabou that has fairly thick fibers all the way to the tips. "It is difficult to create a thick-enough tail if your marabou has very thin tips," Kruse warns.

Body material is even more crucial. A lot of the stuff marketed as "leech yarn" has a white or black core that detracts from the olive. And, says Kruse, "most of the 'mohair' I have seen sold in fly shops is very soft, and I believe it flattens out too much when wet, causing the fly to lose its 'halo.'" He advises using the real mohair sold in specialty yarn stores. Get several tying buddies together, because you'll have to buy a whole skein. If you're lucky, your fly shops will have repackaged the right stuff in smaller packages. Also, some yarn shops have knitting classes, and they sell leftovers.

As you wrap the body, take care not to trap the mohair fibers. To avoid all that tedious teasing out of trapped fibers with a needle or bodkin, tease and stroke the fibers away from the shank as you wrap. "You want a fly that has a 'halo' of long mohair fibers trailing back along the body," Kruse advises.

Fishing Tips

"Normally, I fish this fly as I would a nymph," Kruse writes: "cast upstream and dead-drift under a strike indicator." Fish may strike at any time, but especially as the fly begins to drag at the end of the drift.

In ponds, Kruse fishes his Mohair Leech on a uniform-sink line and uses short strips, a hand-twist retrieve, or both.

ELECTRIC ORANGE LEECH *Tied by John Simonson*

John Simonson, of Corvallis, Oregon, originated this dandy and effective variation on the mohair theme that he fishes in both lakes and rivers, using 3- to 6-inch retrieves "with a pause now and then."

Electric Orange Leech

Hook: TMC 200R, a 3X-long, slightly curved-shank streamer, size 10

Thread: Orange

Tail: Orange marabou with 3 to 5 strands of Krystal Flash as long as the tail on each side (the tips of the body material)

Body: 6 to 10 strands of orange Krystal Flash (including the butts of the tailing strands); *alternatively, use white or pearl*

Palmer "hackle": Orange mohair ("leech yarn") fibers, spun in a dubbing loop, picked out, stroked back, and trimmed so they extend to the tip of the tail

KAUFMANN MINI LEECH *Tied by Umpqua Feather Merchants for Kaufmann's Streamborn*

Many Bugger-like patterns use a marabou tail and either palmered marabou or mohair yarn for the body and "hackle." The best known are Hal Janssen's **Marabou Leech** and the ubiquitous **Mohair Leech**. This pattern by Randall Kauffman has become a western standard. Kaufmann has three excellent bits of advice on fishing this and other leech patterns: tie them small, fish them slowly, and use maroon for lake fishing. If you want to be really prepared, try some of Kaufmann's other Mini Leech colors: red, wine, purple, black, olive, and red/brown. If you don't use a bead head, be sure to fish the Mini Leech on a sinking or sinking-tip line—or use sinking leaders on a floating line.

Kaufmann Mini Leech

Hook: TMC 200R, a 3X-long, straight-eyed, slightly curved-shank nymph, size 10 or 12

Head: *Optionally, a small gold bead*

Thread: Red, fluorescent red, or hot pink

Tail: Maroon or burgundy marabou or "hackle fluff," from a gap-width to half a shank-length long, flanked by a single, slightly longer strand each of wine and pearl Flashabou or Krystal Flash on each side

Body: Maroon-dyed Angora goat and 3 to 5 strands of wine and pearl Krystal Flash, in a dubbing loop and dubbed very shaggily, but fairly sparsely, the strands being stroked backward as you go.

Head/Collar: Tying thread behind the hook eye or bead head

SALMON RIVER MARABOU LEECH

This is a marabou-tailed version of the Fran Verdoliva spring-and-fall pattern, the **Salmon River Leech**. Franze is an opalescent tinsel chenille from Europe; you can use whatever you have.

Salmon River Marabou Leech

Hook: Standard salmon wet-fly, sizes 2 to 6

Thread: Black

Tail: Purple or white marabou, to match the body

Body: Purple or white Franze, or similar opalescent tinsel chenille

Head: Fluorescent-pink chenille wrapped as an "egg"

I don't recall where I picked up this pattern. When I was gathering patterns for this book, I found a piece of note paper on which I had scrawled this recipe, with the notation that the pattern had come from Brent Schlenker, of Cypress Fly Fishing in Medicine Hat, Alberta, via Paul Marriner, of Maritime Canada, whose advise on patterns I always find worth following. According to my notes, either Schlenker or Marriner advises that long, slow pulls work best, the pulls separated by 5-second pauses. Sometimes, he warns, 2-inch pulls work better.

Brent's Blood Leech

Hook: 3X-long streamer, sizes 6 to 10
Head: Red glass bead, small
Thread: Unspecified, but black or dark-red 6/0 should do just fine
Underbody: .020-in lead wire wrapped on front half of shank
Tail: Wine-colored marabou, sparse, with Fire Accent Flash, or similar flash material such as Krystal Flash, on each side
Body: Blended black and red angora goat or mohair—spun in a red wire dubbing loop so the fibers are perpendicular to the hook shank; *alternatively, a suitable commercial dubbing brush (having nothing but black goat and no red mohair, I first wrapped a red Siman Mega Fibers Dubbing Brush then palmered black mohair yarn over)*

This pattern—which looks like nothing in particular but can generally suggest crasyfish, leeches, hellgrammites, baitfish, and the nymphs of damsel and dragonflies—is representative of the patterns Mark Vinsel calls **Shortcut Sparkle Buggers** (I call them **Cactus Blossoms**). Vinsel, the California watercolorist, is particularly fond of this red-and-peacock fly (first tied by his friend David Latham), which he sometimes, but not often, ties with a soft palmer hackle. "Hackles that are too stiff cause a twisting action," Vinsel says. "We usually save time by omitting the hackle, because these flies work as well after fish have torn the hackles away." If you prefer, add a brown or orange hen saddle or schlappen, palmered sparsely over the tinsel chenille.

Christmas Leech

Hook: TMC 5263 (3X-long), TMC 3761 (1X-long), or similar 2X-heavy nymph or streamer, sizes 8 to 12
Thread: Black or olive
Tail: Red or red-orange, soft, webby marabou; *olive, if you suspect fish are feeding on damsel-fly larvae*
Body: Peacock, or green, tinsel chenille, the first turn wrapped under the tail to keep the marabou from fouling the hook
Palmer hackle: *Optionally, a soft hen saddle palmered through the body—left long, clipped short, or clipped to a taper*

Fishing Tips

"Fish the Christmas Leech slowly on an intermediate line to mimic leeches," Vinsel advises, "or fish it near the bottom with twitches to imitate molting crayfish." Either way, he says, the fly draws hard strikes.

Vinsel says Jay Fair, the almost legendary guide from Eagle Lake, California, taught him how to fish leech patterns: "A hand-twist retrieve, with the line going directly from the stripping guide to the left hand, rather than through both hands, will help you detect soft strikes.

Sometimes fish take the leech in completely before closing their mouths."

When trout are feeding in lake shallows, says Vinsel, wading will spook them. So will casting directly to them. "Often, you have to detour around and get ahead of the fish with your line in the water and wait for them to approach your fly" before beginning the retrieve. "Similarly, when wading alongside weed beds, it often pays to cast sidearm—sometimes just ten feet or so—when the fish are in the beds waiting in ambush."

MISSISSIPPI MERMAID

I found this pattern in a back issue of the newsletter of the Ottawa Women Fly Fishers, in an article on fly fishing for upper-Mississippi smallmouths by Rachel Crowder. At this writing president of OWFF, Rachel is a busy woman, being a professional social worker and proprietor of Raven Fly Fishing, a guide and instruction service for women, as well.

Rachel says she developed the Mermaid over several years of fishing for smallies on the upper Mississippi in Ontario, during which field testing the pattern has also proved its worth on brown trout and rainbows. "This fly kicks bass," she says.

Mississippi Mermaid

Hook: Mustad 9672, or similar 3XL streamer, size 6
Head: Medium gold cone
Thread: Unspecified, but black or olive 6/0 will do
Tail: Olive-gold marabou. shank-length, with a few strands of pearl Krystal Flash
Body: Olive-gold Ice Chenille, Estaz, or similar tinsel chenille, wrapped forward in touching turns

ORANGE FRITZ

"Fritz" is a British tinsel chenille, the equivalent of Cactus or Ice Chenille. I found this popular pattern on the Diptera web site (www.diptera.co.uk), where it says, "The Orange Fritz works superbly when fished very fast, ideal when trout are taking *Daphnia*. The Fritz can be tied in a variety of colors and color combinations across the spectrum. Whoever described the pattern comments that "the darker-coloured Fritzes are usually fished more slowly than the lighter-coloured ones."

Orange Fritz

Hook: Kamasan B175, or similar long-shanked streamer hook, sizes 8-10
Head: 3-mm gold bead
Thread: Black 6/0
Tail: Orange marabou
Body: Orange Fritz or tinsel chenille

Tying Note

More recently, but similarly, George Davis, a guide and lodge operator in Cordova, Alaska, has designed what John Randolph of *The Fly Fisherman* has said "may be the best silver [coho] salmon flies ever devised," his **Spanker** series (see page 211).

Sir Kevin Moss's **Claret Damsel** is somewhat similar to both preceding patterns, with a 3-mm brass bead slipped onto a short-shank, gold-plated wet-fly hook (sizes 8 to 12), olive marabou twice as long as the hook (surrounding a few strands of even longer gold Krystal Flash) for the tail, olive chenille on the rear half of the shank and claret tinsel chenille on the front half.

In this other British Cactus Blossom, the key is to keep the tail to shank-length and to use extra-long tinsel chenille and wrap it very closely. Some tiers like to use frayed floss or nylon rather than marabou for the tail, but I have specified marabou to keep to the Bugger tradition. Virtually any "hot" color or color combination can be used, if you think it will attract fish.

Blob

Hook: Standard or heavy-wire nymph or wet-fly, sizes 8 to 12
Thread: Black 6/0
Tail: Black or "hot"-colored marabou, pinched off at shank length (or slightly shorter)
Body/"Hackle": "Hot"-colored or black Grande Estaz, Polar Chenille, or similar long-fibered tinsel chenille, wound very full, in closely touching turns

Tying Tips

As you wrap the tinsel chenille, stroke the long, translucent fibers to keep them from being trapped.

When tying-off, hold the tinsel-chenille fibers back from the eye. After whip-finishing, stroke the fibers forward again so the fly has a popper-like, concave face.

If you want a **Floating Blob**, which should be a good panfish pattern, add a shellback of closed-cell foam. Just tie it in at the bend after tying in the tail and pull it over the body and tie it down at the eye.

But for the bent-shank nymph hook, this is otherwise a fairly conventional flash-bodied Bugger *cum* Cactus Blossom. Dr. Tom Conner (he is a sociology professor at Michigan State) also ties this pattern on heavy, curved-shank scud hooks, but he likes the way this version fishes on the bottom. With the weighted eyes midway between the bend in the shank and the eye of the hook, this pattern produces "a fly that sits and bounces along the bottom with the hook point and marabou tail sticking up a bit higher," he explains. "It also seems to have a better jig-like action when twitched."

Conner's Carp Bugger

Hook: Daiichi 1730 or 1870, Orvis 584E, or similar 3X-long, bent-down-shank nymph, sizes 6 to 10
Thread: Black 8/0
Eyes: Gold bead chain, tied below the shank about midway between the hook eye and the angled bend in the shank
Tail: Light-olive marabou
Body/"Hackle": Olive Ice Chenille, medium, wrapped all the way to the hook eye
Head: Tying thread

The name made this opera fan think immediately of the soprano Kiri Te Kanawa, so I assumed this was a New Zealand pattern. Wrong. It comes from Kim Keeley, co-owner of the Victor Emporium Fly & Tackle Shop in Victor, Idaho, who apparently combined her last name with tequila in naming the fly.

TeQueely

Hook: Orvis 8808, a 4X-long streamer, sizes 2 to 6
Thread: Black
Tail: Black and yellow marabou, mixed
Legs: 12 yellow round rubber, 6 pairs, evenly spaced, 3/4 shank-length
Body/"Hackle": Light-brown Hi-D Krystal Chenille

I found Eric Larsen and this pattern on ROFFT, the fly-tying discussion group (rec.outdoors. fishing.fly.tying). Larsen does much of his fishing up in the mountain lakes around Flagstaff, Arizona, and in the White Mountains of eastern Arizona. This fly was designed as an attractor pattern for trout and only incidentally became a pike fly. Larsen was fishing Long Lake, a typical reservoir with flooded trees for fishing structure. He was fishing for brown trout, using a 5X tippet, and started lip-hooking pike, one of which had one of his flies in its mouth. Now, he uses wire or very heavy mono leaders with his redesignated pike pattern.

Larsen says that, while the colors "are not intended to represent or imitate anything in nature, there is some thought behind the fly design. The silhouette *is* intended to imitate a baitfish. The colors are intended to make the fly visible to the fish at various depths."

In Mesa, the Phoenix suburb where he lives and works as an analyst for the local electrical utility, Eric Larsen is a member of the Desert Flycasters and is much involved with the club's conservation activities.

EZ Pike Bugger

Hook: Mustad 3366, a straight-eyed nymph, sizes 2 to 6
Head: Large red, green, or clear glass bead
Thread: Black, white, or green 6/0
Tail: Bright blue marabou, about half again as long as the shank
Sides: *Optionally, a long strand or two of pearl Flashabou tied in by the middle at each side of the shank at the bend—the aft ends left trailing along either side of the tail, the forward ends later pulled forward along the sides of the body*
Body: Kelly-green Estaz

Tying Tip

Although Larsen has been fishing his pike flies with bright blue tails, he says he intends to start tying them with red, green, white, and other tails as well. Indeed, some of the samples he sent me included red head/pink body/red tail; pearl head and body/green tail; orange head/olive body/black tail; and green-thread head/green body/olive tail

Fishing Tip

Fish the EZ Pike Bugger with a full-sinking line near the bottom, around fish-holding structure. "Use an erratic stripping retrieve," Larsen advises, "to allow the fly to move as a minnow or other small fish that hangs out in structure for protection." And be sure to use wire or other bite-protective leader to guard against the pike's nasty teeth, rather than relying on Larsen's early luck.

CONEHEAD RUBBER BUGGER *Tied by Montana Fly Company*

This pattern, developed by Adam Trina, president of the Montana Fly Company, could be considered just another flash-bodied, conehead Woolly Bugger *except* (and it's a big "except") instead of a hackle feather it uses Tentacles, the company's fine Spandex—similar to SuperFloss, but much finer. That gives the palmer "hackle" even more movement in the water than would the use of feathers. And you can create any color combination you want.

In addition to the listed **Halloween**, the Conehead Rubber Bugger also comes in **Black**, **Brown**, **Olive**, and a

color combo called **Takillya**. The color changes are listed below, in Tying Tips.

Conehead Rubber Bugger

Hook: MFC 7008 or similar 4X-long streamer, size 4
Head: 7-mm gold cone
Thread: Fluorescent fire-orange Nymo
Underbody: 1-mm lead wire wrapped on the shank
Tail: Orange covered by brown marabou blood quill with orange Flashabou, or Flashabou Accent (similar to Krystal Flash), added
Dubbing loop: Fine steel wire, tied in at the bend
Body: Orange Estaz
Palmer "hackle": Black, orange, and yellow Tentacles cut to length and placed in a dubbing loop, or turned into a dubbing brush, and palmered over the body

Tying Tips

The Tentacles should be cut to twice the length you want your palmer "hackle" and should be at right angles to the dubbing loop or wire. When you apply the Tentacles to the dubbing loop or brush, make sure to apply them sparsely and evenly, as they can bulk up very quickly.

Here are the colors substitutions used in tying the other Conehead Rubber Buggers:

Black: black thread, marabou, and Estaz; pearl flash; black and yellow Tentacles
Brown: brown thread and marabou; pearl flash; root beer Estaz, brown and tan Tentacles
Olive: olive thread and Estaz, olive-brown marabou, pearl flash; brown and olive Tentacles
Takillya: black over yellow marabou; copper flash; root beer Estaz; brown and yellow Tentacles

'BOU-LESS BUGGERS

Marabou works best in waters with medium-speed to barely detectable currents, or when retrieved in still water. In slow waters, nothing can quite match the fish-attracting action of marabou. In fast waters, however, marabou slicks back straight and can have the action of a finishing nail; you could use a few strands of tying thread for the tail and get the same result, or lack thereof. To cope with fast water, many tiers resort to different tailing materials: ostrich herl, saddle hackles, hair, or fur. And some saltwater fly fishers like to use craft fur because it's durable under toothy attack and inexpensive to buy (see **Sparky Tarpon Fly** in the previous chapter, page 186).

HERLY BUGGERS

When I tie Woolly Buggers for really fast water, I often substitute a bunch of ostrich herl for the marabou in the tail. This is hardly an original idea, but I don't know who deserves credit for the discovery, but Harry Murray deserves kudos for popularizing it. Depending on the size of the fly, it takes a dozen to two dozen ostrich herls to give the fly the desired action. Ostrich-herl tips are very active, but fragile. For a slightly more durable fly, select herls with very long flues, tie them extra long, and pinch the tail to the desired length, eliminating the fragile tips. Note that I said "pinch," not "clip." Always pinch off the tips to size. Your herly tails will look and work better than if you had trimmed them with scissors. But for their ostrich-herl tails, Herly Buggers are indistinguishable from Woolly Buggers—except in fast water, where they considerably outclass marabou-tailed Buggers.

MURRAY'S HELLGRAMMITE *Tied by Harry Murray*

"Murray" is of course the redoubtable Harry Murray of Edinburgh, Virginia, who literally wrote the book on *Fly Fishing for Smallmouth Bass* (1989). Harry Murray may or may not have invented the Herly Bugger, but he most certainly perfected it. Murray's Hellgrammite is a great pattern for bass and big trout, and deservedly the best-known Herly Bugger in the land.

Murray's Hellgrammite

Hook: Mustad 9672, TMC 5262, or similar 2X- or 3X-long streamer, sizes 4 to 10
Thread: Black 3/0 Monocord
Underbody: Lead wire, about as thick as the hook shank, wrapped over a thread base, centered on the shank and covering about 3/4 of its length, then overwrapped with thread, which is in turn coated with head cement
Tail: Black ostrich herl
Body: Black chenille
Palmer hackle: Soft, webby, dark blue-dun rooster saddle, wrapped forward in 5 evenly spaced turns
Pincers: Black rubber
Head: Tying thread, cemented

Tying Tips

Murray always ties his Hellgrammites heavily weighted. In recent years, he has favored the use of large lead dumbbell eyes, lashed to the front of the shank (leaving room for the rubber pincers and a little more; see below) with figure-8 wraps and cemented in place. He calls this head-heavy version **Murray's Lead-Eyed Hellgrammite**. Murray's Fly Shop now offers the lead-eyed version in three colors: brown, olive, and black.

The important thing in selecting ostrich herl for the tail, Murray says, is that it be strong—ones with thick, hairlike barbules. He says 20 herls is about the right size clump for a size 6 hook. "Holding the clump together," he adds, "break off the weak tips by twisting them between your thumbnail and index finger."

To make the pincers, fold a 2-inch piece of rubber leg material in half, and tie it to the front of the shank, wrapping the thread over the fold. Use figure-8 wraps around the base of each pincer, to make them spread apart at nearly 90 degrees from each other. Pull the pincers forward together, and cut them evenly, about 3/4-inch in front of the hook eye. After wrapping the body and the palmer hackle, build a small thread head over the pincer tie-in wraps.

Fishing Tips

I have fished Murray's Lead-eyed Hellgrammite for smallmouth bass in the South Fork of the Shenandoah (Harry's home water), and I can tell you that nothing else in my box came close to it in effectiveness. That baby *stayed down* in those swift waters! But I can also tell you that, with my flawed casting mechanics, I was left with a lot of stress, strain, and pain in my casting elbow and forearm. I returned to the same waters two weeks later, armed with Airflo sinking leaders and more Murray's Hellgrammites, this time tied much more lightly weighted or completely unweighted. Result? The Hellgrammite showed the same fish-catching effectiveness, and I had more fun and less pain. You've got to keep this fly down on the bottom, but it's the hackle and herl that make it work, not the weight.

This is the red-headed fly-fishing pharmacist's latest creation—it isn't even in the Murray's Fly Shop on-line catalog (www. murraysflyshop.com) as I write this. In addition to the listed **Pearl** pattern, Harry also sent me an all-black version, which was palmered with a longer-fibered saddle hackle.

Murray's Marauder

Hook: 4X-long streamer, sizes 4 and 6
Thread: White
Eyes: Lead dumbbells (1/32-oz or as desired), tied in with figure-8 wraps below the shank not quite a fourth of a shank-length behind the hook eye
Tail: White ostrich herl (as in the Hellgrammite), with 3 or 4 strands of pearl Krystal Flash on either side
Body: Pearl medium Estaz
Palmer hackle: Black, webby, short-fibered saddle hackle, palmered up to the dumbbell eyes
Head: Estaz from the body, X-wrapped around the eyes and tied off at the hook eye

Tying Tips

On the River Smallies web site (www.riversmallies.com), where I first discovered the pattern, the Pearl Murray's Marauder is listed with several differences: the hook is 2X- or 3X-long; the dumbbell eyes are tied atop the shank, painted white with black pupils, and coated with clear Hard As Nails polish; the tail uses white marabou rather than ostrich herl; and the palmer hackle is white and longer-barbed. There, it says the Marauder is "also a great fly in black, olive, root-beer, and purple."

Similar in concept but different in detail is Ed Story's older but hackle-free **Pearl Shiner**, a smallmouth bass streamer that the Feather-Craft (www.feather-craft.com) catalog says is "fished with great success for any gamefish that feeds on baitfish." For example, it calls the Pearl Shiner, "Great for walking the beach & casting for ladyfish." Tied on a 4X-long, 3X-heavy, nickel-plated TMC 9394 streamer hook, sizes 2 through 6, with red, flat waxed nylon or 3/0 UNI-thread, the fly incorporates a nearly shank-length tail of white ostrich herl, a weighted underbody of .020-inch lead wire, a body of pearl Estaz or long-fiber Crystal Chenille, and painted eyes.

FLIGHTLESS BUGGER

All the feathers in this pattern come from two flightless birds (ratites, to the erudite): ostrich and emu. Sometimes, when I'm feeling particularly full of myself, I call this fly the **Ratite Bugger.** (Trivia bonus point: The rhea is the other ratite. Double bonus: Ostriches are native to Africa; emus, to Australia; and rheas, to South America.)

Flightless Bugger

Hook: 3X- or 4X-long streamer, sizes 6 to 10
Thread: Black 6/0
Tail: 20 to 25 black ostrich herls, pinched off at a bit more than hook-length
Palmer hackle: Black emu feather, long-barbed, palmered through the body herl in open spirals, the barbs stroked back with each wrap
Body: Orange or yellow ostrich herl, relatively short-barbed, tightly palmered in touching turns

PEARLY HERLY BUGGER

I like this pale pattern for fishing off-colored pocket water. Tail color is up to you; I lean toward white or natural. Although I usually tie this fly unweighted and fish it on fast-sinking leaders with very short tippets (never more than a yard long), I sometimes slip a bead on the hook before tying on the thread.

Pearly Herly Bugger

Hook: 2X- to 4X-long streamer, sizes 6 to 12
Head: Optionally, a nickel-plated brass or pearl-colored glass bead
Thread: Olive
Palmer hackle: Well-marked grizzly saddle, reverse-palmered from the front
Tail: 15 to 20 white or pale-gray ostrich herls, the frail tips pinched off
Rib: Silver wire
Body: Pearl Mylar tinsel, twisted strands of Krystal Flash, or tinsel chenille—all of them work, but work a little differently; I haven't yet decided on a favorite

Tying Note

Sometimes, I'll use peacock herls for the body (6 herls, twisted in a "rope"), in which case, I call it a **Double Herly Bugger**. If I use peacock herl for both body and tail (at least 15 to 20 herls in the tail cluster, sometimes with a few strands of Flashabou or Krystal Flash added), I'll call it a **Peacock Herly Bugger**. And if I use ostrich herl for both tail and palmer hackle, it's an **Ostrich Herl Bugger**. The herls of both birds make up in fish-attraction what they lack in durability.

HACKLE-TAILED BUGGERS

Almost any sort of feather can be used to tail your Woolly Buggers, as long as you striver for a Buggerish look, either in the vise or in the water. The tail should be roughly as long as the hook shank, to keep your Bugger from backsliding into the Woolly Worm/Palmer Fly category. If you were to palmer-hackle a large, strong, short-shank, corrosion-resistant hook, and use 6 to 8 very long saddle hackles for the tail, you'd have a perfectly acceptable tarpon fly. But that's another story, and belongs in someone else's book. Hackle-tailed Buggers should be fished actively; their tails won't contribute much in a dead drift or wet-fly swing.

PURPLE PEOPLE-EATER BUGGER

The long, multi-hackled tail on this pattern may slightly resemble a tarpon fly from down in Miami Dolphins country, and the name might make old-timers recall Alan Page and the Minnesota Vikings, but M. L. James fishes his Purple People-Eater in Vermont's trout streams—New England Patriot country.

Purple People-Eater Bugger

Hook: 2X-long streamer, sizes 10-14
Thread: Black
Tail: Pink-, purple-, and red-dyed Chinese saddles, hook-length
Body: Purple "semi-metallic" chenille (a tinsel-and-chenille blend such as Sparkle or New Age Chenille)
Palmer hackle: Grizzly saddle, oversize

When I contacted the innovative Hans van Klinken (world famous for his Klinkhamer Special emerger, among others), to see if he had a Woolly pattern to offer, this is what he wrote: "Please don't misunderstand me, the Woolly Bugger is an extremely effective pattern—I just don't like to use patterns that are used by so many people. That's why I never use goldheads or the ordinary CDC. I like designing new patterns with a new look, and my experience is that when certain patterns are used frequently in rivers or lakes, I find that a new or different design attracts the fish more. Maybe that's why I mostly do well in waters where they promote only a few patterns.

"It is not different with the Woolly Bugger. They use it a lot, so that's why I change it, and I catch loads of fish with the different variations—much more than those who still use the standard Woolly Bugger. When they start using my dressing a lot, I change it again. So that keeps me creative and inventive. I will scan some of my Buggers and send them to you tomorrow. I am working on too many stories at the moment to do it today."

What Hans sent was a group shot of 9 Buggers: 6 of them bead-headed, one tied on what looked like a leadhead jig hook;

2 of them forktailed (one of them double-forked); marabou tails ranging from shaving-brush stout to rocket-blast long and slender, from sparse to very full; some prominently tinsel-ribbed, some apparently not; palmered sparsely, heavily, and in between, the barb length varying from shortish to very long, with and without heavy "wet-fly collars" up front; in two cases, palmered only over the front half; the colors ranging from black to yellow, from solid colors to a combination of two or three. I eeny-meeny-miney-moed my way to the one listed below, the particulars of which I am guessing at. But you can be sure that Hans is no longer fishing it, having moved on to something new.

Hans's Bugger-of-the-Moment

Hook: 4X-long streamer, size to suit
Head: Brass bead, medium
Tail: 2 hook-length purple saddles, splayed outward
Rib: Gold flat tinsel, tied in at the bend, wrapped as a tag to secure the palmer hackle, then spiraled through the hackle to the front of the body
Body: Purple chenille or vernille, tied in about an eighth-inch above the bend and wrapped to an eighth-inch short of the bead
Palmer hackle: Purple saddle, tied in by the butt behind the bead and reverse-palmered to the bend— *optionally, using the tip as a third tail*
Collar: Black hen hackle, oversize, tied in behind the bead and wrapped as a wet-fly collar

Tying Note

Superficially, at least, Hans van Klinken's pattern-of-the-moment resembles a commercially available fly, Yvon Gendron's badger-tailed and -hackled **Neptune Streamer** (Neptune Flies, Inc: www.amimoucheur.qc.ca). As far as I can determine, the Neptune is tied without a body, other than a black thread base, bead head, or rib, and the tail hackles are tied in a third of the way up the 4X-long shank.

Paul Milstam is a professional tier from Malmö, Sweden, but the pattern is from Denmark. The Danish name means **Dustball**.

Nullermænd

Hook: Long-shank wet-fly, or single or double salmon, sizes 6 to 10
Thread: Red
Palmer hackle: Brown or fiery-brown saddle, tied in up front and reverse-palmered
Tail: Red body feather from a golden pheasant, about shank-length
Body: Black wool
Rib: Oval gold tinsel
Head: Tying thread, large
Eyes: Painted, yellow with black pupils

STARLY BUGGER

The speckled tail is what gives this pattern its particular fish appeal, so choose your own body and hackle colors. Some days, dark flies work better than light ones, and vice versa. Same difference for the degree of contrast between body and hackle.

At press time, we learned of new research showing that starlings (as well as a few other common, ground-feeding birds) are likely carriers of West Nile virus, so be careful about using starling. My skins are all old enough to be safe; yours may not be.

Starly Bugger

Hook: 1X- or 2X-long wet-fly or nymph, size 10
Head: Copper or black-pearl bead, the color to suit the body and hackle
Thread: Black
Tail: 6 to 12 speckled starling body feathers, however many it takes to give the fly an unruly, featherduster look
Body: Chenille or wool yarn in color of choice
Palmer hackle: Grizzly hen saddle—natural, bleached, or dyed to complement the body

OTHER 'BOU-LESS BUGGERS

SPANKER

This fly, by the outfitter and guide George Davis of Cordova, Alaska, isn't quite a Woolly Bugger, because it lacks both marabou and palmer hackle, but its synthetic materials do a darned good job of standing in. *Fly Fisherman*'s John Randolph and others have called this pattern one of the best flies, if not the very best fly, ever devised for coho (silver) salmon. Rather than quibble over details, I decided to plunk it down here because it just plain belonged.

Spanker

Hook: Standard salmon/steelhead wet fly (alternatively, a heavy-wire, straight-eyed, metallic-green wet-fly), sizes 2 and 4
Thread: Hot lime-green or chartreuse 6/0 or 3/0
Tail: 12 strands of silver Holographic Fly Fiber, covered by a fairly thick bunch of pearlescent fluorescent-green (#6962) Flashabou, all shank-length
Body: Chartreuse, fluorescent-green, or bright-green Cactus Chenille or large Ice Chenille (long-fibered, full-bodied tinsel chenille), wound over wet clear epoxy on the hook shank
Head: Tying thread, long and conical, covered by clear epoxy

Tying Tips

The epoxy on the shank and head will help keep a salmon's teeth from tearing the fly apart.

Take it down to size 10 and you have the **Mini Spanker**.

To make a two-tone version, stay at size 2 and use hot-orange for the front half or third of the body. (This is chromatically similar to the **Fire Tiger Spanker**, which is tied on larger hooks, has a lead-wire underbody, and a long, hot-or fluorescent-orange Flashabou *wing*, taking it out of bounds for this book.)

Tie lead dumbbell eyes on the hook, use pink Flashabou and Cactus Chenille, and you wind up with the **Lady Spanker**, the newest color in the Davis stable, and potentially a good pattern for bonefish, bonito, and other briny species.

Designed by the innovative Swedish tier Erik Andreasson, this is a tinsel-and-mohair hybrid that is both hackle-less and tail-less. *A Bugger without a tail?* Those wraps of mohair on the rear of the shank, behind the body, *function* like a tail plume, and function trumps form in fly fishing.

Like most of Andreasson's innovative patterns, this was designed as a perch fly. (As you can tell from those hook sizes, European river perch tend to be bigger than our yellow perch.)

Colors should suit your purposes, but Andreasson likes these two combinations: white mohair over a purple body and black over orange (the last being good, he says, for night and dawn fishing). I decided to go with a more subtle combination (light-brown mohair over peacock herl) with just a touch of boldness (fluorescent-orange thread).

Woolleech

Hook: 4X-long streamer, sizes 4 to 8
Thread: 6/0 to match yarn color
Underbody: Copper or lead wire, wrapped the length of the shank
Palmer "hackle": Mohair yarn, tied in at the bend and palmered forward over the body, the first wrap or two on the shank behind the body
Body: Long-fiber Crystal Flash Chenille, tied in opposite the hook point and wrapped forward

Although there aren't many pink items on the freshwater menu, I find that on rare occasions pink flies work better than more naturally colored patterns. I discovered this quite by accident while salmon fishing in Scotland. It was a slow day on a dour beat, and I was fooling around with a small pink, molded-plastic Frisky Fly (a Walt Rogers creation you have to see in action to believe) that had somehow found its way into one of my salmon-fly boxes. The brown trout went nuts over it. In waters closer to home, I often take rainbows on patterns tailed with pink hackle fluff.

Flossy Bugger

Hook: Streamer that suits your piscatorial purpose, sizes 6 to 10
Head: Red or pink translucent glass or plastic bead
Thread: Pink 6/0
Tail: Pale-pink poly floss (the kind used in winging streamers or in wind-sailing huge, fluffy dapping flies), combed out, with 2 to 4 longer strands of pearl Krystal Flash mixed in
Palmer hackle: Grizzly saddle
Body: Pink flat floss (see Tying Tips)
Collar: Tying thread—incidental to tying down the hackle and whip-finishing

Tying Tips

Because poly floss doesn't slick down as much as marabou, be careful not to tie too bushy a tail.

For the body, you can use almost any single- or four-strand rayon or silk floss, but I prefer using Dacor Madeira No. 6, a multistranded "100% Viscose filament … lustrous thread for knitting and overlocking" made in Germany. I really like this stuff, and it's worth looking for in sewing shops. The pink color I use is number 1554. I also have some black (1400) and yellow (1423) that I use in other patterns.

Tied on a size 2 to 1/0 stainless-steel hook, and perhaps reinforced with a silver-wire rib, this pattern might be worth casting to Atlantic albacore, something I haven't yet had a chance to try.

HAIRY BUGGERS

Whatever it may use for its body—chenille, yarn, or dubbing—the Woolly Bugger is otherwise based on bird feathers: turkey marabou for the tail, chicken hackle for the palmer rib. (And, as we've just seen, ostrich herl, gamebird feathers, even emu may fill in for either in a borderline Bugger.) A few Bugger-based patterns dispense with either or both of the feathers in favor of animal hair or fur. These really push the limits. But let's look at a few.

HAIR-TAILED WOOLLY BUGGERS

Like ostrich herl, mammal hair or fur works better than marabou in fast currents. Unlike marabou, hair and fur won't slick down straight in fast-streaming water. And unlike most feather tails, hair tails are more "active" in both slow and fast waters. Hair and fur are also more durable than either marabou, ostrich herl, or feathers.

HARE-AND-HERL BUGGER *Tied by Peter Frailey*

Peter Frailey, whose Fishing with Flies web site (www.fishingwith-flies.com) has quickly become a treasure trove of patterns and anecdotes, says this is his "favorite and most versatile wet fly." He attributes its fish-attracting qualities not so much to the iridescence of peacock herl but to "the seductive action of a pulsating tail." On his site he shows a photo with the caption, "If I could only fish a handful of subsurface flies, this would be it"; the photo shows him holding five Hare and Herl Buggers, one of which sports a brass bead head.

Hare-and-Herl Bugger

Hook: 3X-long streamer, size 14 (for trout), or 2X-long nymph, size 12 (for panfish and smallmouth bass); "I think this fishes best in small sizes"

Thread: Black Danville 3/0

Underbody: 8 to 12 wraps of .015-in lead wire, ahead of the hook point

Tail: Rabbit fur (guard hairs and underfur), shank-length; "if you want a fluffier tail, use a bigger clump of hair and pull out most of the guard hairs"

Body: 3 or 4 peacock herls and 2 strands of black Krystal Flash, lashed the full length of the under body and twisted together as a rope before wrapping forward

Palmer hackle: Dun hen neck hackle, the barbs stripped from one side, tied in just ahead of the herl tie-in point, the tip secured to the length of the shank by open thread wraps, then head-cemented to create a secure underbody for the herl; after wrapping the body, palmer the hackle forward in 5 or 6 turns

Head: Tying thread, coated with glossy clear nail polish

Tying Tips

For a neater appearance, tie in the tail clump opposite the barb, snip the butts so they tuck in behind the rear of the lead-wire underbody, then cover the butt hairs lead wire with thread wraps to make a smooth underbody.

"I like to tie in the tail about 2 mm forward of the herl tie-in point," Frailey writes, "so that the herl can be wrapped once or twice behind the feather before being wrapped forward." Before wrapping the body, Frailey coats the underbody (lead wire, herl butts, Krystal Flash, hackle butt, and thread wrap, with head cement. This adds to the fly's durability.

For step-by-step details, see www.fishingwithflies.com/ hareandherlbugger.html.

BABY FUR BUGGER *Tied by Peter Frailey*

Frailey's article, "Building a Better Baby Bugger," on the Global Fly Fisher site (www.-globalflyfisher.com) explains why he designed and uses this diminutive: "Most of my freshwater fishing is done with an 8- or 9-foot 5-weight rod, and chucking a weighted, size-6 Woolly Bugger down and across a river is not exactly a relaxed or smooth operation, especially in wind-assisted conditions." He says he can pleasurably turn these babies over on 4X, 5X, and even 6X tippets. His favorites? Size 14 (3X-long) for trout, size 12 (2X-long) for smallmouth bass and panfish, and size 10 (3X-long) for largemouths.

In Frailey's terminology, "Baby Bugger" applies to any Woolly Bugger tied on a size 10 or smaller hook. In larger sizes, this one is called the **Dubbed Fur Bugger**.

Baby Fur Bugger

Hook: 2X- or 3X-long nymph or streamer, sizes 10 to 16

Head: *Optionally, either instead of or in addition to the underbody, a metal bead*

Thread: Any color 3/0 Danville; 6/0 for size 16

Underbody: 8 to 12 wraps of fine lead wire ahead of the hook point; retain or omit, as desired, if you use a bead head

Tail: Shank-length clump of rabbit or other fur, dyed or natural, as desired

Body: Hare's ear, squirrel, or other fur dubbing, dyed or natural

Palmer hackle: One or more hen neck hackles to match or complement body and tail, the fibers stripped from one side of the quill "for a softer, more subtle appearance;" *use rooster or saddle hackles if you prefer*

THE TINY ONE *Tied by Jay "Fishy" Fullum*

The ever-inventive Jay Fullum of Ravena, New York—"Fishy" to fans, friends, and customers alike—admits that most of the larger fish he has taken on Woolly Buggers were taken on larger flies. "However," he says, "when water levels dictate the use of smaller flies and lighter tippets, I often fish Woolly Buggers tied on hooks as small as 20s." He says you can tie his tiny Buggers in whatever colors you'd like, "but I have found that black, olive, and brown are all that I have ever needed." Instead of marabou, Fishy likes to use rabbit underfur for the tail, "since it is a bit finer than marabou."

The Tiny One

Hook: Standard or long-shank streamer, sizes 10 to 20

Thread: 8/0, color to match the body

Eyes: Fine, black bead-chain, "purchased from a craft store"

Tail: Natural or dyed, fine rabbit underfur

Palmer hackle: Saddle hackle, to match the rest of the fly

Body: Rabbit underfur, as in the tail, dubbed

Head: Rabbit underfur, as in the tail and body, dubbed around the bead-chain eyes after the excess hackle has been clipped

BEAR-HAIR BUGGER

Charles Jardine lists a Bear-Hair Bugger in his *Classic Guide to Fly-Fishing for Trout*. Like the Herly Bugger or Murray's Hellgrammite, the Bear-Hair Bugger "is primarily for fast water," he writes. "The usual tail of marabou, when fished in extreme currents, can be matt[ed] and appear lifeless. But hair reacts and pulsates, and should be chosen for white-water pockets and stretches." Good advice.

However, Jardine omits the palmer hackle in his pattern, using instead a long collar of black rooster hackle. To my mind, this makes it a Bear-Hair Stick Fly, and I really don't think you can eliminate both the marabou tail *and* the palmer hackle and call it a Bugger. So, I'm listing it the way a Bugger-named fly ought to be tied. It should fish as well as Jardine's original. Sorry, Charles.

Bear-Hair Bugger

Hook:	4X-long streamer, sizes 4 to 12
Thread:	Black
Underbody:	Lead wire, wrapped
Tail:	Brown- or black-bear hair
Body:	Black chenille
Palmer hackle:	Black rooster saddle, reverse-palmered
Rib:	Oval silver tinsel
Head:	Tying thread; *optionally, lacquered*

Tying Notes

About that bear-hair tail: If you are lucky enough to own any *legal* brown-bear hair, use it to make a Brown Bear-Hair Bugger instead. The patches of European brown bear I've seen look completely unlike the patches of black bear you see in the fly shops. Where the black-bear hair sold for winging flies is slick, smooth, and well-behaved, brown-bear hair is more often wiry, kinky, and unruly. I suspect the latter pulsates better in the water. If you have some black bear that doesn't behave well as winging material, consider yourself blessed when it comes to fast-water Buggers.

I prefer a weighted head to a wire underbody for deep-fishing flies, but Charles would probably then insist that I call it a Bear-Hair Nobbler. *Touché!* The nuances in fly tying are as much semantic as they are piscatorial.

LLAMA BUGGER

Based on the Llama streamer originated by Mike Tourtilloutt and popularized by Eric Leiser, this one combines four proven trout-taking materials: woodchuck hair, grizzly hackle, red floss, and gold tinsel. My Spanish-speaking friends say it should be pronounced something like 'YAHmah' as in Yamaha.

Llama Bugger

Hook:	4X- to 6X-long streamer, sizes 6 to 10
Thread:	Black 6/0
Tail:	Woodchuck hair, shank length, selected so that all four color bands show
Palmer hackle:	Grizzly hen saddle, tied in behind the eye and reverse-palmered to the bend
Rib:	Flat gold tinsel, used to form a tag *(try to make yours neater than mine)* where it is used to catch and secure the hackle, then wound through the palmer hackle in open spirals
Body:	Red floss, tied in over the hackle tie-in wraps, then wrapped to a point opposite the hook point and back up to the front

Tony Spezio—the Arkansas tier who is better known for his foam Froggies and his bead-headed copper version of Bob Root's Chili Pepper (see page 215)—says he accidentally invented this pattern back in mid-October 1996 while using up leftovers on his tying bench as he waited for his fishing buddy to show up. After catching just two trout in an hour's fishing (limited action for the White River, apparently), he found a pool with "a good number of fish," which refused everything he cast. He decided to try his new creation.

On his first cast, his new fly was taken as it hit the water by a 15-inch rainbow. He caught eight fish on the next eight casts, by which time he had effectively put the rest of the fish down. So he fished his way upstream to join his fishing buddy, during which time Spezio says he "missed a few fish, picked up three more rainbows, and broke off my one-and-only Demon on the fourteenth fish." (Thirteen must be his lucky number, and 14 his unlucky one: "I don't know how many times I have broken off on the fourteenth fish," he says. "I know that sounds funny, but I keep a fishing log and that's what it tells me.") While Spezio was proving the worth of his accidental discovery and the consistency of his numerology, his buddy had risen two fish. Forced to use other flies the rest of the morning, Spezio fished two more hours without a single take.

That afternoon he tied up a few more WRDs, went out that evening, and took 12 more fish on the fly. "The White River Demon never failed me until March 1997, when I fished Pennsylvania with Doug Swisher," he reports. Discouraged by that failure, he didn't fish the Demon all that summer, but resumed using it and catching fish that fall.

He thinks the body material may be the key to its success. "When you wrap the body in two layers," he explains, "the braid traps air and makes the fly slightly buoyant. It sinks with a kind of slow shimmy."

White River Demon

Hook: Eagle Claw LO58, a 3X-long, 1X-heavy streamer, sizes 8 to 14

Head: 4-mm silver plastic bead

Weight: 10 wraps of .010- to .015-in lead wire, jammed into the bead's conical center hole; optionally, after first squirting a drop of superglue gel into the bead's hole

Thread: Fluorescent red

Tail: White rabbit fur, in the same length and fullness as a standard Woolly Bugger tail of marabou

Palmer hackle: White or cream saddle

Body: Pearl plastic canvas braid, tied in at the front and wrapped down to the bend and back

Collar: Fluorescent-red thread, wrapped just behind the bead head

Eyes: Yellow, with black pupils, painted on the bead head (See Tying Tips)

Tying Tips

Spezio says the body material he uses is labeled Rainbow Gallery Plastic Canvas Metallic Needlepoint Yarn. It's a braided plastic or Mylar material available in craft stores.

Before tying on with thread, wrap the lead wire around the bare shank, then slide it forward so that it jams into the conical hole in the bead, filling the space between the bead and the shank. This serves two purposes: putting the weight as far forward as possible (producing a superior swimming action when twitched or retrieved with stop-and-start stripping), and preventing the bead from spinning around the shank, an important consideration on eyed flies. To be extra safe, squirt a drop of gap-filling superglue gel into the bead's hole before sliding the wire wraps forward.

Tony says he uses Slick fabric paint (readily available in craft shops) to paint the eyes. Sometimes, to keep the painted eyes from scraping off, he coats the plastic head with a *water-based* head cement. Solvent-based cement will destroy the paint and the bead.

Fishing Tips

Because both the body braid and the plastic bead are slightly buoyant, partially counteracting the lead's weight, the fly sinks slowly and has a fish-appealing action when strip-retrieved. "When it is retrieved slowly," Spezio says, "you get a jigging, shimmering action that is hard to describe. I have watched trout follow it for several feet, grabbing it as soon as I made a quick, short strip."

"I think the White River Demon is taken for a small shad," Spezio opines. "The WRD seems to do best on bright, sunny days, although I have caught fish on it on rainy days and late evenings."

In an E-mail message, the English–German tier Mike Connors (a displaced Liverpuddlian who has been living in Deutschland almost two decades) told me he has "been using Arctic fox lately as a tailing material" with excellent results and improved durability. Mike fishes his fox-tailed Woolly Buggers in the Baltic Sea for big, toothy, sea-going brown trout.

Arctic Foxy Bugger

Hook: Standard or long-shank streamer, or a swimming-nymph, in a size appropriate to your quarry
Thread: Black or brown
Palmer hackle: Blue dun saddle, reverse-palmered
Tail: Arctic fox, sparse and shank-length or shorter
Rib: Silver wire, closely ribbed
Body: Brown chenille

ARCTIC BUGGER

But for the dimensional proportions, this pattern is essentially similar to the preceding. Whereas Mike Connor fishes his Arctic Foxy Bugger in the brack of the Baltic for sea trout, Armando Quazzo fishes his Arctic Bugger in the Po River and other sweetwater streams of his native Italy for river-run browns. Like Connor, Quazzo switched from marabou to Arctic fox for improved durability. On the Bugger's universal effectiveness, Quazzo

has written, "Should fresh water be found on Mars, Martian trout would rise to a well-presented Woolly Bugger." Now, *that's* having confidence in a pattern!

Arctic Bugger

Hook: 3X- or 4X-long streamer, sizes 2 to 10
Thread: White 6/0
Tail: White Arctic fox fur, flanked by a few strands of pearl Krystal Flash, fairly full and long
Palmer hackle: Grizzly saddle
Body: Polar Aire, or similiar synthetic substitute for polar bear, chopped and spun in a dubbing loop

Tying Notes

In addition to the listed color scheme, Quazzo says, "Black, olive, brown, and yellow are catching colors as well."

A confession: I was fresh out of both white arctic fox and the patience to track down some more, so I used polar bear substitute for the tail as well, figuring what could be more Arctic? Still, Quazzo would probably insist my version be called a **Polar Bugger**.

BADGER BUGGER

This aptly named pattern contains nothing but badger hair and hackle—not counting the hook and thread.

Badger Bugger

Hook: 3X to 4X-long streamer, sizes 4 to 12
Thread: Black 3/0 or 6/0
Tail: Badger guard hairs and underfur, mixed, shank-length
Body: Badger underfur, with a few guard hairs mixed in, in a dubbing loop
Palmer hackle: Badger saddle, grade 2 rooster or whatever you prefer

Tying Tips

I used badger body fur for the sample fly, which contains contains a *lot* of underfur. I like the unruly look of all that underfur in the tail and the dubbed body, but you might not. You can comb out the underfur or use badger tail fur for the tail if you want a sleeker, less bulky look.

I think badger body fur works nicely for the body dubbing, but if you want a slimmer, more compact body, pluck or comb out some of the underfur, chop the fur into shorter pieces, put less material in the dubbing loop, or use a single-thread dubbing technique.

FEENSTRA'S EMULATOR

This pattern probably pushes the Bugger definition right over the edge, but it's sorta close, and it does look awfully fishy. Although designed as a steelhead fly (it's presented in Matt Supinski's *Steelhead Dreams*), Kevin Feenstra's pattern ought to work anywhere trout, bass, or steelhead feed on crayfish. Feenstra, a conservation-minded steelhead guide in Michigan, was quoted in the book as saying, "I enjoy fishing with floating and sink-tip lines with flies that closely imitate naturally occurring food sources." His Emulator (sometimes spelled EMUlator, as you'll shortly see why) is a two-variant pattern, identified in the listing as (1), Possum, and (2), Olive Rabbit. This is **Feenstra's Olive Rabbit Emulator**.

Feenstra's Emulator

Hook: TMC 9395 or similar 4X- to 6X-long streamer; he didn't specify a size
Thread: Unspecified, but black or olive 6/0 should suffice
Antennae: Two sections of barbs from a pheasant tail, longer than the hook—a little cement will keep the barbs from coming "unzipped"
Tail/pincers: Two narrow, hook-length strips of (1) Australian opossum or (2) olive-dyed rabbit strip, one on either side of the shank
Palmer hackle: Two long-barbed emu feathers—one insect-green, the other olive—palmered forward together very closely
Body: Thread base
Head: Long-fibered clump of (1) Australian opossum or (2) muskrat fur wrapped in a dubbing loop around the front of the shank as a shaggy head or collar

HAIR-BODIED BUGGERS

Some tiers forego the chenille body and palmer hackle in favor of a thicvkly dubbed, bristly body of hair or synthetic dubbing. If using animal hair, be sure to include guard hairs in the dubbing mix, comb out the soft underfur, or do both. If using synthetic dubbing, use stuff that has a bit of unruliness about it, so your body will be sheathed in a halo of fibers. Whichever you use, work at giving the fly at least a suggestion of the Woolly Bugger's palmered bugginess.

HAREY BUGGER

I took this pattern from Rob Knisely's excellent Invicta Flies web site (http://members.tripod.com/-invictaflies/). It uses a bristly dubbing brush for the body and omits the palmer hackle.

(*Caveat lector:* I substituted a short-fibered hare-and-synthetic–blend dubbing brush, palmered with a longer-fibered dubbing brush.)

Harey Bugger

Hook: Mustad 9671, a 2X-long streamer, size 10
Head: 5/32-inch gold-plated brass bead
Thread: Brown 6/0 UNI
Tail: Brown marabou
Body: Brown hare's-ear blend dubbing brush, long-fibered and bristly, wound very closely to produce a scruffy, shaggy look; *I used a Mega Fiber Dubbing Brush, a blend of Flashabou, Antron, and hare's mask, belly, and back, then I palmered it with an Oliver Edwards Caddis Legs brush, both from Siman, Ltd.*

The shaggy, beaver-and-Antron body is what gives this Bugger its special appeal. Only marginally bristly enough for inclusion here, the Beaver Leech is a very "fishy"-looking fly. Dub it even rougher, if you want a more Buggery look.

Beaver Leech

Hook: TMC 5262, a 2X-long, 2X-heavy streamer, sizes 2 to 10
Thread: Black or brown
Tail: Brown marabou; *optionally, with a few strands of Krystal Flash mixed in*
Body: 5 parts beaver fur to 1 part Antron, cut in 1/2-inch lengths, blended, and dubbed "rough" in a dubbing loop

PALMERED FUR-STRIP BUGGERS

Palmering a Zonker strip instead of chicken hackle pushes the Woolly Bugger notion to its outer limits, but I decided to include a couple such patterns for your consideration. If you are going up north, to fish for salmon, lake trout, or pike, your fly box ought to include at least one flesh fly pattern, because big fish feed on the rotting carcasses of drowned caribou and other ungulates.

FLESH FLY

Many flies of the same name exist, but this one (listed in the second edition of *Fly Patterns of Umpqua Feather Merchants*) is the most Bugger-like in construction.

Flesh Fly

Hook: TMC 5263, a 3X-long, 2X-heavy nymph, size 4
Thread: White
Tail: Shell-pink marabou
Body: Very-light ginger rabbit strip, palmered the length of the shank

Tying Tip

Even better, palmered-fur Buggers can be made if you use thin "hackle strips" of arctic fox, Finnish raccoon, and other pelts whose guard hairs behave a lot like hackle barbs. The BowTyer hair strips imported from Finland are the best-known of these Arctic fur strips worthy of use in palmering Woolly Buggers. When I use them, I call the resultant flies **BowTye Buggers**.

FURRY BUGGER

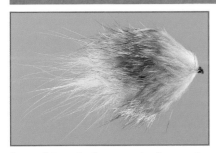

My friend Wayne Mones once shared with me some scraps he'd been given by a relative who is a professional furrier. The bag contained small pieces of all sorts of fur: muskrat, beaver, lynx, fisher, badger, arctic fox, and several colors of fox and rabbit. One of the results of my playing around with these bits of fur was this Furry Bugger, which uses whatever fur or combination of furs strikes my fancy. For the fly illustrated above, I used gray fox fur for the tail and natural rabbit for the body palmer, a combination that somewhat resembles a fat mouse. You may not have as large a variety to choose from, but you can use whatever you have on hand.

Furry Bugger

Hook: 3X- or 4X-long streamer, sixes 4 to 10
Thread: Black or brown 6/0
Tail: Fur plume, not too full, including both underfur and guard hairs
Underbody: Thread base or punch yarn, coated with cement before wrapping body
Body: Thin (1/8-in maximum) strip of soft fur (rabbit, muskrat, fox, etc) wrapped over wet cement

WINGED BUGGERS-IN-NAME-ONLY

Winged flies don't really belong, but these three Bugger-named flies seem a fitting way to conclude our beastly discussion.

ORVIS GIRDLE BUGGER *Tied by Orvis*

This is not a regular Girdle Bugger, which is just a Woolly Bugger with rubber legs. Orvis has done away with the palmer hackle on this one, substituting instead a bushy marabou wing, and added a bright belly. The catalog offers this pattern in just black-and-orange, but don't let that deter you from experimenting with other colors.

Orvis Girdle Bugger

Hook: Orvis 8808, a 4X-long streamer, sizes 4 to 10
Thread: Black
Tail: Black marabou, shank-length
Belly: Orange chenille *(Vernille for the small sizes)*, pulled over the body on the underside of the hook before the fly is ribbed
Body: Black Vernille or chenille
Rib: Fine, clear monofilament
Legs: White rubber, shank-length, 3 per side, evenly spaced and angled 45 degrees backward
Wing: Black marabou, extending back to the tip of the tail
Hackle: Black hen wet-fly collar

ORVIS–HARDER WOOLLY BUGGER

In his *Index of Orvis Fly Patterns, Vol. II* (1987), John Harder list-ed a bizarre, tail-less, winged, inverted, misspelled "Wooly Bug-ger." (Oddly, the Wooll-ly Bugger listed 22 pages later in the "Tying Instructions" section of the same volume is a correctly spelled, olive-and-black fly in the classic Russell Blessing mold.) This one may not be a true Woolly Bugger, but it looks like a good bucktail-and-marabou streamer for weedy waters.

Orvis–Harder Woolly Bugger

Hook: Orvis 1526, a 3X-long nymph, sizes 2 to 10; tied inverted (point up)
Thread: Black
Body: Olive Fuzzy Foam
Palmer hackle: Olive
Wing: Olive bucktail or goat hair, covered by an equal or larger amount of olive marabou, covered by a few strands of pearl Flashabou—tied in on the point side of the shank, extending about a gap-width beyond the bend
Head: Tying thread, very large, coated with high-gloss head cement or clear nail polish
Eyes: Painted or glued-on

WEEDLESS WOOLLY BUGGER *Tied by John Gierach*

This John Gierach transmogrification of the Woolly Bugger is based on the Bend-back series of bonefish flies. "The idea is that the buoyancy of the materials on what would normally be the bottom of the shank counteracts the weight of the bend and makes the fly swim with the point up, to avoid snags," John explains. "I also cheat a little by running a strip of lead wire along the top of the shank (now the bottom), to help change the balance point of the hook."

The marabou in the long wing more or less functionally replaces the Bugger's usual marabou tail. As for the marabou wing's making the fly weedless, John says, "It actually works—as long as you dress the bucktail underwing a little heavy. I call it weed-*resistant.*"

"Color is tier's choice," John says. "I usually tie them in all-black or all-olive, sometimes with brown bucktail." I'm listing it the way John tied the fly shown here.

Weedless Woolly Bugger

Hook: TMC 200R, a 3X-long, straight-eyed, gradually curved-shank nymph, sizes 4 to 10
Thread: Black
Underbody: A strand of lead wire, lashed to the conventional top of the shank (away from the hook point)
Body: Black Furry Foam; *"but sometimes dubbing"*
Palmer hackle: Black saddle
Underwing: Brown bucktail, dressed a bit heavy, tied inverted, on the point side of the shank, and extending past the bend
Overwing: Black marabou, tied inverted, extending a gap-width beyond the bend, tied inverted, on the point side of the shank
Topping: 4 strands of pearl Flashabou or "some sort of tinsel," as long as the wing
Head: Tying thread, large and varnished
Eyes: *Optionally—"I often leave them off"*—painted yellow eyes, with black pupils

EPILOGUE

And that, dear reader, is that. I could have gone on and on, but I think you get the point. Start with the Woolly principles, experiment at the vise and on the water, and you are sure to find a Woolly winner that perfectly suits your fly fishing. But don't be too quick about trumpeting your inventions. Chances are better than good that someone has already been there and done that. Few, if any, other fly patterns have been so often modified and adapted by so many fly tiers and fishers.

The preceding pages have shown you a lot of patterns from all over the world, but I haven't even begun to limn the possibilities of these two fabulous flies. Use your imagination, and don't be afraid to experiment with different colors, materials, tying techniques. And the variations don't stop at the tying table, because these Woolly wonders can be fished in almost every conceivable way.

The basic patterns are easy to tie, but as you incorporate different techniques, you will be honing your tying skills.

The Woolly Bugger has become *the* beginning fly tier's fly. And the Woolly Worm isn't much trickier—unless you insist on having those hackle barbs angled forward. A Catskill dry or full-dress salmon fly that isn't tied just right might look bad and fish worse, but a beginner's Woolly (Worm *or* Bugger) won't disgrace anyone's fly box, and chances are better than good that fish will still find it buggily enticing. And, as with most patterns, the more you tie, the better they work.

No matter your level of tying skills or how you like to fly fish, these flies are for you. In the unlikely event you are a purist (frankly, I can't imagine a purist's picking up a book with this title, let alone reading this far), you can stick to the hatch-matching patterns; see "hatch matching" in the Index.

And let's face it, if you can't catch fish on Woolly Worms, Woolly Buggers, or any of their palmer-hackled kissing cousins, you might as well take up golf or something else to while away your days.

BIBLIOGRAPHY

S ome of the fly patterns and tying procedures in this book were taken from other books, sometimes with slight variation or adaptation by your author. Here are the books from which I most often plucked patterns or inspiration:

—Atkinson, Robert. *Fishing Flies: An Illustrated Album.* New York: Crescent, 1991.

—Buckland, John. *The Simon & Schuster Pocket Guide to Trout & Salmon Flies.* New York: Fireside/Simon & Schuster, 1986.

—Church, Bob. *Bob Church's Guide to New Fly Patterns.* South Hackensack, NJ: Stoeger, 1993.

—Harder, John. *Index of Orvis Fly Patterns.* Manchester, VT: Orvis, 1978.

—Harder, John. *Index of Orvis Fly Patterns, Vol. 2.* Manchester, VT: Orvis, 1987.

—Headley, Stan. *Trout & Salmon Flies of Scotland.* Ludlow, Shropshire, U.K.: Merlin Unwin, 1997.

—Jardine, Charles. *The Classic Guide to Fly-Fishing for Trout.* New York: Random House, 1991.

—Johnson, Gunnar, "Fly Tying," in Göran Cederberg, ed. *The Complete Book of Sportfishing.* New York: Bonanza, 1988.

—Kaufmann, Randall. *Fly Patterns of Umpqua Feather Merchants: The World's 1,100 Best Flies.* Glide, OR: Umpqua Feather Merchants, 1995.

—Kaufmann, Randall. *Fly Patterns of Umpqua Feather Merchants: The World's 1,500 Best Flies. 2nd edition.* Glide, OR: Umpqua Feather Merchants, 1998.

—Koch, Ed and Norm Shires. *Basic Fly-tying.* Harrisburg, PA: Stackpole, 1990.

—Korošec, Tomo, Jože Ocvirk, Lucijan Urbancic, and Božidar Voljc. *Muharjenje.* Ljubljana, Slovenia: Državna založba Slovenije, 1980.

—Kreh, Lefty. *Salt Water Fly Patterns.* Fullerton, CA: Maral, no date.

—Leiser, Eric. *The Book of Fly Patterns.* New York: Alfred A. Knopf, 1987.

—Leonard, J. Edson. *Flies.* New York: Nick Lyons, 1988.

—McClane, A. J. *McClane's New Standard Fishing Encyclopedia and International Angling Guide, Enlarged and Revised Second Edition.* New York: Holt, Rinehart and Winston, 1974.

—Perrault, Keith. *Perrault's Standard Dictionary of Fishing Flies.* Orlando, FL: Kepcor, 1984. [To buy a copy, write to Keith Perrault, P. O. Box 391, Ennis, MT 59729.]

—Price, Taff. *Fly Patterns: An International Guide, 2nd Edition.* London: Ward Lock, 1992.

—Price, Taff. *Tying & Fishing the Nymph.* London: Blandford, 1995.

—Roberts, John, ed. *The World's Best Trout Flies.* London: Boxtree, 1994.

—Roberts, John. *Collins Illustrated Dictionary of Trout Flies.* Edison, NJ: Castle, 1998.

—Stetzer, Randle Scott. *Flies: The Best One Thousand.* Portland, OR: Frank Amato, 1992.

—Tryckare, Tre and E. Cagner (Frank T. Moss, American consultant). *The Lore of Sportfishing.* New York: Crown, 1976.

—Tryon, Chuck and Sharon Tryon. *Figuring Out Flies: A Practical Guide.* Rolla, MO: Ozark Mountain Fly Fishers, 1990.

—Veniard, John, "Making One's Own Flies," in A. Norman Marston, ed. *Newnes Encyclopaedia of Angling.* London: Newnes, 1963.

—Wakeford, Jacqueline. *Flytying Techniques.* New York: Nick Lyons, 1980.

—Wood, Ian, ed. *The Dorling Kindersley Encyclopedia of Fishing.* New York: Dorling Kindersley, 1994

And here are two more books I found invaluable for overall guidance and which no self-respecting tier should try to live without:

—Clarke, Barry Ord and Robert Spaight. *International Guide to Fly-Tying Materials (and Where to Buy Them).* Camden, ME: Ragged Mountain Press, 1997.

—Leeson, Ted and Jim Schollmeyer. *The Fly Tier's Benchside Reference to Techniques and Dressing Styles.* Portland, OR: Frank Amato, 1998.

Appendix: Hooks

Some of the recipes for the patterns listed in this book specify hook styles; others don't. A wide variety of hooks can be and are used to tie Woolly Worms, Bivisibles, Palmer Flies, Woolly Buggers, and similar flies. The patterns listed below can be used—as can other, unlisted patterns by the same manufacturers. Looking at a hook and considering its characteristics counts for more than slavishly following another tier's habits.

To save space, I have not listed every characteristic of the patterns listed. Given the characteristics I have listed, some hooks by the same maker would appear to be identical. But they differ in at least one characteristic: bend, barb, point, sharpening, forging, and others. Besides, I have usually ignored small differences in wire diameter (standard vs. 1X-heavy) and shank length (standard vs. 1X-long).

Unless otherwise specified, the listed hooks have standard or 1X-long straight shanks, turned-down eyes, and barbed points, are made from standard or (in the case of wet WWs and Buggers)

1X-heavy wire, and are bronzed. *Salmon and steelhead hooks*, unless otherwise specified, are black, made of standard or 1X-heavy wire, and have turned-up loop eyes. *Saltwater hooks* have straight eyes and, unless otherwise specified, are either plated against corrosion or are made of stainless steel (SS).

Abbreviations used: BD=bent-down shank ("stonefly nymph"); BL = barbless; BU = bent-up shank ("swimming nymph"); CS = curved shank; SE = straight eye; TUE = turned-up eye; WG = wide gap; X = extra; XF = extra-fine wire; XH = extra-heavy wire; XL = extra-long shank; XS = extra-short shank

Because hook manufacturers frequently add or drop hooks from their catalogs, I cannot claim the following list is utterly completely or absolutely accurate. For example, Partridge has discontinued several hook styles specified in some of the recipes in this book—including CS10/4, CS20, E4A, GRS12ST, J1A, L3AY, L3B, L4A, SH2—but you should be able to find adequate substitutes by looking at the length and weight specs in the recipes and below.

Woolly Worms (wet)

Ashima F30 (2XL), F40, F45 (2XS), F55 (XL, CS). *Note: Ashima shanks are longer than usual; these 2XL hooks are roughly equivalent to 4XL or 3XL hooks by other manufacturers.*

Avalon A1550 or A1710 (2XL)

Cabela's 22 (1XL, 1XH), 23 (2XL), 24 (3XL), 30 (1XS, 2XH)

Daiichi 1120 (1XS, 2XH, CS), 1250 (1XL, TUE, BL, bronze or black), 1260 (2XL, CS, SE), 1270 (3XL, SE), 1273 (3XL, CS, SE, red), 1550, 1560, 1710 (2XL), 1740 (2XL, TUE)

Dai-Riki 060, 070 (1XF), 075 (2XH), 730 (2XL)

Eagle Claw L052 (1XF, CS, SE), L057, L060 (1XF), L063 (2XL), L144 (CS, TUE, X-WG)

Fenwick HQ-BS (SE, black), HQ-NW (3XH), HQ-NW1XL (3XH), HQ-SN (BU, SE), HQ-SN2XL (2XL)

Gamakatsu C12 (CS, WG), C12U (CS, TUE, WG), L10-2H (2XH), P10-2L1H (2XL, 1XH), S10, S14S-3H (3XH)

Kamasan B170 (1XH), B175 (3XH), B830 (2XL)

Montana Fly MFC 7045 (1XS, 1XH, CS, WG), 7076 (1XL, 1XH), 7077 (1XH)

Mustad 3366 (SE), 3399, 3399A (TUE), 3399N (gold), 3906, 3906B (1XL, 1XH), 7948A, 7957B, 9671 (2XL), 80300BR (2XL, 1XF, SE, WG), 81001BR (CS, TUE, WG), C53S (3XL, CS, SE), R48 (2XS), R50, R70 (2XH), R72 (1XL, 2XH), R74 (4XL, 2XH), R90 (4XH)

Orvis 167T, 594F (2XL, TUE), 1524 (2XL), 1638 (2XL)

Partridge CS2 (2XL, loop TDE, black), CS5 (2XL, SE, blue), CS7MW (WG, black), CS28GRS (1XF, 1XL, BL, Grey Shadow), G3A, GRS2A (2XF, WG, Grey Shadow), J1A, H1A (1XF, 2XL, WG), K14ST (2XL, CS, SE, silver), L2A (2XF, WG), SH1 (2XH, Grey Shadow), SH2 (Grey Shadow)

Sprite Trout Wet Fly (TUE, olive), Wide Gape Midge (TUE, nickel)

Targus 3769, 3761 (1XL)

Tiemco TMC 400T (1XF, BU), 700 (black), 3761 (2XH), 3761BL (2XH, BL), 9300

Turrall Barbless Sproat Wet Fly, Bead Standard Nymph (WG), Extra-Long Nymph (1XL), Nymph/Wet Fly

VMC V7071 (2XH), 8526, 8527, 8913 (1XF, 1XS, vertical eye, bronze or nickel), 9279 (2XL), 9410 (loop TUE, double)

Bivisibles & Dry Woolly Worms

Ashima F16

Avalon A1170, A1270 (2XL, CS, SE)

Cabela's 01, 02 (BL), 03 (2XL, 1XF)

Daiichi 1100 (1XF, WG), 1110 (1XF, WG, SE), 1140 (1XS, 1XF, TUE), 1170, 1180, 1182 (silver "Crystal"), 1190 (BL), 1220 (BU), 1222 (BU, silver "Crystal"), 1270 (3XL, CS), 1280 (1XF, 2XL)

Dai-Riki 070 (1XF), 300, 305, 310 (SE)

Eagle Claw L059, L060 (1XF), L061B (BL)

Easy Set 1201 (1XF, BL, Teflon-coated in black, green, blue, brown, white, red, chartreuse, gray, and special-order fluorescent finishes)

Fenwick HQ-D, HQ-DBL (BL), HQ-DH2XL (2XL, 2XF, WG), HQ-DSE (1XF, SE, WG), HQ-DUE (2XF, TUE, WG), HQ-DW1XF (1XF, WG), HQ-EHW (2XF, CS, SE, WG)

Gamakatsu P10, R10-BN (BL, special bend), S10 (black), S10-3F (1XF, black), S10-B (BL, black), S10S (SE, black), S10U (TUE, black), S12S-1F (1XF), S13S-M (1XF, black)

Kamasan B401, B402 (BL), B410 (WG, SE), B420, B440 (TUE)

Montana Fly MFC 7000 (1XF, WG), 7001 (1XF, SE, WG), 7002 (2XL, 1XF, CS), 7004 (1XS, 1XF, WG)

Mustad 3399D (2XF, TUE), 80000BR, 80010BR, 80050BR (3XL), 80300BR (1XF, 2XL, SE, WG), 94831 (2XF, 2XL), 94833 (3XF), 94834 (1XF, gold), 94838 (1XF, 1XS, WG), 94840 (1XF), 94842 (1XF, TUE), 94845 (1XF, BL), 94859 (1XF, SE)

Orvis 170T (1XF), 1509 (WG), 1523 (1XF), 1638 (2XL), 1641 (1XS, 2XH), 1877 (BL), 4641 (large SE), 4864 (large TDE), 8810 (1XF, WG), R30 (2XF), R50

Partridge CS20 (1XF, 1XS, WG, BL, black), CS21 (4XF, black), CS27GRS (2XF, BL, Grey Shadow), CS28GRS (1XF, BL, Grey Shadow), E1A (4XF), E3AY (4XF, BL), E4A (4XF), E6A (4XF, 1XS), GRS3A (4XF, WG, Grey Shadow), K3A (4XF, 2XL, Swedish Dry Fly shank), L3A (4XF, WG), L3AY (4XF, WG, BL, Grey Shadow), L3B (4XF, TUE, WG), L4A (6XF)

Sprite Trout Dry Fly (2XF or 4XF, TUE, nickel), Trout Long Shank Dry Fly (2XL, 4XF, nickel)

Targus 100 (1XF, WG), 103 (1XF, BL, WG), 101 (1XF, SE, WG), 200 (SE, CS), 2302 (2XL, CS), 2312 (SE, CS), 5215 (2XL), 5262 (2XL, 1XF)

Tiemco TMC 100 (1XF, WG), 100BL (1XF, WG, BL), 101 (1XF, SE), 102Y (1XF, black), 103BL (1XF, BL, black), 109BL (3XL, 1XF, BL, black), 200R (3XL, CS), 200RBL (3XL, CS, BL), 900BL (1XF, WG, BL, black), 902BL (2XF, BL, black), 2302 (2XL, CS), 2312 (1XF, 2XL, CS), 5210 (1XF), 5212 (1XF, 2XL), 5230 (3XF), 8089 (1XF), 8089NP (1XF, nickel)

Turrall Barbless Dry Fly (4XF), Extra-Fine Dry Fly (4XF), Keel Dry Fly (2XF, BD keel hook), Mayfly (4XF), Midge (3XF), Sedge (C, TUE, WG), Up-Eye Dry Fly (3XF, TUE)

VMC 7060 (2XF), 7061 (1XF), 7062 (1XF, 2XL), 8913 (1XF, 1XS, vertical eye, bronze or nickel), 9060, 9280 (1XF), 9281 (1XF, TUE), 9282 (1XS, 1XF), 9288 (1XS, 2XF), 9289 (1XS, 2XF, TUE), 9388 (1XS, 1XF, BL, bronze or gold)

Woolly Buggers

Ashima F30 (2XL), F55 (2XL, CS) *Note: Ashima shanks are longer than usual; these 2XL hooks are roughly equivalent to 3XL or 4XL hooks by other manufacturers.*

Avalon A1270 (1XF, 2XL, CS, SE), A1710 (2XL), A1720 (3XL), A2220 (4XL), A1270 (CS)

Cabela's 21 (3XL, CS), 22, 23 (2XL), 24 (3XL), 40 (4XL), 41 (4XL, SE), 42 (7XL, 3XH, SE)

Daiichi 1250 (1XL, TUE, BL), 1260 (2XL, CS, SE), 1270 (3XL, CS, SE), 1273 (3XL, CS, SE, red), 1710 (2XL), 1720 (3XL), 1730 (3XL, BD), 1740 (2XH, 2XL, TUE), 1750 (4XL, SE), 1770 (1XF, 3XL, BU, SE), 1850 (4XL, vertical eye), 1870 (4XL, TUE), 2220 (4XL), 2340 (6XL), 2370 (7XL, 3XH), 2460 (3XL), 2461 (3XL, black), 2462 (3XL, nickel)

Dai-Riki 270 (3XL, CS, SE), 700 (4XL), 700-B (4XL, BD), 710 (3XL), 730 (2XL)

Eagle Claw L058 (3XL), L063 (2XL), L281 (4XL)

Fenwick HQ-NW1XL (3XH, 1XL), HQ-SN (BU, SE), HQ-SN2XL (2XL), HQ-SN4XL (4XL)

Gamakatsu P10-2L1H (2XL), S11-4L2H (4XL, 2XH), S11S-4L2H (4XL, 2XH, SE)

Kamasan B220 (3XL, SE, black nickel), B800 (4XL), B820 (4XL, SE), B830 (3XL, CS), B940 (4XL, SE, black)

Montana Fly MFC 7002 (3XL, CS), 7008 (4XL, 2XH), 7027 (3XL, 2XH), 7030 (6XL, 2XH), 7073 (3XL, BD)

Mustad 3261 (3XL, SE), 3262 (3XL, SE, blue), 3366 (SE), 3399, 3399A (TUE), 3399N (gold), 3665A (6XL), 3906B, 7957B, 9575 (6XL, TD looped eye), 9671 (2XL), 9672 (3XL), 9674 (4XL), 9674A (4XL, gold), 9674B (4XL, nickel), 33956 (4XL, TUE), 33957 (6XL, TUE), 33960 (4XL), 36620 (6XL, SE), 36717 (6XL, 5XH), 79580 (4XL), 80050BR (3XL), 80060BR (3XL, BL), 80150BR (3XL, 1XF, BU, SE), 81002BR (4XL, BD), 94720 (8XL), C53S (3XL, SE, CS), R72 (2XL, 2XH), R74 (4XL, 2XH)

Orvis 0167 (4XL, SE), 594F (2XL, TUE), 596F (7XL, loop SE), 1511 (6XL), 1512 (1XF, 3XL, BU, SE), 1524 (2XL), 1526 (3XL), 8808 (4XL)

Partridge CS2 (2XL, loop TDE, black), CS5 (2XL, 2XH, SE, blue), CS11/1 (4XL, Grey Shadow), CS11GRS (4XL, Grey Shadow), CS15 (10XL, loop TDE), CS17 (6XL, 2XH, loop TDE, black), CS28GRS (1XF, BL, Grey Shadow), CS29GRS (6XL, SE, BL, Grey Shadow), D3ST (4XL, SE), D4A (4XL), D7A (6XL), GRS4A (4XL, Grey Shadow), GRS12ST (3XL, SE, Grey Shadow), K6ST (3XL, 1XF, BU, SE), K12ST (3XL, SE), K14ST (2XL, CS, SE, silver)

Sprite Trout Nymph Hook (3XL, olive), Trout Streamer (3XH, 5XL, TUE, nickel)

Targus 2302 (2XL, CS), 2312 (SE, CS), 5215 (2XL), 5262 (2XL, 1XF), 5263 (3XL), 9394 (4XL, SE, nickel), 9395 (4XL, SE), 300 (6XL)

Tiemco TMC 200R (3XL, CS), 200RBL (3XL, CS, BL), 300 (6XL), 400T (1XF, BU, SE), 700 (black), 947BL (3XL, BU, BL), 2302 (2XL, CS), 3761 (2XH), 3761BL (2XH, BL), 5262 (2XL, 2XH), 5263 (3XL, 2XH), 9394 (4XL, 3XH, SE, nickel), 9395 (4XL, 3XH, SE)

Turrall Barbless Streamer (3XL, BL), Bead Extra-Long Nymph (1XL, WG), Bead Streamer (3XL, WG), Extra-Long Nymph (1XL), Extra-Long Streamer (3XL), Sproat Double (loop TDE, double), Stronghold X-Strong Streamer (3XL, 3XH)

VMC V7070 (3XL, 2XH), V7071 (2XH), 8526, 8527, 9255 (4XL, SE, bronze, nickel, or silver), 9279 (2XL), 9283 (4XL), 9410 (loop TUE, double)

Steelhead & Salmon Woollies

Daiichi 2050 (CS, black, blue, bronze, gold, nickel), 2051 (CS), 2052 (CS, nickel), 2055 (CS, gold), 2059 (CS, blue), 2101 (4XH), 2131 (CS), 2135 (CS, gold), 2139 (CS, blue), 2141 (SE), 2151 (CS, SE), 2161 (CS), 2421 ("low water"), 2441, 3111 (1XS, 1XH, SE), 7131 (double)

Eagle Claw L064B (TDE, BL, bronze), L1197 (TDE, bronze, gold, nickel), L1197G (TDE, gold), L1197N (TDE, nickel)

Easy Set 600 (2XH, BL, Teflon-coated in black, green, blue, brown, white, red, chartreuse, gray, and special-order fluorescent finishes)

Fenwick HQ-SLO (SE)

Gamakatsu L11S-3H (3XH, SE, bronze), T10-3H (1XF, CS, TUE, not looped, bronze), T10-6H (CS, black, red, blue, or green)

Kamasan B180 Salmon Dry Fly, B190 Deep Water Salmon, B220 (3XL, SE, black nickel), B940 (4XL, SE)

Mustad 3406 (SE, bronze), 3406B (SE, nickel), 3582 (TD loop eye, bronze, double), 3582F (double), 3908 (TDE, bronze), 7970 (5XH, TDE, bronze), 9049 (1XF), 36890, 80500BL (2XL), 80501BL (2XL, TDE), 80525BL, (2XL, double), 80526BL (2XL, TD loop eye, double), 90240 (2XF, 1XL), 94863 (2XF, BL, bronze)

Orvis 0528 (double), 1641 (2XH, 1XS, TDE, bronze), 1644 (1XF), 1645

Partridge CS10/1 (2XL, CS), CS10/2, CS10/4 (double), CS11GRS (4XL, Grey Shadow), CS42 (loop TDE, bronze), GRSQ2 (2XL, double, Grey Shadow), M (2XH), N (2XL, "low water"), O1 (6XL), O2 (6XL, double), P (2XH, double), Q1 (2XL, double), R1A (loop TDE, double, bronze), R2A (loop TDE, double, bronze), R3HF (2XS, 2XH, 2XS, loop SE)

Sprite Salmon Double Low Water (2XL), FF (Francis Francis) Salmon Heavy Dee (5XL, 2XH), FF Salmon Heavy Spey (3.5XL, 2XH, 3.5XL), FF Salmon Light Dee (5XL), FF Salmon Light Spey (3.5XL), FF Salmon Light Wire (2XF), FF Salmon Low Water (2XL), FF Salmon Wet Fly (2XH), Salmon Single Dry Fly (4XF), Salmon Single Low Water (2XL), Salmon Single Wet (2XH), Salmon Streamer (7XL, loop TDE, bronze)

Targus 7979 (SE, CS), 7989 (1XF, CS), 7999 (CS)

Tiemco TMC 700 (TDE), 800B, 905BL (1XF, TDE, BL), 7989 (1XF), 7999

Turrall Salmon-Double (double), Salmon-Double Low Water (2XL, double), Salmon Extra-Fine Dry (2XF), Salmon Low Water (2XL), Salmon-Single

VMC 7299 (1XS, TUE, bronze, nickel, red, or silver), 7299SS (1XS, TUE, SS), 7399 (1XS, TUE, BL, bronze, nickel, red, or silver), 9410 (double, bronze)

Saltwater Woollies

Avalon A2500

Daiichi 1182 (TDE), 1222 (TDE, BU), 2546 (2XH)

Dai-Riki 930

Eagle Claw L054SS, L067 Billy Pate, 178 (TDE, gold), 254SS, L256 (2XS, TDE, bronze)

Fenwick HQ-SLO (SE)

Gamakatsu SC15 (WG), SL11H-3H (3XH), SP11-3L3H (3XH, 3XL), SS15

Kamasan B940 (4XL, black), B950U (2XL, XH)

Mustad 3407, 3407SS (2XH), 3408B (TDE), 3498AD (4XL, TDE), 31014, 34005 (2XH, BU), 34007, 34011 (3XL) 34039SS (5XL), 77660SS (1XS), 79666S (keel-fly hook), C70SD (2XH, SE), C71S-SS (1XL, 2XH), S71S-SS (1XL, 2XH, SE)

Orvis 9034 (SS)

Partridge CS11/1 (4XL, TDE, Grey Shadow), CS11/2 (4XL, TDE), CS11/3 (2XL, loop TDE), CS11GRS (4XL, TDE, Grey Shadow), CS29GRS (6XL, BL, Grey Shadow), CS51, CS52 (2XH), CS53 (3XL, 2XH), CS54 (Grey Shadow), GRS S3 (6XL, Grey Shadow), GRS S4 (5XL, 2XH, Grey Shadow)

Targus 800 (2XH), 812S (1XL, 1XF), 4310 (1XH, TUE, reversed)

Tiemco TMC 411S (BU), 800S (black), 811S, 9394 (3XH, 4XL, nickel), 9395 (3XH, 4XL, bronze)

Turrall Salt Water (SS)

VMC 7255, 7299SS Octopus (1XS), 9752 Sea Kirby (WG, silver)

INDEX

KEEPERS OF THE FLAME

*These are the men and women
whose patterns, innovations, and
ideas are featured in this book.
Many of today's tiers have web
sites, so try searching on their
names at www.google.com.*